THE HANDBOOK OF CARBON MANAGEMENT

T0383894

Every manager and every employee in every function can embed climate solutions and reduce greenhouse gas emissions. This book, written by experts in the field of sustainability in business, shows you how.

The climate crisis is one of the greatest challenges we face today, and it affects all aspects of business and society. Consequently, everyone needs to know the best high-impact climate solutions that can be embedded into their organisational area. In this book you will find ideas for your team, your department and your organisation to make this a reality. We provide you with implementation plans and inspiring case studies, with practical and helpful tools that will help you to scale up climate solutions effectively and efficiently. If you are an owner of a company or an executive in any organisation, you will benefit from this step-by-step guide on how to set up your own greenhouse gas management plan, how to set targets and how to reduce the greenhouse gas emissions of your whole organisation. We explain key terms such as *Net Zero, Carbon Neutral, carbon emissions equivalents* and *the three scopes*. In order to halve our emissions worldwide by 2030 to achieve Net Zero by 2050, individual actions on a large scale are required, but also systemic changes. We look at the bigger picture in this book and also how you could effect change.

This is the first book to offer an easy-to-implement approach to decarbonise organisations and transform societies, and is appropriate for managers at any level. This book can also be used in business schools to inspire future managers and business leaders. Last, but not least, everyone can find ideas here that they can implement in their personal lives – let's scale up together!

Petra Molthan-Hill, PhD is Professor of Sustainable Management and Education for Sustainable Development (ESD) at Nottingham Business

School, Nottingham Trent University, UK and Co-Chair of the United Nations Principles for Responsible Management Education (PRME) Working Group on Climate Change and Environment. She is an international multi-award-winning expert for Climate Change Mitigation Education, Greenhouse Gas Management and ESD. Molthan-Hill leads the 'Climate Literacy Training for Educators, Communities, Organisations and Students' (CLT-ECOS) distributed worldwide. She is the editor of *The Business Student's Guide to Sustainable Management* and of *Storytelling for Sustainability in Higher Education: An Educator's Handbook* and led the Green Academy at NTU from 2013–2021.

Fiona Winfield is the School Employability Manager at Nottingham Business School, Nottingham Trent University, and is a Principal Lecturer and a Senior Fellow HEA. Before moving into academia, she spent a decade in sales and marketing in the construction industry. She is involved with Young Enterprise and Enactus, is a Green Gown Award winner (for linking Employability to Sustainability) and a member of the Chartered Management Institute. At NTU, she is part of the Sustainable Development Academic Forum and the Sustainability task group within Employability.

Richard Howarth is a Senior Lecturer in Marketing at Nottingham Business School, Nottingham Trent University. He is an Assistant Course Leader for BA (Hons) Marketing and works closely with organisations and professional bodies (such as the CIM and MRS) to enhance the employability and workplace impacts of students and graduates. He is the Sustainability Coordinator for the Marketing Department. His research interests are related to marketer competences, education for sustainable development, responsible marketer behaviour, sustainability and employability and related learning and teaching interventions.

Muhammad Mazhar is a Senior Lecturer in Sustainability at Nottingham Business School, Nottingham Trent University. He is also the Sustainability Coordinator of the Business School, aiming to help embed sustainability in teaching, research, operational and partnership activities. By background, he is a Civil Engineer with a B.E. in Civil Engineering and MSc. in Construction Management. He received a PhD in Sustainability and Carbon Management. His interest is in sustainability, energy and carbon management, education for sustainable development and low-carbon smart cities.

'Climate change is the existential issue of our age, but with many struggling for guidance this book is a useful and accessible guide to practical actions organisations can take around carbon literacy, reporting and projects to reduce their footprint.'

Andrew Jack, Global Education Editor, Financial Times

'A carbon constrained future is inevitable. For businesses it is a question of competitiveness and survival. This Handbook is a true treasure chest, providing guidance for how to go about it. A must read for executives and practitioners!'

Georg Kell, Founder and former Executive Director of the United Nations Global Compact; Chairman, Arabesque Partners

'This is a refreshingly practical handbook for the many leaders, at all levels, who want to put their organisations in greater service of people and planet – but who don't know how. The clear focus on solutions rings loud.'

Paul Polman, Business leader, campaigner and co-author of *Net Positive*

Net Positive 'A bold resource for contemporary business leaders, this specific yet thorough guide shows how every business can reduce its carbon emissions now and thrive on green energy in the long run.'

**Rae André, Professor,
Northeastern University D'Amore-McKim School of Business;
author of *Lead for the Planet: Five Practices for Confronting Climate Change***

'Finally, a book I have been waiting for. Changing a company's strategy and an individual's mindset on transferring into a sustainable business and behaviour is a complex project. This book gives you well-structured guidelines and covers all required aspects for a considered approach. There is no Planet B – with this book you can get started.'

Marc Oliver Nissen, Director, LinkedIn Talent Solutions, Germany

'Governments, businesses, and universities don't act, people do. *The Handbook of Carbon Management* empowers employees across industries to incorporate climate solutions in the way we live and work.'

Elena Crete, Head of Climate & Energy Program, UN SDSN

'Climate literacy, as illustrated in this book, has become critical knowledge not only for the leaders in organisations to drive the necessary change, but also for those affected by the change to understand the bigger picture, and therefore improve the likelihood of a successful transformation of the organisation.'

**Joris-Johann Lenssen, Project Lead Business & Society,
ZiviZ im Stifterverband (Berlin); Former Managing Director
of ABIS – The Academy of Business in Society (Brussels)**

'This book highlights the importance of effective communication when it comes to climate change, and how marketing is key to changing the course we are on. From educating and raising awareness to shaping new behaviours, both internally and externally, the skillsets of marketers cannot be underestimated.'

Gemma Butler, Marketing Director, CIM

'*The Handbook of Carbon Management* does an excellent job in arguing the case for the rapid reform that is so desperately needed if we are to respond successfully to the chronic and catastrophic climate collapse that is taking place all around us.'

Andy Agathangelou, Founder, Transparency Task Force

'The most frequent question I get asked in my work is not "Shall we act on climate?" but "What should we do?" Having such a comprehensive overview of the best actions that people and organisations can undertake is a really valuable addition to the resources we all need to tackle the climate crisis.'

**Phil Korbel, Co-Founder &
Director of Advocacy, Carbon Literacy Project**

'If you think that climate change is too abstract for you to do anything about it, read this book. This handbook provides a rich resource of concrete inspiration about climate change and how anyone working in an organization can contribute. The book analyses the urgent need for all of us to act and it admirably guides us how to act. This is a book with a clear ambition to have societal impact.'

**Dr Mette Morsing, Head of PRME Principles for Responsible
Management Education, United Nations Global Compact**

'This book is an excellent resource to raise awareness of carbon management. It is essential for all who teach or study any function of business and management, including accounting, banking and finance, supply chain management, marketing and communications, human resource management, strategy and leadership. It provides practical solutions for organisations and individuals to bring about true systemic change in carbon management.'

**Professor Liz Crolley, Chair of QAA Review of Subject
Benchmark Statements for Business and Management**

'This handbook provides inspiration for current and future leaders with actionable steps they can take to implement climate solutions in their work. It is therefore invaluable not only for practitioners, but also students and researchers, potentially benefitting an organisation's financial situation, as well as the environment.'

Stephen Snider, Sustainable Finance Lead, oikos International

'Whether you're new to Carbon Management or have experience in the area, this concisely written book offers you the overview and knowledge you need to take some concrete, practical steps towards reducing your organisation's climate impact.'

Richard Holmes, MEI, MIEMA, C.Env.,
Carbon Management Consultant & Trainer

'This handbook is a must read for everybody who wants to tackle the climate crisis in their workplace. By taking us step by step through the thinking and action needed to embed solutions in strategy and operations, it helps to make sense of the complex, interrelated nature of the change at hand, so we can all turn ambition into impact.'

Gudrun Cartwright, Climate Action Director, BiTC

'This book provides a most useful resource and reference for anyone motivated to address the most pressing threat to the quality of life on our planet. It positively contributes to the process of change needed to generate the paradigm shift in human activity that is urgently required.'

Colin Crawford, CMLI – Chartered Member of the Landscape Institute

'We are living at a time when a fast-growing part of humanity is realizing the havoc our current approaches deal on our livelihood – clients, consumers, investors, politicians, and employees alike. Urgently needed, this handbook provides practical advice on high impact climate solutions that any manager in any organisation can implement to avoid the worst and move towards a positive future.'

Klemens Höppner, CFA, CESFi, Co-Founder & Managing Director,
Mindful Finance Institute

'The Handbook of Carbon Management is the book for any manager to get on the right track in reducing their organisation's carbon impact with its simple and smart quick wins, contributing to a much-needed change from Day 1.'

Favian Munday Alvarado, Project Manager (Toulouse),
Graduate in Architecture (Mexico) and Sustainable Building (France)

THE HANDBOOK OF CARBON MANAGEMENT

A Step-by-Step Guide to High-Impact Climate Solutions for Every Manager in Every Function

Petra Molthan-Hill, Fiona Winfield, Richard Howarth and Muhammad Mazhar

Routledge
Taylor & Francis Group

LONDON AND NEW YORK

Designed cover image: Getty Images / Rawpixel

First published 2023
by Routledge
4 Park Square, Milton Park, Abingdon, Oxon OX14 4RN

and by Routledge
605 Third Avenue, New York, NY 10158

Routledge is an imprint of the Taylor & Francis Group, an informa business

© 2023 Petra Molthan-Hill, Fiona Winfield, Richard Howarth and Muhammad Mazhar

The right of Petra Molthan-Hill, Fiona Winfield, Richard Howarth and Muhammad Mazhar to be identified as authors of this work has been asserted in accordance with sections 77 and 78 of the Copyright, Designs and Patents Act 1988.

All rights reserved. No part of this book may be reprinted or reproduced or utilised in any form or by any electronic, mechanical, or other means, now known or hereafter invented, including photocopying and recording, or in any information storage or retrieval system, without permission in writing from the publishers.

Trademark notice: Product or corporate names may be trademarks or registered trademarks, and are used only for identification and explanation without intent to infringe.

British Library Cataloguing-in-Publication Data
A catalogue record for this book is available from the British Library

Library of Congress Cataloging-in-Publication Data
Names: Molthan-Hill, Petra, author. | Winfield, Fiona, author. | Howarth, Richard B., author.
Title: The handbook of carbon management : a step-by-step guide to high-impact climate solutions for every manager in every function / Petra Molthan-Hill, Fiona Winfield, Richard Howarth and Muhammad Mazhar.
Description: New York, NY : Routledge, 2023. | Includes bibliographical references and index. |
Identifiers: LCCN 2022037806 (print) | LCCN 2022037807 (ebook) | ISBN 9781032227610 (hardback) | ISBN 9781032227603 (paperback) | ISBN 9781003274049 (ebook)
Subjects: LCSH: Management--Environmental aspects. | Carbon dioxide mitigation. | Greenhouse gases--Environmental aspects. | Strategic planning.
Classification: LCC HD30.255 .M65 2023 (print) | LCC HD30.255 (ebook) | DDC 658.4/0830218--dc23/eng/20220811
LC record available at https://lccn.loc.gov/2022037806
LC ebook record available at https://lccn.loc.gov/2022037807

ISBN: 978-1-032-22761-0 (hbk)
ISBN: 978-1-032-22760-3 (pbk)
ISBN: 978-1-003-27404-9 (ebk)

DOI: 10.4324/9781003274049

Typeset in Joanna
by MPS Limited, Dehradun

Access the companion website: www.routledge.com/cw/molthan-hill

IT'S REAL. IT'S US. EXPERTS AGREE. IT'S BAD. THERE'S HOPE.
(John Cook et al 2019)[1]

To Eric, Ansgar and Kiera with the hope that you will have a good future!

−Petra Molthan-Hill

To John, Jack and Kate for all your support and numerous cups of tea

−Fiona Winfield

To Erika, Frances and Tom with all my love − Uncle Quentin!

−Aka Richard Howarth

To Hoorain, Mehwish, Shahnaz and Mazhar for your continuous support over the years

−Muhammad Mazhar

---

1 Cook, J., Supran, G., Lewandowsky, S., Oreskes, N., & Maibach, E. (2019). *America Misled: How the fossil fuel industry deliberately misled Americans about climate change*. Fairfax, VA: George Mason University Center for Climate Change Communication. Available at https://www.climatechangecommunication.org/america-misled/

CONTENTS

FOREWORD

by Dr Peter Young

Whilst the precise occasion may be a point for debate, November 2021 and the Glasgow COP26 being perhaps the most popular, all recognise a tipping point in our climate consciousness has been reached. Climate action is now urgent, cross-economy and a personal responsibility for every decision maker.

Voluntary disclosure of carbon impacts is rapidly becoming a regulated necessity, with mandatory carbon reporting for large organisations in many jurisdictions, including the United Kingdom and Europe. Access to finance increasingly demands alignment to a 1.5°C world ('Paris aligned') or Net Zero ('Carbon Neutral') by 2050 or earlier. ESG (environment, social and governance) investing is the most rapidly growing class of investment products, and must include clear pathways to carbon reduction and climate mitigation and adaptation. Consumer demands are rising and being met through voluntary and regulated labelling schemes. All this means that climate literacy and knowledge of the suite of tools used to measure and manage an organisation's carbon footprint have moved from being a specialist niche to a mainstream skill. No-one from the CEO to support functions, from sales and marketing to procurement, from finance to customer care, can afford to remain ignorant of the basics in how to calculate and explain the climate impacts of their actions. All require new knowledge and extra skill sets in carbon management and climate awareness.

Against this background the timing of this handbook is impeccable. In 15 compressed but accessible chapters, it provides a go-to guide on all the elements necessary to provide a robust understanding of carbon management and options for reducing climate impacts. It is written without regard to previous knowledge of such matters and yet reaches sufficient detail to enable even the most experienced executive to pick up new tips and tools for improving design and execution of climate friendly plans and operations. After explaining how high impact solutions can be prioritised and signposting open-source materials and guided activities, six chapters (3–8) are dedicated to the most fruitful aspects of every organisation's review of carbon reduction potential. The remaining text includes the all-important aspects of reporting and disclosure, marketing and communication, and the underlying metrics and accounting practices which ensure progress is accurately conveyed and understood. Particularly useful are the in-depth de-mystification of the role that pensions and investment decisions can play, how to establish proportionate carbon accounting practices and what 'science-based targets' and other jargonistic phrases actually mean.

The narrative is compelling, but this handbook will not be read once and then put on a shelf afterwards. It should become well thumbed, whether electronically or on paper, as time and again it can be used by every professional to make better decisions and select optimum pathways. Whatever role we play in our organisation, it is our duty to make climate responsible decisions now, and this book will ensure we can play our part in transitioning to a Net Zero future where climate risks are minimised for all. Time is not on our side, so read on and adopt your climate solutions now!

Peter Young
Trustee, Green Purposes Company and Founding
Chair ISO/TC 322 Sustainable Finance

Dr. Peter Young has been an independent advisor to business and governments, established and chaired third sector organisations, and promoted standards, helping to build a low-carbon economy and promote sustainable practices across finance and the real economy.

PART I

NET ZERO AND DECARBONISATION: UNDERSTANDING AND COMMUNICATING THE BASICS

1

FINDING YOUR BEST DECARBONISATION PATHWAY

Petra Molthan-Hill and Fiona Winfield

We have to turn around all our organisations fast to achieve a low-carbon future – some might argue, any sort of positive future – for all! This chapter provides the background to this claim and introduces the key concepts every manager and employee needs to know about climate change, Net Zero and how to achieve a low-carbon future. It also gives an overview of the book and what to find in each chapter.

This chapter is for you if:

- You want to gain an overview of the best high-impact climate solutions
- You want to lead the change in 'Team Humanity'
- You want to understand the greenhouse gas effect and why we have rising temperatures
- You want to appreciate how climate solutions could solve a multitude of other problems related to health and other Sustainable Development Goals (SDGs)
- You want an overview about the chapters in this book and how they are linked.

DOI: 10.4324/9781003274049-2

It will cover:

- Key definitions such as Net Zero and Carbon Neutral
- The greenhouse gas effect and the urgency to act
- How different solutions could bring us on the path to a 1.5°C future
- Sources for high-impact climate solutions
- Multiple health and other benefits of climate solutions
- Earth Index: tracking the G20 response to the climate emergency
- Climate justice and the 5-tonne lifestyle
- Climate leaders – five practices for confronting climate change
- An overview of this book, its sections and chapters.

We have to act now!

The IPCC (Intergovernmental Panel on Climate Change) report 2022 highlights that keeping to 1.5°C is still achievable, but we need to act now and this requires policy makers, organisations and every citizen to achieve dramatic reductions in Greenhouse Gas Emissions (GGE). This book is aimed at achieving such drastic reductions across all functions in all types of organisations, and supporting managers and employees in general in making the right decisions. We will see later, in this and other chapters, that this does not necessarily mean a reduction in lifestyle choices, as there are also very innovative solutions, which might increase our quality of life.

However, before we turn to the solutions, we need to understand the problem. The 2022 IPCC report summarises our current understanding of the interdependencies between climate, ecosystems, biodiversity and human societies, and assesses the risks and impacts of climate change as well as adaptation and resilience. The IPCC is an intergovernmental body of the United Nations and *was created to provide policymakers with regular scientific assessments on climate change, its implications and potential future risks, as well as to put forward adaptation and mitigation options.*[1]

In their 'Climate Change 2022: Impacts, Adaptation and Vulnerability – Summary for Policy Makers' the IPCC summarises:

Risks in the near-term (2021–2040)

Global warming, reaching 1.5°C in the near-term, would cause unavoidable increases in multiple climate hazards and present multiple risks to ecosystems and humans (very high confidence).

The level of risk will depend on concurrent near-term trends in vulnerability, exposure, level of socioeconomic development and adaptation (high confidence).

Near-term actions that limit global warming to close to 1.5°C would substantially reduce projected losses and damages related to climate change in human systems and ecosystems, compared to higher warming levels, but cannot eliminate them all (very high confidence).

Mid- to long-term risks (2041–2100)

Beyond 2040 and depending on the level of global warming, climate change will lead to numerous risks to natural and human systems (high confidence).

For 127 identified key risks, assessed mid- and long-term impacts are up to multiple times higher than currently observed (high confidence).

The magnitude and rate of climate change and associated risks depend strongly on near-term mitigation and adaptation actions, and projected adverse impacts and related losses and damages escalate with every increment of global warming (very high confidence).[2]

The Economist of 09.04.2022 concludes from this IPCC report that emissions must peak by 2025 for the world to have a chance of meeting the Paris goals,[3] others would argue even earlier.[4] It would be possible to achieve this, for example Professor Martin Siegert of Imperial College, London cites estimates that 1% of the United Kingdom's GDP needs to be invested now for the transition, however he also points out that the United Kingdom currently spends only about 0.01% and invests higher amounts in plans that will actually add to our emissions, for example airport expansion plans and new road schemes.[5]

Achieving Net Zero by 2050, a commonly stated goal, might mask this sense of urgency and allow decision-makers in politics, society and industry to postpone urgent decisions to a future date. The IPCC defines **Net Zero** carbon dioxide (CO_2) emissions in their glossary[6] as being achieved when anthropogenic CO_2 emissions are balanced globally by anthropogenic CO_2 removals over a specified period. Net Zero CO_2 emissions are also referred to as carbon neutrality.

In order to achieve this and to limit global warming to 1.5°C, the IPCC stresses that the world needs **to halve CO_2 emissions by around 2030** and reach Net Zero CO_2 emissions by mid-century. In addition, the IPCC emphasises **the need for deep reductions in non-CO_2 emissions across the economy** to achieve this limit. Often commentators concentrate on achieving Net

Zero in 2050, not realising that the reductions need to be planned im-mediately – with the first aim to halve the emissions by 2030! This is quite an ambitious task, but one that is possible.

KEEP 1.5 ALIVE

In order to limit global warming to 1.5°C, the IPCC stresses that the world needs **to halve CO₂ emissions by around 2030** and reach Net Zero CO₂ emissions by mid-century.

What is the greenhouse gas effect?

As just mentioned, global warming is caused by carbon dioxide, but also other greenhouse gases (GHG) such as methane (CH_4), nitrous oxide (N_2O), hydrofluorocarbons (HFCs), perfluorocarbons (PFCs) and sulphur hexafluoride (SF_6).[7] These gases have very different **global warming potentials (GWP)**, which means they may contribute to faster rises in temperature (as they retain more heat than CO_2 – the benchmark gas) and/or they remain in the atmosphere longer. Heat has always been trapped in our atmosphere by the existing GHGs and ensured a good climate, as it allowed for good living conditions for all existing plants, animals and humans. However, since the 'Industrial Revolution', more and more molecules have been sent into the atmosphere by burning fossil fuels and releasing methane through our food waste and other human activities that cause GHG emissions. These molecules have then trapped more and more heat, so that on average, we now have a worldwide increase of 1° Celsius (33.8° Fahrenheit) compared to pre-industrial levels.

An increase of 1°C might not sound like too much, but this has dramatic consequences. For example, sea ice-free summers in the Arctic are predicted to happen once every 100 years if the average temperature worldwide increases by 1.5°C compared to pre-industrial levels. However, it is predicted to happen once every ten years if there is an increase of 2°C, so ten times worse yet only 0.5° more. When the average temperature rises by 1.5° compared to pre-industrial levels, 14% of the global population would be exposed to extreme heat every 1–5 years; this would increase to 37% of the global population at 2°, and so on.[8] The consequences are manifold: shrinking glaciers, rising sea levels, loss of habitat for many species, further decline in coral reefs, higher frequency of floods, fires and other extreme weather events and so forth. If you want to understand the greenhouse gas effect and its consequences in more detail, we recommend watching 'Climate 101: Causes and Effects' by National Geographic, which has also published the article 'Carbon dioxide levels are at a record high. Here's what you need to know'.[9]

Climate change already has dramatic consequences for many nations; the online platform **'Climate Watch'** provides information on vulnerability, climate progress and risk for every country in the world, as well as data on greenhouse gas emissions and a *comprehensive mapping of linkages between Nationally Determined Contributions (NDCs) and the Sustainable Development Goals (SDGs) and associated targets of the 2030 Agenda for Sustainable Development*.[10] It shows us how crucial it is that we limit global warming to 1.5°C.

Designing your own 1.5°C scenario

You might wonder how we can achieve this? A good starting point is the En-ROADS (**En**ergy-**R**apid **O**verview **a**nd **D**ecision-**S**upport) simulator developed by Climate Interactive in collaboration with MIT Sloan and Ventana Systems. This interactive tool can be used by policy-makers and any other decision-makers, as well as any interested citizen, to understand the impact different decisions and policies would have on our future temperature increase. As you can see in Figure 1.1, if we do not change anything, we are currently heading towards 3.6°C by the end of the century. However, we can choose to change the current status quo and introduce for example a carbon price. Setting such a carbon price in the simulator would show us the impact this decision alone would have on the future temperature development. In the background to each of the levers, there are assumptions (behind the three dots) that each user can change and align with their own assessment, for example, to introduce the tax on coal in 2024, rather than 2022. The En-ROADS simulator is a very powerful tool to understand the implications and system-wide interactions each policy would have, and to combine them successfully to limit global

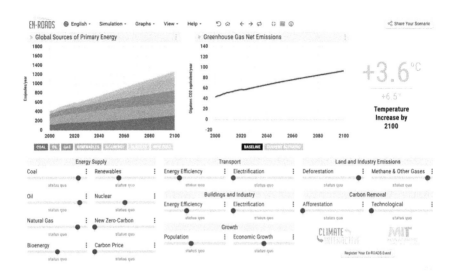

Figure 1.1 En-ROADS Climate Solutions Simulator (2022) reprinted with permission from Climate Interactive.

warming to 1.5°C. You can test various different permutations to set up your own scenario, and we would also encourage you to test the order in which you choose to implement these. For example, what happens when you first introduce a carbon price and then change energy efficiency in transport, or vice versa.

Whilst the En-ROADS simulator produces results within a fraction of a second for anyone who might have very little prior understanding, it is in fact based on an extensive study of the latest research literature on factors such as delay times, progress ratios, price sensitivities, historic growth of energy sources, and energy efficiency potential. This enables En-ROADS to reveal the dynamic interactions between different levers, such as how energy efficiency affects renewable energy, and which feedback loops are most significant.[11] In the extensive guide to En-ROADS, you can find out about its mathematical logic and how En-ROADS uses data from other climate models e.g. the Climate Change Control Scenarios of the Energy Modeling Forum (EMF)[12] – the so-called EMF 22 – to calibrate its own results.[13]

In order to understand the bigger picture, we now invite you to undertake two interlinked activities. This is an exercise designed for all readers (employees, managers, SME owners, CEOs of major corporations). Although it may be tempting to skip this, it will set you up with a solid foundation for the chapters to come.

The first activity uses the En-ROADS simulator and, after watching a short video, you are asked to design your own future scenario to achieve 1.5°C. Please allow at least 30 minutes for the activity in Table 1.1.

Table 1.1 Exercise to design a future scenario to achieve 1.5°C in your organisation

Activity 1 **Design your own future scenario to achieve 1.5°C worldwide with the En-ROADS simulator from Climate Interactive. Then choose three high-impact climate solutions you would like to integrate into your work or organisation.**
1. Watch the video on the relevance of En-ROADS for the business sector. Access YouTube: https://www.youtube.com. Now search for: **Sparking Sustainable Action in the Business Sector with En-ROADS** (https://www.youtube.com/watch?v=92NNRpiQzFA)
2. Design your own 1.5°C future model, combining different high-impact solutions https://en-roads.climateinteractive.org
3. From all the different solutions shown on the model you have designed for the future, choose **up to three high-impact climate solutions** that you could integrate into your work or organisation. Make a note of these and use them in Activity 2 below.

To complement Activity 1, we will now use another tool designed by Climate Interactive: FLOWER (**F**ramework for **Lo**ng-Term, **W**hole-System, **E**quity-based **R**eflection).[14]

This tool allows you to review different climate solutions with respect to other benefits they might have, for example health or jobs and assets. It has a special focus on equity, asking you to reflect on whether a climate solution you have selected only benefits a certain group in society such as the well-off, whether it benefits every citizen, or even whether it might address problems faced by already marginalised communities. An example would be a climate solution that addresses air pollution in a poorer community and improves their health and quality of life. (See Table 1.2 for details of how to use the FLOWER framework – this activity will probably take a further 20 minutes.)

Table 1.2 FLOWER exercise to evaluate your selected solutions

Activity 2
Assess the co-benefits of your chosen climate solutions using the FLOWER framework from Elizabeth Sawin/Climate Interactive.
1. Watch the video that introduces you to the **FLOWER framework**. Access YouTube: https://www.youtube.com. Now search for: **Evaluating Project Benefits with the FLOWER Multisolving Tool** (www.youtube.com/watch?v= byxgfQT8doI)   2. Next apply the FLOWER framework to the solutions you identified in Activity 1   3. If you want to know more about multiple benefits of existing projects, we recommend this additional video - within Youtube, search for: **Multisolving: Connections to Health, Equity, Justice, & Well-being** (https://www.youtube. com/watch?v=NDIp3mpPvVU)   4. Compare the *flowers* you have created for each of your climate actions: which is the action with the most co-benefits?
We hope you will plant at least one of your flowers and wish you lots of success in doing so.

If you are responsible for a larger organisation, we would recommend that you gain an overview of *all* the potential solutions that could be applied. The exercise you have just done could be a starting point, but we will now introduce more solutions and would encourage you to take note of all those which could be relevant to your organisation. In each chapter, you will find further solutions, so you might want to use a mind-map or pull together an overview allowing you to sort the solutions into the functions and departments that are in your sphere of influence.

So many high-impact solutions: Project Drawdown

As the next rich source for finding high-impact solutions we want to introduce **Project Drawdown** to you. Project Drawdown has the mission to 'draw down' the temperature by making use of the available high-impact climate solutions designed and calculated by climate solution scientists. They have summarised and suggested the 100 best high-impact climate solutions based on their calculations for any sector worldwide.[15] There are some unusual ones that might not have crossed your mind before, for example air-conditioning. While Project Drawdown highlights the need to replace the refrigeration gases HFCs, which have 1,000 to 9,000 *times greater* *capacity to warm the atmosphere than carbon dioxide,*[16] the reduction of air-conditioning emissions could also have an enormous impact. For example, by powering air-conditioning units with solar power instead of oil, and not setting the temperature quite so low (you might recognise the experience of entering a bank in a hot country and wishing you had your winter coat with you!). This might be especially important in countries like Qatar, which already air-conditions its outdoor spaces as it experiences average temperatures of 2°C higher than pre-industrial levels.[17] At the same time, Qatar has the second highest emissions of CO_2e per person in the world – at 32.4 tCO_2e.[18] So a vicious circle has been established: the hotter the temperature, the more air-conditioning is used, causing more GHG emissions to be released, which then increases the temperature even further.

Coming back to the high-impact solutions in Project Drawdown, a very entertaining way to encounter a few of them is in the Film '2040'. In this, the director, Damon Gameau, envisions a very positive future in 2040 for his little daughter, who would be an adult by then, and visits changemakers and innovators in agriculture, technology, education, economics, civil society and sustainability to choose and demonstrate the best climate solutions that exist already and could be implemented now and upscaled worldwide.[19]

Another way to find ideas for good solutions is The Climate Game created by the Financial Times in conjunction with Infosys: https://ig.ft.com/climate-game/.[20] The FT states that the basis is the International Energy Agency's (IEA) report 'Net Zero by 2050', with the outcomes being calculated using the MAGICC v7+ (Model for the Assessment of Greenhouse Gas Induced Climate Change) along with the IEA's World Energy Model and the Energy Technology Perspectives (ETP) model. While it is not a perfect simulation of the future, it may be a fun gamified way to engage with the topic and to absorb some of the options. However, it should be noted that the game does not offer as wide a choice of solutions as the En-ROADS simulator or Project Drawdown. It is also more prescriptive, and the underlying assumptions are not as transparent.

Earth Index: tracking the G20 response to the climate emergency

In April 2022, Corporate Knights' Earth Index was launched. Corporate Knights is a media, research and financial information company based in

Toronto, Canada dedicated to achieving what they call *clean capitalism*. According to their thinking, clean capitalism relies on prices that fully reflect social and environmental costs and where every market participant is fully aware of the consequences of their actions. It is especially well known for its ranking of the 100 most sustainable corporations, announced every year at the World Economic Forum in Davos, Switzerland. Its 2022 list also highlighted the climate commitments made by those corporations.[21] In April 2022, they published the **Earth Index** for the first time to measure the *speed at which countries (by sector) are reducing greenhouse gas (GHG) emissions relative to the speed required to deliver on their commitments. Its objective is to create global awareness of whether annual GHG emissions are being reduced fast enough to meet the long-term targets countries have set for themselves. ... [They] focus on G20 countries, which account for about 80% of global GHG emissions.*[22] The Earth Index was developed by the research division of Corporate Knights, experts in the field, and the contributions of the CEOs of the aforementioned 100 most sustainable corporations.

The Earth Index goes into a lot of detail with regard to the reductions per sector in each country, however it also highlights that most countries and sectors need to speed up their efforts: *for the G20 in total, GHG emissions increased in 2019, resulting in an EARTH INDEX score of −15%. The power sector had a score of 5%, indicating that while there was a slight decline in emissions, the pace of reductions would have to be 20 times higher than in 2019 to be on track for meeting the aggregate G20 target. Emissions increased in all the other sectors, yielding negative EARTH INDEX scores and revealing the extent to which outcomes and aspirations are not yet aligned, at least at the level of the entire G20.*[23] In Figure 1.2 you can see how each sector has performed.[24] A negative Earth Index, so for example −35% in the Fossil Fuel sector, indicates that this sector has not achieved the required reduction. In this case, as shown in Figure 1.2, the Fossil Fuel Sector needs a reduction of 104,035 kt CO_2e, but instead of a reduction, there has been an increase of 36,402 kt CO_2e.

While we need to make changes at policy and industry level, as demonstrated in the FT Climate Game and the Earth Index, we also need changes at every other level. We need corporate leaders, managers in all types of organisations, as well as *every* citizen to step up and reduce their GHG emissions. In order to do this, everyone needs to know which activities would reduce emissions the most, and which ones might sound great, but would not have such a big impact.

G20	-15% Earth Index
Stated emissions target	Varies
Emissions in 2019, in kt CO_2e	38,217,786
Target emissions in 2030, in kt CO_2e	25,351,293
Annual kt CO_2e reduction needed to meet target	1,169,681
Emission reduction (or increase) in 2019, kt CO_2e	(180,468)
Average annual emission reduction (or increase), 2016-2019	(407,571)
Earth Index based on 2016-2019 trend	-31%
Power	*5%*
Fossil fuel	*-35%*
Transport	*-31%*
Industry	*-6%*
Buildings	*-39%*
Agriculture	*-15%*
Waste	*-59%*

	Power	Fossil fuel	Transport	Industry	Buildings	Agriculture	Waste
Emissions in 2005, in kt CO_2e	11,551,589	3,299,465	5,768,324	9,236,441	3,066,610	3,948,781	1,346,575
Target emissions in 2019, in kt CO_2e	7,884,000	2,155,079	3,597,617	6,321,035	1,980,243	2,527,259	886,059
Annual reductions needed to meet target, in kt CO_2e	333,417	104,035	197,337	265,037	98,761	129,229	41,865
Annual emission reduction (or increase) in 2019, kt CO_2e	17,432	(36,402)	(61,916)	(15,923)	(38,866)	(20,004)	(24,790)

Figure 1.2 EARTH INDEX scorecard for main sectors in the entire G20 adapted from Corporate Knights, 2022.[25]

In his book 'How bad are bananas? The carbon footprint of everything'[26] Mike Berners-Lee, Professor at Lancaster University, England, shares his calculations for a broad range of products and activities, from the bananas in the title to cryptocurrencies. While written in a very entertaining way, it is based on his extensive research into the best ways to calculate GHG emissions and he helps the reader to understand these calculations and to make the right decisions. We have explained his approach further in chapter 2 'Climate Literacy Training'. The main thing to note is that all the GHG emissions mentioned above are calculated by Mike Berners-Lee in Carbon Dioxide Equivalent Emissions (CO_2e), so in the next section, the 5-tonne lifestyle refers to *all* GHG emissions (not only carbon) caused by consumption, including each product's full life cycle. For more details, please also refer to our Glossary of terms.

Climate justice: a 5-tonne lifestyle?

Another measurement used by Mike Berners-Lee is the **5-tonne lifestyle**, which is quite a powerful way of expressing how much impact one's personal activity might have on the carbon equivalent emissions we cause each year. Berners-Lee suggests that Europe, and we would also add countries such as Australia, Canada, China, Russia, United States of America, Saudi Arabia, Qatar and all the other oil-producing countries, should aim for every citizen having no more than a 5-tonne lifestyle, which would represent an important reduction in the emissions per capita experienced currently. According to data from The World Bank (2018), which is expressed as metric tonnes of CO_2 emissions per capita,[27] in 2018 Australia used 15.48, Canada 15.50, China 7.35, the EU 6.42, Qatar 32.42, the Russian Federation 11.13 and the United States used 15.24 CO_2 metric tonnes per capita. It is interesting to note that the newest data (as at mid 2022) stems from 2018, whereas financial market data movements are broadcast almost daily. In an ideal world, we would regularly be informed as to which countries had achieved reductions in their GHG per capita emissions as well! That aside, you can see from these figures that many countries have a long way to go for their citizens to achieve a 5-tonne lifestyle.

Incidentally, the 5-tonne lifestyle is not a recommendation for what every person on the planet should consume. It is actually important that countries that have much lower GHG emissions per capita (such as Bangladesh at 0.51 tonnes, Brazil 2.04, Kenya 0.36, Rwanda 0.09 and the Solomon Islands at 0.57) do not increase their output to the 5-tonne lifestyle as this would be disastrous. However, it should be noted here that the countries mentioned such as Bangladesh, Kenya and the Solomon Islands are some of the most vulnerable to climate change. In the **World Bank Group's Bangladesh Climate Risk Country Profile** (2021) it is highlighted that *Bangladesh is one of the most vulnerable countries in the world to climate-related hazards such as cyclones and floods. UNISDR estimated the average annual losses to disaster at around $3 billion, or around 1% to 2% of GDP … . These losses are focused particularly on the agricultural sector, but increasingly are impacting Bangladesh's rapidly expanding urban areas … by mid-century, climate change is likely to cost Bangladesh a further 2% of GDP on top of its baseline losses to climate hazards, a figure that potentially rises to 9% of GDP by the end of the century if mitigation action is not increased.*[28]

These Climate Risk Country Profiles show that the countries that emit the least are the most vulnerable to changes in the climate, and they have to bear the consequences caused by the actions of others. **Climate justice** *acknowledges climate change can have differing social, economic, public health and other adverse impacts on underprivileged populations. Advocates for climate justice are striving to have these inequities addressed head-on through long-term mitigation and adaptation strategies.*[29] Coming back to the 5-tonne lifestyle, this would not represent an equitable share of the worldwide carbon emissions, however if every citizen in Australia, the EU, Qatar, the United States of America and so on attempted to achieve a maximum 5-tonne lifestyle, this would be a fantastic mitigation strategy and would reduce carbon emissions in the millions of tonnes when multiplied by the number of citizens of all these countries. Therefore, it is quite a useful measurement to show the magnitude of some actions. For example, according to Mike Berners-Lee's calculations, a premium economy return flight from London to Hong Kong uses 4.5 tonnes,[30] this would leave just 500 kg to do everything else in the whole year: heating, eating, other transport and anything else you might want to consume. As another example, buying a new electric car would cause 11 tonnes CO_2e of embodied carbon (the GHG emissions used to make your car) before you even drive it – so more than twice your allowance for the year! More on this in chapter 4 (Meetings & Transport).

These calculations, and the recommendation to adopt no more than a 5-tonne lifestyle, apply to every citizen and therefore to everyone working in a company. It is therefore good practice to calculate everyone's allowance and usage. As an example, an employee with a company car that they use exclusively could account for more emissions than that person might be allowed for the whole year. Adjustments do of course need to be made according to how many years the car is kept. A vehicle used by several employees in the company on the other hand, would have its embodied emissions divided by the number who use the vehicle. This individual allowance is one level, the other is the company level and identifying who is responsible for which emissions. For this book, we have focused our calculations on the organisational level, and you can find detailed support on how you can calculate the GHG emissions for your whole organisation in chapters 11 to 14.

Will Team Humanity step up to save the planet?

In her ground-breaking book, 'Lead for the Planet: Five Practices for Confronting Climate Change', business professor and best-selling author Rae André points out that for a long time the discussion about whether climate change was really happening dominated the public discourse; the focus has now shifted on how we, all of us, as members of what André calls Team Humanity, are going to solve this challenge.

In order to do so, André highlights that we need climate leadership and more specifically that climate leadership should be systemic leadership. Systemic leaders are not only concerned with leading their organisation or country, they also have a wider vision of what is needed to transform all systems and understand how each system works. As André puts it, Systemic Leaders move beyond individual psychology to weigh the design of organizations and human systems. [...] Systemic Leaders realize that the nature of a problem and the details of its context both matter. For instance, when systemic leaders ponder how they should talk to their followers about climate science, they know they must understand both how their audiences perceive truth and how society influences those perceptions. When they face the conflict between the fossil fuel and renewable energy sectors, they consider the stakes not only for each sector but also for the broader economy.[31]

According to André, systemic leadership is based on three principles. Firstly, all individuals are part of social systems and these systems in turn are embedded in the natural world, hence climate leadership needs to understand these systems and make the right changes, in order to work towards the best climate solutions. Secondly, effective systemic leaders need to understand the power struggles between different competing sectors, such as fossil fuel and renewable energy sectors and other systems and must find ways to manage the power struggles for the collective good.[32] Thirdly, systemic leaders need to base their decisions on moral principles. André contradicts the moral neutrality claimed by some business leaders and highlights that most human beings do not exist amorally[33] and know intuitively the moral dimension at stake with regard to climate change and the survival of different life forms including their own species. Therefore, systemic climate leaders need to lead with moral intent, based on moral reflection.

Drawing on her experience as an organisational psychologist, her social science research and conversations with colleagues in other university disciplines such as business administration, natural resources, engineering and philosophy, André suggests **Five Practices** that guide effective decisions, with the goal to avoid the worst of global warming and create a clean energy future.

Practice 1: get the truth
This section offers guidance on how decision makers can deal with conflicting narratives and weigh up the scientific arguments about global warming, efficacy of solar power and other climate issues. It explores how to deal with different 'facts', when to trust or distrust scientific reports, and how to establish a good basic understanding without being an expert in climate change science.

Practice 2: assess the risks
Here, the focus is on the psychology of risk and how leaders and organisations predict and model risks with regard to climate change and energy, as well as how they attempt to manage these risks.

Practice 3: weigh the stakes
André now turns to the analysis of the different sectors and systems and their impact on the planet. She emphasises the conflicts arising from different interests, for example the often minor interest companies have in the environment and their damaging impact on it, versus the strong interest of governments and other stakeholders to protect citizens from environmental degradation. André uses the *Stag Hunt Dilemma* instead of the *Tragedy of the Commons* to analyse *the roots and limitations of altruism in inter-group conflict.*[34]

Practice 4: define the business of business
Here André explores how business leaders can make profit and reduce costs while simultaneously working towards protecting the planet. She discusses the role of organisational culture to achieve lasting change and utilises traditional tools such as PESTEL and SWOT analyses to highlight climate- and energy-related strengths, weaknesses, opportunities and threats.

Practice 5: engage global leadership
In this final practice, André proposes solutions for how inter-organisational and inter-sector relationships can achieve a positive common future. *Global leaders must think big, and they must think smart. They must understand the psychology and politics of motivation, collaboration and competition, including how to set motivating goals and turn those goals into action. They must be thoughtful about how humanity distributes resources – about economics, including ecological economics and the working of capitalism itself. They must improve the long-term effectiveness of existing global*

institutions or develop new ones. [...] And they must do all this while facing up to psychological factors like human denial and political factors like national sovereignty.[35] André evaluates the strategies used to achieve this, some of them as simple as designing a plan that adds up! Making such a plan could stem from the En-ROADS simulator and the FLOWER framework described earlier in this chapter.

Using a systems approach to analyse an organisation and its connections with other stakeholders, then devising climate solutions based on these insights, is our approach in this book. We hope to inspire you to make a plan that adds up and achieves the positive future we all want!

WANT TO DIG DEEPER?

Lead for the Planet. Five Practices for Confronting Climate Change – by Rae André
We strongly recommend reading the whole of Rae André's book, the key aspects of which we have highlighted here in our introduction. Each of the sections provides many insights, not only for leaders, but for anyone who wants to support *Team Humanity* to make the right choices based on a good understanding of natural science, human nature and the different systems at play.

Net Positive: how Courageous Companies Thrive by Giving More Than They Take – by Paul Polman and Andrew Winston
Former CEO of Unilever, Paul Polman, and Andrew Winston (a globally recognised author and motivational speaker for major corporations such as Walmart, SAP and Pfizer) have written an engaging book on how companies could and should address global challenges such as climate change by becoming a *net positive company*. That is an organisation which:

1. Improves the lives of all its stakeholders
2. Takes ownership of all the environmental and social impacts created by its business model
3. *Partners with competitors, civil society, and governments to drive transformative change that no single group or enterprise could deliver alone.*[36]

What can you find in this book? Overview and structure

This book is for any manager, and indeed any employee or volunteer in any organisation, as well as owners of SMEs or larger businesses. It aims to provide guidance and support for the private, public or third sector, as we have focused on the processes, functions and departments that can be found in most organisations, seeking to provide inspiration for everyone wanting to manage their greenhouse gas emissions. For example, the food chapter is especially useful for someone who orders catering or is the chef in a canteen, but in reality everyone will benefit from reading it, as their food and drink choices can help us all (at work or at home) to make the transition to carbon-friendlier options.

While we only briefly discuss the systemic changes to be made in wider society, we would encourage everyone to strive towards them, along with the changes they make in their working environment and their private life. We have given some ideas in this regard in chapter 15, but it also underpins our chapter 10, where we discuss that we can all potentially use the power of pensions for example to move investments away from the fossil fuel industry.

For all organisations, it is important to distinguish between the core product/service on offer and all the general processes in the organisation, such as the handling of data. While we have focused on the latter, we would also encourage companies to reflect on their core products and/or services, as they might be the biggest contributors to their greenhouse gas emissions. For a telecommunications company for example, this could mean reflecting on their business model: should they focus on contracts that encourage customers to obtain a new mobile phone every two years or could they offer a more modular product where different parts could be replaced or repaired? (See further details in chapter 5, 'Digital Footprint'.)

This book is divided into four parts. The first consists of this and the following two chapters – it sets the scene and offers generic insights such as learning about climate literacy (chapter 2) and communicating climate change to stakeholders (chapter 3). Chapters 4 to 10 provide detailed practical applications that most organisations will find useful, such as reducing GHG emissions in the office, setting up a climate-friendly pension scheme, encouraging a reduction in food waste, or designing a sustainable website. Chapters 11–14 support any organisation, but especially Small and Medium-sized Enterprises (SMEs), to set up their own greenhouse gas management system by identifying their Organisational and Operational Boundaries (chapter 11), measuring their GHG emissions (chapter 12), setting targets on how to reduce them (chapter 13) and finally devising strategies, policies and practices to achieve these targets (chapter 14). The final part contains chapter 15, which suggests further support for any manager and employee, for example networks in different countries, to keep everyone motivated on this journey to a low-carbon society!

In each chapter of this book, you will find an introduction into the topic, where we summarise some of the key insights for you. We then propose high-impact solutions that you could implement in your own organisation. Chapters 2–13 will also contain a case study, which has been written by experts in their field, Quick Wins and Further Resources. On the companion website to this book you can find templates, checklists and further material to help you plan and implement this work.

Detailed summary of each chapter

Part I: Net Zero and Decarbonisation: Understanding and Communicating the Basics

Chapter 2 Climate Literacy and Training for All

Everyone in an organisation needs to understand climate change, its impact on society, on the business itself and the associated sector, as well as the best high-impact solutions to be embedded in their work and private life. In short, everyone needs to be climate literate. This includes the ability to calculate the greenhouse gas (GHG) emissions of every human activity, from using an air-conditioning unit in the office or drinking a cappuccino in the staff room, to buying work clothes or choosing a mobile phone. Additionally, being climate literate provides the tools to help select the climate solutions with the highest impact, which will potentially improve the future for *all* within the organisation, and beyond.

This chapter will introduce the concept of carbon equivalent emissions and how to calculate the greenhouse gas emissions of a wide variety of activities. Utilising the worldwide distributed Climate Literacy Training for Educators, Communities, Organisations and Students (CLT-ECOS), it will offer a detailed plan for an eight-hour training course covering high-impact climate solutions, climate justice, carbon calculations, along with the key insights from climate change science in relation to high-impact solutions. The purchase of the book will give access to all the material needed to run such a training course, along with complementary Online Managers' Notes including slide decks and quizzes. We will also give recommendations in the complementary guide on how to design advanced climate literacy training to cater for the needs of different colleagues, such as those working in accounting or procurement.

Chapter 3 Climate Communication and Reporting to Internal and External Stakeholders

Communication is crucial both strategically and tactically, externally and internally, for an organisation to present its efforts to address climate change, embed climate solutions and improve carbon management. Appropriate communications raise awareness and can be used to define and shape action and progress. This chapter explores various options, looking both at internal communications to employees, and how to have potentially difficult conversations with suppliers.

It seeks to help managers understand central considerations for climate change communication with suggested methods and content for communication such as the role of storytelling and signposting to useful templates. We also look at the use and role of social media in climate change communications and offer guidance on how to ensure it plays both an informational and influencing role effectively.

Regarding more formal communication to external stakeholders, this is explored via a section on reporting and disclosure. Appropriate presentation of relevant information is growing in importance, not only for reporting purposes, but also with respect to applications for tender, or information requested from one's supply chain. For those mystified by the requirements linked to this, it introduces ESG Book, a new initiative from Anglo-German asset manager, Arabesque Partners.

As there are clear links between communications and marketing, and between the contents of this chapter and carbon management, it should be read in conjunction with chapters 9 (Marketing) and 12 (Carbon Accounting).

Part II: High-Impact Solutions: Making a Difference

Chapter 4 Meetings and Transport: Colleagues, Customers and Suppliers

Every organisation is contributing to greenhouse gas (GHG) emissions through meetings held on their premises. This could relate to employees commuting to work, or indeed the recruitment of board members and flying them in for the interview process. In addition, raw materials and ingredients must be sourced from suppliers, and products and processes need to be supplied to customers.

This chapter starts with transportation emissions and how reductions could be achieved. Different solutions are evaluated regarding how meetings could be conducted in a more carbon-friendly way, including recruitment. Innovative solutions will be shared on how employees and customers could be incentivised to choose carbon-friendlier transport. This will include information and solutions regarding embodied carbon in electric (company) cars and vans.

The chapter includes recommendations on how to increase local networks with customers and suppliers, the latter will also be picked up in chapter 7 (Estates & Facilities) and chapter 8 (Procurement & Supply). A case study will look into reducing carbon emissions during the recruitment process. Quick Wins, an implementation plan and Further Resources conclude the chapter.

Chapter 5 Your Organisation's Digital Footprint

An organisation's digital carbon footprint is often regarded as negligible. However the carbon emissions from the world's data centres along with the storage and sending of digital information are massive. The move to using cryptocurrencies increases worldwide emissions enormously and might counteract any savings made in other areas. Finally, the embodied carbon in computers, tablets, smartphones and so on is not usually considered when switching to innovative technologies or devices.

This chapter offers calculations for data centres, cryptocurrencies, websites, social media and different devices such as smartphones. It suggests diverse ways to reduce emissions, especially through behavioural change, improvements to information systems and sustainable website design.

It includes recommendations for changes that can be easily implemented, such as challenging the automatic regular updating of equipment, as well as addressing more complex solutions such as website energy efficiency and data centres. A case study of how an organisation has sought to optimise its web design, along with suggestions for Quick Wins are also included.

Chapter 6 Food Waste and Food for Thought

Food production and food waste contribute to a high proportion of greenhouse gas (GHG) emissions. Many organisations have on-site canteens or buy in outside catering for events and hospitality. The types and provenance of ingredients, the choices of menu offered and the way the food is served, can all have an impact, as can the way in which any leftovers, surplus food or waste are dealt with.

This chapter will provide guidance for anyone who orders catering for events or takes clients out for meals. It will also be useful for managers working in an organisation where there is a canteen or food/drink vending machines on site, to understand the carbon-friendly options available. The chapter will empower managers to select specific climate solutions through an evaluation of the food and beverage provision and improved meal planning to bring food waste to a minimum. It will also look at eco-labelling and how employees can be educated and nudged to change their behaviour. By introducing some of these ideas at work, it may additionally encourage a different attitude to food and food waste outside of the workplace.

It will look at food and beverage sourcing, wastage (prevention and redistribution) and elimination or, at the very least, reduction of single-use plastics. Finally, this chapter's case study contains further hints and tips from an award-winning restaurateur recognised for his sustainability credentials with a Michelin Green Star.

Chapter 7 Estates and Facilities: Building a Better Future

Buildings and infrastructure constitute a significant part of an organisation's total carbon footprint through using energy for heating, powering, lighting and cooling purposes. Demolitions, new builds and refurbishments all cause high emissions, especially where cement and steel are deployed. Increasing energy efficiency of buildings and industry reduces the need for fuel, leading to a reduction in costs and the transition to renewables will be another important lever to reduce related emissions.

This chapter will offer guidance to estates and facilities managers, as well as other employees, on how to manage and reduce GHG emissions in buildings' operations and in construction, to achieve a sustainable built environment. High-impact solutions are provided along with Quick Wins as well as a good practice case study from a business organisation.

It also covers biodiversity, defines carbon sinks and includes strategies on how to attempt to capture greenhouse gas emissions from your organisational property and grounds.

Chapter 8 Procurement and Supply: Pushing the Boundaries to Remove Carbon Emissions

Procurement and supply are responsible for up to 70% of an organisation's revenue and have direct links to profits through the efficiency and effectiveness they facilitate. They are also responsible for the majority of greenhouse gas (GHG) emissions. These are often considered to be outside the control of the organisation, but procurement processes and associated policies can in fact enable the organisation to take control and exert influence. Opportunities arise, not least because of the scale of the emissions and any subsequent reductions will benefit the organisation, its suppliers and its customers. There should be added benefits relating to resilience, relationships and overall engagement, with collaboration and cooperation being key to ensuring a successful reduction in GHG emissions and embedding climate solutions within the organisation and beyond.

The chapter is structured to provide guidance and further support, to facilitate action relating to procurement and supply. It will guide you to design an emissions reduction strategy for the supply chain, suggesting how to work with suppliers. Outcomes have the opportunity to make large impacts on overall GHG emissions and should prove to be mutually beneficial. Included is a case study which examines how UK employers can facilitate the acquisition of electric vehicles for their employees.

Chapter 9 Marketing for a Better Climate

Consumers and other stakeholders are increasingly interested in climate action, and this influences choices about the purchase of materials, products and services at both individual and organisational level, along with wider concerns about health and well-being, good working conditions and how products have been tested. In a business-to-business (B2B) context, an organisation's desire to reposition its brand with regard to emissions to gain new contracts or keep current ones, and its ability to recruit appropriate talent, have gained in importance.

This chapter looks at how core marketing concepts and tools can shape choices and consequent action, with the climate in mind. It looks beyond the core product or service and develops the notion of the creation and delivery of 'value'. Different elements of the marketing mix will be highlighted, such as ensuring a climate-responsible product offer, addressing how price and greenhouse gas (GHG) emissions are interrelated, and how to provide the benefits of online shopping while minimising negative impacts. It also addresses the importance of considering emissions associated with different communication methods, and the overarching requirement for your marketing strategy to address climate change. A case-study on marketing in a hotel is included, along with Quick Wins and Further Resources.

Combined with chapter 3 (Communication & Reporting), this chapter encourages engagement with customers to support their awareness and commitment to climate action, and to enable them to choose climate-friendly products and services. In doing so, this can help them address both their own requirements and those of wider society.

Chapter 10 Pension Funds, Accounts and Other Investments for a Good Future

Every organisation, and to a certain extent every employee, can choose whether their investments, their bank accounts, their pension fund and so on, are benefitting from supporting climate-damaging activities, such as the fossil fuel industry, or are supporting the transition to a low-carbon society by investing in appropriate products and processes. Making bad decisions can result in organisations facing the risk of stranded assets.

This chapter will cover Socially Responsible Investing (SRI) and the difference between investment for impact and investment with impact. It will also include responsible shareholding and Environmental, Social and

Governance (ESG) investing. Leading initiatives such as the United Nations' Principles for Responsible Investment (PRI), the Global Impact Investing Network (GIIN), the Impact Management Project (IMP) and the European Venture Philanthropy Association (EVPA) will be introduced.

More specifically, different investment and screening strategies will be evaluated, the IMP's five dimensions of impact will be introduced, and the chapter will guide managers and employees in organisations to make the right choices based on their own values and financial needs. A case study looking at sustainable investment of a German pension fund is included, along with Quick Wins and Further Resources.

Part III: Carbon Footprinting: Introducing Greenhouse Gas Management for the Whole Organisation

Shaping the journey: guidance for chapters 11–14

This gives you an overview of how these four chapters together help you to set up a greenhouse gas management plan.

Chapter 11 Understanding Greenhouse Gas Management: Scopes and Boundaries for Carbon Footprinting

Greenhouse gas (GHG) emissions, including carbon emissions associated with the core business activities of an organisation, are categorised into three 'scopes' (Scope 1, 2 and 3) as per the Greenhouse Gas Protocol Corporate Accounting and Reporting Standard. The three scopes of GHG emissions cover an organisation's own operations, as well as its wider value chain.

This chapter supports anyone who wants to understand the different reporting scopes and set up a GHG management plan for their own organisation. It is also useful for anyone who wants to participate in discussions around the different scopes and how organisations worldwide report on their greenhouse gas emissions. It explains Organisational and Operational Boundaries (OOB) for carbon footprinting, as well as the associated data requirements for the different scopes. The need for a holistic approach to tackle all three scopes of emissions for effective and impactful Carbon/GHG management processes is also stressed.

This chapter also provides a case study example of a business, focusing on the three scopes and how they developed their OOB. Finally, it offers a checklist for managers to be followed when addressing Scope 1, 2 and 3 for Carbon/GHG management.

Chapter 12 Carbon Accounting: Why What You Measure Matters!
Whilst the adage 'if you can't measure it, you can't manage it' is not necessarily true, it is important for carbon management, as with any other management activity, that information and data are collected to support reporting, decision-making and review. This chapter will introduce the concept of a company's carbon footprint and the Greenhouse Gas Emissions Inventory and how greenhouse gas (GHG) emissions can be calculated, reduced, offset and disclosed.

The processes leading to the compilation of the inventory and footprint must be consistent, accurate and transparent. This is necessary for comparisons and for the communication with other stakeholders such as suppliers, to support decision-making. Internally these decisions will relate to policies and programmes aimed at reducing GHG emissions, and externally they will guide the assessment of what is material, and who is responsible for those reductions.

Advice will be given on how data should be gathered for each of the scopes introduced in chapter 11. We seek to keep carbon accounting simple and adopt a step-by-step approach that provides insights to key guidance and considerations. A case study is included, as well as Quick Wins and Further Resources.

Chapter 13 Setting Science-Based Targets: The Right Approach for Your Business Organisation?
Science-based targets (SBTs) are receiving increased attention in the corporate business world. They support the achievement of an overall Net Zero ambition, in line with the latest climate science and a 1.5°C future. Setting such targets offers a clearly defined pathway for businesses to reduce their carbon emissions, which can add credibility to their overall strategy and objectives.

This chapter introduces the concept of an SBT and outlines its benefits. It then provides an overview of how these might be developed by following certain steps using the process outlined by the Science-Based Targets initiative (SBTi). It also highlights why this could be the right approach for carbon reduction target setting in any organisation.

The apparel and footwear sector is selected as an example to outline the process and to explore sector-specific guidance. The streamlined route for setting SBTs in small and medium-sized enterprises (SMEs) is also discussed. Good practice in science-based target setting from an SME already involved in this approach will be shared through a case study as inspiration for others, and Further Resources are suggested to assist organisations.

Chapter 14 Strategy, Policies and Practices for Carbon Management
Strategy, policies and practices for carbon/greenhouse gas (GHG) management are key to achieving a Net Zero future and mitigating the challenges of climate change for a low-carbon and sustainable economy.

This chapter supports managers in designing relevant strategy, policies and practices for the effective implementation of GHG management – in any sector. It suggests a planned approach through all hierarchy levels from 'elimination' to 'compensation' to reduce GHG emissions. 'Carbon offsetting' as a concept is also discussed and evaluated, for organisations with residual emissions to become Carbon Neutral or Net Zero. A related case study explores this further.

Example policies are presented, which can easily be replicated or adapted for any organisation. The chapter concludes with a list of Quick Wins for managers who want to get started on this journey, as well as suggested Further Resources.

Part IV: The Road to Net Zero: Making it a Reality

Chapter 15 Team Humanity on the Road to Net Zero: Will You Make it Happen?
The transition to Net Zero and to a low-carbon society should be our key priority, and action is needed right now. We have summarised in this final chapter some of the main insights from the book. However, the focus is on giving further support to managers, and indeed all employees of an organisation, to ensure we keep global warming to 1.5°C maximum.

Diverse incentives are given in many countries, from awards to accreditations to funding opportunities. Besides these 'carrots', many also use a 'stick' approach by making certain types of reporting mandatory and by increasing regulation. We have highlighted a few in this chapter and we provide links to more information which will be of benefit for those in some of the higher-emitting countries.

Recommendations are given on how to find support and mentoring schemes within various countries and internationally. Networks in different parts of the world such as Australia, Canada, Europe, Qatar and the United States of America are introduced, with some focus on the United Kingdom, and we also include networks targeted at accountants or investors for example. Several awards and accreditation schemes are highlighted, along with suggested news organisations that offer regular updates and resources on climate change.

A section is dedicated to help you connect all the dots and suggests how to develop, transition, and sustain an organisation's strategy to remove greenhouse gas (GHG) emissions. Integrating the elements into the organisation's overall strategic plan, and that of its customers, will be key. However, it is noted that individuals and organisations will not have all the answers and there are significant benefits from partnerships and working collaboratively, as work related to the UN Sustainable Development Goals and others suggests. This collaboration should be internal, with your supply and value chains, and beyond. Education and training also need to be at the heart of organisations, schools and higher education, with Business Schools having an important role to play.

We finish this final chapter with the bigger picture – how systemic changes worldwide could be achieved and sustained. The companion website provides up-to-date ideas for useful websites about awards, accreditations and networks, in order to support readers on their journey.

Notes

1. IPCC: https://www.ipcc.ch/about/
2. IPCC (2022) *Climate Change 2022. Impacts, Adaptation and Vulnerability – Summary for Policy Makers:* https://report.ipcc.ch/ar6wg2/pdf/IPCC_ AR6_WGII_SummaryForPolicymakers.pdf
3. Economist (2022) *The latest IPCC report argues that stabilising the climate will require fast action:* https://www.economist.com/science-and-technology/

2022/04/09/the-latest-ipcc-report-argues-that-stabilising-the-climate-will-require-fast-action

4. https://unfccc.int/news/the-evidence-is-clear-the-time-for-action-is-now-we-can-halve-emissions-by-2030

5. McKie R (2021) It's now or never: Scientists warn time of reckoning has come for the planet, *The Observer* (15 August): https://www.theguardian.com/environment/2021/aug/15/its-now-or-never-scientists-warn-time-of-reckoning-has-come-for-the-planet

6. IPCC, 2018: Annex I: Glossary [Matthews JBR (ed.)]. In: *Global Warming of 1.5°C. An IPCC Special Report* [Masson-Delmotte V P *et al* (eds.)]. In Press.: https://www.ipcc.ch/sr15/chapter/glossary/

7. Water vapour, ozone and CFCs are other GHGs not covered by the Kyoto protocol, please see: Brohe A (2016) *The Handbook of Carbon Accounting*, London & New York: Routledge, p. 183

8. Climate Council Australia (2018) *Infographic: the difference between 1.5 and 2 degrees warming*: https://www.climatecouncil.org.au/resources/infographic-the-difference-between-1–5-and-2-degrees-warming/

9. National Geographic (2019) *Carbon dioxide levels are at a record high. Here's what you need to know*: https://www.nationalgeographic.com/environment/article/greenhouse-gases; the video mentioned is available via this website

10. Climate Watch (2022) https://www.climatewatchdata.org/about/description

11. En-ROADS User Guide (2021) *About En-ROADS*: https://docs.climateinteractive.org/projects/en-roads/en/latest/guide/about.html

12. Energy Modeling Forum: https://emf.stanford.edu/

13. En-ROADS User Guide (2021) https://docs.climateinteractive.org/projects/en-roads/en/latest/index.html

14. The Framework For Long-Term, Whole-System, Equity-Based Reflection (2015) by Elizabeth Sawin: https://img.climateinteractive.org/wp-content/uploads/2017/09/Flower-Writeup-Long.pdf. More information about her and the Multisolving Institute https://www.multisolving.org/about-us/

15. Project Drawdown (2022) *Table of Solutions*: https://drawdown.org/solutions/table-of-solutions

16. Project Drawdown (2022) *Refrigerant Management*: https://drawdown.org/solutions/refrigerant-management

17. Washington Post (2019) *Facing unbearable heat, Qatar has begun to air-condition the outdoors*: https://www.washingtonpost.com/graphics/2019/world/climate-environment/climate-change-qatar-air-conditioning-outdoors/

18. The World Bank – *consumption per capita (tCO$_2$/person)*: https://data.worldbank.org/indicator/EN.ATM.CO2E.PC

19. Film 2040: https://whatsyour2040.com/see-the-film/

20. FT (2022) *The Climate Game* https://ig.ft.com/climate-game/ and then click on 'Created by The Financial Times' to find this quote/information

21. Corporate Knights' *100 most sustainable corporations ranking 2022*: https://www.corporateknights.com/rankings/global-100-rankings/2022-global-100-rankings/100-most-sustainable-corporations-of-2022/

22. Corporate Knights (2022) *Earth Index: Tracking the G20 response to the climate emergency*: https://www.corporateknights.com/wp-content/uploads/2022/04/2022-Earth-Index-Report.pdf p3

23. Corporate Knights (2022) *Earth Index: Tracking the G20 response to the climate emergency*: https://www.corporateknights.com/wp-content/uploads/2022/04/2022-Earth-Index-Report.pdf p. 12

24. Corporate Knights, *Earth Index*: https://www.corporateknights.com/wp-content/uploads/2022/04/2022-Earth-Index-Report.pdf

25. Corporate Knights, *Earth Index*: https://www.corporateknights.com/wp-content/uploads/2022/04/2022-Earth-Index-Report.pdf

26. Berners-Lee M (2020) *How bad are bananas? The carbon footprint of everything*. London: Profile Books Ltd

27. The World Bank (2018), *CO$_2$ emissions (metric tonnes per capita)*: https://data.worldbank.org/indicator/EN.ATM.CO2E.PC

28. World Bank Group, *Climate Risk Country Profile: Bangladesh (2021)*: https://climateknowledgeportal.worldbank.org/country/pakistan

29. Simmons D (2020) *What is 'climate justice'?*: https://yaleclimateconnections.org/2020/07/what-is-climate-justice/

30. Berners-Lee M (2020) *How bad are bananas? The carbon footprint of everything*. London: Profile Books Ltd, p. 12 and p. 145 for the next calculation

31. André R (2020) *Lead for the Planet: Five Practices for Confronting Climate Change*, University of Toronto Press, p. 3

32. André R (2020) *Lead for the Planet: Five Practices for Confronting Climate Change*, University of Toronto Press, p. 4

33. André R (2020) *Lead for the Planet: Five Practices for Confronting Climate Change*, University of Toronto Press, p. 5
34. André R (2020) *Lead for the Planet: Five Practices for Confronting Climate Change*, University of Toronto Press, p. 9
35. André R (2020) *Lead for the Planet: Five Practices for Confronting Climate Change*, University of Toronto Press, p. 165
36. Quote taken from https://netpositive.world/book/ where you can also find more information about the book

2

CLIMATE LITERACY TRAINING FOR ALL

Petra Molthan-Hill and Fiona Winfield

Every manager and every employee of every organisation needs to be climate literate, and therefore enabled to choose the best high-impact climate solutions to be embedded in their own work and that of the wider company or organisation. Leading employers in both the public and private sector are now implementing such training as part of their in-house offer to their staff at all levels. As every human activity is linked to carbon equivalent emissions, this chapter also offers insights for changes to be made at home or in the community.

This chapter is for you if:

- You are a manager, an employee or a volunteer in any organisation
- You work in the HR department of an organisation
- You are responsible for corporate training or staff development, or work in the Learning & Development department
- You are interested in climate literacy for yourself, friends, family and colleagues.

DOI: 10.4324/9781003274049-3

It will cover:

- What impact can I have as an individual?
- What will my future look like if I make changes?
- What is climate literacy and what is a carbon footprint?
- What are carbon equivalent emissions?
- How can I make sure that I choose high-impact climate solutions?
- What training is on offer?
- What is typically covered in a Climate Literacy Training course?

What can I possibly do to make a difference?

As people learn that climate change is anthropogenic (i.e. caused by humans), they realise they hold the key to mitigate it by embedding appropriate high-impact climate solutions in every aspect of their professional, personal and community life, and may in some cases be in a position to influence institutional policies in their organisation. This all starts with individual action. People might wonder whether the activity of one single person can make a difference, but as we will show in this chapter, it really can.

Let's assume you decide to have one meat-free day per week in your organisation and also discontinue the purchase of beef imported from the other side of the world. Let's assume meat-eaters throughout your country make the same decision; with a minor change in everyone's diet, you would reduce the meat consumption by at least 180 tonnes per million people per week![1] That equates to savings of 26.4 tonnes of CO_2e! Even without having a weekly meat-free day, replacing any imported beef consumed with locally sourced beef, would save 12 kg CO_2e per 8 oz (c225 g) steak per person. If everyone consumed a steak once a week, this would amount to weekly savings of 12,000 tonnes CO_2e per million people. Clearly if you were calculating any savings for your country, you would need to discount those who are already vegetarian or vegan, as the savings would not apply to them.

Additionally, the more people who change their eating habits, the more it becomes the norm, which might give other people permission and inspiration to take similar action. Turning from our food choices to our buildings, '**green curtains**' for example have become a new feature in architecture and are immensely popular for example in Japan.

WHAT ARE GREEN CURTAINS?

A green curtain consists of plants grown down the side of buildings – a sort of living wall. They have become commonplace in Japan over the last few years. By 2012, over 80% of Japan's local authorities supported and encouraged installing green curtains within their cities.[2]

According to the US Environmental Protection Agency (EPA), these plant installations serve two purposes. They add greenery to urban areas and they mitigate against the 'heat island' effect. These are *built up areas that are hotter than nearby rural areas*, and because they encourage greater use of air-conditioning in warmer months, these areas consume more energy during the summer, and create more air pollution and emit more greenhouse gases all year round.[3] The plants also absorb the sun's rays, which would otherwise be absorbed by the building materials used in the nearby structures and roads.

Green curtains can be built in both industrial and residential areas. In the former, they can be as tall as 20 feet (over 6 metres) and are often built using steel frames attached to the side of the building. Residential green curtains tend to be shorter, typically 5–10 feet high (2–3 metres approximately). The latter only require a few materials and can be quite simple to install and, as a bonus, certain types of fruit and vegetables can be grown on them.[4]

Similar developments can be seen in other countries such as the **Bosco Verticale** (**Vertical Forest**),[5] a pair of residential towers in Milan, Italy. They are 111 metres (364 ft) and 76 metres (249 ft) high respectively and contain more than 900 trees over 8,900 square metres (96,000 sq ft) of terraces, as well as shrubs and other plants. Residential buildings such as these offer accommodation for many people using minimal space, while the 'vertical forest' increases biodiversity and green spaces, reduces noise pollution, and improves the air quality. Trees and plants are a very efficient and cost-effective way to absorb carbon dioxide, one of the so-called carbon sinks. According to the National Geographic Society, a **carbon sink** is an area that absorbs more carbon than it releases, while a carbon source releases more than it absorbs. Trees might be the best-known carbon sinks, and initiatives such as 'planting a tree' is one of the favoured actions to increase carbon sinks worldwide. Other examples are peatlands, oceans and coastal areas, such as mangroves, salt marshes and sea meadows. Regenerative practices in the oceans and along the coasts could and should receive more attention, providing carbon sinks, while supplying food, improving fisheries and supporting storm protection.[6]

Returning to the *Bosco Verticale* which you can see in Photo 2.1, the approximately 900 trees, 5,000 shrubs and 11,000 plants growing on the buildings will convert around 2 tonnes of carbon each year into oxygen. Additionally, they moderate the internal temperature by shading the interiors from the sun in the summer and reducing the need for air-conditioning

Photo 2.1 Bosco Verticale – Milan, Italy photo by Daniel Seßler on Unsplash.

to cool down the internal temperature, as well as blocking fierce winds in the winter. The buildings themselves are self-sufficient by using renewable energy from solar panels and filtered wastewater to sustain the buildings' plant life. In chapter 7 (Estates & Facilities) we will explore further how this technology is used for example in Singapore, which is leading the way and seeks to green at least 80% of its buildings by 2030.[7]

The changes discussed here have an impact on people, organisations, companies and economies. They create for example a demand for tools and plants related to vertical farming and green technologies, and provide employment for gardeners and horticulturalists who understand vertical farming and how to look after the plants in buildings transformed into 'vertical forests'. The growing of fruit and vegetables on the estate or buildings might even inspire the organisation to offer more vegetarian or vegan food in their canteen.

A positive future is within our grasp

Often people associate the changes required to reduce carbon emissions with personal lifestyle changes, sacrifices and a poorer quality of life. This might be partially true in some cases, such as a reduction in travel to distant tourist locations, however the potential for a better quality of life is often less well understood. Imagine for example a city like New York full of green plants on all its tall buildings. People can sit nicely shaded on their balconies and terraces; a recent article in the UK's *Guardian* newspaper even shared the story and pictures of a New Yorker making his own wine from his mini vineyard on the tenth floor! Imagine additionally that no one gets stuck in traffic in New York anymore, as personal cars are replaced by bicycles with rain shields for added comfort, everyone cycling in fresh air to work, improving their own health and mobility at the same time. No one is stuck in a yellow cab or a traffic jam anymore, desperately trying to get to a meeting on time. Pedestrians are exposed to fewer exhaust fumes, and space on the streets is dedicated to more outdoor dining and green spaces for children and teenagers to play games or cycle in a safer environment. Taxi drivers have retrained as gardeners or youth workers, or are driving older people around in rickshaws. Some electric vehicles are allowed in the city such as ambulances or fire engines. A 'side benefit' is that ambulances no longer get stuck in traffic and patients with acute conditions are more likely to survive.

The associated reduction in carbon emissions (fewer cars and less air-conditioning required due to the 'green curtains') and the additional benefit of plants acting as carbon sinks, combine with many other benefits that increase the quality of life for all citizens. This may especially benefit marginalised citizens who often live in the centre of large cities next to major roads: less noise, less air pollution, better health, increased mobility and better mental well-being. Bogotà in Colombia is one city that has already realised the benefits of such changes and since 2000 has closed its centre to traffic on car-free days (and since 2021 has extended this to a car-free week).[8] This has inspired other cities such as Jakarta, Washington, DC and Montreal.

In his film '2040', the director, Damon Gameau, motivated by concerns for his four-year-old daughter, is inspired to go on a journey around the world to find the best high-impact climate solutions available now, so that his daughter will have a good life in 2040. He talks to changemakers and innovators in agriculture, technology, education, economics, civil society and sustainability, to choose and demonstrate the best solutions that are available to us already and are being implemented now, or could be in the future. He is impressed by the solutions already put in place, from marine permaculture to decentralised renewable energy projects. His journey is as summarised on the film's website: *the central premise for the documentary '2040', a story of hope that looks at the very real possibility that humanity could reverse global warming and improve the lives of every living thing in the process. It is a positive vision of what 'could be', instead of the dystopian future we are so often presented.*[9]

Knowledge is power

In order to make appropriate choices, everyone needs to be climate literate. Just as every child needs to learn to read, write and count, everyone needs to have a basic understanding of carbon or more specifically carbon dioxide equivalents. Furthermore, everyone needs to be carbon management literate, so that they can manage their own carbon dioxide equivalent emissions with the aim to reduce them as much as possible, especially at work.

Carbon dioxide equivalent, as defined by the OECD is: *a measure used to compare the emissions from various greenhouse gases based upon their global warming potential. For example, the global warming potential for methane over 100 years is 21. This means that emissions of one million metric tonnes of methane are equivalent to emissions of 21 million metric tonnes of carbon dioxide.*[10] All activities undertaken by humans release greenhouse gases, whether it is methane when eating or throwing away food, a refrigeration gas when using air-conditioning or a fridge, or carbon dioxide when burning fossil fuels, see Figure 2.1 for the different types of greenhouse gases. We will explore this topic further in chapter 12 (Carbon Accounting), where we will talk about the conversion factors issued by governments so that companies and other organisations can calculate their own emissions in a consistent manner.

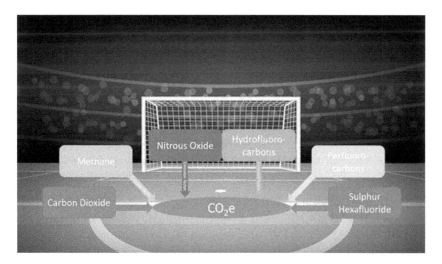

Figure 2.1 Carbon dioxide equivalents – Achieving the goal figure copyright: Carbon Literacy Training for Business Schools 2020.[11]

Being carbon management literate would enable supermarket shoppers to spot immediately the right choices, and they would not have to think twice about whether asparagus flown in from another country out of season would produce higher carbon emissions than a cheese produced locally. It would also enable them to put the right processes in place, whether in a private or work context.

What effect am I having on the planet?

Another term to clarify is **'carbon footprint'**. There are different definitions, the World Health Organization (WHO) for example offers: *a measure of the impact your activities have on the amount of carbon dioxide (CO_2) produced through the burning of fossil fuels ... expressed as a weight of CO_2 emissions produced in tonnes.*[12]

However, many provide a broader definition such as the following from 'youmatter': *A carbon footprint corresponds to the whole amount of greenhouse gases (GHG) produced to, directly and indirectly, support a person's lifestyle and activities. Carbon footprints are usually measured in equivalent tonnes of CO_2, during the period of a year, and they can be associated with an individual, an organisation, a product or an event, among others.*[13]

It is important to note that a carbon footprint can be calculated not just for every product or service, but also for the whole company/organisation; we will discuss this in more detail in chapter 12 (Carbon Accounting). Here, however, we would like you to explore your own *personal* footprint, which will encourage you to reflect on your own lifestyle and consumption patterns. You could for example use the following UN calculator: https://offset.climateneutralnow.org/footprintcalc.

After this analysis you could choose to offset, but it might be even better if you reflected on the areas where you have the highest personal carbon footprint and decide whether you could make any changes in your personal life. If for example you realise that the biggest component is your leisure travel, perhaps you enjoy long weekends abroad on a regular basis, you might decide to reduce the frequency. This approach can also be applied to your work life. You might want to reflect on how many of your business meetings really need to be in person. We will discuss this topic further in chapter 4 (Meetings & Transport).

Often people realise that they do not have a deep enough understanding as to which of the different solutions on offer would really have an impact, or they would like to know which changes would really make a difference. This becomes even more complex when you take other solutions into account, such as setting a carbon price or improving the carbon sinks associated with the activities of your organisation. Here the demand for training arises, in order to fill the gaps in understanding.

WANT TO DIG DEEPER?

How bad are bananas? The carbon footprint of everything – book by Mike Berners-Lee
Professor Berners-Lee shares in this book his calculations for a broad range of products and activities, from the bananas in the title to cryptocurrencies. Written in an entertaining way, it is based on his extensive research into the best ways to calculate carbon equivalent emissions, and helps readers to understand these calculations and make the right decisions.

Drawdown: Climate Solutions at work – unleashing your employee power (Sept 2021) https://drawdown.org/sites/default/files/210920_Drawdown_AtWork_06.pdf
Project Drawdown was already introduced in chapter 1 and also inspired film director Damon Gameau to make the film '2040' mentioned in this chapter. This Drawdown guide helps employees to understand the transformative climate actions their organisation could, and indeed should, be taking.

The climate literacy training for educators, communities, organisations and students (CLT-ECOS)

In this next section, we will present a specific training course in more detail, however there are others available, and recommendations for alternative online and virtual courses are given at the end of the chapter.

The Climate Literacy Training for Educators, Communities, Organisations and Students (CLT-ECOS) is a virtual 'train the trainer' programme, empowering people to embed high-impact climate solutions in their personal, professional and community life. Professor Petra Molthan-Hill, one of the authors of this book, led the design of this training course.

Many sustainability, climate and carbon literacy training courses focus on climate science and individual action, which are essential, but insufficient. The CLT-ECOS integrates the foundational carbon science from leading think tanks, alongside social science insights and change theory, and also focuses on high-impact climate solutions from a systems perspective. The CLT-ECOS synthesises key points from top sustainability training resources with an action-learning focus. It integrates tools and examples of how climate solutions contribute to other Sustainable Development Goals (SDGs) beyond SDG 13: Climate Action, generating synergy between the goals. Learners explore climate solutions individually and in groups, then evaluate them against other SDGs, choosing impactful actions to be taken by themselves and their communities. A vision is developed for the whole world based on an understanding of the systems at play, and is then put into action within the area of influence of each learner. Tools offered can be used at any level, by a student, CEO, vice-chancellor or prime minister! CLT-ECOS alumni ambassadors are invited to share the practical outcomes of their plans six and more months down the line, to share best practice and to inspire a new generation of changemakers. This is underpinned by positive and persistence-focused framing, and a clear and strong message of hope and possibility.

The CLT-ECOS was inspired by the Carbon Literacy Training in the British television sector (BBC & ITV), which is covered in this chapter's case study. The CLT-ECOS demonstrates a strong commitment to the common good as well as several instructional design innovations. CLT-ECOS is free for anyone: the materials are Open Source for participants and available for adaptation to one's national, institutional, or community context. With the training delivered virtually, participants from around the world can learn together synchronously through the creative use of video conferencing, virtual whiteboard tools (Padlet & MURAL) and curated websites. This accessibility allows scalability beyond the usual face-to-face classroom or professional development training. This 'train the trainer' content is a thoughtful synthesis of cutting-edge climate change science, climate justice and practical solutions from numerous thought-leaders (c.f. Al Gore's Climate Reality Project, Climate Interactive and MIT's En-ROADS simulator and Project Drawdown). These combined with insights from behavioural science enhance the learners' climate literacy and empower them to make high-impact changes to their own carbon footprint and that of their organisations. The last distinctive feature is a certificate from the Carbon Literacy Project (CLP), linked to the Carbon Literacy Trust, a Charitable Incorporated Organisation based in Manchester (England), for participants who complete all sessions, pass an assessment and develop an action plan.

Table 2.1 CLT-ECOS training course – overview of content and timings

CLT-ECOS OVERVIEW	
Session 1: High-Impact Climate Solutions	
Content	**Timings**
Overview of training • Why should we engage with Climate Literacy Training? • Why do 99% of climate scientists agree that climate change is caused by humans? • What benefits or other Sustainable Development Goals (SDGs) could we achieve if we increase SDG 13: Climate Action?	60 minutes
Quiz 'Project Drawdown': Which climate solutions have the highest impact? Breakout session: Our favoured solutions Quiz: Calculating your own footprint Introducing the Assessment Form	15 minutes 20 minutes 15 minutes 10 minutes
Session 2: Climate Justice and Future Scenarios	
Content	**Timings**
• Kahoot Quiz: Climate Justice • Activity: High emitters of carbon and vulnerability	30 minutes 30 minutes
Storytelling (group activity) • Troubled Future Scenario • Positive Future Scenario • Discussion	60 minutes
Session 3: Climate Change Science and Carbon Calculations	
Content	**Timings**
Climate Change Science: • What is the greenhouse gas effect? • What is a carbon sink?	60 minutes
Carbon Calculations: • How do we calculate greenhouse gas emissions? • Activity: Carbon-friendly food, drinks and meals • Quiz: Transport and communication emissions • Group Activity: Cryptocurrencies, data centres and the World Cup emissions	10 minutes 15 minutes 15 minutes 20 minutes

(continued)

Table 2.1 (Continued)

Session 4: Systems Thinking – Bringing it all together	
Content	Timings
• Game: Can we achieve a 1.5°C future, combining different high-impact solutions using the En-ROADS Simulator from Climate Interactive	30 minutes
• Requirements for the assessment and review of sessions	15 minutes
• Video: FLOWER framework	10 minutes
• Evaluating the additional benefits of climate solutions	15 minutes
• Group Action Plans: making a plan for a high-impact climate solution to be embedded in a work and/or policy context	40 minutes
• Sharing ideas	10 minutes

CLT-ECOS is run over eight hours and delivered virtually in four sessions. Table 2.1 highlights the key topics covered in each session and indicates the different activities involved, with timings. The training is very interactive and a special focus is given to peer-to-peer learning, hence every session includes a breakout element and participants are encouraged to share their own insights in the chat function, as well as posting their ideas and the resources they find on the linked Padlet. Between Sessions 3 and 4, participants are asked to model a 1.5°C scenario and the trainer invites one or two participants in Session 4 to share their screen to explain their workings to the other participants. The trainer provides feedback and uses these to highlight the complexities at policy level for carbon reduction measures and the many high-impact solutions that need to be brought in simultaneously. The trainer refers back to other solutions shared during the course and recommends additional reading.

After the completion of the eight hours, participants are encouraged to submit their assessment form to the Carbon Literacy Project in Manchester (England) to receive a certificate, as this will give them the evidence (assuming they pass) that they have acquired sufficient knowledge and understanding to design high-impact climate solutions. They are also encouraged to become trainers themselves and scale up the knowledge and actions of their peers, thereby contributing to a snowball effect of increased climate and carbon literacy across the world!

CLT-ECOS can be used by anyone who has been through the training and completed the assessment, to train up their colleagues, people in their community or other stakeholders. The CLT-ECOS is designed so that everybody can understand each session, however we recommend using relevant examples in order to tailor the course to the context of the learners in question.

- If delivered to academics as part of our UN PRME Working Group on Climate Change and Environment,[14] we use examples such as integrating climate change mitigation education tools into teaching content and/or into a research design to illustrate certain points.
- If delivered to a specific part of the world, we recommend contextualising the examples such as talking about a typical diet in that region and how this could be made into a lower carbon (dioxide equivalent) diet taking into account cultural preferences.

CLT-ECOS covers general climate and carbon management literacy, which could be the starting point for *every* employee in an organisation. This could be followed by more specific detailed climate training courses, for example 'carbon accounting' for accountants in an organisation. Alternatively, the training for accountants could take some elements of CLT-ECOS and combine them with guidance as covered in chapter 12 (Carbon Accounting).

The CLT-ECOS course described in this chapter is one of several Carbon Literacy Training courses accredited by the Carbon Literacy Project (CLP), and any organisation using the course is encouraged to contact the CLP[15] to certify their learners. At the time of writing, CLP has certified nearly 42,000 learners, involving around 400 courses delivered in 18 nations across a wide variety of sectors. The CLP offers a unique externally-verified adaptable framework for a day's-worth of consistently relevant climate action training. It is owned by the British NGO The Carbon Literacy Trust. Employers, educators and communities can work with them to design and accredit customised courses and certify their learners, or they can create shareable sector-wide training toolkits. The latter approach is in use across the UK public sector – in central government, local authorities, the health service, universities and colleges.[16] There are other sector toolkits available for the automotive sector and museums, with more planned for the construction, fashion and legal sectors.

Case study

The following case study will show how a Carbon Literacy Training programme, in this case the one designed for the television industry, transformed a whole organisation. The project was led by Dan Jackson, whose work on a long-running British television programme resulted in the world's first sustainable TV production and went on to inform best practice and industry standards for sustainable production across the TV industry, both in the United Kingdom and internationally.

Sustainability street: reducing emissions in the television sector

By Dan Jackson (Director of Production, Koolstof) and Lee Rayner (Head of Production, Coronation Street, ITV)

Originally, the Granada Television studios were home to many quintessentially English TV programmes. However, a change in the way shows were made and a shift in viewing habits meant the studios found themselves increasingly empty, all bar one part – the home of the fictional Northern English town of Weatherfield since 1960, where a close-knit, working-class community lived, laughed and loved, on and off the cobbles of Britain's most famous street – **Coronation Street**. To this day, it's the UK's most successful, and the world's longest-running, continuing drama.

In 2012, an opportunity arose to move into a new, purpose-built home in what was to become Europe's largest media hub, MediaCity (Salford Quays). The show's production team had the promise of a sparkling new, high-tech facility that would see them through future decades of fictitious weddings, murders, scandals, scams, heartbreaks and disasters, all weathered with Coronation Street's characteristic Northern charm and heart-melting comedy.

But there was a problem; the planet, both on and off-camera, was also melting.

Climate change has been in the public consciousness for decades, but as late as the 2010s it was still largely misunderstood, ignored, dismissed or denied. One cold February morning, representatives from across the city of Manchester assembled to listen to Cooler Projects, presenting their ideas to position modern-day Manchester as the Scrooge of Christmas future, recognising its own ills of a Christmas long past; if Manchester had been responsible for starting the Industrial Revolution, it must be Manchester who would start a new, sustainable revolution. Acceptance is the first step to recovery, after all.

While planning for the big move, ITV's Production Management team saw an opportunity to build back better, way before anyone else coined the phrase. There was a real excitement about the possibility of doing things differently and of improving the production's environmental impact. With buy-in from senior management, the production team had the blessing to forge ahead.

But there was another problem – fear of the unknown.

Climate systems are chaotic, interconnected, and bewilderingly complex to understand. As elsewhere, climate change education in the United Kingdom had been missing from mainstream education for most. As the ITV production team mulled over how best to tackle the show's carbon footprint, it was clear that the crews were hampered by a lack of knowledge and understanding of the subject. For Northern, hard-working TV crews – the sort who wear shorts all year round – admitting you don't know how something works takes courage.

Because the climate doesn't count carbon emissions according to where they arise, it was clear that a holistic approach was required to boost the knowledge levels of everyone involved. The answer – 'Carbon Literacy Training', which does what it says on the tin: to increase an understanding of *the carbon dioxide costs and impacts of everyday activities, and the ability and motivation to reduce emissions, on an individual, community and organisational basis.*[17]

Under the supervision of Cooler Projects, representatives from across Media City (UK), including ITV, the BBC and Peel worked with experts to develop the world's first course of accredited Carbon Literacy Training for Television Production. It combined climate science with practical ways to reduce carbon emissions, specific to TV production, and was piloted at Coronation Street. This training invited participants to take an active role in owning their own carbon emissions and proposing their own solutions to reduce them.

Initially, the courses were met with a degree of scepticism. For hard-working crews, spare time for external training is lacking. What was so astonishing though, was the shift in attitude and levels of engagement the training always elicited. Afterwards crews were buoyed by feelings of empowerment and enthusiasm to apply their new knowledge. There was a buzz and it was contagious.

Following the training, crews had to report back to the production management team quarterly with their commitments to reducing their environmental impacts. Changes to working practices included a move to LED lighting in studios, and to 100% renewable energy, a reduction in the buying of props, costumes and sets, with departments favouring instead the Waste Hierarchy, or, as described in the North: 'make, mend or make do'. Electronic working was introduced for scripts, schedules and continuity, vastly reducing the printing required, while allowing teams to be more agile and responsive. Transportation emissions were reduced through careful planning and digital working, while single-use plastics were completely removed from catering. Recycling increased to over 90%, while water and energy use plummeted.

But perhaps the most uplifting aspect was the way in which the audience was actively engaged. When appropriate, climate-positive storylines were introduced, stories that saw characters and locations shift towards more sustainable choices, ranging from organic vegetable-growing competitions to upcycling, with plenty of fun and drama included. Scripts were amended to model sustainable choices, electric vehicles drove up the Street and recycling bins even made appearances in the famous Corrie back-alley on the appropriate transmission days. This built sustainability into the fabric of the show, so that its daily UK audience of about 6 million viewers might adopt some of the positive examples in their own lives. Even now, if you watch the end credits of Coronation Street, the famous green mallard reminds the audience that the programme was made responsibly, and as sustainably as possible.

Coronation Street is an employer that promotes from within. With little employment churn, teams learn best practices from their peers and managers. There is a mandatory digital training module for all new starters, which must be retaken annually.

As John Whiston, the MD of Continuing Drama at ITV Studios, says *the fact that sustainability is built into annual mandatory training for everyone at ITV, shows the level of importance the Board and Management now put on this area. ITV has made bold commitments to getting to Net Zero and it sees continual education as a vital tool in changing the culture of ITV from within, changing the way we do things and so achieving those climate targets. The success of the Carbon Literacy Training programme at Coronation Street, and the way it shifted the responsibility for climate change action from the corporate to the personal, engaging with the whole work-force and making everyone working on the show feel responsible for their own behaviour and work practices, persuaded the bosses at ITV that real, lasting change starts with education and awareness and not with top down edicts. As a consequence, climate change awareness and climate change action is baked into everything we do on Coronation Street, and now at ITV.*

For its work on Carbon Literacy and sustainability more generally, Coronation Street won various awards, including the Observer's prestigious Ethical Business Award (2015). Its pioneering work went on to influence the rest of the industry with other shows following its example. Today BAFTA, and others, work across the industry to educate TV professionals in sustainability and examples of best practice in the United Kingdom continue to make waves internationally as the world wakes up to the climate challenge.

The unintended consequences of becoming Carbon Literate were a more engaged and empowered workforce, and a more dynamic, efficient, creative and responsive production. But the best thing about carbon literacy on Coronation Street was a sustained and steady drop in the production's carbon emissions. There's always more to do, but while drama of all kinds will likely thunder down Coronation Street for years to come, the show is playing its part to set the scene for future generations of sustainable production.

Dan Jackson, is Director of Production at Koolstof (www.thekoolstof.com) and Head of Production at Reduced Listening, making arts and current affairs content for the BBC, Spotify, Audible and others. With two decades of production experience with the BBC, ITV and others, Dan also works with content creators and cultural organisations to help transition them to sustainable working.

Lee Rayner is Head of Production, Coronation Street, ITV.

As shown in the case study, a good approach for embedding such training in an organisation is to prioritise the senior managers. When interviewed by one of this book's authors, the head of departments in 'Coronation Street' highlighted the importance for them of the training culminating in the design of an action plan for the whole team. They considered it a really useful takeaway, allowing them to work immediately through all required steps in the next team meeting, in order to embed the necessary techno-logical and behavioural climate solutions as soon as possible.[18] Depending on the organisational culture, a bottom-up approach might also work. For example, starting first by training 'Climate Champions' in each department and using a 'train the trainer' approach could bring the training to all employees in no time. It is important that the training is supported by the

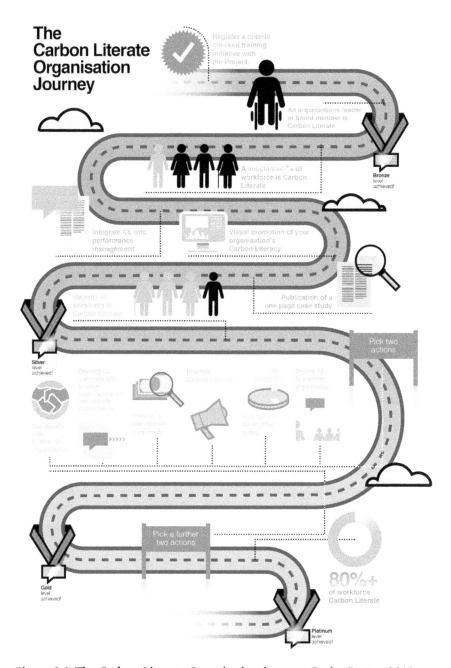

Figure 2.2 The Carbon Literate Organisation journey Cooler Project 2019.

incentives, such as performance management and costs, allowing teams to purchase appliances that are more energy efficient to support the carbon reductions they want to make. We have covered some further ideas in chapter 14 (Policies & Practice), where we discuss the 'Green Rewards Scheme' allowing employees to collect points in a gamified approach when undertaking appropriate actions such as cycling to work.

Beyond offering training and toolkits, the Carbon Literacy Project has also designed a scheme that supports organisations to increase their commitment to climate solutions step by step and achieve the accreditation of a Carbon Literate Organisation (CLO) (see Figure 2.2). Even the best training requires support in its aftermath to optimise the actions enabled by the training. Without it, motivated and enabled Carbon Literate learners could be frustrated in their ambition to optimise their climate action within their organisation, and this is why the Carbon Literacy Project has created its CLO scheme. It enables internal and external recognition of the training and allows internal systems to be created to support climate action from the learners. The awards run from bronze to platinum, broadly representing the number within the organisation certified as Carbon Literate. Criteria include a leader being trained for bronze; the embedding of climate action in performance management in silver and a menu of actions to support other organisations with their carbon literacy for gold and platinum. Some organisations have devised sector-facing shareable training toolkits as their action for these last two.[19]

Outlook – what next?

It is worth investigating the toolkits and courses available to your organisation, having first established whether anyone has already undergone training. The more colleagues you can involve the better, and the easier it will be to start to reduce your organisation's emissions and improve its carbon footprint.

Further Resources

In the website companion guide to this book, you will find more information on how to run such a training course, which you can download to help you plan this work. These resources will be updated regularly, and new developments integrated.

As mentioned earlier, several **online courses** are available, which could be a good first step to gain a better understanding of the different topics raised above. We will give a few recommendations here. Please note however, that this list is not exhaustive:

Climate Change: The Science and Global Impact

https://sdgacademy.org/course/climate-change-the-science-and-global-impact/

Climate science expert Professor Michael Mann introduces the basic scientific principles behind climate change and global warming. *The course covers the basic principles of atmospheric science and methods of climate data collection and interpretation. It introduces basic climate modelling and explores the impact of various greenhouse gas emissions scenarios. Finally, it outlines the impacts of climate change on social, economic, cultural, urban and human systems.*

Climate Solutions 101 presented by Project Drawdown

https://www.drawdown.org/climate-solutions-101

This programme takes a positive outlook and focuses firmly on climate solutions, rather than on problems and challenges. It is based on its own rigorous scientific research and analysis. It includes video units and in-depth conversations, combining Project Drawdown's own resources with inspirational speakers.

FutureLearn Climate Action Initiative

https://www.futurelearn.com/courses/collections/climate-action

Here you can find a range of online courses from free short courses to master's degrees, such as MSc Disaster Management and Resilience. You can also find a short course there from this chapter's authors: 'Climate Literacy and Solutions for Everyone' and from 2023 a microcredential course: 'Climate Solutions for a Net Zero Future'.

Often people prefer **interactive learning**, and we would recommend the following **virtual training courses**, each with a different focus:

Mastering En-ROADS Training Course

https://learn.climateinteractive.org/

En-ROADS by Climate Interactive in collaboration with MIT offers an easily understood overview of the changes needed worldwide to reduce our emissions so that 1.5°C stays in reach. You will learn what impact each change, such as stopping deforestation, could have on decreasing further temperature rises.

The Climate Reality Leader Training

https://www.climaterealityproject.org/video/apply-climate-reality-leader-training

This training course by Al Gore and his team has a focus on climate justice, the impacts climate change is having on different communities in the world. It will give you a detailed understanding of how every country in the world is already affected by climate change and how the latter has affected the different systems in these countries such as agriculture, health and so on.

Climate Literacy Training for Communities, Educators, Organisations and Students CLT-ECOS

The CLT-ECOS described earlier in the chapter would be another option. You could also become a member of the UN PRME Working Group on Climate Change and the Environment – register for free here: https://www.unprmeclimate.org/. That will give you access to newsletters including invitations to the next training course and interesting webinars. On the companion website to this book, you will find more information on how to run such a training and further quizzes and other material to integrate into your training offers.

And last, but not least, something to read:

Srkoc, MMM, Pontoppidan, CA, Molthan-Hill, P and Korbel, P, Exploring Carbon Education for All: The Carbon Literacy Project. In: M Lackner, B Sajjadi and W-Y Chen, eds. (2022) *Handbook of Climate Change Mitigation and Adaptation*, 3rd edition, New York: Springer, pp. 1–37.

This book chapter introduces Carbon Literacy Training and covers both the CLT-ECOS and the television sector's version, as mentioned earlier. It is one of many recommended chapters in the *Handbook of Climate Change Mitigation and Adaptation* that would enable readers to design their own climate change mitigation strategies and tools.

Notes

1. For this calculation, we have used figures from Mike Berners-Lee's (2020) book, *How bad are bananas? The carbon footprint of everything* (pp. 87, 101). For the meat-free day, we assume that 180 g of chicken is replaced with 125 g of chickpeas, 100 g tofu and 100 g of nuts. This would save almost 2.4 kg CO_2e to obtain one day's portion of protein (50 g). This then equates to saving 2,400,000 kg (2,400 tonnes) CO_2e per million people/week. For the second calculation, if UK inhabitants regularly consume steak once a week, and if instead of buying beef imported from deforested land in Brazil, they were to buy British beef, this would save 12 kg CO_2e per week/person, so 12,000 tonnes per million people. These two changes alone would therefore amount to a total of 14,400 tonnes of CO_2e savings per week.

2. Green curtains spread nationwide: https://www.japanfs.org/en/news/archives/news_id032073.html

3. Heat islands: https://www.epa.gov/heatislands

4. Building a green curtain in your own backyard: https://willamette.edu/org/jssl/culture-resources/green-curtain/index.html

5. Milan's vertical forests: https://www.theverge.com/2017/8/9/16112758/milan-vertical-forest-stefano-boeri-video

6. Project Drawdown: https://drawdown.org/sectors/coastal-and-ocean-sinks

7. Singapore, Building and Construction Authority (BCA) (2010) p. 3

8. Colombia's car-free days initiative: https://www.treehugger.com/bogota-changes-car-free-day-car-free-week-4849029

9. To view the film '2040' check: https://whatsyour2040.com/see-the-film

10. OECD: https://stats.oecd.org/glossary/detail.asp?ID=285

11. The Climate Literacy Training for Business Schools was developed by Nottingham Business School, United Kingdom, in collaboration with the UN PRME Champions, the international student organisation 'oikos International' and the Carbon Literacy Project; please contact petra.molthan-hill@ntu.ac.uk for more information.

12. World Health Organization, *Reducing your carbon footprint can be good for your health:* https://www.who.int/globalchange/publications/factsheets/Kit2008_annex1_2.pdf

13. YouMatter.World – carbon footprint definition: https://youmatter.world/en/definition/definitions-carbon-footprint/

14. PRME working group on climate and environment: https://www.unprmeclimate.org/
15. To find out more about being involved in Carbon Literacy Training, contact: info@carbonliteracy.com
16. Carbon Literacy Project toolkits for the public sector: https://carbonliteracy.com/toolkits/
17. The Carbon Literacy Project: https://carbonliteracy.com/
18. For more details about this research, see: Chapple W, Molthan-Hill P, Welton R and Hewitt M (2020) Lights off, spot on: carbon literacy training crossing boundaries in the television industry. *Journal of Business Ethics*, 162 (4), pp. 813–834. ISSN 0167–4544.
19. Full details of the Carbon Literate Organisation scheme can be found here: https://carbonliteracy.com/wp-content/uploads/2018/12/CLO.zip

3

CLIMATE COMMUNICATION AND REPORTING TO INTERNAL AND EXTERNAL STAKEHOLDERS

Richard Howarth

Action to address climate change stands and falls with communication. This includes internal communication to colleagues and employees, as well as external communication to customers, suppliers, investors, communities and other stakeholders. Some external communication falls into the category of reporting and disclosure, which will also be addressed.

This chapter is for you if:

- You work in any function where you communicate with stakeholders
- You are responsible for internal bulletins or newsletters
- You prepare briefing notes or executive summaries for senior management
- You contribute to your organisation's social media presence and communications
- You write annual or other reports for your organisation.

DOI: 10.4324/9781003274049-4

It will cover:

- The purpose of climate change communication (CCC)
- The features of successful climate change communication
- The power of stories and the narrative
- Reporting, reports and disclosure
- Guidance on communication with colleagues, suppliers, investors, in social media and reports
- A case study about ESG book, which helps to demystify data disclosure.

The role and importance of Climate Change Communication

Deloitte identifies that the moment to act and communicate on climate change is **now**.[1] This is because of the heightened awareness of the risks posed, and the consequent need to act quickly. It is also because governments, business leaders and individuals are keen to know more and are actively listening. From a business perspective, many customers especially younger ones are prioritising action in this area and seeking to change their consumption behaviour (see chapter 9, Marketing). If you do not make them aware of the benefits of your products, services, or company, it will be a business and climate opportunity missed. The same goes for investors. However, businesses must be careful not to exaggerate or make false claims. In the United Kingdom, the Green Claims Code[2] seeks to regulate what is known as 'greenwashing'; that is, the provision of false or misleading information or impressions about the environmental or climate credentials of a product or organisation without clear evidence to substantiate. This is where reporting and disclosure can come in, alongside external verification or certification of claims, with the aim of supporting the credibility and impact of one's communications.

According to the Yale Programme, climate change communication (CCC) is *about educating, informing, warning, persuading, mobilizing and solving this critical problem*.[3] CCC is an important tool in the fight against climate change, not least because of its role in raising awareness, providing information and supporting action through persuasion. To motivate others, it will be crucial to engage individuals, groups and organisations across all sectors by facilitating their understanding of the role *they* can play and the direct and wider benefits. Those are key to engendering interest in the topic; ensuring it's prioritised; that there is a desire to act, and action does indeed follow; and where appropriate, it leads to sustained behaviour change.

When it comes to the process and the basic principles of communication, most marketing texts make reference to the 'radio concept', with a sender of information communicating via messages to passive receivers. In reality, communication and certainly CCC are more complex, not least because the science-based nature and the use of data might alienate or simply be a barrier to reception for some people. Culture will also have an influence, as will personal values and one's own life experiences. Michael Mann describes in his book 'The New Climate War'[4] how values, especially political preferences, influence how messages around climate change are perceived, but also how 'fake news' is created and distributed. We have discussed his insights further in chapter 15.

Some communications will be information-based, with eco-labelling and recycling messages on packaging being two examples, which we have further explored in chapter 9 (Marketing). Others will involve dialogue and feedback, for example with suppliers and customers (see also chapter 8, Procurement & Supply). In this current chapter, we will cover informal as well as more formal communication, in the form of reporting.

So much noise: what do we need to know?

Apart from the complexity of communications relating to climate change and the impacts of this on the communication process, there can also be a lot of 'noise'. This includes conflicting messages on the same topic, the fact that some messages do not reach the customer, or they are mis-interpreted, or even ignored. The impact of existing knowledge, the setting and context, current practices and priorities, along with values and beliefs, further contribute. They are particularly relevant when people are *active* participants and there is two-way dialogue.

When engaging in climate change communication, the Yale Programme identifies the importance of identifying the:

* **Strategy** and the **aims** of the message (raising awareness or seeking action)
* **Audience** (and what is their current level of understanding)
* **Messenger**, the **message** and its **content**
* **Channels** to be used and their efficacy (will they cut through the noise)

- **Context** and where/when the message is communicated
- **Integration** with other messages (are there conflicts)
- **Evidence** to back up any claims
- **Feedback** and **metrics** to support understanding of the outcomes and the overall efficacy.

The latter elements, and specifically evidence, feedback and metrics, are important. They recognise and seek to address, for example, concerns about potential gaps between what the company is saying and what they are actually doing to address climate change, and thus false or unsubstantiated claims, or simply an attitude-behaviour gap (see, for example, Marketing Week).[5] This gap exists when anyone commits to a target, such as reducing greenhouse gases in their operations or achieving Net Zero by 2025, but the announcement is not followed by recognisable action. Either there is no action at all, or the company is not able to evidence or communicate it appropriately to its stakeholders. Gaps and mixed messages can also occur when an organisation for example purports to be concerned about climate change, then sends a glossy brochure in a plastic wrapper in the post, rather than electronically. Or where a climate-responsible product is packed in multiple layers made from different materials, making recycling difficult.

The Intergovernmental Panel on Climate Change (IPCC) has also published a guide on communicating climate change[6] that offers 'hands on' guidance and identifies the importance of understanding and capitalising on the opportunities. The guide covers six key principles, relevant both to scientists and lay people:

- **Be confident** – maximise trust and support authenticity
- **Avoid abstract ideas** – use day-to-day examples that everyone will understand, rather than big global numbers
- **Connect through what matters** – understand that scientific knowledge does not necessarily lead to action
- **Tell a story** – do not overwhelm with statistics, focus on the narrative
- **Lead with what is known** – unknowns cause stumbling blocks, so start with points of agreement
- **Use effective visual communications** – these can be more important than written communication. The cartoon below, Image 3.1, connects a number of these important elements (telling a story, avoiding abstract ideas, using images to support visual communication) and humour, both to challenge and get a message across.

Image 3.1 Example of integrated communication: What If Climate Change Is a Big Hoax?
Joel Pett Editorial Cartoon used with permission of Joel Pett and the Cartoonist Group. All rights reserved.

The most important thing to remember is that your message needs to reach the right people, who can hear and understand it, then translate it into action. This is particularly important when considering the role and power of social media as a specific communication tool. Social media has brought the world within reach of individuals and has significantly lowered the cost of getting messages out to specific and wider audiences. The ACCEPT project recognises all of this and how social media both enables and challenges work to support the fight against climate change.[7] ACCEPT identifies the important role of influencers and key opinion leaders, the reach and breadth of the audience available and how one voice can make a large difference. Algorithms embedded in websites and social media can either help reinforce beliefs, or create harmful ones, and polarise opinion. For example, researchers Taha Yasseri and Mary Sanford have raised concerns about how social media is reducing climate change debates to views on topics such as veganism.[8]

We are not all Shakespeare but ... the power of stories and the narrative

In his book, 'The Tipping Point', Malcolm Gladwell[9] refers to the concept of the 'stickiness' of a message and how this contributes to message or information retention. This will resonate with many when thinking about great speeches or even adverts or slogans from childhood. Even when a message is sticky, it is also necessary to think about how it is framed, and how its 'content' is presented. So, what is the narrative and how does this fit into the overall story that is being told, and who tells it?

Stories facilitate the sharing and presentation of information and are key to ensuring reception and engagement with the information transmitted. Creating an effective supporting narrative is key, certainly when seeking to communicate a complex subject like this, with sometimes conflicting views and perspectives. The IPCC's work on climate change communications can assist. The IPCC suggests that much of the focus will be setting the scene, describing the problem, laying out the consequences and talking through the solutions. This last element is really important, as the nature of the problem can lead people to feel overwhelmed if the way forward is unclear and they cannot easily identify action they can take. Without a clear flow to the narrative, the audience can become confused or just get bored. Randy Olson's 'And|But|Therefore' (ABT) framework[10] can help address this, as it provides a simple structure and supports the IPCC's guidance, by addressing: the Set up (And), the Problem (But) and the Solution/Action required (Therefore). An illustration would be: Food waste results in up to 10% of emissions caused by humans,[11] but customers do not like misshapen vegetables. Supermarkets such as Tesco, Waitrose and others meet the challenge head on by labelling items as 'Imperfectly Perfect' or 'A Little Less than Perfect' and use taste not shape as the important choice criteria, changing perceptions along the way.

Reporting, reports and disclosure – the point and purpose

It is important to understand the terms used:

- **Disclosure** – the act of making available to others: information, data and a '**report**' about an organisation's performance, and in the current context, its GHG emissions and associated performance
- **Reporting** – the process that supports the production of the report itself and the act of disclosure.

For some organisations in certain parts of the world, disclosure of greenhouse gas (GHG) emissions, and possibly wider Environmental, Social and Governance (ESG) issues, is a legal requirement. However, there are concerns about clarity, consistency and reporting outputs, as there are many different approaches and guidelines available.[12] This can be an issue even in a specific part of the world such as the United Kingdom, as discussed in a recent article by Professor Ian Thompson and colleagues at the University of Birmingham.[13]

Work is being undertaken to try and resolve such inconsistencies. For example, in the United States of America the Securities and Exchange Commission (SEC) has introduced rules to lead to the standardisation of disclosures within its sphere of control.[14] As regards the United Kingdom (similar to the United States of America), from April 2022, there is a requirement for larger listed and some non-listed companies to include information on climate risks in their annual reports.[15] The hope is that in requiring businesses to measure their climate impact to underpin reporting, those organisations may understand the need to be more ambitious and as a result actively reduce their emissions and move towards Net Zero. A bonus is that this may lead to operational cost savings. Although in the first instance the requirement affects mainly larger businesses, it will doubtless have an impact on others in their supply chain, and is likely to be extended to smaller organisations either now or in the coming years. The information provided by those disclosing must be in line with the guidance from the Task Force on Climate-related Financial Disclosures (TCFD), which was set up as part of the Financial Stability Board (FSB) and its work to promote and facilitate better quality climate-related financial disclosure.

Apart from potential costs savings, there may be other benefits of reporting and disclosure. In 2019, the Carbon Trust[16] surveyed some of the United Kingdom's top companies to find out what they thought the benefits of reporting were:

- 72% reported increased brand value
- 37% cited reduced shareholder pressure and activism
- 29% reported an increased diversity of investors
- 21% reported a higher company valuation
- 31% reported positive financial impact.

Because there are real advantages, some organisations will report and disclose information voluntarily, even when not required to do so. Whatever the reason or motivation, reporting and disclosure should provide a consistent and complete insight into an organisation's position, intentions and progress. To enable benchmarking and the opportunity for comparison, any potential conflicts, information gaps or uncertainties should be fully documented, as their relevance and accuracy will underpin assessment of the organisation's effectiveness and performance.

As seen later in this chapter (and in others, such as chapter 12, Carbon Accounting), there are various principles and protocols that facilitate and guide how to bring together an effective inventory, how to account for GHG emissions, and how to ensure their effective disclosure. What will also be seen is that there are different approaches that can be followed to support all aspects of disclosure: when, what, where, how and why. As this is likely to become mandatory for more businesses in the future, it is worth understanding the requirements and this is covered in the high-impact solutions section below.

Whatever the reporting approach or accounting tools used, it will be essential to declare this and adhere to the requirements and processes. Reporting should ultimately be supported by appropriate objectives, targets and metrics, and should ideally be grounded in the organisation's overarching strategy and governance processes.

To facilitate consistency and comparison, completeness and accuracy, we recommend that the data and information collected should include:

- **Headline company information** (size, turnover, ownership, market data, etc.)
- The **timing of the report** and details of whether it is to comply with specific requirements (or whether it's voluntary)
- How the organisation identifies and defines the '**boundaries**', '**scopes**' and **timeframes**, and how those were selected (these terms are explained in detail in chapter 11)
- What **specific data** were collected, how and why they were selected
- Any **assumptions**, **uncertainties** and **estimates**, and any consequent implications
- Details of the **underpinning methodology**, conversion tools and factors selected (more detail on this and the next points in chapter 12)
- The **targets, ratios or benchmarking metrics** being used, and why these were selected
- The **base year** and why this was chosen
- **Performance** and **progress** against objectives, targets and metrics as necessary (with clear evidence)
- Grounding of **performance assessments** over time
- Any **other relevant comparisons** – product lines, activities, external benchmarking to illustrate
- Note of any **removals** or **additions** related to GHG emissions and any **offsetting**
- Details of the **management system** employed
- **Risks and opportunities** – internal and external (and any fines incurred)
- An **overall assessment** of performance, governance, strategy and management, and any subsequent recommendations.

To summarise, when making disclosures and undertaking reporting, it will be essential to understand the purpose, intention and outcomes and, as with any communication, the audience involved.

WANT TO DIG DEEPER?

#TalkingClimate Handbook: How to have conversations about climate change in your daily life
https://climateoutreach.org/reports/how-to-have-a-climate-change-conversation-talking-climate/
This useful handbook looks at how to have constructive day-to-day conversations about climate change and the climate crisis. The work seeks to normalise these conversations and recognises that this is essential to raising awareness and facilitating action. The handbook is for anyone, whether in a formal setting, at home over dinner or on the bus. It seeks to empower us all to talk about the subject.

Climate Communication Project
https://theclimatecommsproject.org/
A collaborative project involving academics and researchers, charities, partner organisations and individuals taking stock of knowledge about engagement with climate change. A wide range of information, sources and tools to support understanding and action in this topic area.

SME Climate Hub
https://smeclimatehub.org/
The SME Climate Hub is a global initiative that empowers SMEs to take climate action and build resilient businesses for the future. Included are some useful communications resources, such as templates and sample reports.
The Hub is an initiative of the 'We Mean Business Coalition', the 'Exponential Roadmap Initiative', the UN 'Race to Zero' campaign and the International Chamber of Commerce, in collaboration with Normative and Oxford University.

High-impact solutions

As discussed above, communications, raising awareness and persuading individuals, groups and other organisations are fundamental to securing commitment, action and ongoing behaviour change. However, as identified by Climate Outreach,[17] and specifically in the context of change through engagement, climate change communication (CCC) seems to be the most under-used and least understood tool, despite probably being the most powerful.

Embedding high-impact solutions into your work and daily life requires effective communication with others who can help you achieve each solution. It might be about convincing your work colleagues to change a well-established practice, or perhaps explaining to your stakeholders why you have invested in something that will support the transition to Net Zero. In this section, we have chosen examples that most people will find relevant. This is by no means exhaustive, but we hope that each topic provides inspiration on how to communicate in those settings, and we provide some of the core approaches and principles that should translate to other contexts.

Our starting point has to be a strategic review of the organisation's CCC. So, our first question is: **how do I improve my organisation's climate change communications?**

In order to get the message right for external audiences, it is good to start with the internal messaging, so that everyone is singing from the same song sheet. Formally, these communications can be part of 'internal marketing',[18] which is linked to employee engagement and priority setting. The second question is, therefore: **how do I talk with my colleagues about climate change?**

Following this, we should consider procurement and the supply chain, and so our third question is: **how do I engage my suppliers with climate solutions?**

Retaining the external focus, but thinking about the development of GHG inventories and accounts (see also chapter 12), we need to address formal reporting and disclosure of climate change commitments, activity and outcomes and how we decide what is relevant (or material). In doing this, we address our fourth question: **how do I report and disclose to key stakeholders?**

Finally, thinking about both internal and external audiences, we need to consider one of the most powerful, but challenging tools for communication – social media. Our fifth question is: **how should I present the organisation's climate action on social media?**

How do I improve my organisation's climate change communications?

When seeking to communicate internally and externally about climate change, the organisation needs an overall plan or strategy. This will ensure more effective climate change communications, and the messaging around the 'Race to Zero' campaign (see chapter 1 for more information on Net Zero). Efficiency is required, which here includes the avoidance of multiple messaging and reducing the risk of overwhelming the audience. Many organisations have started to take action, not least since the Paris Agreement and the more recent COP26 pact in 2021, with commitments made to climate change emissions reductions, Net Zero carbon, the management of climate risks and business transformation.

As Deloitte identifies however, it will be important that commitments and pledges are turned into action, and that communication has effective and solid foundations, otherwise they will lack substance and credibility.[19] As a starting point, in line with any strategic communication campaign, Deloitte suggests there should be a clear communication strategy and primarily an external focus, which:

- **Is anchored in the company's purpose** – it must be embedded in the core purpose of the organisation, if not there will be conflicts and major challenges. Given the importance of climate change (to society, customers and other stakeholders), it may be necessary to review the organisation's *core* strategy and purpose, so that climate change is embedded and a good fit can be achieved.
- **Talks about business change** – climate change and sustainability communications are more powerful and effective if they demonstrate innovation and developments with quantifiable impacts that can be understood and are clearly connected to associated challenges.
- **Mobilises the executive team** – without leadership commitment and action, it is likely that both those inside and outside the organisation will be sceptical of the claimed commitments. It is important to develop bold and ambitious, relevant but achievable plans that resonate with all stakeholders (internal and external).
- **Finds the big conversations** – ensure the communications and action are relevant and recognise and align activities to high-profile solutions.

This will help engagement with customers, stakeholders and policy makers too. Be careful however to ensure relevance for the organisation and avoid paying lip service through action and evidence.

- **Shares stories** – use examples of achievements to share with stakeholders, including customers, to support their engagement and action. Share with other organisations too, specifically those in the supply and value chains. Ensure there is two-way dialogue to support the outcomes and learn from each other in the process.
- **Measures performance** – connecting achievements and outcomes to recognised measurement frameworks will add credibility and support consistency and comparisons. As with any reporting or disclosure, robust data should be underpinned by clear insights. This will also be picked up in our fourth question below.

Deloitte further identifies that because communication teams (including those within Public Relations and Marketing) are tuned to the needs of stakeholders, and specifically customers, they are well placed to identify shifts in expectations and the necessary response. As such, the Communication team should act as the conscience of the organisation, and both advocate and lead change.[19] Again, with some similarity to core marketing and communication theory, Deloitte proposes that future organisational climate change communication plans should:

- **Use targeted communications** – selecting channels and methods to ensure messages are tailored to different stakeholders.
- **Be forward-looking** – recognising what is needed now, but also taking a strategic long-term view of both climate change specifically and sustainability in general. Also recognising what this means in the future for the business, its strategy and purpose. Will priorities of the business and its customers change? If so, when, why and how?
- **Turn information into action** – communicating with stakeholders and customers about your actions and achievements, sharing insights into what works and why, in order to support behaviour change.
- **Move from the margins to the mainstream** – climate change is now mainstream and is no longer a niche issue. If you do not feel this is recognised in your organisation, demand clear answers as to where it fits in the organisation's purpose and associated narrative.

- **Make it permanent** – as well as no longer being a niche issue, climate change and sustainability are not just about the here and now, and what is on trend. Climate change, and sustainability communications more widely, must be a *core* dimension of your communications moving forward.

Reflecting the guidance on how to approach communication above, it will also be essential to recognise the extent of the greenhouse gas (GHG) emissions of the communication tools and approaches used by your organisation, and this is discussed in more detail in chapter 9 (Marketing). Mike Berners-Lee's book 'How bad are bananas?' – introduced in chapter 1 – is of some use here to aid the quantification of different methods such as a sending leaflets or catalogues by post versus an email. Work by organisations such as AdNetZero, which is dedicated to responsible advertising, also helps.[20] The key is taking an informed decision regarding GHG emissions when selecting the communications channel. Without this, conflicts between what you are trying to communicate and the means of doing so can exist and are likely to undermine the message. Because of its specific role and its potential impact from a messaging and communication perspective, and because of the potential links to the GHG emissions from the channel too, social media is discussed in the fifth question in this section of the chapter.

How do I talk with my colleagues about climate change?

Internal communication supports the implementation element of an organisation's policies, strategies and associated objectives and targets. The latter two give direction to the activities and the means of assessing progress. As noted above, the Communication team is likely to have some involvement in this process, to ensure consistency between external and internal communication for example, but others will be involved as well. Internal communication, within the wider area of internal marketing, is therefore an important dimension of the communication approach of *any* organisation.

Internal marketing has traditionally been seen as particularly important for service organisations, which historically relied heavily on people and their interactions with customers. The aim is to ensure that employees fully understand the offer, their role in creating value, and in supporting the customer experience and satisfaction. It is important to ensure employees' interactions and behaviour with customers are 'on message' and consistent with the promises made by the organisation in its external marketing to the customer. In doing this, 'gaps' between what is promised and what is delivered can be managed and minimised.

As with external marketing communication, it is important to be clear on who the audience is so that the messages can be tailored and appropriate communication channels employed. Feedback should be taken into account to improve the overall approach and to address any gaps along the way. Below are the factors identified by Forbes[18] to help ensure success.

- **Appoint champions and encourage collaboration**: these are key within an organisation, and there will be benefits from identifying leaders and influencers in each area of the business. A range of voices and insights must be listened to, and opinions shared as appropriate. Champions are key to developing positive communications and outcomes, and should be involved in regular meetings, where the objectives can be reviewed (see below for further guidance).
- **Focus on the primary communication channels**: recognise which ones are most suited in your circumstances, and do not overload people. Messages themselves can lose impact if shared via the 'wrong' channel, while too many messages via different channels can overwhelm and disengage colleagues.
- **Provide training, tools and budgets**: if training is required, decide if this should be deemed 'essential learning' which everyone must undertake. Whether a short webinar will suffice, or if full climate literacy training is more appropriate (see chapter 2 Climate Literacy Training, for suggestions). The organisation must be prepared to invest the appropriate amount of time and money, and there needs to be buy-in and full engagement from the very top.
- **Establish metrics and objectives**: these need to tie in with the overall aims and strategy. Review and report on these as necessary.

In doing this, it must not be forgotten that the shape and culture of many organisations have changed and continue to do so. Traditional top-down approaches will not always be the best and one that recognises this and leads through live conversations between all levels is likely to reap rewards.

R espect your conversational partner and find a common ground
E njoy the conversation
A sk questions
L isten and show you have heard

T ell your story
A ction makes it easier, but does not fix it
L earn from conversation, and
K eep going and keep connected.

Figure 3.1 REAL Talk principles Webster and Marshall, 2019.[21]

To support the detail of the conversations that will be needed, the work of Climate Outreach provides very useful guidance and identifies how to focus on constructive climate conversations in a range of settings. The basis of their work **REAL TALK** (Figure 3.1).

A link to their work is contained in the 'Further Resources' section and can be of benefit for anyone seeking to improve climate change communications, either as part of a business strategy, in their own area or in life in general.

How do I engage my suppliers with climate solutions?

As the majority of an organisation's GHG emissions are usually outside of its control (and fall into Scope 3, see chapter 11, Scopes & Boundaries) it will be essential to discuss emissions with your suppliers.

If you are unsure how to start the conversation, it is worth consulting the website of the Exponential Roadmap Initiative.[22] This is a collaboration between many different organisations and companies, whose aim is to halve emissions by 2030 *through exponential climate action and solutions*. The website provides access to the 1.5°C Supplier Engagement guide[23] and the SME Climate Hub[24] and includes the 1.5°C Business Playbook.[25] The initiative is also an accredited partner of the United Nations' Race To Zero.[26]

Included on the website are examples of reports to help ensure the 'Foundations' put in place to cut emissions are solid – such as IKEA's Climate Positive report and Unilever's Climate Action Plan. Bearing in mind that in some organisations it will be necessary to convince one's own top management before working more closely with external partners, these can be used as inspiration to get you started.

Within the 'Procurement' area of the website, there is a general template letter that can be sent to suppliers requesting them to halve their emissions by 2030. Alongside that is a sample letter from, for example, Telia to its suppliers, requesting they join with them in setting a Net Zero target. Ericsson's supplier code of conduct is also provided. And in case further persuasion is required, Ericsson's slide deck, which sets out their expectations of suppliers' climate action, is also shared.

To further facilitate 'Supplier engagement', there are examples of other communications that might be useful, including a questionnaire that can be sent to suppliers.

As can be seen from the above example, this resource provides a detailed level of information and is very practical, which should provide the impetus for anyone feeling unsure how to start the conversation with their suppliers.

How do I report and disclose to key stakeholders?

As explained earlier, the requirement for reporting and disclosure varies in different parts of the world, but in the United Kingdom it is required of certain larger organisations since 2022, and is likely to become more widespread in the future. It is important that you are aware of the requirements and any new obligations in your part of the world.

The Task Force on Climate-related Financial Disclosures (TCFD) provides guidance and recommendations[27] for the following, in relation to climate-related risk and opportunities:

- **Governance**
- **Strategy and financial planning**
- **Risk management** – identifying, assessing and managing
- **Metrics and targets** – to assess and manage, where such information is material.

The TCFD's recommendations can be used for *all* organisations in *all* sectors. This adds real value to anyone looking to embed reporting and disclosure in a consistent manner.

Climate metrics and targets are covered, as well as how to use them.

These have implications for inventories, accounting and reporting, and according to the TCFD[28] should be:

- **Decision useful** – they must be relevant to the organisation's own risks and opportunities
- **Clear and understandable** – with clear context; narrative and notes should support where necessary
- **Reliable, verifiable and objective** – the metrics should be free of bias
- **Consistent over time** – to support tracking and interpretation and other characteristics.

To assist the setting of targets and metrics, the TCFD recommends that calculations of GHG emissions are based on the Greenhouse Gas Protocol (GHGP).[29] That covers both accounting and reporting aspects, and clarifies the definition of the different scopes. These are covered in more detail in this book in chapter 11 (Scopes & Boundaries) and chapter 12 (Carbon Accounting).

The work of the CDP[30] is also relevant. This not-for-profit charity has produced a Climate Disclosure Framework for SMEs[31] in conjunction with the SME Climate Hub[32] (see 'Dig Deeper' earlier in this chapter). This is a really useful guide that supports both awareness and action in SMEs in this important area of measuring and effecting change regarding GHG emissions and climate action. There are modules covering:

- **Energy reporting**
- **Value chain emissions**
- **Management and resilience**
- **Climate solutions.**

Similar to the implementation guidance from the TCFD mentioned above, the CDP's Climate Disclosure guidance contains clear detail of what is needed and how to achieve it. As a result, it is a really practical and usable resource. Also, the case study in this chapter introduces ESG Book, another tool to support SMEs needing or wanting to understand how to disclose data.

A core element in reporting and disclosure related to climate change and GHG emissions is the question of materiality. This term has traditionally been used in financial, legal and accounting contexts and more recently extended to include wider sustainability and climate-related impacts of a company. It is important to recognise as it is a core principle that underpins the relevance and the usefulness of communication through these formal channels.

Materiality refers to where an issue has a major bearing on the economic, financial, legal or reputational aspects of the business. Any communication, reports and disclosures must recognise this and ensure that matters deemed 'material' are identified. Materiality is included in the guidelines for the Global Reporting Initiative (GRI) as the cornerstone of the GRI Sustainability Reporting Framework. In its 'Materiality Definition: The Ultimate Guide', Datamaran claims that the materiality concept has: *quickly become essential for stakeholder engagement exercises and topic mapping while appearing as a keyword in consultant pitches.* As a concept borrowed from the accounting and auditing domain: *materiality represented the perfect idea to foster the integration of non-financial issues in the mainstream business thinking and decision making. It sounds professional, financially relevant, familiar to investors and auditors.*[33]

Essentially, if information is considered important by a reasonable person, then it must be disclosed – this is the core of materiality. Following GRI and TCFD work, climate-related impacts on a company would be considered important and therefore 'material', and they must be reported and disclosed. Because of the nature of sustainability and climate change, the GRI also recognises what is known as 'double materiality'. In simple terms, this is both what is important (or '*material*') financially to the organisation itself, and also the impact the organisation has on others. In formal terms, according to the GRI,[34] double materiality relates to:

- **Financial Materiality** – information on economic value creation at the level of the reporting company for the benefit of investors (shareholders)
- **Impact Materiality** – information on the reporting company's impact on the economy, environment and people for the benefit of multiple stakeholders, such as investors, employees, customers, suppliers and local communities.

Double materiality tends to be elusive and a challenge according to the GRI. This is because it requires both the reporting organisation and interested parties to consider the dynamic nature of any impacts, the organisation's consequent financial performance and external parties impacted

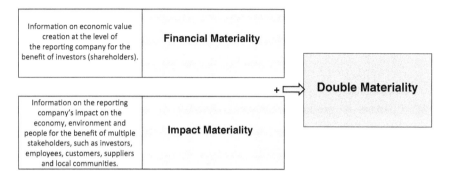

Figure 3.2 Connecting elements of materiality to double materiality adapted from GRI, 2022.[34]

by its emissions. Within the context of reporting and disclosure, double materiality will be important and will also support clarity and account-ability (Figure 3.2).

How should I present climate action on social media?

Whether communicating internally or externally, to individuals, groups, organisations or government departments, social media will have an im-portant influencing and informational role to play.

In a timely and useful piece in The Conversation, Professor Tenbrick of Bangor University suggests how to ensure social media posts relating to climate change matter in eight simple steps:[35]

1. **Relevance matters** – although the article is written from an individual perspective, the key is that in all cases, the message needs to resonate with the audience and needs to be framed appropriately.
2. **Conciseness helps** – given the abundance of information available, the opportunity to overwhelm is ever present. Some tools use short format messaging and, whether we think that is good or not, they do shape reactions. Being to the point and brief is key in this environment.
3. **Chase positive, realistic targets** – climate anxiety is real and global threats can lead to a sense of powerlessness. Communicate positive messages, which are fact-based and realistic, and bring action within the realm of the audience.

4. **Avoid misleading terminology** – climate change and related communications are messy subjects with many dimensions, debates and perspectives. Choose your words and terms carefully and aim for precision. Consider the context too, for example use the term 'upward trend' rather than 'negative trend' when talking about temperature rise, so it seems less alarming.

5. **Climate is global, weather is local** – be clear that the two are different. People often talk about specific weather events to support or deny climate change. Stick to the facts about climate change (which occurs over time) not the weather (happening outside on a given day).

6. **Avoid uncertainty** – this is a big one and has also been looked at specifically by Climate Outreach who have produced a handbook to support understanding and action.[36] Framing uncertainties as risks is more relevant for the general public, but may not be for other audiences. Professor Tenbrick gives the example of Greta Thunberg, as her social media posts connect directly, and leave little scope for uncertainty or misunderstanding (clear framing supports here too). The key is to ensure language is clear, suitably direct and targeted at the audience in question.

7. **Suggest concrete action** – use appropriate references to evidence that the audience can relate to. Provide practical and impactful advice that people can action and so feel they are making a difference as a result, such as reducing food waste. This advice is more likely to stick and be followed.

8. **Listen** – be aware of when your audience is struggling to understand issues regarding climate change and what to do. Listen carefully, to aid understanding and behaviour change, by demonstrating that their concerns have been heard.

With respect to the potential challenges, concerns and opportunities related to social media, the work of Tuitjer and Dirksmeier[37] is also helpful. Not least their questioning as to which platforms have the greatest negative or positive impacts; this is particularly important given the role of channel choice in effective communication and dialogue.

As circumstances will vary widely, it is hard to provide tailored guidance regarding the selection of the social media platforms to use, but the most relevant selection criteria will be:

- **Who is the audience?**
- **What role does the channel play** – is it more for information giving or for dialogue seeking?

Only by identifying the target audience and the role, and by understanding the advantages and downsides of the different channels and platforms, can an informed selection of appropriate channels be undertaken. Please see the 'Further Resources' section below for general guidance regarding social media for SMEs.

Case study

The case study below presents a solution for companies on how they can collect and present all the data required by their external stakeholders. While aimed at SMEs, it can also be of benefit to larger organisations.

ESG book: data disclosure demystified

By Herman Bril (Managing Director & Head of Responsible Investment at PSP Investments) and Parul Gupta (Partner, Arabesque Group)

Investors across the world are today looking for sustainability information, not only on the largest listed global companies, but increasingly on smaller, private enterprises. In this new data ecosystem, there is a wide range of stakeholder activity ranging from supply chain analysis and regulatory reporting, to procurement and vendor selection, with corporations facing an ever-growing stream of questions around their environmental, social and governance (ESG) footprint.

In short, companies can no longer escape requirements to disclose ESG data. Common metrics might range from greenhouse gas emissions, waste and water management, to human rights, labour conditions, community impact, diversity and inclusion policies. In the face of rising sustainability reporting, the burden is greatest for SMEs who often lack the resources, knowledge, systems and standards to meet requirements. Even sizable corporations with greater financial capacity can struggle to disclose ESG data in alignment with the many reporting frameworks now in place, such as the Sustainability Accounting Standards Board (SASB), the Global Reporting Initiative (GRI), the Task Force on Climate-related Financial Disclosures (TCFD) and the EU Taxonomy.

From 2023 onwards, corporate ESG disclosures in Europe will be regulated through the EU Corporate Sustainability Reporting Directive (CSRD). Bruno Le Maire, French Minister for Economic Affairs, Finance and Recovery announced in February 2022 that *companies with more than 250 employees or listed companies will now have to translate their environmental, social and governance policy into standardised, justified and certified information documents. This means greater transparency for citizens, consumers, and investors so that businesses can play their full part in society. This is the end of greenwashing. Today, Europe is setting the rigorous non-financial reference standards of tomorrow, in line with our environmental and social ambitions.*[38]

Sustainability data is too often unstructured, fragmented, qualitative, outdated, and uncentralised, regardless of a company's financial data, systems, reporting, standards and resources. And while large corporations are committing significant budgets to process the increasing flow of ESG disclosure requests, smaller organisations are at risk of being left behind.

Sustainability reporting is a costly process, and moreover, there is a chronic lack of market guidance on how to properly gather this information, as well as on the most relevant metrics to report against. Small and medium businesses are understandably at a loss on how best to communicate their progress on ESG topics, and in turn attract greater capital towards sustainable activities.

ESG book

In response to these growing market issues, the technology company Arabesque launched ESG Book in 2021 with a mission to reshape the future of ESG data. Supported by a global alliance of leading financial institutions and organisations, including the International Finance Corporation (IFC), UN Global Compact, GRI, Allianz, Bridgewater Associates, HSBC and Nikkei, ESG Book is a new central source for accessible and digital corporate sustainability information, directly connecting investors and companies.

The platform uniquely maps corporate ESG data to commonly-used frameworks, making it highly efficient for companies to disclose information, and enabling free public access to pre-populated data for thousands of corporations. It aims to address one of the most important challenges in the mainstreaming of sustainable finance, which is the lack of transparency around ESG data. With the market still overly reliant on estimates, companies themselves no longer recognise the data that investors have on them.

ESG Book however, has been developed as a tool that guides companies around multiple frameworks, and allows them to be custodians of their data by updating their information in real time with clear evidence. Companies can benchmark themselves against their peers, identify the gaps in their reporting and improve their sustainability performance more effectively.

Available for corporates of all sizes, investors, standard-setters and other stakeholders, ESG Book follows five principles based on a mission to create ESG data as a public good:

1. **Companies control their own data**
   Corporates should have control of their sustainability data by having autonomy over the disclosure and maintenance of data in real time, unrestricted by the annual reporting cycle.

2. **Transparency on data usage and interactions brings more meaningful reporting**
   Companies should be empowered to report on the most material and valuable issues requested by investors, thereby reducing the noise in reporting and enabling data gaps to be more clearly identified.

3. **Accessibility and impartiality**
   ESG data should be reported by companies in a clear and consistent manner, and should be readily accessible for all stakeholders.

4. **Framework-neutral**
   ESG data should be framework-neutral and provide a level-playing field for all market participants.

5. **Easing the reporting burden**
   Reported ESG data can be mapped across a range of frameworks simultaneously over time. This frees up company resources for greater action-driven insights.

Through ESG Book, the disclosure of sustainability data for SMEs has become easier and also free. Companies can sign up at www.esgbook.com and request access. Once signed up, they can choose with key stakeholders which sustainability frameworks to use, and the minimum level of data required. The platform's automated workflow then guides the company to upload their evidence-supported data, with options to provide restricted access to supply chain and other clients.

As with all corporations, SMEs need to maintain their societal licence to operate. The disclosure of corporate ESG data to all relevant stakeholders is no longer an opt-in; it is mandatory for successful capital markets. And by integrating ESG into the core of their long-term profitable business models, companies can ensure they remain future-fit on a Net Zero, sustainable pathway. Through ESG Book, the journey ahead has become clearer.

Herman Bril recently started as Managing Director & Head of Responsible Investment at PSP Investments in Montreal. He has 30 years' experience in international financial institutions across investment management, derivatives, treasury and development finance. He is co-editor of Sustainable Investing – A Path to a New Horizon (2020), and Sustainability, Technology, and Finance - Rethinking how markets integrate ESG (2022).

Parul Gupta is a Partner at Arabesque, based in London. She is responsible for business development and strategic partnerships at the group. Parul has more than 15 years' experience in providing portfolio recommendations and ESG integration advice to asset managers and family offices globally. Prior to joining Arabesque, Parul was Head of Strategic Asset Allocation at Citi Private Bank and a member of the Global Investment Committee.

Further Resources

On the companion website to this book will be further material to help you plan and implement this work, including some detailed examples on how to communicate to different audiences and some sample reports.

Below you can find some links that go into more detail on the above and are provided in addition to the ones mentioned in the endnotes, and further solutions on how to communicate best.

General

The Climate Communications Project: https://theclimatecommsproject. org/ (search for additional input also via #theclimatecommsproject) Although this project (which included academics from UK universities and the climate charities 10:10 and Climate Outreach) has come to an end, its website has a useful set of blogs that discuss the many ways in which climate change is being communicated.

Climate Outreach: https://climateoutreach.org/
A British-based charity that seeks to help people understand the complex issue of climate change in ways that resonate with their sense of identity, values and worldview.

Social media tips for small business owners: https://blog.hootsuite.com/social-media-tips-for-small-business-owners/
This blog provided by Hootsuite gives 12 simple tips on how an SME can start engaging successfully with social media.

Video

Introduction to TCFD recommendations: https://www.youtube.com/watch?v=fxSvBEL1–5M
In this video, the managing director of the Climate Disclosure Standards Board gives an introduction and overview of the TCFD recommendations.

Notes

1. Deloitte: *Communications for a Changing Climate* https://www2.deloitte.com/global/en/blog/responsible-business-blog/2021/communications-for-a-changing-climate.html
2. Greenwashing – CMA puts businesses on notice: https://www.gov.uk/government/news/greenwashing-cma-puts-businesses-on-notice
3. The Yale Programme, *Climate Change Communication*: https://climatecommunication.yale.edu/about/what-is-climate-change-communication/
4. Mann M (2021) *The new climate war*: https://michaelmann.net/books/climate-war
5. Jefferson M (2021) Marketers urged to bridge the 'say-do' gap, *Marketing Week* (19 Oct): https://www.marketingweek.com/marketers-so-do-gap/
6. IPCC (2018) *Principles for effective communication and public engagement on climate change*: https://www.ipcc.ch/site/assets/uploads/2017/08/Climate-Outreach-IPCC-communications-handbook.pdf
7. ACCEPT – ASEAN Climate Change and Energy Project: https://accept.aseanenergy.org/the-power-of-social-media-to-fight-climate-change/

8. Yasseri T and Sanford M (2021) Social Media is reducing climate debates to your views on veganism, *The Conversation* (1 Oct): https://theconversation.com/social-media-is-reducing-climate-change-debates-to-your-views-on-veganism-167931

9. Gladwell M (2002) *The Tipping Point*: https://www.littlebrown.com/titles/malcolm-gladwell/the-tipping-point/9780759574731/

10. Olson R, #199: *How to Use the ABT to Focus Your Brand Stories*: https://businessofstory.com/podcast/abt-brand-stories/

11. IPCC (2019), *Climate Change and Land: an IPCC special report on climate change, desertification, land degradation, sustainable land management, food security, and greenhouse gas fluxes in terrestrial ecosystems* [P.R. Shukla *et al* (eds.)]: https://www.ipcc.ch/srccl/

12. UNFCCC, *Harmonization of Standards for GHG Accounting*: https://unfccc.int/climate-action/sectoral-engagement/ifis-harmonization-of-standards-for-ghg-accounting

13. Thomson I *et al* (2021) *Net Zero Accounting for a net zero UK* (October): https://www.birmingham.ac.uk/documents/college-social-sciences/business/research/responsible-business/net-zero-accounting-for-a-net-zero-uk-report-final.pdf

14. US Securities and Exchange Commission (2022): https://www.sec.gov/news/press-release/2022-46

15. TCFD mandate (2022): https://www.edie.net/tcfd-mandate-everything-you-need-to-know-about-the-uks-new-climate-disclosure-requirements/

16. The Carbon Trust, *Briefing TCFD disclosures*: https://www.carbontrust.com/resources/briefing-tcfd-disclosures

17. Climate Outreach: https://climateoutreach.org/reports/theory-of-change/

18. DesRochers M (2019) Internal Marketing, *Forbes* (5 August): https://www.forbes.com/sites/forbesbostoncouncil/2019/08/05/internal-marketing-what-it-means-and-why-its-important/?sh=2a109a5e4086

19. Deloitte: https://www2.deloitte.com/global/en/blog/responsible-business-blog/2021/communications-for-a-changing-climate.html

20. Advertising Association: https://adnetzero.com/

21. Webster and Marshall (2019), *The Talking Climate Handbook*: https://climateoutreach.org/reports/how-to-have-a-climate-change-conversation-talking-climate/

22. Exponential Roadmap Initiative: https://exponentialroadmap.org/

23. 1.5° Supplier Engagement Guide: https://exponentialroadmap.org/supplier-engagement-guide/

24. The SME Climate Hub: https://smeclimatehub.org/

25. Exponential Roadmap Initiative – 1.5° Business Playbook: https://exponentialroadmap.org/wp-content/uploads/2020/09/1.5C-business-playbook-version-1.1.pdf

26. UN Race to Zero: https://climatechampions.unfccc.int/

27. TCFD Implementing Guidance: https://assets.bbhub.io/company/sites/60/2021/07/2021-TCFD-Implementing_Guidance.pdf

28. TCFD Metric Targets Guidance: https://assets.bbhub.io/company/sites/60/2021/07/2021-Metrics_Targets_Guidance-1.pdf

29. GHG Protocol: https://ghgprotocol.org/

30. CDP: https://www.cdp.net/en

31. CDP SME climate framework: https://cdn.cdp.net/cdp-production/cms/guidance_docs/pdfs/000/002/852/original/SME-Climate-Framework.pdf?1637746697

32. SME climate hub:https://smeclimatehub.org/

33. Datamaran, *Materiality Definition*: https://www.datamaran.com/materiality-definition/

34. GRI, *The Materiality Madness: Why Definitions Matter*: https://www.globalreporting.org/media/r2o0jx53/gri-perspective-the-materiality-madness.pdf

35. Tenbrick T (2021) Eight ways to make your climate change social media posts matter, *The Conversation* (17 June): https://theconversation.com/eight-ways-to-make-your-climate-change-social-media-posts-matter-from-a-communication-expert-161026

36. Climate Outreach: https://climateoutreach.org/reports/uncertainty-handbook/

37. Tuitjer L and Dirksmeier P (2021) Social media and perceived climate change efficacy: A European comparison, *Digital Geography and Society* (vol 2): https://www.sciencedirect.com/science/article/pii/S266637832100009X

38. European Council (2022) *Council adopts its position on the corporate sustainability reporting directive (CSRD)*: https://www.consilium.europa.eu/en/press/press-releases/2022/02/24/council-adopts-position-on-the-corporate-sustainability-reporting-directive-csrd/

PART II

HIGH-IMPACT SOLUTIONS: MAKING A DIFFERENCE

4

MEETINGS AND TRANSPORT: COLLEAGUES, CUSTOMERS AND SUPPLIERS

Petra Molthan-Hill and Fiona Winfield

Meetings will be one of the most common features in most organisations, and many will involve travel. This includes the commute by employees to their place of work, but also longer-distance travel to visit customers and suppliers, or to attend an interview. In this chapter we will explore different solutions for how greenhouse gas (GHG) emissions could be reduced in relation to the different travel needs in an organisation.

This chapter is for you if:

- You have a company car or van
- You organise meetings
- You work in HR or recruit staff
- You travel for work.

DOI: 10.4324/9781003274049-6

It will cover:

- Reducing GHG emissions through electrifying transportation
- Videoconferencing
- The Climate Gap Report: Transport Report Card
- The consumer actions which cut the most carbon in relation to transport
- Local networks
- Embodied carbon of electric cars
- Incentives for employees to 'travel green'
- A case study on how to reduce carbon emissions in recruitment
- Quick Wins, an implementation plan and Further Resources.

Speed and scale

The venture capitalist and New York Times number-one bestseller author John Doerr highlights in his new book 'Speed & Scale: A Global Action Plan for Solving our Climate Crisis Now' how electrifying transportation, along with decarbonising the grid, could reduce our current worldwide emissions of 59 gigatons (GT) by 27 gigatons. He sets up specific Objectives and Key Results (OKRs) to do so; his top-line OKR is to reach net-zero emissions by 2050 – and to get halfway there by 2030, a critical milestone.[1]

In order to achieve a reduction worldwide in transportation emissions, from the current 8 GT to 2 GT by 2050, John Doerr has chosen the following key results for his first Objective which is to 'Electrify Transportation':

KR 1.1 Price – electric vehicles (EVs) to achieve price-performance parity with new combustion-engine vehicles in the United States (US$35K) by 2024, and in India and China by 2030 (US$11K)

KR 1.2 Cars – half of all new personal vehicles purchased worldwide to be EVs by 2030 and 95% by 2040

KR 1.3 Buses and Trucks – all new buses to be electric by 2025, and 30% of medium and heavy trucks purchased to be zero-emission vehicles by 2030, with 95% by 2045

KR 1.4 Miles – 50% of the miles driven on the world's roads to be in electric vehicles by 2040, and 95% by 2050

KR 1.5 Planes – 20% of miles flown to use low-carbon fuel by 2025, and 40% of miles flown to be Carbon Neutral by 2040

KR 1.6 Maritime – shift of all new construction to 'zero-ready' ships by 2030.[2]

The Climate Interactive tool En-ROADS, introduced in chapter 1, also suggests that energy efficiency and electrification in transport are key levers to reduce worldwide greenhouse gas emissions.[3] In this chapter we will cover both, but we will also explore behavioural change, away from using transport as we do currently, and replacing it with video calls, car-sharing, cycling and walking!

Project Drawdown, also introduced in chapter 1, was already listing teleconferencing back in 2018 as one of its 100 most impactful climate solutions and calculated that *[b]y avoiding emissions from business air travel, telepresence can reduce emissions by 2 gigatons of carbon dioxide over thirty years. That result assumes that over 140 million business-related trips are replaced by telepresence in 2050. For organizations, the investment in telepresence systems pays off with $1.3 trillion worth of savings and 82 billion fewer unproductive travel hours.*[4] During the Pandemic in 2020–22, those able to work from home realised how fast such a shift could be made. However, in the coming years the question will be whether organisations will use tele-conferencing (and videoconferencing) as their main approach to communication between employees, clients or other stakeholders, or whether there will be a return to travelling everywhere to meet in person.

Companies, governments and consumers can only achieve these targets together

Achieving these reductions in carbon emissions requires the joint efforts from everyone in society: governments, organisations, companies and consumers. Rob Harrison and Josie Wexler have published a very interesting approach identifying the gaps between the targets set for a whole country (UK) and how this could be achieved when government, companies and consumers work together, while highlighting the gap that needs to be closed. This approach could be applied to other countries.

From their Climate Gap Report published in the Ethical Consumer – an independent UK not-for-profit, multi-stakeholder co-operative with open membership based in Manchester and dedicated to helping consumers make ethical buying decisions since 1989 – we have chosen their Transport Report Card 2021 (see Figure 4.1) printed here with their permission. In that report, they also provide cards for food, heating and selected consumer goods, along with an overall Summary Report Card 2021, showing that 75% of total consumer emissions could be reduced if the actions suggested on the different cards were achieved.[5]

TRANSPORT REPORT CARD 2021 (c 25% total emissions)	Annual emissions from cars	Annual emissions from aviation	Electric car registrations
Consumer-related actions needed by 2030 in the CCC's 'Balanced Scenario' (from a 2019 baseline)	c.40% reduction	c.13% reduction	97% of registrations by 2030
Where are we in the most recent figures?	74.7 million tonnes CO2e (2019)	38 million tonnes CO2e (2019)	6.5% (2020)
The current climate gap. What is still needed?	40% reduction (30 million tonnes)	13% reduction (4.94 million tonnes)	93.5% of registrations
What were the figures from the previous year?	75.1 million tonnes	38 million tonnes	3.5% of registrations
Are we moving fast enough?	No	No	No
What does government need to do?	Decarbonise electricity supply. Sense check road building. Support walking, cycling and public transport.	Halt airport expansion. Frequent-flyer levy. Encourage efficiency gains. Aviation tax reform.	EV purchase subsidies. Support rapid rollout of charging infrastructure. Mandatory zero-emission sales targets.
What do companies need to do?	Sell more electric vehicles. Continue innovating on decarbonising HGVs. Reduce distance travelled.	Replace business travel with online working. Increase plane efficiency. Develop sustainable aviation fuel.	Switch to electric cars and vans. Invest in charging infrastructure.
What do consumers need to do?	Electrify. Reduce distance travelled. Switch to lower carbon travel where possible.	Reduce flying if possible.	Replace cars with a fully electric vehicle as soon as possible.
Where are consumer intentions?	35% willing to reduce car travel	30% will fly less after pandemic	24% plan to buy an EV or a (much less good) PEHV in next five years

Key to tables: c. = circa or approximately CCC = Climate Change Committee	Going in the wrong direction	Not moving fast enough	On target	No year on year data available

Figure 4.1 Transport Report Card 2021 reprinted with permission from the Ethical Consumer.[6]

The Climate Gap Report is mostly based on data provided by the Climate Change Committee (CCC) in the United Kingdom. The CCC was set up under the Climate Change Act 2008 to advise the UK government and the devolved administrations on emissions targets, and to report to Parliament on progress made in reducing greenhouse gas emissions and preparing for, and adapting to, the impacts of climate change.[7] For the Climate Gap Report, these data were simplified and presented as a list of key actions for consumers, companies and governments. Using the 'balanced scenario approach' introduced by the CCC, the Climate Gap Report identifies targets that only require modest changes to the way we live now, although the authors do highlight that we might have to move faster. However, seeing as we appear unlikely to achieve even the modest targets identified, the authors recommend that we focus all our efforts on at least achieving those.

We can see in Figure 4.1 that these actions combine electrification of transportation with reduction of travel. However, the electrification alone would not allow us to meet our reduction in carbon emission targets worldwide, as every new car purchased, including electric cars, causes additional carbon emissions, due to their **embodied carbon**. In this case, embodied carbon includes everything that is needed to make a car: extracting metal and ores, sourcing all the parts such as rubber tyres, plastic dashboards, paints and their transport, assembling the car and transporting it to the consumer. An SUV for example would be responsible for emitting 25 tonnes CO_2e before it is even driven.[8] This would equate to five years of the recommended 5-tonne lifestyle (see chapter 1), so someone buying an SUV would use all their annual allowance for five years on acquiring the vehicle itself, with nothing left over for any food or drink, or even for driving the vehicle anywhere!

While an electric car does not have an internal combustion engine, it does have a battery, so with respect to embodied carbon, an electric car has a greater carbon footprint (when comparing cars of the same size). However, the difference is in the electricity used to run the car, which has a smaller footprint than the fossil fuel alternative. Mike Berners-Lee therefore concludes after his calculation that *overall you can think of electric cars as being about half as carbon-unfriendly as petrol cars*.[9]

It should be considered, however, that carbon footprinting is a static representation of the current emissions associated with the production of electric vehicles. It does not account for the contribution early adopters of the technology will have on market development by generating economies of scale, reducing costs, driving innovation and making it more likely that future consumers will purchase electric vehicles, which might have a lower embodied carbon due to lower carbon production processes.

In Figure 4.1, you can also see that this transition to electric cars is nevertheless important, so new cars purchased *should* be electric (and should be small). However, this ought to be accompanied by a reduction in travel, either by switching to public transport, cycling or walking, or replacing travel with video- or teleconferencing.

Building on the actions identified in the Transport Report Card (Figure 4.1), Josie Wexler published further details on the consumer actions that would cut the most carbon in relation to housing, transport, food, products and waste in the following issue of the Ethical Consumer.[10] Figure 4.2 in this chapter shows the conclusions regarding consumer action in relation to transport. While these actions focus on consumers in general, they could also be applied to employees of an organisation, or managers encouraging their colleagues to make changes, such as taking fewer long-haul flights to meet with customers or suppliers.

WANT TO DIG DEEPER?

Project Drawdown Transportation
https://www.drawdown.org/sectors/transportation
Here you can find both an overview and detail about transport-related climate solutions suggested by Project Drawdown: bicycle Infrastructure, carpooling, efficient aviation, ocean shipping and trucks, electric bicycles, cars and trains, high-speed rail, hybrid cars, public transit, telepresence and walkable cities.

Road Freight Zero: Pathways to faster adoption of zero-emission trucks
https://www.mckinsey.com/industries/automotive-and-assembly/our-insights/road-freight-global-pathways-report
This is a joint publication by the WEF and McKinsey that describes how the Road Freight Zero (RFZ) initiative can help countries reach their emissions goals. The initiative, established in September 2020, is designed to help industry leaders jointly develop solutions. The target audience includes stakeholders on both the demand and supply sides, including manufacturers, consumer-goods giants, logistics majors, fleet operators, energy, tech and infrastructure firms, innovators, finance companies, academic institutions and civil-society groups.

Transport – The UK has one car per two people, so relevant figures should be divided by 2 to get average per capita figures.[10] Approximately 40% of the UK takes one or more short haul flights a year, 20% long haul, 50% don't fly at all.[11]

Action	Role in decarbonisation	Average carbon saving for the year 2021	Average carbon saving in tonnes by 2030 (9 years)
✳ Take one fewer long-haul flight a year	Extremely helpful.	A London-Beijing roundtrip, including an 'uplift' factor for indirect warming effects, is about 2.5 tonnes.[12] A London-Sydney roundtrip is about 5 tonnes.[13]	23 tonnes or 45 tonnes respectively.
✳ Switch from a conventional car to an electric car	In the long run, necessary for those who own cars.	Saves about 1.5 tonnes a year during driving, although there is a manufacturing cost which has to be paid back. This cost is disputed and also varies hugely on the car, but one average estimate is about 7 tonnes for a conventional car, and 10 for an electric.[14] (This too will drop with time, as much of it is the electricity used to make the car and battery). The average UK car lifespan is 13 years, so if the grid mix didn't change, savings minus payback would average to 0.7 tonnes a year.	With grid decarbonisation, savings from driving will be 15 tonnes to 2030. If you subtract the payback for manufacturing emissions mentioned, averaged over the 13-year lifespan, it leaves about 7 tonnes.
✳ Switch one trip per day from driving to cycling	Very helpful.	A recent study based on real world behaviour found a reduction of about 0.5 tonnes over a year.[15]	Over 9 years this is 4.5 tonnes.
✳ Car sharing	Very helpful.	The 7 tonnes estimate for making a conventional car, averaged over the 13-year lifespan, comes to 0.5 tonnes per year. However, real-world studies of car pools have suggested that actual savings are much less because of how people use them.[16]	About 4.5 tonnes.
✳ Take one fewer short-haul flight a year	Very helpful.	A London-Madrid roundtrip, including an 'uplift' factor for indirect warming effects, is about 0.4 tonnes.[17]	About 3.6 tonnes.

Figure 4.2 Which consumer actions in relation to transport cut the most carbon? reprinted with permission of the Ethical Consumer.[11]

High-impact solutions

According to EU data, passenger cars and vans (also known as 'light commercial vehicles') are respectively responsible for around 12% and 2.5% of total EU emissions of carbon dioxide (CO_2).[12] While the aviation sector creates 13.9% of the emissions from transport, making it the second biggest source of transport GHG emissions after road transport.

- If global aviation were a country, it would rank in the top 10 emitters.
- Someone flying from Lisbon to New York and back generates roughly the same level of emissions as the average person in the EU does by heating their home for a whole year.

Before the Covid-19 crisis, the International Civil Aviation Organization (ICAO) forecasted [sic] that by 2050 international aviation **emissions could triple** compared with 2015.[13]

With this in mind, anything that a company could do to replace global networks with local networks, especially with regards to their suppliers, or their employees commuting to work or meeting up with other stakeholders, would be a positive development, hence our first question we will answer is: **networks: how to move from global to local?**

Video calls use between 2g and 50g CO_2e per participant/hour depending on the device (although this does not allow for the embodied carbon from the device's manufacture).[14] If instead of the video call, you were to travel to the meeting, you would have emitted that amount after driving just a few metres in your car. For example, going to a meeting in a mid-sized five-door electric car will cause 180g CO_2e per mile.[15] In other words, video calls are almost certainly going to be better for the climate than meeting in person. Therefore, our second question is: **travel and video-conferencing: how do we meet the sustainable way?**

As pointed out before, the embodied carbon of electric cars is higher than that of other cars, however over their lifetime electric cars are better than fossil-fuel powered cars and will become better still in the long run, therefore our third question is: **embodied carbon: when should I replace my company vehicle with an electric one?**

Finally, you might need employees to commute to work, and customers might need to visit your site, in which case such travel can potentially be reduced or improved, hence our fourth question: **employee and customer journeys: how can you incentivise them to 'travel green'?**

Networks: how to move from global to local?

Anne Hidalgo, mayor of Paris (as at autumn 2022), is a keen promoter of the '15-minute city' where everything is in close vicinity so that people can live, go to school, work, shop and spend their leisure time within a fifteen-minute walking or cycling radius of their home. In order to achieve this, 60 km of cycling paths within Paris have been made permanent in the last two years, along with a reduction in the number of parking spaces, an increase in the number of EV charging points and a decrease in the speed limit in the French capital to just 30 km per hour. Reporting on these achievements, an article by the CTNG, an international English-language Chinese state-run cable TV news service based in Beijing, China, concludes that the 15-minute city plan works well in rich countries like France, but could also be the right approach in India or China for big metropolises.[16]

Cities as different as Paris, Melbourne and Portland (Oregon) are working to reimagine their cities using the lens of walking/bike travel time.[17] Carlos Moreno, Professor at the Panthéon Sorbonne University in Paris, and creator of the 15-minute city concept, argues that *neighbourhoods could be designed to contain all the amenities we need to live, no more than 15 minutes' walk from a person's front door. Not only would it negate the need for such regular use of fuel-burning transport but would give us back valuable time spent travelling or commuting each day.*[18]

In addition to planning workspaces this way in collaboration with local councils, companies and other organisations need to rethink their supply chains. Which of the products needed for their own products and process could be sourced locally? This topic is discussed in more detail in chapter 8 (Procurement & Supply).

Travel and videoconferencing: how do we meet the sustainable way?

One business-class flight from London to Hong Kong and back is 10 tonnes CO_2e, or approximately 1,700 locally produced steaks.[19] Offsetting this one flight would require replanting 200 m^2 of broadleaf forest in the United Kingdom. But as we have shown in chapter 1, any form of afforestation or moving to a vegan diet alone cannot solve climate change; it needs to be part of a portfolio of solutions, which includes a reduction in our travel.

Some travel can be replaced with more carbon-friendly travel options. For example, a short haul flight of 411 miles, such as the distance between Glasgow and London, uses 368 kg CO_2e (economy class per person) for the return journey. Going the same distance by train uses only 64 kg CO_2e (per person). If you travel the same distance by car, you will use between 148 kg CO_2e (small electric car, driver only) and 1.02 tonnes CO_2e (large SUV, driver only). Either taking the train (or indeed a coach with 40 kg CO_2e per person) would be the more carbon-friendly option and something that perhaps every organisation should have as a requirement for their employees. For example, all organisations based in Europe should require their employees to travel by train if going to any other European city, as this could cut their emissions by a fifth. Furthermore, compared to travelling by car, the time spent on the train can be very productive as it allows employees to work on projects, writing and reading, which is obviously not possible when driving a car![20]

However, the best option would be to meet up using video- or tele-conferencing, which causes only a fraction of the emissions. Mike Berners-Lee calculates that a meeting using an averagely efficient laptop uses 10g CO_2e per hour and suggests that replacing a meeting in Hong Kong with two people flying in from Europe, with a virtual meeting could save 20 tonnes CO_2e! Replacing conferences or other large-scale gatherings can easily reach millions of tonnes CO_2e. For example, the 2018 football World Cup, where 74% of the 2.2 million tonnes CO_2e were attributed to transport. The biggest share was taken by the estimated 3 million spectators who saw matches live, at approx. 700 kg per spectator. In contrast, the 3.6 billion people worldwide watching the 64 matches on television and online used only 62g CO_2e per hour of entertainment (per spectator).[21] Many companies and organisations will have the possibility to reduce their carbon footprint by reducing attendance at, and organisation of, large gatherings and replacing them with well organised videoconferences; substituting individual meetings with video meetings will also add to the savings an organisation could make. Recruitment can likewise be conducted differently; please refer to our case study in this chapter.

Embodied carbon: when should I replace my company vehicle with an electric one?

As mentioned before, the embodied carbon of a car often has a very high impact on the car's emissions over its lifetime. *Manufacture of a top-of-the-range*

Range Rover Sport HSE that ends up being scrapped after 100,000 miles accounts for about two-thirds of its lifetime exhaust pipe emissions.[22] Consequently keeping a car longer reduces the carbon equivalent emissions as its embodied emissions are spread over a longer lifetime. For example, for the Range Rover Sport HSE, it drops from 493–513g embodied emissions/mile when only driven for 100,000 miles to 247–257g embodied emissions/mile when driven over 200,000 miles. So overall it is better to keep a car for longer as the embodied carbon causes the most emissions; buying a new car will cause these upfront emissions even if it is an electric vehicle. Furthermore, a car replaced at lower mileage will be driven for longer in the used car market, continuing its lifetime in-use carbon emissions, in addition to the new car that replaced it.

If, however, your car needs replacing and/or the fuel consumption is extremely poor, it is better to buy a new car. In this case, an electric vehicle is better, as the emissions of the electricity you use (especially if from renewable sources), are much lower than the fossil-fuel alternative per mile, despite the embodied carbon of an electric car being slightly higher. Over the lifetime of a car, especially if you use it for longer as just outlined, the electric car will only cause half of the emissions or even less.

When buying a new vehicle, consider the alternatives, could you buy a second-hand car or van? Buying a second-hand vehicle means that the embodied emissions per mile will be lower as it will be used over a longer lifetime. Also consider the size of the vehicle. How big does it need to be to carry all the tools you need for the job? Consider taking only certain tools for that day's jobs or rotate the tools depending on the jobs planned. By selecting a smaller vehicle, more embodied carbon will be saved, but also more fuel/electricity will be saved, as extra weight will use more fuel or electricity. Also, you can consider whether you need to replace the vehicle at all, could you do your work with the remaining fleet, or could you set up a roster or booking system to optimise the use of the company vans, lorries or cars? Finally, check out the case study in chapter 8 (Procurement & Supply) where we look at 'harmoto', a business offering EVs available via salary sacrifice in the United Kingdom.

Employee and customer journeys: how can you incentivise them to 'travel green'?

Aim to make it as easy as possible for your employees to commute to work, and for your visitors to reach you, using public transport. If you are not too remote, encourage those who do not live too far away to consider using a bike. Once at work, if travelling to other sites or meeting clients and suppliers off site is essential, make it easy for your employees to use carbon-friendly modes of transport.

If your company is not connected to the public transport network, it might be good to provide shuttle buses at key times to the nearest public bus stop, train, tram or underground station. If there are other organisations based nearby, you might be able to share the cost, or even lobby for such a connection to be supplied, especially if it attracts other passengers.

Depending on where you are based, check out what schemes exist to support and encourage the use of bikes by your employees. In the United Kingdom, the Cycle to Work scheme allows employees to save 25–39% of the cost of a new bike and accessories, while spreading the cost. It is completely free for a company to join and is reported to be easy to administer online.[23] There is also information available from a social enterprise called the Green Commute Initiative which you might find useful.[24] Meanwhile, in some European countries such as Belgium, France and the Netherlands, it is possible to pay commuters or give them tax breaks to incentivise them to cycle to work.[25]

For employees needing to move around, ensure you have small electric vehicles available and have an easy-to-use booking system. If you are a small organisation and prefer not to own your own vehicles, perhaps tap into a commercial operation such as the Enterprise Car Club scheme.[26]

Also, as mentioned in chapter 6 (Food), waste from food and drink production can be used to produce bio-gas which can power vehicles. While electrification might be the ideal overall goal, at least in this situation, waste matter is being put to good use and is not ending up in landfill.[27]

Case study

In this chapter, we look at how interviews can be conducted in a carbon-friendly way. The case focuses on SMEs but can also be applied to larger organisations. Given that one long-distance flight as outlined above causes 10 tonnes CO_2e, you can imagine how much carbon could be saved if international recruitment were carried out virtually rather than in person.

Recruitment and selection doesn't need to cost the Earth

By Ani Raiden (Associate Professor – Nottingham Business School, UK)

This case study focuses on recruitment and selection practice in Small and Medium Enterprises (SMEs), although the problems and solutions offered can apply to organisations of any size, and there is further exploration of practices in larger organisations later on. The company A. Aldridge Designs (a designer and producer of niche greeting cards) does exist, but the name, location and other details have been changed as the organisation prefers to remain anonymous.

The business is based in the affluent Stoke Newington area in North London (England), with a factory in a nearby industrial estate that employs 25 people. Given the recent success of their greetings cards, they are looking to expand their marketing and distribution teams. These roles can be fulfilled remotely, which allows the company to widen its employee base to include people from isolated rural communities, deprived areas, or even internationally.

SMEs operate across many industries and play an essential role in the economy of a country, and according to the European Commission account for 99% of all firms in some countries.[28] SMEs usually have a business presence within a specific location, and they tend to tap into relatively local labour markets. While such a place-based approach can be a distinct business advantage, and contributes to healthy regional development, it can limit access to talent and hinder the potential for growth and innovation. SMEs have the potential to offer employment opportunities to people locally and nationally (and sometimes globally too).

People's identification with the founding purpose and values of the organisation is important to SMEs, and it is the employees' sense of shared purpose, teamwork and a set of common objectives that steer the collaborative working style found within many small businesses. Thus, recruitment and selection practices tend to be friendly and less formal than those found in larger organisations.

A desk and webcam are all you need

An interview, whether with a panel or one-to-one, is a central element of the selection process. Even though they have low predictive validity (i.e. they are relatively poor in determining how well a person will perform in the job they're being hired for, and the potential for distorted judgements is significant because of bias and differences in expectations), establishing the 'human' connection between the hiring organisation and the candidate is valued highly. The Director of A. Aldridge Designs is certainly very keen to meet all suitable candidates in person and give them a tour of the premises. She is very proud of the company success and considers the employees as part of the Aldridge family. At the same time, she is focused on finding the best people for the new marketing and distribution roles, and the A. Aldridge Designs management team is increasingly aware of the local labour market limitations. Hence, they have decided upon a national recruitment campaign, targeting leading universities in order to source graduates.

Meeting selected candidates in person will mean extensive travel; either the candidates would need to go to London, or the team would need to tour the universities. In the United Kingdom, the national rail network serves the country well and so public transport should be feasible. Electric trains emit 60% less carbon than their diesel counterparts, but only 42% of the UK rail network is currently electrified, which places the United Kingdom far behind European neighbours, such as the Netherlands, where 76% of the network is electrified.

Domestic flights and travelling in a medium-sized petrol or diesel car have the highest carbon footprints of all different modes of transport. Taking a train instead of a short flight can lower emissions by 84%. In an international context, travel for interviews leads to a considerable environmental burden if shortlisted candidates are invited to attend interviews in person; medium and long-haul flights also have a high carbon footprint.

The Covid-19 pandemic has accelerated the uptake of remote working across all sectors and industries, and has influenced patterns of work and organisational practice, even in SMEs that had previously been slow adopters of virtual teamwork. Use of videoconferencing has been normalised as part of the repertoire of tools and methods to establish contact with people, even when they live and work geographically close by.

Selection interviews can be conducted online with minimal disruption and expense to all – the organisation, the individual and the planet. Socially and environmentally responsible organisations are also 'selling' remote working as an opportunity to engage and attract a wider pool of people who may be unable or reluctant to travel for work. This can help reduce the organisational and the individual employees' carbon footprint, and it helps in expanding the talent pool with which SMEs engage. It signals commitment to flexible working, innovation and valuing the environment, thereby strengthening the company ethos on sustainability.

Solutions to reduce the carbon footprint

For A. Aldridge Designs, the following are real options to reduce the carbon footprint of their recruitment and selection practices:

• **Advertising the new graduate roles on national/international recruitment sites and social media** to tap into a wider pool of suitable candidates. Signalling that A. Aldridge Designs is a socially and environmentally responsible employer can help target communities and individuals that need jobs but find it difficult to secure work locally. Offering flexible and remote working can encourage applications from people in rural areas or further afield where there are candidates with relevant skills. For example, St Andrews (Scotland), a top 5 UK university for marketing, and Durham University (NE England), a top 5 university for supply chain logistics, could be targeted. Opportunities for remote working would also allow for targeting less affluent communities within the Greater London area, for example Tower Hamlets which is approximately a 50-minute commute.

• **Conducting selection interviews online** (at least the first round) thus cutting carbon emissions by not flying candidates for interviews from St Andrews (Dundee or Edinburgh airports) or Durham (Teesside airport) to London. The distance from Dundee airport to London is 460 miles, and Edinburgh and Teesside airports are 400 and 260 miles, respectively.

• **Encouraging use of trains instead of planes for essential travel** where face-to-face interviews are deemed necessary.

• **Shared files** – beyond the travel arrangements, the organisation's carbon footprint can also be reduced by hosting relevant documentation on a shared drive compared to emailing an attachment or posting paper copies.

Many large national and multinational companies (MNCs) grapple with similar issues. The most common approach to internationalisation for MNCs is an ethnocentric model whereby subsidiaries are managed by expatriates from the parent company. This is compounded by many being in geographical locations where demand for staff is high, but the supply of available workers is low. Better understanding of the benefits of employing a diverse workforce, some countries introducing quotas for female board members, and an increasing availability of self-initiated expatriates, can encourage MNCs to adopt a more geocentric mindset and recruit globally. If establishing an in-person 'human' connection between the hiring organisation and the candidates remains a highly valued aspect of the recruitment and selection practice, it will demand extensive travel across different countries and continents.

Using a combination of selection methods, so called 'assessment centres', can embrace technology-enabled solutions to test the candidates' job-specific skills and competencies in a much more accurate way and they can also be largely virtual. The assessment centre can include online psychometric tests, a presentation, case study work, virtual group work and interviews.

So, although some organisations will cling to the traditional face-to-face methods of recruitment and selection, many have realised that interviews and assessment centres can be carried out effectively virtually, reducing both paperwork and travel, which need not cost the earth!

Dr. Ani Raiden is a Carbon Literacy Project accredited Carbon Literacy Trainer and Associate Professor at Nottingham Business School (UK). Principles of sustainability are integral to Ani's research on managing people, quality of working life and social value. She is the lead author of *Social Value in Construction* (2019) and *Social Value in Practice* (2022), and an editor of the Routledge *Social Value in the Built Environment* book series.

Quick Wins

Overall, we recommend that you develop a Travel Plan and a Travel Policy (see chapter 14) for your organisation with targets to reduce carbon emissions, and adopt new approaches, but that may take some time, so start with the suggestions below.

1. When scheduling a meeting, does this need to be in person? You might be able to reduce the number of face-to-face meetings considerably without impairing results. An additional benefit might be that employees save on travel time and could fit in other tasks on the same day.
2. When your meetings are over, switch off your devices completely, do not leave on stand-by!
3. Can you travel by bike, rent an electric scooter or walk to a meeting?
4. If commuting, could you join a car-share scheme or use a carpool?
5. If there isn't one already, could your organisation introduce a car-share scheme? Or could you find a car-sharing partner through your company's intranet?

6. Has your organisation investigated if there's a 'cycle to work' scheme in your country, to encourage employees to commute by bike (in some cases saving money on purchasing the bike)?

7. Avoid transporting unnecessary items: the heavier the vehicle, the more fuel you'll need to move it around, so just keep things in there that you need for the job on the day.

8. Drive more efficiently! Save up to 33% on your fuel bill (and your emissions) by 'eco-driving': check your tyre pressure (under-inflated tyres use more fuel); *where safe* keep moving instead of stopping, and don't drive too fast, e.g. driving at 80 mph can use up to 25% more fuel than driving at 70 mph. Check the full list of suggestions to save fuel on the AA's website.[29]

9. Introduce telematics to improve journey planning.

10. Use the most fuel-efficient route, such as avoiding steep hills or roads where you need to brake a lot; Google Maps for example has introduced eco-friendly routes: https://blog.google/products/maps/3-new-ways-navigate-more-sustainably-maps/

11. Monitor the energy performance of any company vehicles to create a benchmark against which to judge future emissions.

12. Set a maximum acceptable CO_2 emission level and remove high emission vehicles from the fleet and company car choice list.

13. Offer incentives when employees travel by train instead of flying. (Trains cause approximately one-fifth of the carbon emissions compared to planes over the same distance.)

Outlook

As shown in this chapter, there are many climate solutions that would help you reduce the greenhouse gas emissions related to transport and travel in your organisation. We recommend that you draw up an implementation plan similar to the one suggested in Figure 4.3 for all your transport and travel-related reduction possibilities. As a next step, you could create specific implementation plans for each of the high-impact climate solutions outlined above, such as how to incentivise 'green travel' by your employees. You might also want to read other chapters such as the one on the Supply Chain (chapter 8) to optimise the transportation of your goods.

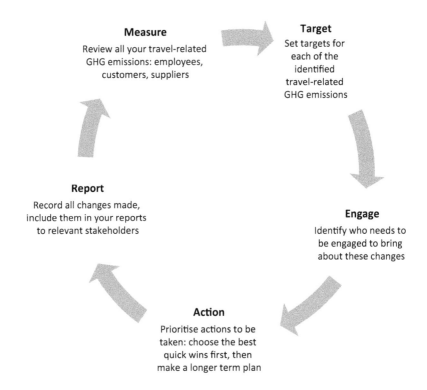

Figure 4.3 Implementation plan for the reduction of travel-related GHG emissions.

If your organisation is larger than an SME, an audit of transport may have been carried out under the EU Energy Efficiency Directive (2012/27/EU) or the Energy Saving Obligation Scheme (ESOS) in the United Kingdom.

Further Resources

On the companion website to this book you can find further material to help you plan and implement this work. We especially recommend the Climate Literacy Training, which you can download from the companion website and which we explained in more detail in chapter 2; transport solutions are included in the slide deck and could be used to train your colleagues and other stakeholders.

Below are links which go into more detail on the above, or suggest further solutions that might be of interest in addition to the ones mentioned in the endnotes. We have also included some references to initiatives that could be copied in other countries such as 'The Sustainable Transport Alliance'.

General

The Sustainable Transport Alliance
https://como.org.uk/sustainable-transport-alliance/
Established by several groups in the United Kingdom: the Community Rail Network; the Campaign for Better Transport; Bus Users UK; the Community Transport Association; Living Streets; Sustrans; the London Cycling Campaign; and Collaborative Mobility UK (CoMoUK). Their vision of future transport is that *all communities can develop into healthy, unpolluted, inclusive, prosperous places to live, work and enjoy, well-connected and served by green and fair transport that works for everyone.*

UN Sustainable Transport
https://sustainabledevelopment.un.org/topics/sustainabletransport
The United Nations highlights that sustainable transport could contribute to achieving several of the UN Sustainable Development Goals (SDGs) such as SDG 3 – *Ensure healthy lives and promote well-being for all at all ages*, SDG 9 – *Build resilient infrastructure, promote inclusive and sustainable industrialization and foster innovation* and SDG 11 – *Make cities and human settlements inclusive, safe, resilient and sustainable.* Information on how to do this can be found on this website.

Notes

1. Doerr J (2021) Speed & Scale. *A Global Action Plan for Solving our Climate Crisis Now*, London: Penguin, pxxiv
2. Doerr J (2021) Speed & Scale. *A Global Action Plan for Solving our Climate Crisis Now*, London: Penguin, p. 6; please see also his whole chapter on 'Electrify transportation' for further information
3. En-ROADS: https://en-roads.climateinteractive.org/scenario.html?v=22. 3.0

4. Hawken P (2017) *Drawdown. The most comprehensive plan ever proposed to reverse global warming*, London: Penguin, p. 155

5. *Ethical Consumer* 193 Nov/Dec 2021, pp. 32–37. A summary can be found here: https://www.ethicalconsumer.org/climate-gap-report

6. Ethical Consumer (2021) *Climate Gap Report:* https://research. ethicalconsumer.org/sites/default/files/inline-files/climate-gap-2021-main-report4.pdf, p. 15

7. More info about the Climate Change Committee can be found here: https://www.theccc.org.uk/

8. Berners-Lee M (2020) *How bad are bananas? The carbon footprint of everything*, p. 145; here you will also find detailed information on how this is calculated

9. Berners-Lee M (2020) *How bad are bananas? The carbon footprint of everything*, p. 148

10. Wexler J (2022) Which consumer actions cut the most carbon? *Ethical Consumer* 194 Jan/Feb 2022, pp. 45–47

11. Wexler J (2022) Which consumer actions cut the most carbon? *Ethical Consumer* 194 Jan/Feb 2022, p. 46

12. European Commission, CO_2 *emission performance standards for cars and vans*: https://ec.europa.eu/clima/eu-action/transport-emissions/road-transport-reducing-co2-emissions-vehicles/co2-emission-performance-standards-cars-and-vans_en

13. European Commission, *Reducing emissions from aviation*: https://ec.europa.eu/clima/eu-action/transport-emissions/reducing-emissions-aviation_en

14. Berners-Lee M (2020) *How bad are bananas? The carbon footprint of everything*, p. 25

15. Berners-Lee M (2020) *How bad are bananas? The carbon footprint of everything*, p. 62

16. CGTN, *Is France's 15-minute city a game changer for climate change?*: https://newseu.cgtn.com/news/2021-11-09/Is-France-s-15-minute-city-a-game-changer-for-climate-change--13XuEL9rngI/index.html

17. This website offers detailed guidance on how to design a 15-minute city: https://www.15minutecity.com/blog/hello

18. Further information on the 15-minute city: https://ww3.rics.org/uk/en/modus/built-environment/homes-and-communities/living-differently--how-does-a-15-minute-city-work-.html and a useful link to understand more about the concept

19. Own calculation based on figures provided by Mike Berners-Lee (2020) *How bad are bananas? The carbon footprint of everything*, p. 101 and p. 140

20. Berners-Lee M (2020) *How bad are bananas? The carbon footprint of everything*, p. 114

21. Berners-Lee M (2020) *How bad are bananas? The carbon footprint of everything*, p. 25 and p. 162

22. Berners-Lee M (2020) *How bad are bananas? The carbon footprint of everything*, p. 146

23. UK Cycle to Work scheme: https://www.gov.uk/government/publications/cycle-to-work-scheme-implementation-guidance

24. Green Commute Initiative: https://www.greencommuteinitiative.uk/

25. Countries incentivising their workers to ride to work: https://electrek.co/2022/02/03/these-countries-pay-people-to-ride-bicycles-and-e-bikes-to-work-shouldnt-the-us-too/

26. Enterprise Car Club Scheme: https://www.enterprisecarclub.co.uk/gb/en/home.html

27. Food Manufacture (2021) *Black Sheep Brewery signs three year biogas sustainability deal:* https://www.foodmanufacture.co.uk/Article/2021/08/16/Black-Sheep-Brewery-signs-three-year-biogas-sustainability-deal

28. European Commission: https://ec.europa.eu/growth/smes/sme-definition_en

29. AA, *Save fuel and money with eco-driving*: https://www.theaa.com/driving-advice/fuels-environment/drive-economically

5

YOUR ORGANISATION'S DIGITAL FOOTPRINT

Petra Molthan-Hill and Fiona Winfield

Every organisation will use data to a certain extent, whether its employees are using computers for their daily tasks, the company website promotes the organisation's products and services, or financial transactions are made with credit cards, Bitcoins or similar. Many organisations will have very complex information systems and might have their own data centre.

This chapter is for you if:

- You are an employee using a computer, tablet or smartphone
- You design or update websites or anything else on the internet
- You are a software developer or coder
- You have set up a data centre
- You produce and stream videos.

DOI: 10.4324/9781003274049-7

It will cover:

- The contribution of the Information and Communications Technology (ICT) sector, including cryptocurrencies, to global greenhouse gas emissions
- Improving data centres
- Reducing carbon emissions from cryptocurrencies
- Web design optimisation, linking experience and energy reduction
- Embodied carbon reduction in relation to smartphones
- A case study, Quick Wins and some Further Resources for the 'Internet of Things'.

Data – do we have our heads in the clouds?

The Information and Communications Technology (ICT) sector encompasses data centres, networks, streaming devices, teleconferencing, computers, smartphones, tablets and videogames, along with cryptocurrencies including Bitcoins. Calculating the greenhouse gas (GHG) emissions for all these different devices and infrastructures, as well as the energy to power all of them, is quite an undertaking. Hence, the estimates for the GHG emissions for the whole ICT sector, including the supply chain and life cycle analysis, vary from 1.8 to 3.9% of global GHG emissions.[1]

Cryptocurrencies alone accounted for 68 million tonnes CO_2e (see glossary) in 2019, and if the take-up is as great as other new technologies, could emit 1.2 billion tonnes in 2030 alone.[2] In 2020, the total crypto-mining power consumption was equivalent to the annual carbon footprint of Argentina; a single transaction made with Bitcoin has the same carbon footprint as 680,000 Visa card transactions or 51,210 hours of watching YouTube.[3] To help understand the impact of cryptocurrencies, the Cambridge Bitcoin Electricity Consumption Index (CBECI) offers comparison between various energy-intensive activities, see Table 5.1. The CBECI website also provides an up-to-date estimate of the Bitcoin network's daily electricity load, which is useful if you want to understand this topic better.[4]

While some argue this is not a problem if the energy used is from renewable sources, others point out that miners will go to countries where

Table 5.1 The energy consumption of energy-intensive activities (as of April 2022)[5]

Activity	Energy Consumption per year
Bitcoins	137 TWh
Gold mining	131 TWh
Data centres	200 TWh
Data networks	150 TWh

energy is cheaper, and this might favour countries using predominantly coal, such as China. While generally the move to decarbonise the whole ICT sector with renewables is a positive development, renewables still have their own carbon footprint, and although lower than all the other energy sources, this is not negligible (see chapter 7, 'Estates & Facilities'). Hence, using unlimited energy for cryptocurrencies, storing information in the 'cloud', and staying connected and informed all the time, might not be the right way forward for the planet.

We can turn this around!

Project Drawdown[6] highlights telepresence as one of their 100 most impactful solutions: *by avoiding emissions from business air travel, telepresence can reduce emissions by 1.0–3.8 gigatons of carbon dioxide over 30 years. That result assumes that more than 486–676 million business-related trips are replaced by telepresence in 2050. For organisations, the investment of US$104–366 billion in telepresence systems pays off with US$1.2–4.4 trillion worth of business travel savings and 107–143 billion fewer unproductive travel hours.* During the Covid pandemic, many organisations realised that business trips could be replaced by virtual meetings, however the question after the pandemic is whether tele- or video presence will replace, or be used in addition to, business travel. We discuss this question further in chapter 4 (Meetings & Transport) and offer solutions there.

Generally, careful management of ICT could cut GHG emissions in industries such as travel, and therefore reduce the overall emissions of a country; an organisation embracing this could thereby contribute to the shift. However, we need to be aware of the so-called **rebound effect** – the idea that when something is more carbon-efficient and therefore cheaper, we end up doing more of it.[7] This is especially true for how we deal with data. In the last ten years we have grown accustomed to finding immediate answers from the internet if we want to increase our knowledge about a topic, research laws and regulations, track down a suitable supplier or research a future employee, or search for a product or service and read user feedback. Also, we expect to store more and more data in the 'cloud' and hold onto documents and photos that we might have shredded or thrown away in the past. We have embellished our websites and social media accounts by adding videos and special images that use more data than the previous versions. We store lots of information about our customers and target them with tailored advertisements. This has all resulted in the requirement for infrastructure and data centres with more capacity. We therefore need to focus our attention on how to reduce the associated GHG emissions, as well as the quantity of data used, employing Search Engine Optimisation (SEO) for example. In improving the user experience, enabling a quick response to an enquiry, we also reduce the number of irrelevant websites returned in the search and reduce the associated energy needed to upload these.

We will focus in the next section on other high-impact solutions that will bring down emissions. Recent research[8] calculated the contribution of each ICT category in 2020: the biggest chunk was data centres (45% of emissions), followed by communication networks (24%) and smartphones (11%).

As the topic is so wide, we cannot cover all solutions in detail in this chapter, for example the topic of whether energy efficiency in processor technology can be further improved. So far, the semiconductor industry has followed what is known as Moore's law – which states that the number of transistors on a microprocessor chip will double approximately every two years, and hence allow for ever faster transmission of data. In the future, new applications might be developed to overcome problems like the heat generated when more silicon circuitry is jammed together on a tiny chip.[9] We will therefore leave this aside when we focus on solutions in the next section, as we will concentrate on those which not only have a high impact, but can also be easily implemented immediately in any organisation.

WANT TO DIG DEEPER?

Wholegrain Digital:
https://www.wholegraindigital.com/blog/website-energy-efficiency/
This resource offers 17 ways to make your website more energy efficient. Written by Tom Greenwood, one of the two founders of Wholegrain Digital, industry leaders in web sustainability and performance, to help the industry to shift to a zero-carbon future.
The company might also offer inspiration through their case studies for different sectors: https://www.wholegraindigital.com/work/

The Climate Impact of ICT: A Review of Estimates, Trends and Regulations – book by Charlotte Freitag and Mike Berners-Lee, available at: https://arxiv.org/ftp/arxiv/papers/2102/2102.02622.pdf
This report gives a detailed overview of current trends in the ICT sector and explains in detail the underlying calculations and methodologies used in this chapter.

High-impact solutions

In this section we have ranked the potential solutions that would make a difference according to their impact (highest first) and would be the most likely to be implemented. As mentioned above, data centres account for 45% of carbon emissions and therefore our first question in the next section will be **data centres: how do we cool them and power them more sustainably?**

Data centres and networks are also used excessively for so called **blockchains** in cryptocurrencies, where transactions are recorded digitally so that they cannot be forged. Our second solution is therefore focused on cryptocurrencies, especially as some people are worried that *Bitcoin emissions alone could push global warming above* 2°C.[10] So our second question is **cryptocurrencies: assuming they're here to stay, how can their impact be reduced?**

The demand on data centres and infrastructure is lower when people research information on the internet using an optimised search, therefore we have chosen sustainable web design as the third question which is **sustainable web design: how to ensure findability?**

Embodied carbon varies from one device to another,[11] here we focus on smartphones, as they currently account for 1% of global emissions and their popularity continues to increase worldwide. There are several billion people without smartphones currently, and existing users tend to replace their phones frequently and use them more extensively for all parts of their life, keeping up to date with friends and family, checking the latest news, listening to music and so on. So our final question is **embodied carbon: how to reduce it in our smartphones and other devices?**

Data centres: how do we cool them and power them more sustainably?

The three most important solutions for achieving a Carbon Neutral or even carbon negative data centre depend on the use of renewable electricity, choosing the right geological location and appropriate cooling techniques. The Positive Internet Company[12] for example builds its data centres in a naturally windy spot, which helps to cool down the servers. The wind is also used to generate energy and power the centres. The main data floor runs using adiabatic 'free' cooling systems, which are low-energy and make use of evaporative cooling. Overall, they have succeeded in being carbon negative, so they produce more energy than they consume for the running of their data centres.

Different cooling technologies have been developed. For example, *Iceotope's chassis-level precision immersion cooling solution removes the heat from every part of the system reliably and efficiently. Precision delivery of dielectric coolant mitigates the need to constrain the design of the IT solution, while maximising the cooling directly to the hotspots. This means there are no performance-throttling hotspots and no front-to-back air-cooling, or bottom to top immersion constraints.*[13]

Another option is heat recovery so that the heat generated in the data centre is reused and redirected into the local district heating network. For example, the Swedish company Conapto collaborates with Stockholm Exergi and Sollentuna Energi for heat recovery, and is part of the 'Climate Neutral Data Centre Pact' to make data centres Carbon Neutral by 2030.[14] Conapto also holds the Fossil Free Data label from Node Pole.[15]

Cryptocurrencies: assuming they're here to stay, how can their impact be reduced?

With regards to cryptocurrencies and blockchains, we will focus here on the solutions regarding the hardware or the calculation process; solutions regarding cryptocurrencies in financial markets will be discussed in chapter 10 (Pensions & Investments).

Cryptocurrencies are one of the many uses of blockchains – *the system's distributed and immutable electronic database – a ledger of every transaction that has ever taken place on the network. Data are stored as cryptographically secured 'blocks', strung together in a 'chain'.*[16] The energy consumption of these blockchains can be reduced by up to 99% if the currently used proof-of-work (PoW) is replaced by building an entirely new blockchain based on the proof-of-stake (PoS) algorithm.[17]

With regards to the hardware, the graphics processing unit can be changed to a more energy efficient Application-Specific Integrated Circuit (ASIC) miner.[18] Many of the solutions outlined above for locating data centres can also be applied to mining rigs, such as placing them in a desert to make the best use of solar power.[18] Another interesting new technology to cope with our increasing demand for data centres and mining rigs could be *heating houses with nerd power* as the BBC entitled an article in 2015.[19] 'Cloud and Heat' is an organisation that offers such technology and solutions for companies using artificial intelligence and machine learning, along with a carbon calculator.[20]

Sustainable web design: how to ensure findability?

When it comes to web design, there are technical solutions and improvements to the code being used, but there are fundamental decisions that can be made when designing a website. It is firstly worth considering anything that improves the user experience: to make sure that our customers, investors and other stakeholders are directed to the appropriate resources for their information needs at the first attempt. This will obviously have multiple benefits beyond the carbon saved by not uploading unnecessary websites, it will help customers to find the products they want to buy without spending too much time, it will direct investors to the right financial information without wading through additional information or giving up altogether, it will direct potential new employees to the relevant organisational and job details to help them decide if they should apply for the post, and so on.

The same applies to Search Engine Optimisation (SEO), *which is the process of getting traffic from free, organic, editorial, or natural search results in search engines. It aims to improve your website's position in search results pages. Remember, the higher the website is listed, the more people will see it.*[21] You would clearly want your organisation's website to appear on the first page when your customers or other stakeholders search for your products or services. By optimising this, people will spend less time browsing through different websites, an action which uses a lot of energy to visit content they were not even interested in, adding to their frustration as well! These changes to reduce carbon emissions will potentially benefit your organisation in so many ways.

Many other changes can be made to the website, for example reducing images, videos or using system fonts. The website carbon calculator located on websitecarbon.com helps you to identify ways in which you can reduce the CO_2e per page. Along with the calculator, there are examples of many companies that have optimised their websites. Riverford Organic, the United Kingdom's leading seasonal organic veg box delivery company, only uses 0.23 grams CO_2 per page view, whereas *the average web page tested produces approximately 0.5 grams CO_2 per page view. For a website with 10,000 monthly page views, that's 60 kg CO_2 per year.* Riverford therefore saves over 30 kg of emissions per annum.[22]

A full list of improvements and carbon reductions applicable to web design can be found in the book 'Sustainable Web Design'[23] by Tom Greenwood, the co-founder of Wholegrain Digital, a specialist in web performance and sustainability, and editor of the monthly green web newsletter: Curiously Green. He has also authored '17 ways to make your website more energy efficient',[24] which covers recommendations such as using less JavaScript, optimising images and using a data centre close to your users (as the further the data has to travel, the more energy it uses to reach the audience). If your audience is spread across the world, he recommends using a CDN (Content Delivery Network), which makes sure the largest files will be loaded from the CDN location in the user's own region, simultaneously improving energy efficiency and page load times. Another way to reduce energy consumption would be to block bots as they *often use up 50% of resources such as processing and bandwidth.*[24]

Embodied carbon: how to reduce it in our smartphones and other devices?

Smartphones are one example where the embodied carbon – the greenhouse gas emissions caused by mining, manufacturing and transport – outweigh the electricity used to run the device. In this case it would take on average 34 years until the footprint of the electricity used to run the device equals the footprint of manufacturing the phone.[25] This is due to the precious metals and rare earths needed to be mined for a smartphone's chip and motherboard. One solution could be new technology that does not use these metals, although this is not very likely, in the near future.

A more practical solution would be for everyone to keep their smartphone for longer. Most people discard their phone after two years, which is also encouraged by the regular introduction of upgraded models, the length of contract and type of subscription. Based on the average two-year ownership, the production footprint of 40 to 80 kg CO_2e must be divided by two accounting for 20 to 40 kg CO_2e of its footprint per annum.[26] If people decided to keep their phones for four years, it would come down to 10–20 kg CO_2e per annum. In the United Kingdom, The Big Repair Project is trying to work out how to make this more likely and how to ensure the 'Right to Repair' is fully implemented and accepted as the norm for electronic devices and equipment.[27]

Another option would be to buy second-hand or go for modular mobile phones, where you can replace the module when you want a new feature such as a better display, without replacing the whole phone.[28] The life of the battery can be a limiting factor too, and it has become more difficult to replace that in some smartphones. This approach could be applied to all devices and would allow companies to update each model as required for their operations. However, it would also mean that telecom companies, manufacturers of phones and other devices would need to change their business model.[29]

Case study

In the following case study, the web team at Nottingham Trent University (NTU) in the United Kingdom describes in detail how they optimised the university website, improving user experience while simultaneously reducing carbon emissions.

One small step – reducing our digital carbon footprint

By Claire Miller (Web & Digital Content Officer, Nottingham Trent University) Max Wakelin (Web Developer, Nottingham Trent University)

Inspired by a presentation by Tom Greenwood, CEO of Wholegrain Digital, about reducing the carbon footprint of a website, Nottingham Trent University's Web team began discussing methods of improving their website's impact on the environment in January 2021. At this time, NTU's website caused approximately 2.38 g of carbon equivalent per page view, according to Wholegrain Digital's Website Carbon Calculator.[30] Over a year, based on the 19 million views that ntu.ac.uk received between January 2020 and 2021, this equates to approximately 45,220 kg of annual CO_2 emissions. The calculator specifies that 1.76 g per page view is the average amount of carbon equivalent caused by websites at this time, so this became a **target of the project**.

The team also realised that the larger the overall file size of a webpage, the longer it takes to load and the more energy intensive it becomes. This 'page weight' is one of the few digital sustainability factors over which a Web team has influence, as a webpage's file size and associated assets can be altered. Project planning sessions were therefore focused on identifying **'Quick Win' opportunities** and areas with the biggest impact on page weight. These mostly fell under the remit of the developers, in particular:

- Reducing and limiting the file size and dimensions of images
- Reducing and limiting the file size of documents
- Removing unused or conflicting code
- Removing unused fonts and their variants such as bold, italic, etc.
- Minifying JavaScript and CSS files.

Other potential improvements included auditing content to reduce duplication and unnecessary pages, improving content processes around archiving content, and best practice guidance for CMS (Content Management System) users, amongst others. Several actions that would improve the carbon footprint of a website would also improve its accessibility, user experience and SEO, and therefore its findability. For example, reducing duplicated content would reduce cannibalisation of content in search engines, and help users find content more efficiently, reducing the amount of energy used in browsing.

Measuring success

To benchmark progress, a number of different page types including landing pages, forms and search results were put through multiple load speed tools on a weekly basis. The NTU project used the following:

- GTMetrix for performance, structure and contentful paint (time to load first elements) [31]
- Google PageSpeed Insights for mobile and desktop scores [32]
- Website Carbon Calculator for approximate carbon equivalent per page view. [33]

One of the issues posed in measuring digital sustainability is the lack of accuracy in reporting impact. Digital sustainability is not yet a commonplace practice, so there are few guides on how to measure it. There are also several variables that cannot easily be measured, including millions of users' internet connections and devices, variance in page weights across the site, how traffic is split across those pages and more, making it nigh on impossible to give accurate data. Monitoring load speed gives only an indication of success.

Solutions for a difficult problem

Media file size was identified as a major area for improvement, with some individual images on the website reaching 19.5 MB. To tackle this, the Web team wanted a way to compress images uploaded into the CMS automatically. The main obstacles presented by this solution were limitations in the CMS, including lack of backend querying tools, no root access to the server, and no CDN (Content Delivery Network) integration with image compression capabilities. Because of this, an NTU developer created an automatic image compression script from scratch to work around the limitations.

A web server was created to analyse and manipulate data within the University CMS. This server was used to automatically identify and compress oversized images on the site, to generate the appropriate reports that monitored overall effectiveness, and to identify improvement opportunities within the script. A failsafe was written into the script in the event of image pixelation, but has not yet been required. The image compression identified and reduced all images above 1,800 pixels wide by 600 pixels high (the maximum size for NTU banner images) and above 512 KB, to below this threshold. Of the 19,315 total images, 1,470 were eligible for compression. These images were reduced by approximately 88.5%, from 3.51 GB to 407 MB, taking the total media folder size from 5.34 GB to 2.38 GB by compressing only a thirteenth of the total images.

After ongoing work around accessibility, SEO and UX throughout the year, and the completion of the first round of image compression, **NTU's carbon equivalent per page view dropped to approximately 2.09 g, which equates to 9% fewer carbon emissions per year.** According to the EPA's Carbon Equivalencies calculator, this saving is the same as charging a smartphone 827,060 times or driving over 17,000 miles in an average passenger vehicle.[34]

Further refinement can be made to the image compression work by separating banner images from standard images used across the site. Standard images can then be reduced to 881 × 585 pixels and below 100 KB where possible, without losing image quality. Investigation has also begun into compressing document files and automatically archiving expired events content. The digital sustainability project is still ongoing, but the Web team at NTU is on target to reach the average website carbon equivalent when the project is complete.

Claire is a Web & Digital Content Officer at Nottingham Trent University, UK working to improve the user experience of the NTU website through more useful, accessible and better optimised content.

Max Wakelin is Web Developer at NTU, working to optimise and autonomise technological processes to more effectively achieve sustainability objectives amongst other business goals.

Quick Wins

1. Develop your overall ICT strategy to move away from reliance on new equipment and enable reuse and retention of existing hardware as much as possible, for example delay replacing your smartphone and laptops so frequently.
2. Only gather and retain data that you absolutely need, e.g. what information do you require about your customer in relation to your product/service?
3. Compress the customer data where you can, e.g. just the house name or number and post code.
4. Switch off your router and other devices overnight, at weekends and during holidays (and do not leave on stand-by).
5. Choose hardware that does not need moving parts, such as a fan or a hard disk, for example a Raspberry Pi.[35]

6. Use an open-source operating system such as Linux to avoid advertisements (and thereby reduce the energy needed for these to pop up on your screen).
7. Make your website darker, preferably black in some places, as OLED Monitors will then use less power.
8. Avoid cryptocurrencies!

Outlook

As shown in this chapter, there are many climate solutions that would help you to reduce the greenhouse gas emissions related to data used in your organisation. We recommend that you draw up an implementation plan like the one suggested in Figure 5.1 for **all** your data/ICT-related reduction possibilities. As a next step, you could review your ICT in more detail, and draw up specific implementation plans for each of the high-impact climate

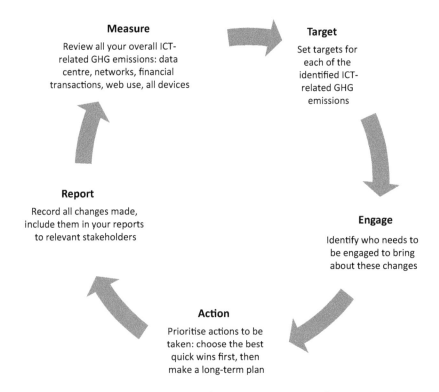

Measure
Review all your overall ICT-related GHG emissions: data centre, networks, financial transactions, web use, all devices

Target
Set targets for each of the identified ICT-related GHG emissions

Engage
Identify who needs to be engaged to bring about these changes

Action
Prioritise actions to be taken: choose the best quick wins first, then make a long-term plan

Report
Record all changes made, include them in your reports to relevant stakeholders

Figure 5.1 Implementation plan for the reduction of ICT-related GHG emissions.

solutions outlined above, such as the devices used in the organisation or the web design. You might also want to read other chapters such as the one about Marketing (chapter 9) and optimise your web design with regards to user experience and your marketing communications.

Further Resources

On the companion website to this book you can find further material to help you plan and implement this work.

Below you can find resources that go into more detail on the above, or suggest further solutions that might be of interest in addition to the ones mentioned in the endnotes. These additional topics such as Artificial Intelligence (AI) or the Internet of Things (IoT) – the interconnection and communication of devices, objects and sensors, such as the case of Smart Cities – really deserve their own full chapter as, while they can optimise energy efficiency on the one hand, they require more networks and data centres on the other. The references and courses suggested below offer a starting point to understand these emerging topics.

General

The alarming environmental impact of the Internet and how you can help:
https://medium.com/wedonthavetime/guest-blog-post-the-alarming-environmental-impact-of-the-internet-and-how-you-can-help-6ff892b8730d
This blog written by Ben Clifford offers some easy to implement re-commendations on how an individual can reduce their own carbon emissions, such as deleting any unused apps.

Carbon impact of video streaming:
https://www.carbontrust.com/resources/carbon-impact-of-video-streaming
This white paper discusses the carbon impact of video on demand and was funded by Netflix.

Artificial Intelligence (AI)

O Mulhern, Can AI Help Achieve Environmental Sustainability?:
https://earth.org/data_visualization/ai-can-it-help-achieve-environmental-sustainable/

This article explores how AI can address sustainable challenges such as the Sustainable Development Goals and climate change.

Internet of Things (IoT)

DR Kiran, Internet of Things: https://www.sciencedirect.com/topics/engineering/internet-of-things
A good starting point to understand the 'Internet of Things' is chapter 35 in Kiran's book 'Production Planning and Control' published in 2019 by Elsevier, which offers different commonly used definitions of the 'Internet of Things'. The link also connects to other articles that might be useful to understand this topic.

'Internet of Things (IoT) and Sustainability' online course
https://www.futurelearn.com/courses/internet-of-things-iot-and-sustainability
This FutureLearn course explores how the rise of smart devices can lead to a sustainable future. It introduces the technical dimensions of the Internet of Things (IoT) including hardware and software essentials and the role of technology platforms. It evaluates the IoT's role in addressing sustainability challenges in a range of case studies in key industry contexts.

Notes

1. Small World Consulting, *The climate impact of ICT*: https://arxiv.org/ftp/arxiv/papers/2102/2102.02622.pdf p. 1
2. Berners-Lee M (2020) *How bad are bananas? The carbon footprint of everything*, p. 164 and p. 259
3. Aratani L (2021) Electricity needed to mine bitcoin is more than used by 'entire countries', *The Guardian* (27 Feb): https://www.theguardian.com/technology/2021/feb/27/bitcoin-mining-electricity-use-environmental-impact
4. The Cambridge Bitcoin Electricity Consumption Index (CBECI) provides an up-to-date estimate of the Bitcoin network's daily electricity load. As the precise electricity consumption cannot be determined, the CBECI provides a hypothetical range and within those boundaries it provides a best-guess estimate of electricity consumption: https://ccaf.io/cbeci/index/methodology

5. Cambridge Bitcoin Electricity Consumption Index (April 2022): https://ccaf.io/cbeci/index

6. Project Drawdown, *Telepresence*: https://drawdown.org/solutions/tele-presence; for more about 'Project Drawdown', see chapter 1 of this book

7. Berners-Lee M (2020) *How bad are bananas? The carbon footprint of everything*, p. 166

8. Belkhir L & Elmeligi A (2018) Assessing ICT global emissions footprint: Trends to 2040 & recommendations, *Journal of Cleaner Production*, Vol 177 (10 March) pp. 448–463

9. Waldrop M (2016) *The chips are down for Moore's Law*: https://www.nature.com/news/the-chips-are-down-for-moore-s-law-1.19338

10. Nature - *Climate Change*: https://www.nature.com/articles/s41558-018-0321-8

11. Detailed calculations can be found here for computers, tablets etc.: https://www.sciencedirect.com/science/article/pii/S095965261733233X

12. The Positive Internet Company: https://positive-internet.com/

13. Iceotope: https://www.iceotope.com/technologies/kul-chassis-level-precision-immersion/

14. Conapto, *How to create a sustainable IT environment*: https://content.conapto.se/how-to-create-a-sustainable-it-environment/

15. Node Pole, *Fossil-free data label*: https://www.nodepole.com/news-and-insights/node-pole-launches-fossil-free-data-label

16. Nature, *Tackling climate change with block chain*: https://www.nature.com/articles/s41558-019-0567-9 p. 644

17. Bitcoinist, *'Ethereum 2.0' PoS Blockchain Aims to Cut Energy Use by 99%*: https://bitcoinist.com/ethereum-pos-blockchain-cut-energy/

18. Coindesk, *Building a greener bitcoin*: https://www.coindesk.com/markets/2014/04/09/building-a-greener-bitcoin-how-to-reduce-carbon-emissions/

19. BBC, *Heating houses with nerd power*: https://www.bbc.co.uk/news/magazine-32816775

20. Cloud and Heat, *The Green Cloud for AI and ML*: https://thinkgreen.cloudandheat.com/en/

21. Digital Marketing Institute, *What is SEO?*: https://digitalmarketinginstitute.com/blog/what-is-seo

22. Website carbon calculator: https://www.websitecarbon.com/

23. Book can be ordered here: https://abookapart.com/products/sustainable-web-design/

24. Wholegrain Digital, *17 ways to make your website more energy efficient*: https://www.wholegraindigital.com/blog/website-energy-efficiency/

25. Berners-Lee M (2000), *How bad are bananas? The carbon footprint of everything*, p. 116

26. Belkhir L & Elmegi A (2018) Assessing ICT global emissions footprint: Trends to 2040 & recommendations, *Journal of Cleaner Production*, Vol 177, pp. 448–463: https://doi.org/10.1016/j.jclepro.2017.12.239 (here you will also find calculations for all other devices)

27. The Big Repair Project: https://www.bigrepairproject.org.uk/

28. Android central, *Best sustainable and repairable phones 2022*: https://www.androidcentral.com/best-sustainable-repairable-phones

29. Sustainable Brands, *Fairphone forges ahead with longer-lasting, e-waste-neutral smartphone*: https://sustainablebrands.com/read/product-service-design-innovation/fairphone-forges-ahead-with-longer-lasting-e-waste-neutral-smartphone

30. Wholegrain Digital, *Website Carbon Calculator,* https://www.websitecarbon.com (NB: the number is approximate for various reasons, including the fact the calculator only uses the website's homepage to calculate the figure)

31. GTmetrix, *How fast does your website load?*: https://gtmetrix.com

32. Google, *PageSpeed Insights*: https://pagespeed.web.dev/

33. Wholegrain Digital, *Website Carbon Calculator:* https://www.websitecarbon.com

34. Environmental Protection Agency, *Greenhouse Gas Equivalencies Calculator,* https://www.epa.gov/energy/greenhouse-gas-equivalencies-calculator

35. Raspberry Pi Foundation: https://www.raspberrypi.org/

6

FOOD WASTE AND FOOD FOR THOUGHT

Fiona Winfield and Petra Molthan-Hill

This chapter gives you an overview of some of the major issues concerning food and drink and provides potential climate-friendly solutions (Quick Wins and longer term) that an employee in any industry could implement.

This chapter is for you if:

- You want to understand how food contributes to greenhouse gas emissions and what we can all do (at home or at work) to reduce its impact
- You want to make improvements to the catering service provided on your premises (or want to encourage others to do this)
- You are deciding policies on the sourcing of food and drink, or setting up supplier contracts and procurement
- You want to address the disposal of waste and surplus food
- You, or your colleagues, order outside catering for events or take clients out for meals.

DOI: 10.4324/9781003274049-8

It will cover:

- Food policies and strategies for every organisation
- Food and drinks sourcing – for your canteen and hospitality events
- Food and drinks wastage – prevention and redistribution
- Elimination/reduction of single-use plastics and other packaging
- Inspiration for the food and beverage sector about the perspective of their consumers.

From Farm to Fork – food has an enormous impact on emissions

Food and drink production and consumption contribute significantly to greenhouse gas (GHG) emissions. It is estimated that around 30% of total GHG emissions are from global food production[1] and more than half of these relate to animals and meat, with beef and lamb being the worst.[2] European livestock for example is estimated as being responsible for 81% of Europe's agricultural emissions, with a global warming impact equivalent to almost 20% of EU total emissions.[3] In the USA meanwhile, it was estimated in 2018 that the agricultural sector accounted for 10.5% of their overall GHG emissions.[4] A special problem is the deforestation of the Amazon to grow soya, with 80% of all the soya grown globally being fed to livestock, thereby enabling the production and sale of cheap chicken, for example. The resultant demand for soya has contributed to the 22% annual increase in deforestation of the Amazon rainforest in 2020/21.[5]

Managers responsible in any way for the choice of food and drinks available on their premises need to understand, and take into account, the whole life cycle of the products on offer, which is commonly referred to as 'farm to fork'. This includes agriculture, transportation and refrigeration of produce, food processing, retail logistics, food and drink offered across the hospitality sector, food preparation, meal and menu planning, food and drink packaging, and finally the consumption or disposal of food and drink. Several countries are working on policies that address the impact of food on climate change. For example, the European Union's Farm to Fork Strategy 2020 *aims to accelerate [their] transition to a sustainable food system that should ... help to mitigate climate change and adapt to its impacts.*[6]

Not only does our food system create a high percentage of the total GHG emissions, it can also contribute to global warming and climate change when we allow it to be wasted across the entire supply chain. Food waste is biodegradable and it releases methane (a greenhouse gas) during decomposition. This occurs when we leave food produce to rot, whether it is in the field or on a landfill site. The Intergovernmental Panel on Climate Change (IPCC) report 'Climate Change and Land' estimates: *[d]uring 2010–2016, global food loss and waste equalled 8–10% of total anthropogenic GHG emissions.*[7] If you carry out a food and beverage audit, it will not only help you to understand the food and drink requirements of your organisation, it will also help you to identify areas that require and how to avoid waste. There are financial benefits to be made when you reduce food waste to a minimum and these financial savings can in turn be invested in additional food and drink climate solutions.

Carbon-friendly catering

Many of the high-impact climate solutions from Project Drawdown (see chapter 1 of this book) are linked to changes in diet, agriculture, cooking methods and food waste. In addition, there are more complex decisions to be made by the wider industry relating to gases used in the refrigeration process (unlikely to be in your control, although if replacing equipment, you could take this into account). Reducing the need for refrigeration and freezing, by sourcing more locally produced products in the first place, is something we could all address. A product as simple as a fruit yoghurt might be produced in one place, with imported fruit and milk from two different parts of the world, and packaging from yet another country. These transport miles add up and could be reduced by using local in-gredients and packaging, and creating the end product closer to home.

It is especially important to avoid ingredients that will have been air-freighted or grown in artificially heated greenhouses, as they are probably out of season in the country where they're consumed. Asparagus flown from Peru to the United Kingdom represents 18.7 kg CO_2e per kilo of vegetable. Grown locally and consumed in season in the United Kingdom, would reduce the footprint by over 90%. If selecting imported food, when brought in by plane, it will typically have a footprint 100 times more than if shipped in by sea.[8]

THE CLIMATE CONSCIOUS FOOD OFFER[9]

1. Reduce meat consumption, especially red meats (beef and lamb for example).
2. Plan menus and meals by conducting a demand analysis with a view to sourcing/ preparing/serving only the amount required.
3. Embed a leftover food and drink plan into your policy – this could include an employee leftovers scheme, subscribing to an initiative such as 'Too Good To Go', or donating to your local foodbank or charity.
4. Source in season ingredients where possible through careful meal/ menu planning.
5. Choose locally sourced ingredients and food produce.
6. Opt for food and drink items with less packaging.
7. Avoid disposable plates, cutlery and cups, or where necessary, use compostable items.
8. Encourage a 'Bring your own container/cup/bottle' scheme for employees.

Whilst food production is important to consider as it uses energy, water[10] and land, unless we are farmers or part of the food supply chain, it is probably outside of our control. The issue of food waste however is something we *can* all address. According to WRAP,[11] the Food and Agriculture Organization (FAO) of the United Nations estimates that approximately a third of all food produced for human consumption is wasted globally every year. In the United States of America, it is claimed to be nearer to 40%.[12] This feeds into global GHG emissions and the IPCC calculates that up to 10% of man-made emissions are due to food waste.[13]

Surplus food intended for human consumption can be redistributed to food banks and other charities, diverted to energy creation or food for animals. It is however more resource efficient to reduce food waste in the first place. Within the UN Sustainable Development Goal (SDG) 12, *Sustainable Production and Consumption*, target 12.3 specifically addresses food waste reduction. To support this, various initiatives are being introduced across the globe. In the United Kingdom, the Courtauld Commitment aims to help organisations and households cut their food waste in half by 2030 (compared to 2007).[14] In China, legislation was introduced in 2021 to allow restaurants to charge extra if customers order too much and then waste it.[15] In Spain, where it is estimated that people throw away on average 31 kg of food annually, a food-saving law was introduced in 2021. That aims to steer towards a more efficient production system [which] focuses on development of a circular economy, and requires all industries throughout the food chain, from the primary or agricultural sectors through to tertiary or retail and hospitality businesses, to have a plan in place to cut waste.[16] Local, in season and organic produce will be encouraged, with fines of up to €150,000 for non-compliance.

Such actions will hopefully lead to a significant reduction in CO_2e emissions. Project Drawdown estimates that if, between 2020 and 2050, we achieved a 50% reduction in food loss and wastage globally, there would be a reduction of 90.7 gigatons of CO_2e emissions; 13.6 gigatons due to diverted agricultural production, 76.3 gigatons from avoided land conversion and 0.8 gigatons from ecosystem protection.[17] In France, the aim is to achieve a 50% reduction in food waste sooner than 2050. Their 'Loi Anti-Gaspillage' (anti-waste law) was passed in 2020 and amongst other things, it requires food retailers and factory/school canteens to reduce their waste by 50% between 2015 and 2025, with food producers having until 2030 to meet such a reduction. Wholesalers must also donate any unsold produce to charitable organisations for re-distribution.[18]

After considering food waste and how to reduce it within your organisation, another area worth addressing is the type of food you are ordering and consuming. Turning again to Project Drawdown, if 50% of the world's population adopted a plant-rich diet by 2050, the total cumulative emissions reduction would be 65.0 gigatons of CO_2e gases; 43.0 gigatons due to diverted agricultural production, 21.8 gigatons from avoided land conversion, and 0.2 gigatons from ecosystem protection (savings between 2020 and 2050).[19]

Finally, in terms of how food is cooked, consider how much energy different appliances consume. In many circumstances, a microwave oven will probably be more energy-efficient than a conventional one. In domestic kitchens, using a slow cooker might be a good alternative. See also the Case Study in this chapter. As of 2018, nearly half of the developing world relies on stoves that burn wood or charcoal. If these were replaced by cleaner technology, Project Drawdown estimates that reductions in emissions could amount to between 31 and 73 gigatons.[20] While this might not affect all readers of this book, if you are based in a country where you *do* rely on wood or charcoal, you might consider switching to solar-powered cookstoves in your canteen or sourcing your food supplies from caterers with such technology. It is important to ensure the solar stoves are designed so the food is cooked by being exposed to the sunlight, without the need to use any electricity from renewables or fuel such as wood or charcoal.

WANT TO DIG DEEPER?

Carbon footprint calculators
Below are examples, and similar calculators exist in many parts of the world.

BBC Food Carbon Footprint Calculator https://www.bbc.co.uk/news/science-environment-46459714
This food calculator helps you gain a basic understanding of the carbon equivalent emissions associated with certain food and drinks. From the perspective of a company based in the United Kingdom, you can for example calculate whether offering potatoes or rice in your catering would make a difference.

Food Carbon Emissions Calculator by CleanMetrics https://www.foodemissions.com/Calculate
This US food calculator can work out the emissions in CO_2e of ingredients. The calculation covers emissions from production, processing and transport of the item. You can select the ingredient, quantity and approximate distance (food miles).

Carbon Positive Australia https://carbonpositiveaustralia.org.au/calculate/
Useful for Australian-based organisations and individuals.

Omni Calculator – Meat Footprint calculator https://www.omnicalculator.com/ecology/meat-footprint
The website of this Polish start-up allows you to focus on the effect of meat consumption with a view to helping you reduce this once the impact on the environment is understood.

High-impact solutions

In this section we will offer recommendations as to how some of the high-impact climate solutions identified above could be introduced into your organisation. We will order them according to importance of impact, taking into account feasibility, so that these changes can be embedded by any organisation, whether you order food in from outside caterers, prepare and serve food in a canteen or only provide occasional snacks for your employees.

Earlier we identified that food transported by air has a much higher footprint, typically around 100 times the carbon impact of the same product being transported the same distance by sea. Many of the foods that are airfreighted, soft fruit for example, also need to be refrigerated during the flight, and kept in cold storage at either end of the journey. Most will also need careful packaging to avoid damage. Any form of transport, refrigeration and packaging adds to the carbon impact, so we will first discuss: **how can you change your food offer to include more seasonal and local food with less packaging?**

A third of all food produced and prepared is not consumed. In high-income countries this is often due to the produce being perceived as imperfect or ugly. In some cases, too many meals are prepared, or maybe people help themselves to overly generous portions that they cannot consume. Therefore, our second question is: **how can you reduce food waste through your catering practices in the whole food production chain, from farm to fork and beyond?**

One of the biggest changes that can be made is reducing meat in one's diet and replacing it by vegetarian or vegan options. Using Mike Berners-Lee's book (p. 86), if a day's protein (assumed to be 50g) is consumed through pulses, such as chickpeas or lentils rather than red meat, this represents emissions of approximately 420g of CO_2e for the pulses, compared to 10 kg CO_2e for lamb, or as much as 25 kg of CO_2e if imported beef raised on deforested land is chosen, so our third question is: **can you replace some meat-based meals with vegetarian or vegan options?**

In order to benefit from other energy savings within the supply chain, for example by choosing drink containers with the lowest emissions, such as a refillable glass bottles containing locally sourced (oat) milk – our fourth question relates to how your organisation sources its food: **what are the best criteria to help us distinguish between different suppliers?**

All these changes can only be made if your employees and colleagues support them. There might be resistance in some places if meat is suddenly removed from the menu, and people might vote with their feet. Our final question is, therefore: **how can you get buy-in from colleagues eating in your canteen or ordering outside catering?**

How can you change your food offer to include more seasonal and local food with less packaging?

Start by selecting your suppliers based on whether they offer products in season, where they source their products, how they package them and how they transport them to you.

For those preparing the menus or choosing ready-prepared food items to be served at your workplace, it is especially important to have a good understanding of the carbon emission equivalents (CO_2e) of food. While the climate benefits of changing from beef to chicken or to beans as a protein source is quite widely understood, few may be aware of the carbon impact in many parts of Europe of replacing rice with potatoes, for example.

Avoiding food that includes airfreighted ingredients and replacing these with local and seasonal alternatives is another effective climate solution. Your caterers (whether in-house or external) will need a good knowledge of what is in season in your part of the world, and should plan meals using those ingredients. For example, a vegan meal might at face value be assumed to be better for the environment, but if it included rice and asparagus served in the United Kingdom in winter, it would produce more carbon emissions than a cheeseburger.[21]

Consider also any packaging, as its production will probably involve resources that require energy and water. If we consider food and drink consumed regularly in the United Kingdom, it is not unusual for the raw materials for the packaging to have been extracted in Australia, processed in Asia, shipped to Europe to the plant where it is used as primary packaging for the food or drink in question, before it finally arrives at the retailer. Again, by selecting local seasonal ingredients, the emissions throughout the entire chain of the primary and secondary packaging of the food and drink that you offer can be significantly reduced. Such ingredients will typically need less packaging, due to less handling and shorter journey times. Where sourcing products locally, if you regularly use the same suppliers, ask them to provide the food in reusable crates rather than cardboard boxes, for example. Packaging contributes approximately 5.4% of global food-system emissions, more than any other supply chain factor, including transportation.[22]

Another consideration is to reduce or even eliminate single-use plastics (both for packaging and implements offered).

- Take stock of what you currently use
- Ensure all future supplies are made from sustainable materials
- Buy in larger quantities or opt for refillable plastic/glass containers instead of single-use plastic
- Discontinue the use of plastic straws, use glass not plastic cups, create incentives for people to bring their own cup and food containers for takeaway meals, or use recyclable cups and cutlery or compostable plant-based plates and cutlery such as those produced by Vegware[23] (sold in 70 countries – throughout Europe, the Middle East, South America and the Caribbean, and with a presence in the United States of America, Hong Kong and Australia).

How can you reduce food waste through your catering practices in the whole food production chain, from farm to fork and beyond?

There are various initiatives packed with resources and ideas on reducing food waste such as the United Kingdom's 'Love Food Hate Waste'.[24] On their website, they recommend three easy actions:

a.   Menu planning
b.   Adequate food storage
c.   Using up leftovers and surplus food.

When planning your menus and sourcing your ingredients, consider preparing meals or ordering food made from produce that is less than perfect. For example, 'wonky vegetables' for soup or stews, as these will not even be noticed by those consuming them. You could also sign up to a box scheme that delivers leftover produce from the food production process, for example 'wonky bread'.[25] Ensuring surplus ingredients and leftovers are incorporated into the menu the following day is also an option for those organisations that have food preparation facilities on site. For those without such facilities, there needs to be a plan that ensures the surplus ingredients and food is not lost.

It is worth assessing your storage facilities to ensure they are sufficient, and that you have energy-efficient fridges and freezers. Small actions, such as investing in plenty of reusable air-tight food storage containers, can prevent surplus ingredients and food from going to waste.

If you cannot store the leftovers adequately, consider offering them to your staff to take home, or signing up to a public-facing scheme such as 'Too Good To Go'[26] (started in Denmark in 2015 before spreading within Europe, and entering the United States in 2020). Other public-facing schemes to which you could donate surplus food include Olio[27] (available in over 100 countries by late 2022 via their app) and Foodwise[28] in Australia. Alternatively, you could work with your local food bank or charity of choice (maybe a homeless shelter or refugee camp). In Rome (Italy) the city introduced food waste hubs in 2019, using NGOs to distribute surplus food to residents in need, with the aim of halving food waste (mainly from supermarkets and company canteens) by 2030. This citywide policy was recognised as being an initiative that could be copied elsewhere and in 2021 won the Earthshot prize in the 'Build a waste-free world' category.[29]

While minimising waste would be ideal and diverting surplus food to those in need would be the next best solution, being realistic there will often be scraps and surplus food, which may not be suitable for human consumption. One option is to have a worm composting (or vermicomposting) unit, suitable for both domestic and catering kitchens. In the United Kingdom there is the Urban Worm[30] for example, and their website explains the principles and shows how to build your own unit. A simple internet search reveals that worm composting is popular in many parts of the world and suitable worms can usually be sourced without too much difficulty.

The main thing to avoid is sending your waste to landfill, where it will produce methane. In Mike Berners-Lee's book 'There is no Planet B', he explains how, with the exception of donating waste food for human consumption, all other options are rubbish![31]

Can you replace some meat-based meals with vegetarian or vegan options?

Having understood what your current offer is, and the makeup of your supply chain, the next step is to examine its impact on the environment and establish where improvements could be made. Here is the opportunity to consider the choice you offer from various angles: looking at quality vs nutritional content vs value for money, as well as food miles and carbon emissions. Remember to include food and drink bought in from outside caterers, as well as any produced in-house.

Depending on your starting point, you could offer a greater variety of vegetarian meals. If you do this already, consider offering more vegan options, for example by having plenty of choice for those who sign up to 'Veganuary'.[32] In 2021, more than half a million people in over 200 countries and territories signed up to go vegan in January. By making it easy for your staff and colleagues through offering an interesting range of food, you might stimulate the demand for such meals and snacks throughout the year and not just for the one month. Researchers from the United Kingdom's University of Westminster found that making vegetarian food more available on menus significantly encourages people to switch to more sustainable food choices. In their research study (published in 2021), meat-eating participants were found to be more likely to opt for vegetarian dishes when these made up 75% of the menu, with the likelihood of selecting a vegetarian meal being nearly three times greater than when the menu was half vegetarian and half meat-based.[33] The message seems to be that if you decide to increase the choice of plant-based meals, be bold and offer a wide range; do not just state that vegetarian options are available on request.

When planning a buffet, rather than serving both meat and plant-based versions of a dish, consider offering only the plant-based options. Or perhaps introduce 'meat-free Mondays' in your canteen. While offering just vegetarian or vegan food could appear to be a good option, this may be discouraged, as it might prove too expensive. Caterers tend to have contracts with suppliers, especially when buying in bulk. If the norm in your organisation is to serve meat-based meals, the contracts with the meat suppliers may be much better value than the contracts for vegan produce, where smaller less frequent orders may be placed. If your organisation switched to vegetarian or even vegan meals as their main offer, you would clearly need to negotiate bulk orders with suppliers of the plant-based produce instead.

Some might question the approach of favouring or imposing plant-based meals, as they would not want to be so prescriptive. There was a huge backlash in spring 2021 in Lyon (France), a city renowned for its gastronomic meat-based cuisine, when the green party mayor decreed that school lunches in the city would all be vegetarian.[34] Likewise, the suggestion by the Spanish Consumer Affairs Minister in July 2021 that less meat should be consumed led to a national row,[35] and in the Netherlands, the possibility of a meat tax was also met with consternation.[36]

If you think there may be resistance in your organisation, consider labelling the food you currently offer with a traffic light system – perhaps a green cloud for a low-carbon emission meal at one extreme, and a red one for a high-carbon emission meal at the other. In the Further Resources section there is a link to a website that can help you calculate the emissions of your menu items. The University of California, Berkley, has done this and has introduced CO_2 labelling on their menus. As a result, they have seen an impact not only on their students' menu selection, but on the dishes designed by their chefs in the first place.[37] This sort of action starts to educate diners and hopefully nudges them towards opting for meals with a lower impact on the environment. Some food producers are already starting to use carbon labelling and this is likely to become more prevalent in the future.[38] Foundation Earth for example, a not-for-profit organisation supported by various international food producers and supermarkets, started a pilot in autumn 2021 to introduce eco-labels on certain foods – similar to the colour-coded approach used for nutritional purposes. Their aim is to introduce a Europe-wide system of labelling in 2022.[39] Working with 'My Emissions' is another British option for food producers.[40] Taking a slightly different approach, the German supermarket chain Penny, in collaboration with two German universities, decided in 2020 that they wanted to inform their customers of the true cost of a selection of their products.[41] They introduced dual labels for certain foods on sale, showing the selling price alongside the true cost, taking into account a variety of factors. This showed for example that some meat would be nearly treble the price if the true costs were factored in, and cheese would be approximately double the price charged. Another option is to avoid making a big issue out of a product being vegan, but to convince customers through the better taste of the vegan option. This approach has been taken by some French pastry chefs.[42] There are clearly different ways of approaching this, but educating and nudging need to be considered, even if restricting choice feels inappropriate in the short term.

What are the best criteria to help us distinguish between different suppliers?

Managers and employees involved in food procurement need to consider the entire chain when determining the choice of food and drinks available, both on and off site. Additionally, managers responsible for the food policies in their organisation should consider the packaging of the food and drink they purchase. Thinking about cold drinks for example, it is important to consider whether to select reusable clear glass bottles, recycled green glass bottles, new brown glass bottles, aluminium cans or plastic bottles (the list is ordered from low to high emissions in this example).

Try to work with your suppliers, question them about their plans and their own sustainability credentials. Ask where they source their ingredients and what sort of energy they use in their production facilities. Ask if they could label their produce clearly with respect to carbon equivalent emissions, so you can then pass on that information to your own employees. In the 'High-impact solutions' section of chapter 3 (Communication & Reporting), we discuss how to have that sort of conversation with your suppliers and we give links to template letters that could be used.

You might also want to think about favouring suppliers who are innovative about any surplus or residues in the production of their food and drink. The Black Sheep Brewery for example (a British company) has signed a deal where by-products of their beer production including used grains, hops and yeast are purchased and collected by a local biogas producer, Warrens Group, along with food waste from the brewer's visitor centre restaurant. These items then go into the production of biogas and also fuel Warrens' fleet of gas-powered vehicles.[43]

To sum up, request information from your suppliers about:

- The raw materials and ingredients they use, and their data for food waste and loss
- The shelf life of supplies and the balance between frozen, fresh and tinned produce

- The types of packaging they use
- Using eco-labelling
- Their policies for their own supply chain and how others in the supply chain deal with food waste and loss.

Then work with your suppliers to improve their carbon footprint as well as your own, and maybe include a carbon footprint clause in the contract when it is next up for renewal.

How can you get buy-in from colleagues eating in your canteen or ordering outside catering?

For many, changes in food habits will be gradual. Someone who has always eaten meat for their main meal might vote with their feet and boycott the canteen if all they can eat there is vegetarian or vegan food. It might be preferable to offer plant-based options alongside traditional food and support these changes with an effective communication campaign (see also third question above). One option could be to offer both meat-based and vegetarian versions of the same dish in parallel, and promote the latter with a 'Can you spot a difference in taste?' campaign. The vegetarian version could also be offered at a lower price to be more appealing. More ideas on communication to colleagues can be found in chapter 3 of this book.

Another more extreme way to influence people would be to offer vegetarian or vegan meals as the *default* option, giving people the chance to specify meat as a 'special dietary requirement' (alongside allergies, food intolerances and so on). At the annual United Kingdom's EAUC (Environmental Association of Universities and Colleges) conference, there is choice, but the default is vegetarian/vegan dishes, and those who declare their dietary requirement as meat are asked to identify themselves to catering staff by wearing a red sticker.[44]

Gradual changes could be made by replacing some meat with other proteins such as pulses, increasing the amount of red kidney beans for example compared to the beef in a 'chilli con carne'. Another gradual change could be achieved by offering meats with a lower meet our protein requirements, but have lower CO_2e emissions. Beef from deforested land can have a carbon footprint that is nine times that of chicken for instance.[45] Again, this can be communicated to colleagues by visual displays for example as per the photo in 6.1. This is from Green Week in Nottingham Trent University, UK, where visual displays were used comparing beef burgers to those made from chicken and soy, to educate and encourage staff and students to make more sustainable food choices.

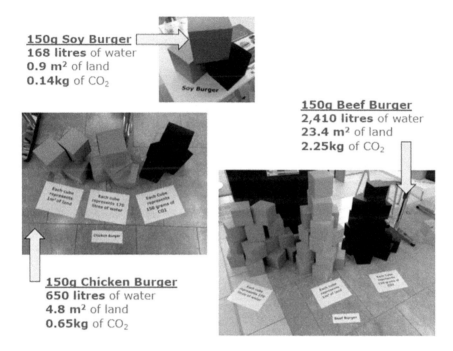

150g Soy Burger
168 litres of water
0.9 m² of land
0.14kg of CO_2

150g Beef Burger
2,410 litres of water
23.4 m² of land
2.25kg of CO_2

150g Chicken Burger
650 litres of water
4.8 m² of land
0.65kg of CO_2

Photo 6.1 Food impacts visual display (NTU Green Academy/Vanessa Odell 2019).[46]

After having reviewed and addressed the five areas above, it's time to create a low-carbon communications plan for all staff, visitors, clients and suppliers. Communicating climate solutions maximises the impact of the solutions identified for food and beverage procurement and provision within the organisation. It offers a platform for a sense of belonging and shared purpose among employees. It serves as a talking point with your suppliers, and potentially attracts new climate conscious customers. Please refer to the 'High-impact solutions' of chapter 3 (Communication & Reporting) for guidance on involving your employees and suppliers.

Case study

In this chapter, our case study features a well-respected and award-winning chef, who has embraced sustainability. He discusses his motivation and shares some hints and tips to reduce emissions, that could be applicable in any kitchen.

Going green: restaurant Sat Bains and the Michelin Green Star

By Kirsty Hunter (Senior Lecturer in Nutrition, Nottingham Trent University) and Sat Bains (Chef-Proprietor, Restaurant Sat Bains)

Sat Bains is the chef-proprietor of the Michelin two-starred Restaurant Sat Bains (RSB) in Nottingham, England. The restaurant was one of 23 recipients of a Michelin Green Star when it was first introduced for Great Britain and Ireland in 2021 and RSB retained the Star in January 2022. This accolade is awarded to restaurants which combine *culinary excellence with outstanding eco-friendly commitments*[47] and recognises those at the forefront of the industry when it comes to their sustainable practices.[48] RSB is open four days a week during which it caters for 160 covers weekly.

Prompted by increasing utility bills, and the notorious wastage associated with restaurants, Sat decided to investigate strategies to reduce both. Below, we explore how Sat has turned his desire to be more sustainable into reality within the constraints of elite gastronomy. He shares his tips for those head chefs and heads of catering who are looking to become more sustainable.

Tip 1 – Partner with experts and develop win:win strategies

Sat sought out local experts in the field of sustainability and linked with Dr Mark Gillott from the University of Nottingham (UoN). The relationship has been fruitful for both parties, including a review of how the restaurant can become more sustainable, produced by a PhD student. Through this review, which included an analysis of the restaurant's energy consumption profile, Sat was provided with valuable intelligence to inform his planning.

Tip 2 – Making sustainable changes can result in unforeseen benefits

In 2007, RSB converted all cooking appliances to electric, including induction hobs. Using a hob which switched off immediately after the cooking vessel was removed reduced energy usage, but it also reduced the temperature in the kitchen! The staff said that they were cold, so Sat installed a wood-fired oven, introducing a new way of cooking into the kitchen. Later, he realised that the residual heat of the new oven need not be wasted. He now uses it to cook tomatoes and mushrooms in earthenware pots overnight, so they are ready for breakfast service – cooked slowly with reduced water content, thus concentrating the flavour. As Sat says, this is not a new idea, attributing it to French bakers who used their ovens to cook potatoes.

A state-of-the-art composter also brought additional benefits and facilitated the introduction of a closed-loop system. The composter uses heat and water extraction to turn 100 kg of kitchen wet waste into 10 kg of dry matter. The extracted water is stored in a water butt and used for irrigation of the garden while the dry matter product matures for 3–6 months and is then used as compost in the garden. Waste going to landfill has been reduced by 70% with the associated saving in landfill charges.

In 2012, Sat introduced multiple growing systems in the land around the restaurant. With the limited space, Sat concentrated on growing micro-herbs and small intensively flavoured ingredients. Two gardeners maintain the pair of greenhouses and 16 beds. In addition, he has installed growing walls around the car park. Having products on site allows the chefs to adapt quickly when dishes need adjusting. They also have two beehives that produce up to 60 kg honey per year for the restaurant and bring the environmental benefits of bees to the local area.

Tip 3 – Be innovative

Sat does not like to rest on his laurels. Two years ago, for example, with support from UoN academics, he secured a grant to purchase solar panels. He is now investigating solar batteries so he can harness the energy stored during the three closure days each week to use when RSB reopens. He believes you should keep the green agenda in mind at all times; always considering energy efficiency and waste reduction as integrative parts of your planning programme.

Tip 4 – Ingredients

Sat uses the highest-quality ingredients as is expected by his fine dining clientele. Ninety percent of the ingredients are sourced from Britain, and are local when possible, but to maintain the excellence required at this level of gastronomy, some have to come from further afield – seafood for example which is procured from sustainable sources. He also chooses seasonal produce so, during the game season for example, main courses will always include game as the meat component. He also ensures he taps into the knowledge of suppliers to provide expert and current information for the development team.

Tip 5 – Communicating to customers

Sat places a lot of importance on this aspect and welcomes questions from guests. He operates an open kitchen, and his front of house team is fully briefed on the finer details of the menu and the provenance of ingredients. He has also co-authored papers with UoN academics and uses social media to promote his sustainable activities.

Tip 6 – Involve everyone in the organisation – education is paramount

The educational aspect of the business is really important to Sat. He operates a 'whole team' approach to ensure that every staff member understands why RSB does things in a certain way and this includes the many sustainable initiatives. Sat hopes that staff will follow his lead and, if they move on, hopefully they will take his ethos with them. He also welcomes students, thus facilitating a real-world experience for them that cannot be replicated in college or university.

Tip 7 – Little wins

- All bin liners are clear allowing easy identification of anything that could be recycled.
- Each section of the kitchen has a box for food waste; anything that is still edible is utilised for staff food e.g. soup or stew.
- To reduce the environmental costs of using bottled water in the restaurant, Sat installed a filter system which produces highly purified water, still and sparkling, from tap water. The water is served in glass bottles which are washed and reused.
- During a recent refurbishment of the restaurant, Sat used natural materials including English oak. He chose a designer who calculated the number of trees used in the refurbishment and planted the same number to offset the carbon footprint.
- He has also stopped using chemical sanitising products in the kitchen. Instead, he uses electrolysed water.

So, whilst working within the restraints of fine dining, Sat has made changes which reflect those discussed in the 'High-impact solutions' section this chapter. His ethos is a holistic one and he believes that every little change is worth making, as they add up to large impacts on the environment.

Dr Kirsty Hunter is Senior Lecturer in Nutrition at Nottingham Trent University and author of 'Addressing food waste through university and community partnerships'.[49]

Sat Bains is Chef-Proprietor of the Michelin 2-star Restaurant Sat Bains, Nottingham.

Following Sat Bains' tips, which should inspire any cook or chef, below are some further 'Quick Wins', which could be implemented in your organisation. (Please also refer to the 'Climate Conscious Food Offer' box earlier in this chapter.)

Quick Wins

1. Where possible, source your canteen's food locally and in season, or use caterers and outside venues who do the same.
2. Offer more vegetarian and vegan dishes in your canteen, placing them at the top of the menu.
3. If catering for a buffet, offer only vegetarian dishes, rather than a choice of meat and vegetarian. Maybe even change the order form so that vegetarian options are at the top, or people have to opt in for meat-based menus.
4. Encourage staff to bring containers to take home leftover food and make it the norm for people to bring their own cup or glass to use at work.
5. Sign up to a local initiative to give away leftover and surplus food.
6. Do a stocktake of the packaging and type of cutlery offered for takeaways (food to go) within your canteen. After using up current supplies, stop buying products using single-use plastic; switch to plates, cutlery and containers that are reusable or compostable.
7. Think about the cooking methods and appliances used (certainly at home, if not in the work situation). Using a microwave rather than a conventional oven, for example, should save energy, and therefore money.[50]

Outlook

As shown in this chapter, there are many climate solutions that would help you to reduce the greenhouse gas emissions related to food and drink offered in your organisation. We recommend that you draw up an *overall* implementation plan like the one suggested in Figure 6.1. Then, having established your overall objectives and timelines, break it down and draw up implementation plans for each of the high-impact climate solutions outlined above, such as a detailed plan to reduce food waste.

To do this, you will need to carry out a comprehensive audit of the current situation. This will allow you to understand the demand for different types of food and drink in your canteen, the quantity and ratio of hot to cold meals and snacks, etc. Remember to include all food and drink,

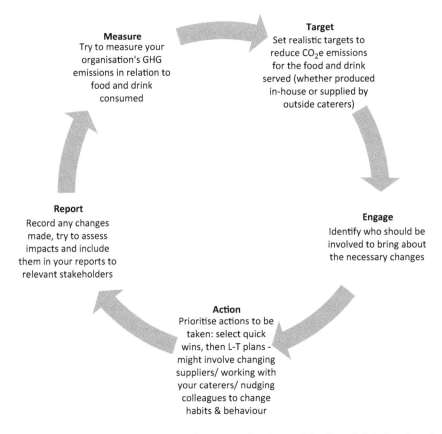

Figure 6.1 Implementation plan for the reduction of food and drink-related GHG emissions.

both the ingredients used by an in-house catering team and food supplied by outside caterers. This should allow you to calculate the carbon equivalent footprint of all the food and beverages served on and off site. There are various open-source carbon footprint calculators for food and drinks that can be used (see suggestions in the 'Want to Dig Deeper?' section in this chapter); start by selecting the one you will employ, or researching a more appropriate one for your part of the world.

How you approach this will depend on the size of your organisation, the number of sites and types of facilities. If all food and beverages are procured centrally in the organisation, then a strategic policy approach would be more feasible, see chapter 14 (Policies & Practices) for guidance. If you have a multi-site operation, you may prefer to issue general guidance, but allow each location to decide on what works best for them.

The key thing is to work with and educate your employees and suppliers, and ensure you get buy-in from your catering staff or outside caterers from the start.

Further Resources

On the companion website to this book you can find further materials to help you plan and implement this work.

Below is a link to support you to reduce your GHG emissions, and further links to help you track down more information regarding food waste and its reduction, and useful sites for locating food banks and where to send surplus food in different parts of the world.

General

World Resources Institute: https://www.wri.org/research/tracking-progress-toward-cool-food-pledge and the **Cool Food Pledge**: https://coolfood.org/
This is a global initiative that helps caterers and other food suppliers to provide dishes with smaller climate footprints. The resources on offer help organisations to set targets to reduce their food-related GHG emissions. It helps users to use appropriate metrics, establish a baseline and track progress towards their targets. Those signing up to the initiative should aim for an absolute reduction of 25% (when comparing 2030 to 2015).

Sustainable Food at NTU (March 2022): https://www.ntu.ac.uk/__
data/assets/pdf_file/0032/1048649/sustainable-food-ntu.pdf
This might act as inspiration for an organisation looking to implement
some of the ideas in this chapter. It details what Nottingham Trent
University is doing to reduce emissions, by working with local suppliers,
to reduce packaging, and to ensure spare food does not just get thrown
away. It also explains how NTU works with the waste management contractor 'ENVA', and how plate waste or food that cannot be re-distributed
is collected and goes to produce electricity and bio-fertiliser.

Future food movement: https://futurefoodmovement.com/
Launched 2022, their aim is to *radically empower the food industry at all levels to help
fight climate change. [...]. We want to really help businesses deliver a Net Zero culture,
because all the targets have been set. We all know where we need to go, but we need our
workforces to get behind it and actually become activists.* They state they *are on a mission
to close the climate skills gap in the food industry by upskilling today's business leaders and
inspiring tomorrow's rising stars to step up on climate.*

Reducing food waste

There are many resources available to help reduce food waste. In Table 6.1
a few of these are signposted, and may provide inspiration.

**Table 6.1 Some useful resources for further information on how to reduce
food waste**

International
• UN Environment Programme – Food Waste Index 2021: https://www.unep.org/resources/report/unep-food-waste-index-report-2021
• The Global Food Banking Network: https://www.foodbanking.org/stateofglobalfoodbanking/index.html
• UN FAO (Food & Agriculture Organization) Make #NotWasting a way of life: https://www.fao.org/3/C0088e/C0088e.pdf
United Kingdom
• DEFRA, Food and drink waste hierarchy: deal with surplus and waste (statutory guidance): https://www.gov.uk/government/publications/food-and-drink-waste-hierarchy-deal-with-surplus-and-waste/food-and-drink-waste-hierarchy-deal-with-surplus-and-waste

- WRAP Food & Drink Surplus Network: https://foodsurplusnetwork.wrap.org.uk/
- Selecting food that emits fewer emissions: https://wrap.org.uk/taking-action/food-drink/actions/reducing-greenhouse-gas-emissions
- WWF: https://www.wwf.org.uk/what-can-i-do/10-tips-help-you-eat-more-sustainably
- GIKI (Get Informed, Know your Impact): https://giki.earth/

Australia

- Department of Agriculture, Water and the Environment: https://www.awe.gov.au/environment/protection/waste/food-waste

Canada

- Love Food Hate Waste (Canada): https://lovefoodhatewaste.ca/about/food-waste/

Europe

- Zero Waste Europe (ZWE) https://zerowasteeurope.eu/about/about-zero-waste/
- Food banks in Europe: https://www.eurofoodbank.org/
- Redistributing surplus food in the EU: https://ec.europa.eu/food/system/files/2019-06/fw_eu-actions_food-donation_ms-practices-food-redis.pdf

India

- No Food Waste: https://nofoodwaste.org/about

New Zealand

- Love Food Hate Waste: https://lovefoodhatewaste.co.nz/food-waste/what-we-waste/

Nigeria

- To reduce waste: https://www.africa.com/cool-scheme-to-reduce-food-waste-in-nigeria/

South Africa

- WWF: https://www.wwf.org.za/our_work/initiatives/food_waste/

United States of America

- USDA (Department of Agriculture) – Food Loss & Waste: https://www.usda.gov/foodlossandwaste
- Supporting surplus distribution: https://www.nutrition.gov/topics/food-assistance-programs/food-distribution-programs

Notes

1. WRAP (Waste Resources Action Programme): https://wrap.org.uk/taking-action/food-drink

2. BBC: https://www.bbc.co.uk/news/science-environment-46459714

3. Leip A, Carmona Garcia G and Rossi S (2017) *Mitigation measures in the Agriculture, Forestry, and Other Land Use (AFOLU) sector*, EUR 28680 EN. Luxembourg (Luxembourg): European Union

4. USDA (United States Department of Agriculture): https://www.ers.usda.gov/topics/natural-resources-environment/climate-change/

5. Wasley A, Jordan L and Mendonça E (2022) Feed supplier to UK farm animals still linked to Amazon deforestation, *The Guardian* (14 Jan): https://www.theguardian.com/environment/2022/jan/14/feed-supplier-to-uk-farm-animals-still-linked-to-amazon-deforestation

6. European Commission (2020) *Farm to Fork Strategy*: https://ec.europa.eu/food/system/files/2020-05/f2f_action-plan_2020_strategy-info_en.pdf

7. IPCC (2019) *Climate Change and Land: an IPCC special report on climate change, desertification, land degradation, sustainable land management, food security, and greenhouse gas fluxes in terrestrial ecosystems* [P.R. Shukla *et al* (eds.)]

8. Berners-Lee M (2020) *How bad are bananas? The carbon footprint of everything*, p. 80

9. See also Berners-Lee M (2020) *How bad are bananas? The carbon footprint of everything*, p. 199

10. UN Environment Programme (2021) *UNEP Food Waste Index Report 2021*: https://www.unep.org/resources/report/unep-food-waste-index-report-2021

11. WRAP (Waste Resources Action Programme): https://wrap.org.uk/taking-action/food-drink

12. NRDC (2017) *Wasted: How America is losing up to 40 percent of its food from farm to fork to landfill*, https://www.nrdc.org/sites/default/files/wasted-2017-report.pdf

13. IPCC (2019), Summary for Policymakers. In: *Climate Change and Land: an IPCC special report on climate change, desertification, land degradation, sustainable land management, food security, and greenhouse gas fluxes in terrestrial ecosystems* [P.R. Shukla *et al* (eds.)]

14. Courtauld Commitment: https://wrap.org.uk/taking-action/food-drink/initiatives/courtauld-commitment

15. Caiyu L (2021) China adopts law against food waste; binge eating, excessive leftovers to face fine, *Global Times* (29 April): https://www.globaltimes.cn/page/202104/1222490.shtml

16. ThinkSpain.com, *Spain's first ever anti-food waste law*: https://www.thinkspain.com/news-spain/33095/spain-s-first-ever-anti-food-waste-law-here-s-what-s-involved

17. Project Drawdown: https://www.drawdown.org/solutions/reduced-food-waste

18. Ministère de la Transition Ecologique (2022): https://www.ecologie.gouv.fr/gaspillage-alimentaire-0

19. Project Drawdown: https://www.drawdown.org/solutions/plant-rich-diets

20. Project Drawdown: https://www.drawdown.org/solutions/improved-clean-cookstoves

21. See for example p. 32 and p. 113 of Mike Berners-Lees' book, *How bad are bananas*

22. UN International Day of Awareness on Food Waste and Loss Reduction: https://www.un.org/en/observances/end-food-waste-day/background

23. Vegware: https://www.vegware.com/uk-en/

24. Love Food Hate Waste (2018) *What to do:* https://www.lovefoodhatewaste.com/what-to-do)

25. An example of a UK scheme would be 'Earth and Wheat': https://www.earthandwheat.com/

26. Too Good to Go: https://toogoodtogo.org/en

27. Olio (2021) *Office Surplus Food*: https://olioex.com/office-surplus-food/

28. Foodwise (2012) *The Food Donation Toolkit*: http://www.foodwise.com.au/wp-content/uploads/2012/09/DoSomething-Food-Donation-Toolkit.pdf

29. The Earthshot Prize: https://earthshotprize.org/london-2021/the-earthshot-prize-winners-finalists/waste-free/

30. The Urban Worm: https://theurbanworm.co.uk/

31. Berners-Lee M (2021) *There is no Planet B*, Cambridge: Cambridge University Press

32. Veganuary: https://veganuary.com/

33. Parkin BL and Attwood S (2022) Menu design approaches to promote sustainable vegetarian food choices when dining out, *Journal of Environmental Psychology*, Volume 79 (Feb)

34. Henley J (2021) Meatless school menu sparks political row in France, *The Guardian* (24 Feb): https://www.theguardian.com/world/2021/feb/24/meatless-school-menu-sparks-political-row-in-france

35. Henley J *et al* (2022) Greens v 'beefatarians', *The Guardian* (21 Jan): https://www.theguardian.com/environment/2022/jan/21/the-greens-want-to-take-our-meat-away-europeans-go-to-war-over-their-dinner

36. Dutch News (2021): https://www.dutchnews.nl/news/2022/03/dutch-look-into-taxing-meat-as-part-of-shift-towards-vegetable-protein/

37. University of California, Berkley, *Fight climate change with food*: https://menu.dining.ucla.edu/Pages/CarbonFootprint

38. Evans J (2020) Will carbon labelling soon become routine? *Financial Times special report* (19 Nov)

39. Foundation Earth: https://www.foundation-earth.org/

40. My Emissions (eco-labelling for food): https://myemissions.green/about-us/

41. Green Queen (2020) *Meat should cost three times more*: https://www.greenqueen.com.hk/meat-should-cost-3-times-more-german-grocer-shows-consumers-hidden-environmental-price-of-food/

42. https://www.theguardian.com/food/2022/jul/15/croissants-are-moving-on-the-vegan-chefs-reinventing-french-patisserie

43. The Business Desk (2021) *Sustainability on the menu at brewery with energy from waste deal*: https://www.thebusinessdesk.com/yorkshire/news/2079844-sustainability-on-the-menu-at-brewery-with-energy-from-waste-deal

44. EAUC annual conference: https://www.eauc.org.uk/a_sustainable_conference2

45. A comparison between the different sources of protein and their CO_2e is given in: Berners-Lee M (2020) *How bad are bananas? The carbon footprint of everything*, p. 86

46. Odell V, Molthan-Hill P, Erlandsson I and Sexton E (2019) http://irep.ntu.ac.uk/id/eprint/38516/ Visual displays of the sustainable development goals in the curricular and extra-curricular activities at Nottingham Trent University - a case study. In: W Leal Filho et al (eds.) Universities as living labs for sustainable development: supporting the implementation of the sustainable development goals. World sustainability series. Cham, Switzerland: Springer, pp. 227–246

47. The Michelin Guide (2021): https://guide.michelin.com/gb/en/article/features/new-michelin-green-star-for-restaurants-in-england-scotland-wales-ireland

48. Michelin Green Star restaurants: https://guide.michelin.com/gb/en/restaurants/sustainable_gastronomy

49. http://irep.ntu.ac.uk/id/eprint/28403

50. https://www.theguardian.com/money/2022/aug/27/best-ingredients-and-appliances-to-save-cash-when-cooking

7

ESTATES AND FACILITIES: BUILDING A BETTER FUTURE

Muhammad Mazhar, Petra Molthan-Hill and Fiona Winfield

This chapter guides estates and facilities managers, as well as other employees in an organisation, on how greenhouse gas (GHG) emissions can be managed and reduced in building operations, refurbishment and new construction, to have a sustainable built environment, as well as capturing carbon on the estate. Climate solutions are introduced, such as increasing the energy efficiency of buildings, thereby reducing costs and emissions.

This chapter is for you if you are:

- Part of the senior management/executive team of an organisation
- An estates director, manager or officer within the estates or facilities management team
- An environmental, sustainability, carbon or energy manager within an organisation
- An employee in any department within an organisation using buildings and facilities
- A landlord, renting a property, or a builder.

DOI: 10.4324/9781003274049-9

It will cover:

- The role of the built environment in reducing GHG emissions
- Increasing energy efficiency in existing and new buildings
- GHG emissions reduction in building operations and retrofits
- Terms such as carbon sink and decarbonisation of the grid
- Capturing carbon on the estate
- Certifications, codes, standards and benchmarks for buildings
- A case study of a small business showcasing actions through which buildings can operate in a low-carbon way.

The built environment – scale of the problem and its solutions

While buildings and their operations have always been a major contributor to global greenhouse gas (GHG) emissions, their share is increasing, for example, in line with the need for more air-conditioning in buildings, due to rising outdoor temperatures in many countries. *Buildings are currently responsible for 39% of global energy related carbon emissions: 28% from operational emissions, from energy needed to heat, cool and power them, and the remaining 11% from materials and construction.*[1] In their recent report, the Intergovernmental Panel on Climate Change (IPCC) has highlighted the importance of changes in the built environment for keeping global warming to 1.5°C and reducing worldwide carbon emissions by half in 2030.[2]

Due to the scale of the problem and the increasing GHG emissions from buildings, organisations of all types and size need to identify and implement high-impact solutions that can significantly reduce carbon emissions. Key areas that organisations need to address are **1) energy efficiency, 2) electrification** and **3) decarbonisation of the grid**.

En-ROADS (introduced in chapter 1) also stresses the first two areas listed. They say we should focus on increasing energy efficiency of buildings, appliances and other machines, which may be used in our organisations on a daily basis. This can be achieved through measures such as insulation in buildings and optimising energy use in manufacturing or factories. Energy efficiency can help save costs and improve the health and well-being of people (the users) in buildings.

Secondly, En-ROADS highlights electrification of buildings and industry, meaning the increased use of electricity (instead of fossil fuels such as oil and gas) in buildings, heating systems, appliances and other equipment or machines. Electrification can help reduce emissions if the electricity is from renewable sources, for example, solar and wind.[3] According to the Architecture 2030 initiative [a]chieving zero emissions from new buildings will require energy efficient buildings that use no on-site fossil fuels and are 100% powered by on- and/or off-site renewable energy. Energy-efficient new construction ensures that total building energy demand is minimal, enabling carbon-free renewable energy sources to easily meet demand.[4]

The latter is linked to the decarbonisation of the grid, which means reducing the power sector's carbon intensity: that is, reducing the emissions per unit of electricity generated (often given in grams of carbon dioxide per kilowatt-hour).[5] As renewables produce fewer emissions per unit of electricity generated than fossil fuels, a shift to renewables in the power sector is crucial. That will entail installing more wind and solar farms, and utilising hydro-electric sources of power. When the electricity from such sources is fed into the central grid, this allows the grid to be 'decarbonised'.

With respect to the built environment, it also includes the generation of power from and around individual buildings. This allows communities to generate their own electricity through renewables, rather than rely on the grid, so-called stand-alone power systems (SPS).[6] Where connected, surplus energy generated on site can feed back into the grid. This could be for example solar panels on the roofs of buildings, warehouses and factories. Hermann Sheer, German politician and founder of the International Renewable Energy Agency (IRENA), pioneered the concept where anyone can produce solar energy in their facilities and estates and feed it into the grid. The German Renewable Energy Act (EEG), also known internationally as Scheer's Law,[7] has provided the supporting means to ensure this shift away from fossil fuels. Fareed Zakaria sums up this success story in the Washington Post:

> A German politician, Hermann Scheer, managed to pass a feed-in tariff, which entered into force in 2000, that paid subsidies for solar panel installations in homes. Private sector entrepreneurs began to innovate and come up with better and cheaper panels. Then the Chinese government decided to fund this nascent industry. The result is that between 2010 and 2020, the world has gone from 40 gigawatts of installed solar capacity to 700 – an increase of almost 1,700 percent.[8]

In his new book 'Speed & Scale: A Global Action Plan for Solving our Climate Crisis Now', the venture capitalist and *New York Times* number-one bestselling author John Doerr sets out specific objectives and key results (OKRs) to reduce current emissions. His *top-line OKR is to reach net-zero emissions by 2050 – and to get halfway there by 2030, a critical milestone.*[9]

In order to achieve a reduction worldwide from the current 27 GT to 3 GT by 2050 through decarbonisation of the grid, John Doerr has chosen the following key results (KRs):

KR 2.1 Zero Emissions – 50% of electricity worldwide to come from zero-emission sources by 2025, 90% by 2035 (up from 38% in 2020). This would remove 16.5 GT.

KR 2.2 Solar and Wind – these power generators to be cheaper to build and operate in 100% of countries in 2025 (up from 67% in 2020).

KR 2.3 Storage – electricity storage to cost less than $50 per kWh for short durations (4–24 hours) by 2025, and $10 per kWh for long durations (14–30 days) by 2030.

KR 2.4 Coal and Gas – no new coal or gas plants after 2021; existing plants to retire or zero out emissions by 2025 for coal, and by 2035 for gas.

KR 2.5 Methane Emissions – eliminate leaks, venting and most flaring from coal, oil and gas sites by 2025. This will remove 3 GT.

KR 2.6 Heating and Cooking – cut gas and oil for heating and cooking in half by 2040. This will remove 1.5 GT.

KR 2.7 Clean Economy – reduce reliance on fossil fuels and increase energy efficiency to quadruple energy productivity rate (GDP + fossil fuel consumption) by 2035.[10]

As John Doerr points out, this is the timeline for *developed* countries, with others maybe taking five to ten years longer. However as discussed in chapter 2, developing countries are not the high emitters, so the action needs to be taken by those that are, such as Australia, Canada, Europe, the Gulf States, United States of America and their citizens. Everyone who owns and uses buildings could potentially make the necessary changes to support decarbonisation, by turning down the thermostat, for example; this cannot just be the responsibility of built environment professionals.

Electrification of buildings, energy efficiency and decarbonising the grid

Based on geographical location, the transition in some countries will be easier than others. Places with high average temperatures and an abundance of sunshine, such as Saudi Arabia and Qatar, should ideally switch their energy production to solar, and retrofit their buildings to use solar energy for their air-conditioning, for example. This could sit alongside new building designs aimed to ensure the interiors stay cool.

For cooler climates, one of the pioneers of energy efficiency Amory Lovins has been developing innovative ways to make buildings more energy efficient and reduce the dependency on the grid, for over 50 years. This includes his own house, as described in a 2022 article:

> Temperatures dropped far below freezing this week in Snowmass, Colorado. But Amory Lovins, who lives high up in the mountains at 7,200ft above sea level, did not even turn on the heating. That's because he has no heating to turn on. His home, a great adobe and glass mountainside eyrie that he designed in the 1980s, collects solar energy and is so well insulated that he grows and harvests bananas and many other tropical fruits there without burning gas, oil or wood.[11]

Designing a new building makes it easier to reduce the energy consumption by applying some of the principles that professionals such as Amory Lovins have been developing for decades. Far more difficult is insulating the existing building stock, especially considering the scale and speed that is required to do this. In the EU, about 75% of existing buildings are energy inefficient and represent a source of energy wastage.[12] Hence, existing non-domestic buildings need significant improvements, for example through retrofit measures. To tackle this strategic problem, the Life-Cycle Assessment (LCA) is increasingly being used as it is a state-of-the-art tool that assesses the environmental impacts of a product over its service life. The methodology highlights the impacts related to different phases of a process. It can facilitate decision-making to support GHG management and emissions reduction throughout the life cycle of a building, from planning, construction, operation, renovation to deconstruction,[13] in order to bring transformative change to the sector. The impact of demolition on emissions is often underestimated and it is far better to view existing buildings as *material banks*[14] and the starting point for new buildings.

If materials are not reused, and new ones are selected, it is important to consider the GHG emissions released during their production. *Materials and products used in buildings, such as steel and aluminium, are created by a production process of raw material extraction, raw material process, melting, manufacture to final products, and transportation to building sites. Each of the steps consumes energy, which is also expressed in terms of carbon emissions. Total carbon emissions of all building materials and products and the construction involved to put them together is known as a building's embodied carbon.*[15]

The move to electrification in buildings is another way to achieve better GHG management in the built environment. In this context, *[e]lectrification refers to the processes through which … [equipment and appliances] currently powered by fossil fuels are powered instead by (renewably sourced) electricity. Examples … include heat pumps, electric vehicles connected to buildings via vehicle-to-home (V2H) technologies, and heat pump water heaters.*[16]

For decarbonisation, it is argued that *the least-cost and most flexible path is to electrify buildings.*[17] Taken together, electrification of your building services (installing an electric heat pump for example, for both heating and cooling), integrated with energy efficiency measures and a renewable energy system, will provide you with solutions to support effective carbon management in your estate and buildings.

Using renewable energy can be part of the solution to deliver a zero-energy building, which is one where, *on a source energy basis, the actual annual delivered energy is less than or equal to the on-site renewable exported energy.*[18] In other words, a building that produces enough energy from renewable sources to meet its own annual energy consumption needs. Renewable energy comes from a sustainable and low-carbon source, and technologies such as solar panels, wind turbines or heat pumps can be used with few or no carbon emissions. Provision of renewable energy in both new and existing buildings can make a significant difference in terms of carbon emissions reduction, and buildings powered by such energy, on and/or off site, can help achieve Net Zero.[19] See Table 7.1 for options available to organisations wishing to install renewable and other sustainable technologies.

Table 7.1 Common sustainable technologies

Activities	Sustainable Technologies
Heating, Ventilation and Air Conditioning	Biomass Boiler Ground and Air Source Heat Pumps (GSHP/ASHP) Solar Thermal (ST) Mechanical Ventilation and Heat Recovery (MVHR)
Power	Solar Photovoltaics (SPV) Micro-Combined Heat and Power (CHP) Micro-Wind Generation Voltage Optimisers
Lighting	LED Lighting

Source: Finnegan, Jones and Sharples, The embodied CO_2e of sustainable energy technologies used in buildings: A review article: https://www.sciencedirect.com/science/article/pii/S0378778817323101

While renewables are better than coal or gas, a few further points need to be made. Firstly, although onshore wind turbines for example do not cause GHG emissions during their lifetime, the embodied carbon (i.e. the carbon emitted by mining the resources for the wind turbine and constructing it) can range from 59t CO_2e to 1046t CO_2e for a large structure.[20] All other renewable energy forms also have this embodied carbon, and the production is therefore not Carbon Neutral, but adds to GHG emissions. In addition, we need to consider that most technologies need resources that might be limited. The Institute for Sustainable Futures (ISF) in Sydney has for example highlighted that *demand from renewable energy and storage technologies could exceed reserves for cobalt, lithium and nickel, and reach 50% of reserves for indium, silver, tellurium. Primary demand can be reduced significantly, with the greatest potential to reduce demand for metals in batteries through high recycling rates, and for PV metals through materials efficiency.*[21] So while it is advisable that we switch to renewables, we also need to use less energy, in order to reduce the embodied carbon associated with renewables.

Turning to biomass, it has also been questioned by some scientists as to whether it is really a good renewable energy source. One reason cited is the number of mature trees being cut down to run Drax (United Kingdom) for example, considered to be the largest biomass plant in the world. While supporters highlight the ability of forests to regrow and continue acting as carbon sinks (covered later in the chapter), opponents have questioned the ability of a small sapling to absorb as much carbon as a mature tree.[22] Biomass can be positive when by-products of other industrial processes such as furniture making are used. Another example would be a potato snack company that uses its vegetable peelings to power their ovens. In this case, carbon would be released if the peelings went to landfill, therefore burning them to make power is the better option. However, where resources are used that could be employed to feed humans, we might find that the biomass is viewed similarly to Mike Berners-Lee's conclusion for biofuels: [i]f carefully handled … [biofuels] can provide a small but worth-having part of the energy mix. If an unregulated free market were allowed to run its course in a transition to a low carbon world, they could be a disaster. We could see biofuel for the rich becoming more profitable than providing essential food for the poor, and we could see yet more natural habitats trashed in exchange for monocultures.[23] In conclusion, other renewable energies should be given preference over biomass, and if biomass is selected, the preference should be to deploy by-products of other manufacturing processes.

Energy efficiency – the human and non-human factors

The negative aspects of fossil fuels are usually well-understood, and many will assume that the best option is to focus on switching to renewable sources of energy. However, as explained above, by continuing to consume the same quantity of electricity, the amount of embodied carbon in the renewable sources means we would still produce a lot of GHG emissions. The key is therefore to improve energy efficiency, as that has a significant role to play in achieving Net Zero, and organisations need to keep it at the heart of their carbon management strategy (see chapter 14 – Policies & Practices). When thinking about energy efficiency, we need to address technological means of reducing and we also need to encourage users and occupants to find ways to consume less. Buildings that are more energy-efficient should help reduce global carbon emissions, and the lower demand for energy should lead to less air pollution, fewer respiratory problems, lower healthcare costs and higher productivity.[24] Energy efficiency should therefore benefit the bottom line, the investors and the employees and users of your buildings.[25]

Looking first at the non-human factors, your organisation needs to focus not only on your buildings, but also on the equipment, appliances and other machines within them. The buildings themselves should be well insulated, and the amount of energy used for lighting, air-conditioning and heating should be reduced. According to the European Commission, [t]he *'energy efficiency first principle' means taking utmost account of cost-efficient energy efficiency measures in shaping energy policy and making relevant investment decisions.*[26]

When it comes to human factors, building users are key stakeholders in organisations. They can play a critical role in driving energy and carbon emissions down, however that role is not generally well understood in the context of the built environment.[27] A building can include all sorts of smart technologies and can be well designed, but it may not work in an energy-efficient way if the users are not on board. Ideally all users and employees should be consulted at the design and construction stage of any new building. This can also apply if any existing buildings are being retrofitted or refurbished. This allows you to understand and incorporate their needs and expectations, and building solutions can be co-created, leading to a sense of ownership. Effective carbon management demands behaviour change within organisations; this may involve education, awareness raising, incentivisation, persuasion and enabling. A good summary to support this is Michie, Atkins & West's 'Behaviour Change Wheel: A Guide to Designing Interventions'.[28]

Carbon sinks – natural, artificial and building materials

A major solution in the built environment is the increased use of carbon sinks, either by turning every possible location inside and outside the building into a green space, or through using carbon-absorbing building materials. A carbon sink is defined as *anything that absorbs more carbon from the atmosphere than it releases – for example, plants, the ocean, and soil.*[29] The protection of existing carbon sinks and the creation of additional ones are important means of mitigating climate change. The role of trees in reducing GHG emissions is generally well understood and often used in offsetting schemes, such as those where they are planted to compensate for taking a flight. The role of others, such as soil, seems less well known. For example, having a lawn or even a meadow on your estate absorbs carbon and is far better than laying artificial grass.[30] There is also a tendency in some countries to replace front gardens of houses or the green spaces on company premises with concrete driveways and parking for vehicles. Here we have a double negative impact, these parking areas replace the soil and plants that reduce GHG emissions from the atmosphere, and at the same time more cars can be accommodated, adding GHG emissions to the atmosphere.

In many organisations there will be potential to increase the amount of green spaces.[31] A rooftop for example could become a welcoming area with an array of diverse plants. This would not only help to absorb carbon from the atmosphere, it could also provide a sanctuary for bees and other pollinators, increasing biodiversity and offering employees an outdoor space to enhance their well-being and health, all while reducing air pollution. Building green walls (introduced in chapter 2) and green roofs, or introducing pots with native plants, are all solutions that could improve the situation, and these are likely to be within the sphere of influence of the organisation. Depending on your location, other less well-known carbon sinks such as hedgerows and seagrass could be cultivated, while peatland could be protected. Seagrass for example absorbs carbon from the atmosphere up to 35 times faster than tropical rainforests, whilst offering a home for fish nurseries and endangered species such as seahorses.[32] The magazine 'Resurgence & Ecologist' portrays some of these new initiatives focusing on cities and the built environment, and in a recent issue discusses how art and design institutions across Europe are creating urban forests.[33]

Using alternative building materials is another solution. Firstly, consider specifying materials made from natural products that absorb carbon while they grow, such as hemp, wood fibre, straw or other grasses. The 'Flat House' in the United Kingdom, for example, is a home built using timber and local hemp, and the architects who designed it boast that it is made from the plant which grows around it.[34] Similar concepts can be used for non-domestic buildings for organisational use. Secondly, consider substituting traditional building materials with bio-based alternatives, which have the capacity to store carbon.[35] So-called carbon sink building materials are mainly sourced from harvested wood products (HWPs), using wood from trees that capture carbon through the process of photosynthesis. It is important to source from sustainably managed plantations and not from illegal forest logging, which would not be Carbon Neutral and might destroy biodiversity. However, not all building materials can act as carbon sinks and in such cases, it is worth seeking out low-carbon alternatives. Such products would typically be manufactured from materials with low embodied energy and carbon in their production, assembly and transportation.[36]

Other eagerly awaited technological solutions are ones which remove carbon from the atmosphere. They are mostly in their infancy; it is not clear when artificial carbon capture will be fully developed and there is concern that it may be highly risky.[37] However, these solutions are needed sooner rather than later, to reduce the impacts that climate change is already having on many people worldwide (see also chapter 1).

Geoengineering is another solution in the making. In the case of solar geoengineering for example, particles are sent into the atmosphere like ashes from a volcanic eruption to reflect sunlight back into space, so that the rays do not warm the planet further, hence cooling the temperature on Earth. However, as Gernot Wagner, the founding executive director of Harvard's Solar Geoengineering Research Program, points out in his book 'Geoengineering: The Gamble', this could have a lot of unintended consequences, such as changes in rainfall and ozone depletion,[38] so we should perhaps think twice before embarking on such a risky mission, when we have all the solutions shared here already to absorb carbon naturally (natural carbon capture).

Building certifications, codes and standards

Different countries have their own building standards and certification schemes, which can offer your organisation a framework to develop sustainable and low-carbon buildings, the most common being LEED and BREEAM. The latter certification scheme is available in 77 countries and is *the world's leading sustainability assessment method for masterplanning projects, infrastructure and buildings. [It] does this through third-party certification of the assessment of an asset's environmental, social and economic sustainability performance ... Assessment and certification can be at a number of stages in the built environment life cycle, from design and construction through to operation and refurbishment.*[39] Various features of a building are reviewed, such as energy, waste, transport and water.

LEED is another building certification scheme, developed by the US Green Building Council. It *provides a framework for healthy, efficient, carbon and cost-saving green buildings which is a globally recognized symbol of sustainability achievement and leadership. Their vision is to transform the way buildings and communities are designed,* built and operated, enabling an environmentally and socially responsible, healthy, and prosperous environment that improves the quality of life.[40] In addition to BREEAM and LEED, some countries have their own certification schemes.

Various countries also have building energy codes that play a key role in setting standards to help reduce energy and carbon emissions in building construction. We would recommend that you check if your country of operation has any such codes in place. Two examples are the US building energy code, and the Rwandan Green Building Minimum Compliance System.[41] Apart from codes, building energy certification is a further policy instrument to drive carbon emission reductions in buildings. The aim is to evaluate a building's energy performance and, as of 2018, 85 countries had introduced such schemes.[42] Depending on location, certification may focus on rating a building's operational or expected energy use, and might be voluntary or mandatory for a particular building sector. These schemes address domestic and/or non-domestic buildings.

Other initiatives include the World Green Building Council's Net-Zero-Carbon-Buildings Commitment,[43] which challenges businesses and organisations to reach Net Zero operating emissions by 2030, and advocates for all buildings to be Net Zero by 2050. A country-specific example is the Building Efficiency Accelerator (BEA) project in Dubai, UAE, to benchmark energy performance of existing hotels, schools and shopping malls.[44]

In terms of standards, in order to support businesses and professionals in the built environment to achieve the United Kingdom's ambitions to reduce GHG emissions by 2050, the BRE (Building Research Establishment) is working with RIBA (Royal Institute of British Architects), the UK Green Buildings Council and various other organisations to produce a new standard. It will cover both new and existing buildings and will set out performance targets addressing operational energy and embodied carbon emissions to align with the UK's 2035 and 2050 emissions targets (78% reduction and Net Zero respectively). It will also cover the procurement of renewable energy and the treatment of residual emissions, including carbon offsetting.[45]

As there is such a wide variety of initiatives, schemes, codes and certifications, which cannot all be listed here, local intelligence will be essential. It is therefore advisable to work with relevant stakeholders for the design, construction and operation of your organisation's buildings, to ensure you are compliant with local requirements and regulations.

WANT TO DIG DEEPER?

Net Zero by 2050 –A Roadmap for the Global Energy Sector – International Energy Association (IEA) Report
https://iea.blob.core.windows.net/assets/deebef5d-0c34–4539-9d0c-10b13d840027/NetZeroby2050-ARoadmapfortheGlobalEnergySector_CORR.pdf
The IEA has produced this comprehensive report, considered as one of the most important and challenging undertakings in its history. It sets out clear milestones spanning all sectors and technologies for what needs to happen, and when, to transform the global economy, from one dominated by fossil fuels into one powered predominantly by renewable energy. Infrastructure and buildings are a key part of this decarbonisation.

Flourish: Design Paradigms for Our Planetary Emergency by Sarah Ichioka & Michael Pawlyn
https://www.flourish-book.com/
In this book, the two authors – both built environment professionals – share ideas and principles about how their profession could be part of the solution and not one of the big problems. This includes principles such as sourcing locally or using old buildings as 'material banks', as well as many innovative ideas and best practice examples including constructing integrated renewables and the 'Edible Garden City' in Singapore.

Better business guide to energy saving – The Carbon Trust
https://prod-drupal-files.storage.googleapis.com/documents/resource/public/Better-Business-Guide.pdf
This introduces measures to help businesses reduce their energy consumption and subsequent GHG emissions in non-domestic buildings. It covers the key energy and cost saving opportunities for small businesses.

High-impact solutions to reduce GHG emissions from buildings

In this section, we have ranked the potential solutions that would make a difference according to their impact and to the likelihood of being implemented by your organisation. As mentioned above, one of the best solutions is to design buildings so that they do not need any energy at all, or very little, to heat them if you live in a cooler climate, or to cool them if you live in a hotter climate. Additionally, the construction itself should cause as few GHG emissions as possible by reusing material where feasible, and then opting for materials with lower embodied carbon. Therefore, our first question will be: **how do we design and build new buildings using as little energy as possible to construct them and minimise heating/ cooling?**

Many organisations have buildings that are inefficient and are energy and carbon intensive. As part of improvements and any retrofit strategy, your organisation can install energy-efficient and carbon reduction measures to lower your energy consumption and reduce costs. Therefore, our second question will be: **retrofitting –how can we reduce energy consumption in existing buildings?**

Clean and renewable energy markets are evolving rapidly across the world and many organisations are now using renewable energy as part of their investment decisions. It is important to explore which technology is right for you in the context of your organisation. Our third question is, therefore: **renewable energy production –how should we produce our energy, once we are energy-efficient?**

After considering and implementing technical measures and renewable energy installations, behaviour change is paramount to engage building users as they can support the carbon management journey of your organisation. So, our fourth question is: **behaviour change –how can we engage building users in our efforts to reduce energy and carbon?**

Finally, another key area that has started to attract more attention recently is the improvement of biodiversity and carbon sinks. Therefore, our last question is: **how do we introduce more carbon sinks around our estate?**

How do we design and build new buildings using as little energy as possible to construct them and minimise heating/cooling?

The first thing to consider is your geographical location and to make a plan for the renewable resources you could use. For example, in a country where you have good access to solar energy and where you could harness this to power everything you need in your buildings and factories, you might prioritise designing a roof that would hold photovoltaic (PV) panels. You could even plan to produce excess energy to feed into the grid or sell to other organisations. You might want to use this energy to air-condition your buildings or to power your refrigeration. However, as mentioned before, we suggest combining the switch to renewable energies with energy reduction, so for example you could design the building so that it stays cooler using natural solutions:

> For more than a thousand years, windcatchers have existed in and around the Persian Gulf. These architectural towers are perfect examples of natural ventilation and passive cooling – ideas that have become increasingly relevant in sustainable design.

This is one of many examples in the guide 'How to build a house that stays cool without AC' which also cites David Wright, an architect who has been in the sustainable design movement for nearly five decades: [p]assive solar design … is all the things that you can do when you're designing a building to basically naturally condition it and make it a better place to live.[46]

This will include an understanding of wind patterns, which we also mentioned in chapter 5 when finding the best location for a data centre. Generally, it is good to know which parts of your building might need cooling down and to ensure these are in the shade of other buildings or in a windy location. You might also want to capture excess heat, produced for example in the kitchen of a restaurant, to warm other rooms. Natural light can also be used in your design, ensuring that for most of the day you do not need to buy or use additional electricity. The British engineer Max Fordham had very innovative ideas on how to design buildings so that they make the best use of daylight as well as innovative heating systems and ventilation.[47] Last, but not least, you might want to consider current or upcoming climate risks in your part of the world, such as flooding or hurricanes, in your building design.

The Passivhaus Standard (see Further Resources) allows buildings to demonstrate energy savings for both non-domestic and domestic/residential buildings. It has been successfully implemented in offices, factories, administrative buildings, sports halls and schools.

The second high-impact solution in the design of new buildings is the concept of using old buildings as a *material bank* with closed-loop cycles of repair und reuse.[48] This might include using as much of an old building in the new design as possible. The American Institute of Architects has outlined the main steps to reduce embodied carbon emissions in buildings:[49]

- Reuse buildings instead of constructing new ones
- Specify low-carbon concrete mixes
- Limit carbon-intensive materials (for example, aluminium and plastics)
- Choose lower-carbon alternatives (for example, wood structures instead of steel and concrete)
- Choose carbon sequestering materials such as wood
- Reuse materials whenever possible (for example, brick, metals, broken concrete or wood)
- Use high-recycled content materials such as metal
- Minimise waste and maximise structural efficiency.

Singapore is another good example where sustainability innovations are integrated into built infrastructure at scale. Singapore's 'green buildings' (including offices, university and public transport buildings and other facilities) have adopted principles of circularity where recycled materials and green technologies are used in their design.[50]

Retrofitting – how can we reduce energy consumption in existing buildings?

Existing buildings can be energy intensive, and they need to be improved to save energy consumption and reduce carbon emissions. As an organisation, you need to take a decision as to whether you want to demolish and construct a new building (see above) or retrofit an existing one. For an informed decision, the cost implications must be considered, but so should the carbon emissions impact associated with retrofit versus new build. By taking action to retrofit your building now, you will put your business/ organisation in a favourable position as energy prices rise and as legislation tackling carbon reduction changes in the future.[51] Energy retrofit can help reduce consumption of existing buildings by 30–50% or even more, leading to cost savings.[52]

An important driver for many businesses in the United Kingdom is that most non-domestic rented buildings will need to meet Energy Performance Certificate (EPC) B by 2030; this certificate might be useful and applicable to other countries and the link to an example is shared in the endnotes.[53]

According to research from the former UK Department of Energy & Climate Change (now subsumed into the Department for Business, Energy and Industrial Strategy), the average UK SME can reduce its energy bills by up to 25% by installing energy efficiency measures and implementing behavioural change. This is particularly valid for offices and retail businesses.[54] It is also worth consulting 'Retrofitting: A guide for non-residential buildings', which contains useful guidance and includes case studies of organisations that have adopted such solutions.[55] Another useful resource is the UKGBC's 'Delivering Net Zero: Key Considerations for Commercial Retrofits'.[56]

Firstly, implement measures that can help you reduce the energy needs of your buildings, for example:

*   Roof insulation
*   Wall insulation (cavity, internal and external)
*   Draught-proofing
*   Floor insulation
*   Replacement of windows
*   Secondary glazing
*   Replacement of doors.

Also look at the energy efficiency of your buildings, this might include:

*   Building and energy management systems
*   Smart controls: temperature, lighting and ventilation system controls and sensors, as well as energy metering
*   Review of heating, hot water and ventilation
*   Review of other equipment and appliances
*   Having a robust feedback system, providing information to help building users and other stakeholders to make better informed decisions.

Some of these solutions may cost money, but the payback is normally achieved as you save money on energy bills. The UK Energy Saving Trust has also developed an 'Energy Walkaround Checklist', which you could use and complete regularly. The aim is to review the performance of your infrastructure and equipment, and identify areas such as heating, lighting, offices and behaviours that can be improved to reduce energy consumption and carbon emissions. From this, an action plan can be developed for implementation.[57]

Renewable energy production – how should we produce our energy, once we are energy-efficient?

The first and easiest step is to change your energy supplier. You could switch to a 'green tariff' with your existing provider, but the better option would be to choose a supplier that invests exclusively in renewable energy, or even purchases the excess energy from homeowners who produce their own. This could be done through a company such as Good Energy that buys from over 1,900 independent generators[58] or with a company such as Sunrun in the United States, where homeowners create their own electricity and take control of their rising energy costs.[59] You could also investigate if any local organisation is producing energy, from waste products for example, and seek to purchase from them.

Another option would be microgrid, which is a localized grouping of distributed electricity generation technologies, paired with energy storage or backup generation and tools to manage demand or 'load'.[60] This is one of the solutions proposed by Project Drawdown, introduced in chapter 1, you might also want to explore their other solutions relating to renewable energy, such as geothermal power or high-efficiency heat pumps.[61]

If you want to install your own renewable technology, there are many options and the prices have dropped in recent years. The recent IPCC report (2022) highlights that there have been sustained decreases in the unit costs of solar energy (85%), wind energy (55%), and lithium-ion batteries (85%), and large increase in their deployment, e.g. >10x for solar and >100x for electric vehicles (EVs), varying widely across regions.[62] Harvard Business Review points out that [t]he market for clean energy technologies is changing fast, and companies need to understand both the technologies and their financing options. Firms that aren't aggressively incorporating renewables and other new energy technologies into their overall energy strategies are overlooking important benefits and exposing themselves to an array of risks.[63]

Behaviour change – how can we engage building users in our efforts to reduce energy and carbon?

People as building users are key stakeholders. They need to be seen as an opportunity rather than a problem in terms of reducing energy and carbon emissions. The following ideas are therefore suggested:

- Develop a Building User Guide to set out the organisation's intentions for how the building should be used, and to communicate the key processes to the users. The awareness of the building's design intentions, policies and processes is important for building users;[64] they use the facilities on a regular basis and can make a contribution towards efficient operations of the building, reduce energy and carbon emissions.
- Use innovative tools such as apps and energy dashboards to provide feedback to, and engage, building users. For example, the EU-funded horizon 2020 project eTEACHER proposes the use of Information and Communication Technology (ICT) solutions to encourage and enable behaviour change of building users towards energy efficiency.[65]
- Design activities that will engage your employees. For example, to encourage the use of the stairs instead of the lifts by introducing the 'Mount Everest Challenge', where they log how many flights of stairs they have climbed each day, with the chance to win a prize. Or consider making your staircases into a piano as shown in this video: https://www.youtube.com/watch?v=SByymar3bds, an initiative of Volkswagen.

How do we introduce more carbon sinks around our estate?

Your organisation needs to ensure that there are carbon sinks in your estate and building portfolio. Based on the work that the UN Climate Technology

Centre and Network has undertaken, we present below some examples of recently developed low-carbon materials and products based on recycled materials and by-products. Some of these construction materials, such as wood or bamboo, are also carbon sinks. By using them, the carbon does not get released again.[21]

1. Low-carbon bricks (including 40% fly ash to help reduce embodied carbon)
2. Green concrete where the raw material to make conventional concrete is substituted with by-products of industrial processes and other recycled materials
3. Green tiles made of ceramic material from over 55% recycled glass and other minerals
4. Recycled metals, as the production of metal products is very carbon intensive
5. Harvested wood building materials and products, including flooring and cladding materials, window frames, doors, furniture, structural columns, beams and rafters. Bamboo is also now increasingly being used in construction.

Several examples of how we could introduce more green space have been shared above and some are highlighted in the 'Quick Wins' below. A building that has green walls can reduce the need for air-conditioning, as covered in detail in chapter 2. For example, there is a plant-covered 20-storey building in Silicon Valley that was designed by Japanese studio Kengo Kuma and Associates with a green atrium at its centre.[66] Green roofs with planted vegetation can provide nature-based solutions in buildings and mitigate solar heat gains.[67]

As mentioned above, soil also acts as a good carbon sink and is a natural way to store carbon and represents the second largest carbon sink after our oceans, with the capacity to store three times more carbon than is in our atmosphere.[68] Figure 7.1 shares some ideas on how soil can be improved as a carbon sink and how this could be communicated to stakeholders.

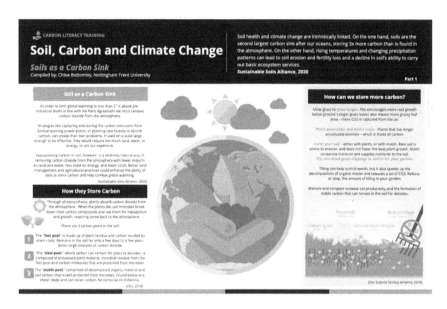

Figure 7.1 Engaging stakeholders to improve non-domestic green spaces
Source: Chloe Bottomley/NTU.[69]

Case study

The following case study is focused on how a small business is managing and reducing its GHG emissions within its estate and facilities.

Spenbeck achieving net zero within the built environment

By Helen Taylor (Sustainability in Enterprise NBS Consultancy Projects Coordinator) and Becky Valentine (Co-owner and Lead – Sustainability, Wellbeing and Building Health, Spenbeck, Nottingham)

Founded in 1981, Spenbeck is a multi-award-winning micro-SME, specialising in providing bespoke, sustainable and inclusive office spaces in Nottingham's historic Grade II listed former lace warehouses. Throughout its 40-year history, this second-generation family business has been synonymous with regenerating The Lace Market area of Nottingham (England). It has recently diversified into sharing its expertise in sustainability, building health and interior design through the launch of its consultancy support. Despite limited resources, the Spenbeck ambition is to maximise opportunities on offer to support Net Zero and carbon management initiatives within the commercial portfolio. Spenbeck is embedding ESG (environmental, social and governance), 'Triple Bottom Line' and the Sustainable Development Goals (SDGs) framework within its vision, values and culture, decision-making and planning processes.

Heritage sector net zero challenges and opportunities

Spenbeck's Grade II listed office portfolio causes specific challenges in responding to the UK Government's Heat and Buildings Strategy. Though achievable, the practicality of implementing carbon reduction strategies is constrained by a building's heritage status and the specialist conservation advice required alongside a shortage of heritage and conservation skills. Installation of heat pumps or solar panels requires a thorough understanding of their application to the structure of a heritage building, potential restrictions and associated costs on any structural changes necessary. Spenbeck is at the forefront of awareness raising of this issue within the heritage office sector, lobbying both central and local government via its established relationship with Historic England (HE), to ensure the heritage sector context features in future carbon management discussions.

The company has made various improvements to its estate, which are embedded into its overall efforts to reduce GHG emissions in all it does, and to have a coherent strategy aligned with all its stakeholders. Various actions have been taken including embedding Environmental, Social and Governance (ESG) aspects in its strategy, carbon reduction measures in its building portfolio, energy efficiency retrofitting and developing relevant expertise.

Collaborations with stakeholders

Spenbeck is aligning its Net Zero strategy and sustainability policy with the Nottingham City Council (NCC) Carbon Neutral 2028 target, action plan and Business Charter Environmental Checklist. The business is partnering with HE's climate team to lobby local and central government for clearer guidance on how the recent Heat and Building's Strategy will impact the listed heritage buildings sector, increasing risk of obsolescence resulting from the 2030 legislated energy efficiency targets. Furthermore, Spenbeck is supporting HE with a Birkin Building case study to research the impact of weather events on listed buildings, to inform the heritage sector's climate mitigation and response efforts.

Building in-house carbon management expertise

Spenbeck is a Carbon Literate SME, having completed Certified Carbon Literacy Training (CLT). (More information on training available can be found in chapter 2.)

- Supporting and developing tenants' Environmental Management System requirements e.g. B Corp and ISO 14001 certification.
- Empowering SMEs to commit to Net Zero through sharing their experiences via webinars, podcasts and expert panels.

Spenbeck has specifically improved its buildings and the following section presents some of the actions that have been implemented recently. Building in-house capacity and gaining relevant expertise has helped Spenbeck in its carbon management journey.

Carbon management actions in buildings and facilities

- Installing 100% renewable energy, improved thermal health measures and LED lighting.
- Developing low-carbon creative spaces through initiatives like waste composting and battery recycling.
- Supporting health and wellbeing via chemical-free cleaning, cross ventilation, natural light and minimal touch washrooms.
- Promoting low-carbon transport options for all, through lockers and secure bike storage, and providing showers, within the built environment.

Energy efficiency: Retrofitting the heritage property portfolio

Spenbeck has implemented a number of actions to reduce operational Scope 1 and 2 carbon emissions within its property portfolio:

- Improved environmental performance to reduce energy use intensity (resource consumption, lower emission of pollutants, waste generation and noise).
- Switched electricity provider in 2021 to 100% renewables reducing the carbon footprint.
- Prioritised works to reduce thermal leakage including window replacements and refurbishments and sympathetic brickwork repairs during Phase II of the Heritage Action Zone (HAZ) renovation project, thereby reducing tenants' energy bills.

- Commercial portfolio energy efficiency upgrades via the installation of secondary glazing, app-controlled heating and zoned LED lighting, PIRs, calculated to make over 30,000 kg CO_2 equivalent savings per year, a figure due to double by the end of the upgrade project.
- Designed a contractor pre-qualifying questionnaire (PQQ) to embed environmental sustainability along Spenbeck's supply chain and address Scope 3 emissions.
- Collaborated with stakeholders, such as the University of Nottingham's Energy, Innovation and Collaboration team, which has funded internships and provided expert advice and Nottingham Trent University's Sustainability Team to receive sustainability consultancy and participate in carbon management workshop programme via ERDF Sustainability in Enterprise Project.
- Building resource capacity through student consultancy projects and graduate internships offering the dual benefit of SME support, along with student and graduate experience in business GHG emissions reduction.

The changes made to the property portfolio have also supported and encouraged other carbon reduction initiatives:

- Responsible consumption to minimise resource use and implement low-carbon and circular economy principles.
- Sourcing Forest Stewardship Council (FSC)-certified, locally produced and recycled materials.
- Food composting via Stonebridge City Farm.
- Battery recycling.
- Large windows and high ceilings, allowing high levels of natural light and cross ventilation.
- HAZ work has significantly reduced thermal leakage and increased tenants' thermal comfort.
- Retrofitting to improve building fabric, meet functional needs and improve occupants' health & wellbeing.

Conclusion

Spenbeck is a market leader in heritage eco-office provision and has been categorised as an early adopter of using sustainability for competitive advantage by the Chartered Institute of Marketing (CIM). By explicitly supporting its tenants' Net Zero, B Corp and ESG aspirations, currently rare among landlords,

Spenbeck has seen increased demand for its offices, despite the move to hybrid-working practices through the pandemic, resulting in 75% of its vacant offices (over 12,000 ft²) being let in the last 12 months, leading to increased turnover and growth despite a tumultuous economic environment.

Helen is currently the ERDF-funded Sustainability in Enterprise Nottingham Business School (NBS) Consultancy Projects Coordinator (https://www.ntu.ac.uk/business-and-employers/financial-and-funded-support/sustainability-in-enterprise). Helen has supported a broad range of SMEs, throughout all stages of their sustainability and Net Zero journey, through bespoke consultancy and within sustainability projects at NTU, including The British Business Bank with the launch of its nationwide SME support package and 'Green Decoder'.[70]

Becky Valentine is a multi-award-winning expert in sustainable buildings and operations. Grounding the Sustainable Development Goal framework in commercial reality, she delivers bespoke consultancy support in decarbonisation, climate change mitigation and building health. Becky is a Carbon Literacy Project accredited Facilitator, delivering Carbon Literacy training for NBS as an Associate Lecturer. She is also an Active Travel Associate Practitioner and regular contributor to sustainability leadership expert panels, podcasts and webinars. More info: http://www.spenbeck.co.uk.

Quick Wins

Reduce energy consumption:

1. Start with low or no cost measures, for example, turn off lights, equipment, and heating when not in use.
2. Do not leave anything on stand-by.
3. Install light sensors that allow lights to switch on and off depending on movement in the building.
4. Switch sensors off when not needed e.g. if you use them for your staff kitchen but there is daylight during working hours in the summer, switch the sensor off during these months.
5. Install LED lighting and smart timers to help your organisation save energy and reduce costs.
6. Use energy-saving electrical sockets.
7. Use easy-to-install aluminium foil for windows or blinds to keep rooms cool.

8. Gather and share energy and carbon data to the building users regularly, so they understand their personal impact and will hopefully be more engaged.

Change to renewables:

1. Switch to a renewable/green energy tariff if possible.
2. Choose an energy provider that invests only in renewables.
3. Check that your energy provider is not using biomass, or if they are, establish whether it is biomass from waste products, rather than from plants grown specifically for this purpose.

Increase carbon sinks in your garden and/or estate:

1. Do not use artificial grass anywhere on your organisation's estate (or your own garden) nor artificial plants in your office.
2. Use living plants in your office that also purify the air such as the Peace Lily.[71]
3. Engage your employees (estate users) by empowering them through information such as infographics (see for example Figure 7.1).
4. Improve the well-being of your employees by designing green spaces, consider using rooftops or small outdoor spaces. Choose the plants that absorb the most carbon in your geographical location. Simultaneously, you might want to choose plants that are good for pollinators in your area to increase biodiversity.
5. Include employees in the design and running of green spaces including those indoors. Also, consider growing edible plants that they could take home in exchange for their work in planting and harvesting them.
6. Design green walls (more information in chapter 2).

Outlook

As shown in this chapter, there are many climate solutions that would help you to reduce the carbon emissions related to estates and facilities within your organisation. We recommend that you draw up an implementation plan like the one suggested in Figure 7.2 for **all** your estates, buildings and facilities-related carbon reduction possibilities.

Figure 7.2 Implementation plan for the reduction of estates and buildings-related GHG emissions.

Further Resources

On the companion website to this book you can find further materials to help you plan and implement this work.

Below you can find some links that go into more detail on the above or suggest further solutions that might be of interest in addition to the ones mentioned in the endnotes.

Audiovisual resources

How to decarbonize the grid and electrify everything

https://www.youtube.com/watch?v=d4Cy16uOdLM

In this TED Talk, John Doerr, author of 'Speed & Scale. A Global Action Plan for Solving our Climate Crisis Now' (see Dig Deeper), talks to climate policy expert Hal Harvey on *why humanity has to act globally, at speed and at scale, to meet the staggering challenge of decarbonizing the global economy (which has only ever increased emissions throughout history) – and share helpful examples of promising energy solutions from around the world.*

Bringing Embodied Carbon Upfront: The World Green Building Council
https://www.youtube.com/watch?v=2h0WxP3jJPU&t=139s
This video explains embodied carbon, the importance of addressing it and the key actions required.

What is a Zero Energy Building?
https://www.youtube.com/watch?v=FysJKq5yCfg&t=38s
This short video explains zero energy buildings and may inspire those looking to build or commission such a building.

Flourish Systems Change
https://www.flourish-book.com/flourishsystemschange-podcast
This is the podcast series that complements 'Flourish', the book featured in Dig Deeper. In this series, the two authors, Sarah Ichioka and Michael Pawlyn speak to various specialists about different aspects of regenerative design. They offer *ideas and solutions for designers, clients and inhabitants alike to build a thriving future, together.*

Reports, articles and standards

Practical Tips to Reduce Energy and Carbon Emissions
https://www.churchofengland.org/sites/default/files/2021-01/the-practical-path-to-net-zero-carbon-numbered-Jan2020.pdf
This offers recommendations to help churches reduce their energy use and associated carbon emissions. It will also be useful for your own organisation to find carbon management ideas.

Mackay Carbon Calculator by the UK Department for Business, Energy & Industrial Strategy (BEIS)
https://tinyurl.com/2p8fx2pk
This provides a model of the UK energy system, that allows us to explore pathways to decarbonisation including Net Zero by 2050. Buildings are part of this tool.

A Growing Embodied Carbon Library
https://www.buildinggreen.com/newsbrief/growing-embodied-carbon-library
The Carbon Leadership Forum has published a whole library on embodied carbon emissions. It is part of a crowdsourcing initiative where resources are added daily.

Energy Technology List (ETL)
https://www.gov.uk/guidance/energy-technology-list
This is a UK government list that provides details of energy-saving products for businesses and public sector organisations. It is created and updated monthly by the UK government's Department for Business, Energy, and Industrial Strategy (BEIS).

The Passivhaus Standard
https://bregroup.com/a-z/the-passivhaus-standard/
This is an international energy performance standard, and this web-based resource provides the related information and the associated certification standard for buildings.

Organisations

The International Renewable Energy Agency (IRENA)
https://www.irena.org/
IRENA is an intergovernmental organisation that supports countries in their transition to a sustainable energy future, and offers a repository of policy, technology, resource and financial knowledge on renewable energy.

BioRegional
https://www.bioregional.com/about-us
This organisation aims to make it easy for people around the world to live sustainably. They do this by working with developers and delivering projects worldwide to help communities build environmental resilience.

Notes

1. Word Green Building Council, *Bringing Embodied Carbon Upfront:* https://www.worldgbc.org/embodied-carbon

2. IPCC (2022) https://report.ipcc.ch/ar6wg3/pdf/IPCC_AR6_WGIII_FinalDraft_ FullReport.pdf and solutions for building sector recommended in the full report (pp. 64–66: 6.3.5.2 Building Design and Construction): https://www. ipcc.ch/report/ar6/wg2/downloads/report/IPCC_AR6_WGII_FinalDraft_ Chapter06.pdf

3. En-ROADS: https://www.climateinteractive.org/en-roads/

4. Architecture 2030, *Actions for Zero Carbon Buildings – New Buildings*: https://architecture2030.org/new-building-actions/

5. LSE and Grantham Research Institute (2020) *What is 'decarbonisation' of the power sector … in the UK?*: https://www.lse.ac.uk/granthaminstitute/ explainers/what-is-decarbonisation-of-the-power-sector-why-do-we-need- to-decarbonise-the-power-sector-in-the-uk/

6. Western Power, *How is WA decarbonising the grid*: https://www. westernpower.com.au/community/news-opinion/what-is-decarbonisation/

7. Hermann Scheer: https://www.hermann-scheer-stiftung.de/en/about- hermann-scheer/

8. Fareed Zakaria (2021) *On climate, we need to run fast — but not run scared*: https://www.washingtonpost.com/opinions/2021/11/04/climate-we- need-run-fast-not-run-scared/

9. Doerr J (2021)*Speed & Scale. A Global Action Plan for Solving our Climate Crisis Now*, London: Penguin, p. xxiv

10. Doerr J (2021)*Speed & Scale. A Global Action Plan for Solving our Climate Crisis Now*, London: Penguin, p. 34; please see also his whole chapter on 'Decarbonize the grid' for further information

11. Vidal J (2022) Energy efficiency guru Amory Lovins: 'It's the largest, cheapest, safest, cleanest way to address the crisis' *The Guardian* (26 Mar): https://www.theguardian.com/environment/2022/mar/26/amory- lovins-energy-efficiency-interview-cheapest-safest-cleanest-crisis

12. European Commission, *In focus: Energy efficiency in buildings*: https://ec. europa.eu/info/news/focus-energy-efficiency-buildings-2020-lut-17_en

13. Chau CK, Leung TM and Ng WY, *A review on Life Cycle Assessment, Life Cycle Energy Assessment and Life Cycle Carbon Emissions Assessment on buildings*: https://www.sciencedirect.com/science/article/pii/S030626191500029X? via%3Dihub

14. Ichioka S and Pawlyn M (2021) *Flourish: Design Paradigms for Our Planetary Emergency* https://www.flourish-book.com/

15. UN Climate Technology Centre and Network, *Carbon sink and low-carbon building materials:* https://www.ctc-n.org/technologies/carbon-sink-and-low-carbon-building-materials

16. Penttinen S-L *et al, Chapter 8 - Electrification and energy efficiency in buildings: Policy implications and interactions (p175):* https://www.sciencedirect.com/science/article/pii/B9780128221433000044#

17. Green Biz, *Building electrification is key to a safe climate future:* https://www.greenbiz.com/article/building-electrification-key-safe-climate-future

18. Finnegan S, Jones C and Sharples S, *The embodied CO₂e of sustainable energy technologies used in buildings: A review article:* https://www.sciencedirect.com/science/article/pii/S0378778817323101

19. Architecture 2030, *Why the Building Sector:* https://architecture2030.org/why-the-building-sector/

20. Berners-Lee M (2020) *How bad are bananas? The carbon footprint of everything*, p. 153

21. Dominish E, Florin N and Teske S (2019) *Responsible Minerals Sourcing for Renewable Energy*. Report prepared for Earthworks by the Institute for Sustainable Futures, University of Technology Sydney, p. iii

22. Reuters (2017) *Biomass a burning question for climate*: https://www.reutersevents.com/sustainability/biomass-burning-question-climate

23. Berners-Lee M (2019) *There is No Planet B. A Handbook for the Make or Break Years*. Cambridge University Press, p. 79

24. Climate Interactive, *Buildings and Industry – Energy Efficiency*: https://docs.climateinteractive.org/projects/en-roads/en/latest/guide/buildings_ee.html

25. World Economic Forum, *Why buildings are the foundation of an energy-efficient future:* https://www.weforum.org/agenda/2021/02/why-the-buildings-of-the-future-are-key-to-an-efficient-energy-ecosystem/

26. European Commission, *Energy efficiency first principle*: https://ec.europa.eu/info/sites/default/files/energy_climate_change_environment/events/documents/in_focus_energy_efficiency_in_buildings_en.pdf

27. Janda KB, *Buildings don't use energy: people do:* https://www.tandfonline.com/doi/abs/10.3763/asre.2009.0050

28. Stuart-Smith R, *Behaviour Change Interventions For Reduced Energy Use –Best Practices for Universities:* https://www.sustainabilityexchange.ac.uk/files/energy_behavior_case_study_v2_-_university_of_oxford.pdf

29. ClientEarth, *What is a carbon sink?:* https://www.clientearth.org/latest/latest-updates/stories/what-is-a-carbon-sink/

30. Laville S (2022) Eden Project installs plastic grass to stop children getting muddy, *The Guardian* (29 April): https://www.theguardian.com/uk-news/2022/apr/29/eden-project-cornwall-installs-plastic-grass-to-stop-children-getting-muddy

31. euronews.green (2020) *Europe's hidden green spaces: from flowering roof tops to bus stop gardens* https://www.euronews.com/green/2020/04/23/europe-s-hidden-green-spaces-from-flowering-roof-tops-to-bus-stop-gardens

32. Finding a solution – naturally in: Resurgence@Ecologist, Issue 328, September/October 2021, p. 38

33. A growing trend in: Resurgence@Ecologist, Issue 328, September/October 2021, pp. 52–54. You can find more inspiration also in relation to other climate solutions in this magazine: https://www.resurgence.org/magazine/issues.html

34. Horton H (2021) What will our eco-friendly homes of the future look like? *The Guardian* (27 Aug): https://www.theguardian.com/environment/2021/aug/27/what-will-our-eco-friendly-homes-of-the-future-look-like

35. Pomponi F *et al*, *Buildings as a Global Carbon Sink? A Reality Check on Feasibility Limits:* https://www.sciencedirect.com/science/article/pii/S2590332220303626#:~:text=Carbon%2Dstoring%20materials%20are%20most,drives%20buildings%20to%20be%20taller

36. UN Climate Technology Centre and Network, *Carbon sink and low-carbon building materials*: https://www.ctc-n.org/technologies/carbon-sink-and-low-carbon-building-materials

37. McKinsey Sustainability (2022) *The net-zero challenge: Accelerating decarbonization worldwide* (Jan): https://www.mckinsey.com/business-functions/sustainability/our-insights/the-net-zero-challenge-accelerating-decarbonization-worldwide

38. Wagner G (2021) Geoengineering. *The Gamble*, Cambridge: Polity

39. LEED vs BREEAM: https://www.vts.com/blog/leed-vs-breeam-understanding-the-differences https://www.vts.com/blog/leed-vs-breeam-understanding-the-differences

40. USGBC, *LEED*: https://www.usgbc.org/about/mission-vision

41. IEA, *2019 Global Status Report for Buildings and Construction:* https://iea.blob.core.windows.net/assets/3da9daf9-ef75-4a37-b3da-a09224e299dc/2019_Global_Status_Report_for_Buildings_and_Construction.pdf

42. Global Alliance for Buildings and Construction, *2018 Global Status Report*: https://www.worldgbc.org/sites/default/files/2018%20GlobalABC%20Global%20Status%20Report.pdf

43. World Green Building Council, *The Net Zero Carbon Buildings Commitment*: https://www.worldgbc.org/thecommitment

44. IEA, *2019 Global Status Report for Buildings and Construction:* https://iea.blob.core.windows.net/assets/3da9daf9-ef75-4a37-b3da-a09224e299dc/2019_Global_Status_Report_for_Buildings_and_Construction.pdf

45. BRE, *BRE joins forces with industry leaders to develop UK Net Zero Carbon Buildings Standard*: https://bregroup.com/news/bre-joins-forces-with-industry-leaders-to-develop-uk-net-zero-carbon-buildings-standard/

46. How to build a house that stays cool without AC (2021): https://www.popsci.com/science/keep-home-cool-without-ac/

47. *The Guardian* (2022) Max Fordham obituary: https://www.theguardian.com/technology/2022/jan/14/max-fordham-obituary

48. Ichioka S and Pawlyn M (2021) *Flourish: Design Paradigms for Our Planetary Emergency* https://www.flourish-book.com/

49. The American Institute of Architects, *10 steps to reducing embodied carbon:* https://www.aia.org/articles/70446-ten-steps-to-reducing-embodied-carbon

50. Singapore's Green Buildings: https://wedocs.unep.org/bitstream/handle/20.500.11822/34976/SGB.pdf

51. BioRegional and Association for the Conservation of Energy, *Retrofitting a-guide-for-non-residential-buildings:* https://www.hertfordshire.gov.uk/media-library/documents/environment-and-planning/building-futures/retrofitting-a-guide-for-non-residential-buildings.pdf

52. IEA, *2019 Global Status Report for Buildings and Construction:* https://iea.blob.core.windows.net/assets/3da9daf9-ef75-4a37-b3da-a09224e299dc/2019_Global_Status_Report_for_Buildings_and_Construction.pdf

53. Energy Performance Certificate (EPC): https://assets.publishing.service.gov.uk/government/uploads/system/uploads/attachment_data/file/5996/2116821.pdf

54. Energy Saving Trust, *A guide to energy efficiency for employees:* https://energysavingtrust.org.uk/a-guide-to-energy-efficiency-for-employees/

55. BioRegional and Association for the Conservation of Energy, *Retrofitting a-guide-for-non-residential-buildings:* https://www.hertfordshire.gov.uk/media-library/documents/environment-and-planning/building-futures/retrofitting-a-guide-for-non-residential-buildings.pdf

56. UKGBC: https://ukgbc.s3.eu-west-2.amazonaws.com/wp-content/uploads/2022/05/05110851/Commercial-Retrofit-Report.pdf

57. Energy Saving Trust, *Energy walkaround checklist:* https://energysavingtrust.org.uk/wp-content/uploads/2022/02/Energy-checklistv3.pdf

58. Good Energy: https://www.goodenergy.co.uk/our-energy/electricity/

59. Sunrun: https://www.sunrun.com/

60. Project Drawdown, Microgrids: https://drawdown.org/solutions/microgrids

61. Project Drawdown, Sector Summary Electricity: https://drawdown.org/sectors/electricity

62. IPCC (2022) https://report.ipcc.ch/ar6wg3/pdf/IPCC_AR6_WGIII_FinalDraft_FullReport.pdf see Figure SPM.3

63. Winston A *et al* (2017) Energy Strategy for the C-Suite, *Harvard Business Review:* https://hbr.org/2017/01/energy-strategy-for-the-c-suite

64. Better Building Partnerships, *Building User Guide:* https://www.betterbuildingspartnership.co.uk/node/1114

65. eTEACHER: http://www.eteacher-project.eu/

66. Dreith B (2022) Kengo Kuma breaks ground on plant-covered Silicon Valley building with "green lung", *Dezeen:* https://www.dezeen.com/2022/05/05/kengo-kuma-park-habitat-silicon-valley-green-lung/

67. Global Alliance for Buildings and Construction, *2019 Global Status Report for Buildings and Construction:* https://wedocs.unep.org/bitstream/handle/20.500.11822/34976/SGB.pdf

68. EEA, *Soil and climate change*: https://www.eea.europa.eu/signals/signals-2015/articles/soil-and-climate-change

69. Based on the work produced by Chloe Bottomley at Nottingham Trent University, UK

70. British Bank (2022) *Green Decoder*: https://www.ntu.ac.uk/about-us/news/news-articles/2022/05/nbs-co-create-the-british-business-banks-green-decoder

71. 15 Indoor Air Purifying Plants According to NASA Study https://gardenerknowhow.com/15-indoor-air-purifying-plants-according-to-nasa-study and NASA Study: BC Wolverton; WL Douglas; K Bounds (1989). Interior landscape plants for indoor air pollution abatement (Report). NASA. NASA-TM-101766.

8

PROCUREMENT AND SUPPLY: PUSHING THE BOUNDARIES TO REMOVE CARBON EMISSIONS

Richard Howarth and Fiona Winfield

This chapter looks at removing greenhouse gas (GHG) emissions and embedding climate solutions through the important areas of procurement and supply. There are specific roles for these two business areas because of their influence over material, product and service specifications and contracts, as well as transport, distribution and logistics. Collaboration and cooperation are especially important as many different stakeholders need to be engaged in this joint effort.

This chapter is for you if:

- You have responsibility for procurement, buying and supply strategy and policy
- You want to know more about the role of procurement and supply in the management of GHG emissions
- You want to understand which actions are likely to lead to the highest reductions in GHG emissions

DOI: 10.4324/9781003274049-10

- You have heard about Scope 3 GHG emissions and the link with procurement and supply, but are not sure what this means and the implications.

It will cover:

- The core questions and elements to consider in relation to GHG emissions when establishing strategies and approaches to sourcing and management
- An insight into related actions in an organisation and its supply chains
- Key areas to consider with respect to future action and GHG emissions.

Supplying a better climate, now and in the future

The Chartered Institute for Procurement and Supply (CIPS), an organisation with global reach and standards, identifies that the processes of procurement and supply are essential to organisations.[1] These processes are responsible for up to 70% of an organisation's revenue and have direct links to profits through the efficiency and effectiveness they facilitate. When it comes to greenhouse gas (GHG) emissions, procurement and supply processes also have an important role to play. CDP, formerly known as the Carbon Disclosure Project, a charity that helps organisations manage their environmental impact, estimates that emissions from supply are over ten times higher than those from an organisation's own operations.[2]

It is therefore crucial for all organisations to have an understanding of these issues. Action starts with buy-in from top management, so that relationships with other parts of the supply chain are based on a mutual desire to work together to reduce GHG emissions as far as possible. Many will be 'indirect', being connected to 'upstream' operations (the input of materials into the production process for example) or 'downstream' operations (the production and distribution processes). The Greenhouse Gas Protocol[3] (introduced further in chapter 12), clarifies that 'upstream' operations include goods and services required for the production process, along with their transportation. While 'downstream' covers activities and processes following production, resulting from the sale, storage and distribution of products and services to the end users Figure 8.1.

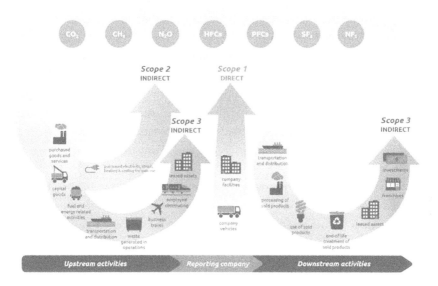

Figure 8.1 Overview of the GHG Protocol scopes and carbon emissions across the value chain.[4]

The indirect emissions above are classed as 'Scope 2 and Scope 3'. Direct emissions from an organisation's own activities are at the centre of Figure 8.1 and are classed as 'Scope 1'. More information on these categorisations can be found in chapter 11 (Scopes & Boundaries) and chapter 12 (Carbon Accounting).

Decisions regarding procurement affect the company itself, its customers, other stakeholders, the climate and environment, and overall sustainability. The Ellen MacArthur Foundation,[5] which has done extensive research into the circular economy (CE), identifies key areas where procurement can have an influence, since CE relates to the elimination of waste and the decoupling of economic activity from the consumption of finite resources.[6,7] The areas to address include:

- **Strategy for procurement, supply and logistics**: articulating the needs of the business and the expectations, standards of behaviour and performance requirements of suppliers.

- **Specification and sourcing of products and services required by an organisation**: operationalising performance standards and expectations, supporting awareness raising, education and learning.
- **Evaluation and selection criteria for suppliers and contractors**: public sector 'Green' Procurement Policies (GPP) are being introduced in many parts of the world and these ensure that contracts are written to support the purchaser's GHG strategy.[8] Such contracts are relevant for the private sector too. In Scotland for example, the government advice to procurement professionals is to reflect on: Whether, What, How and How Much to buy in all situations.[9]
- **Associated management processes**: organisations such as CDP (see 'Want to Dig Deeper' box in this chapter) help by defining the data and information needed by members of each network. They facilitate the disclosure and sharing of information and support learning from the process. Also important will potentially be: auditing your suppliers to lead to insights into their performance against specifications and requirements, along with the identification of what support, guidance and training may be needed. Aim for dialogue and facilitating action rather than simply checking compliance. Outcomes from reviewing data, information and performance will inform the strategy for procurement, supply and logistics moving forward.

The scale of the task means opportunities for all

Many businesses have focused on direct Scope 1 and indirect Scope 2 emissions (the latter being mainly purchased electricity) because they are within the organisation's control, and because this is what the regulations, and perhaps their customers, require. However, in most sectors, those classed as Scope 3 account for between 70% and 90% of the total GHG emissions.[10,11] The Boston Consulting Group (BCG) identifies that the supply chains with the largest GHG emissions are: food, construction, fashion, fast moving consumer goods (FMCG), electronics, automotive, professional services and 'other freight'.[12]

Figure 8.2 provides some insight into the key environmental impacts from the coffee capsule supply chain, which have direct impacts on climate

Figure 8.2 Coffee supply chain and key emissions and other impacts.[13]

change too. Using the Scopes from Figure 8.1, it can be seen that the stages of production include, for example:

- **Scope 1** – direct emissions from the use of fuel to heat buildings during final processing and packaging stages (assuming this is undertaken by the reporting company) and fuel used in transport, if the vehicles are owned by the reporting company.
- **Scope 2** – emissions from electricity usage at final processing and packaging stage (again assuming this is undertaken by the reporting company).
- **Scope 3** – production and management of waste from the reporting company. Upstream emissions related to production of coffee beans and associated processing (e.g. related to energy use and wastage), transportation to the reporting company and so on. Downstream emissions relate to usage by customers (including energy used to brew the coffee) and onward, to end of life and disposal.

Some businesses have therefore recognised the advantages of working with their suppliers in this respect and, as a result, sizeable GHG emission reductions have been identified and have followed.[14] This can benefit a range of stakeholders and lead to improved data and information sharing. This is also important when assessing organisational and supplier performance, both for establishing the effectiveness of processes and reporting. (See also chapter 3 – Communication & Reporting.)

Moving materials and products

It has long been recognised that the supply chain can result in significant and maybe excessive emissions. A classic article by Böge[15] presented the example of strawberry yoghurt and illustrated the emissions from its production and distribution. The article identified an overall increase in the use of goods vehicles, due to their availability and low cost, which led to the negative consequences. It demonstrated how many different parties were involved in various countries and how that led to excessive road miles and journeys, and associated emissions. Given the increased cost of fuel, associated emissions and also questions of resilience, models of supply and production such as this will require change.

According to the International Maritime Organization's (IMO) third GHG study, maritime transport emits around 940 million tonnes of CO_2 annually and is responsible for about 2.5% of global GHG emissions. The IMO estimates that if everyone continues with business as usual, shipping emissions could increase between 50% and 250% by 2050.[16] According to EU data, trucks, buses and coaches are responsible for about a quarter of CO_2 emissions from road transport in the EU and approximately 6% of total EU emissions. Furthermore, *the aviation sector creates 13.9% of the emissions from transport, making it the second biggest source of GHG emissions after road transport.*[17] It is evident therefore that many supply-related GHG emissions result from transport, distribution and logistics decisions.

In their report 'Your Supply Chain Needs a Sustainability Strategy', BCG identifies **'levers'** for change,[18] and the recommended action that is most likely to contribute to improvements in procurement, supply and logistics:

- **Enhanced sustainability of inputs and suppliers**
  - Opt for suppliers who meet specific environmental performance standards

- o Focus on raw materials with smaller environmental footprints, perhaps from renewable sources
- o Use recycled, reusable or alternative materials and packaging where possible
- o Use energy and fuels which cause fewer or no GHG emissions
- o Investigate alternative fuelled vehicles such as electric and hydrogen and think about how these are procured.
- **Increased efficiency in the use of operational resources**
  - o Ensure production facilities are as efficient as possible, that resources are used effectively and waste is minimised
  - o Efficiency from a logistics perspective might include a reconsideration and change to the types and size of vehicles.
- **Optimisation of the supply chain network**
  - o Focus on directly reducing climate impacts from the movement of materials and products through the supply chain
  - o Localise supply and production where viable
  - o Adopt 'circular economy' models, taking a fully integrated view of what's produced, how it's produced, the materials and inputs involved and what happens at the end of the product's life.

In the BCG report, there are also examples of companies that have put some of the above into practice.

- A collaboration between Kellogg's and the brewers Seven Bro7hers means that by-products from the former's production process are being used to make beer
- PepsiCo's water conservation has not only saved the company more than US$80 million between 2011 and 2015, it has reduced its reliance on resources that might well be affected by climate change in the future
- Alcoa (an aluminium producer with its HQ in the United States of America) is working with the auto industry to co-design metal that weighs less, to reduce vehicle emissions.

The Ellen MacArthur Foundation also works with organisations such as BioPak to close the loop on single-use food packaging.[19] Scottish ice-cream maker Mackie's is another good example, producing energy on site to support its manufacturing process, using milk from its own farm and producing its simplified packaging on site.[20]

Every organisation will be different, but the examples and the additional sources mentioned above will hopefully give you some inspiration for where to start in your business. Further suggestions of resources to assist you are featured in the next sections.

WANT TO DIG DEEPER?

SME Climate Hub: 1.5° Supply Chain Leaders
https://smeclimatehub.org/supply-chain-leaders/
A good set of free resources for SMEs to help them establish how to work with their supply chain to reduce emissions.

BCG: Supply Chains as a Game-Changer in the Fight Against Climate Change
https://www.bcg.com/en-gb/publications/2021/fighting-climate-change-with-supply-chain-decarbonization
A recent report from the Boston Consulting Group that provides relevant information and guidance on the benefits, challenges and opportunities, from action within supply chains to counter climate change.

CDP: Changing the Chain – Making Environmental Action in Procurement the New Norm
https://cdn.cdp.net/cdp-production/cms/reports/documents/000/004/811/original/CDP_Supply_Chain_Report_Changing_the_Chain.pdf
The CDP is a not-for-profit charity that supports a range of organisations, partners and suppliers to manage their own and their wider environmental impacts. This report looks specifically at the supply chain and the work of a wide range of organisations, and provides insights into the action they have undertaken and what can be learnt from them.

High-impact solutions

As noted earlier, transporting raw materials and finished products are major contributors to GHG emissions, so anything a company could do to replace global with local networks, especially with regard to their suppliers, would be a positive development. Hence, our first question is: **networks – how can a local system of supply be established?**

Besides reducing transportation via roads, water and air, emissions from all types need to be reduced as far as possible, therefore our second questions relates to: **efficiency and effectiveness – how can you improve transport, distribution and logistics?**

Throughout the production process, it's important to think about design, material selection, reuse and recycling, the use of new or alternative or even recycled materials, and their impacts, in both products and their packaging. This leads us to the third question: **materials – what steps can be taken to reduce GHG emissions through specification and production processes?**

Despite the importance of procurement and supply, when it comes to GHG emissions and achieving Net Zero, there is broadly a lack of connection currently between statements of intent, where they even exist, and action. The fourth question is, therefore: **procurement and supply – how can action be initiated and facilitated?**

Finally, getting your own house in order will be important, but supporting others – suppliers, customers and particularly SMEs within supply chains – will be essential. This will involve information and data sharing, and potentially the provision of training. Our final question is, therefore: **awareness raising and training – will engagement and dialogue be important?**

Networks – how can a local system of supply be established?

Potentially large benefits can be achieved through localising supply and production nearer to where materials, products and services are consumed. In the case of food or other perishable items, knock-on benefits come from a lower reliance on refrigeration leading to decreased use of energy, refrigeration materials and gases. Reducing air-conditioning and refrigeration was identified in Project Drawdown as one of the best high-impact solutions (see chapter 1).

Businesses could make a positive contribution towards addressing the historic lack of consideration of the negative impacts from production and supply, and the apparent failure of some procurement processes to recognise those impacts. It is, therefore, important to think about this in your own context and consider how your current operations could be reconfigured to support GHG emission reductions, wider sustainability activity and resilience.

It may not be possible to change your *whole* business model and supply chain for *all* products and services, particularly if your organisation is large and complex. Careful prioritisation will be important and selection may be based on volume or value of sales, the current and future needs of your customers and your organisation, and so forth. Dialogue with your current and new suppliers will be key, as your organisation is unlikely to have all the data and information needed, and it is unlikely to have all the answers either. Working through options and scenarios, paying attention to each one's pros and cons, and remaining open-minded, are therefore crucial.

Efficiency and effectiveness – how can you improve transport, distribution and logistics?

Your overall focus should be on the reduction or elimination of GHG emissions from transport, distribution and logistics. This will require decisions about whether vehicle movements are even needed and, depending on your current situation, whether you should switch to zero emission (ZE) vehicles.

Associated with this will be the optimisation of both route planning (i.e. scheduling) and routing (the actual routes to be taken). Within the EU alone, 70% of road freight GHG emissions are from heavy-duty vehicles, made up of large or heavy-duty trucks (HDTs)[21] and medium-freight trucks (MFT).[22] Using the most appropriately sized vehicles will be critical, whenever possible.

According to the Exponential Climate Action Roadmap, published in 2018,[23] the electrification of vehicles and adapting the global shipping fleet, will be two important ways to reduce emissions. It was estimated that these could lead to reductions of more than half by 2030, but would require policy shift in many parts of the world. In 2022, the international retailer Tesco confirmed that it is starting to fit refrigerated trailers with solar panels, which should lead to an estimated saving of 2,000 litres of diesel (and 5 tonnes of carbon emissions) annually per trailer.[24] All organisations can do their bit and a useful source of ideas is 'Road Freight Zero' (RFZ) published by the WEF and McKinsey.[25]

To summarise the RFZ report, you could start by thinking about:

- **Route length**
    - The current length of your routes and whether you have any influence on the type and size of vehicle used

- Alternatives with ZE options; route length is influential for electric transport due to the battery size requirements and the time taken to charge
- Available infrastructure, if many routes are long, the current infrastructure may limit your options.
- **Payload**
  - The weight, volume and nature of the items transported
  - For bulky or difficult-to-move loads, there may be a financial incentive to source or produce nearer to customers or production facilities.
- **Routes and routing**
  - Current and future depot types and how they are integrated
  - Whether your depots support battery charging. It is estimated that 60–90% of the electric vehicle charging infrastructure (trucks, vans and cars) will be located within logistics and distribution hubs, these may be your own or those operated by others. This could require collaboration and relationships with other stakeholders (organisations, governments, local authorities, community groups etc.) with benefits for all
  - The number of drivers needed, the scheduling of driver breaks and operating hours, etc.
- **Structure**
  - The ownership model for any vehicles within a fleet and the use of third-party operators
  - How in-house vehicles are financed, and how are they maintained
  - The gap in direct and life cycle cost differences between ZE vehicles and current alternatives, particularly in relation to residual values and finance options.

Specialists, such as freight forwarders, have a role to play here, as they can help ensure that vehicle movement and payload efficiencies are maximised. But the model of the business, and whether your production and supply are local, will have an impact too.

Your starting point should be an audit of your organisation's current situation regarding the above issues and their associated GHG emissions. The specific issue of 'last mile delivery' and the associated downstream GHG emissions and their calculations are discussed in chapter 9 (Marketing) and chapter 12 (Carbon Accounting). By carrying out such an audit, you will have evidence to present to colleagues, to ensure buy-in at senior level.

Materials – what steps can be taken to reduce GHG emissions through specification and production processes?

To reduce the GHG emissions related to packaging (primary, secondary or tertiary), it may be that your organisation is already doing some, or all, of the following. If not, this checklist compiled with reference to various sources, including BCG[26] and WEF,[27] will hopefully prompt discussion and action, ensure effective assessments and calculations of current and new emissions, and support decision-making.

- **Elimination:** take a critical look at the types of packaging currently used and consider their purpose – can any be removed or simplified without affecting the protection and presentation of the product? WEF highlights the work by retailers ASDA and Tesco in eliminating plastic film in multibuy packs, and Carlsberg's multipacks of beer which are held together with glue dots, instead of plastic rings.
- **Reusable packaging:** the work of Earthshot Prize nominees PR3 could be beneficial here as they are seeking to establish global standards for reusable packaging.[28] PR3 estimates that, if it were reusable, up to 90% of packaging produced and 80% of associated GHG emissions could be eliminated. Also, check if any tertiary packaging is being reused, if not, check if that's feasible.
- **Recycled or alternative content:** check if recycled materials could provide a revenue stream to increase your company's income, which may lead to cost savings. If you are not already using packaging materials made from recycled or alternative materials (such as plant-based plastics), establish if this would work for you.
- **Reductions in the type and quantity of packaging:** if multiple layers of packaging from different materials are used, see if the number of layers can be reduced. Mixed packaging materials can cause increased emissions for your customers, especially if the materials are not designed with reuse, recycling or recovery in mind. Seek out packaging products made from single materials, for example, padded envelopes made from just paper and card.

- **Environmentally-friendly packaging:** examples include biodegradable tea bags and compostable stickers for fruit. Look out for packaging materials made from corn, sugar cane or bamboo for example.
- **Refills:** if packaging cannot be eliminated, think about refilling it. McKinsey and WEF see this as an important trend that is supported by many retail customers, with various supermarkets and others seeing positive outcomes from trials. Refills and reusable containers can work well in specific business-to-business settings too. For example, Nottingham Trent University's catering department has worked with its fruit and vegetable suppliers to switch to reusable containers, eliminating cardboard waste, which has probably also cut the supplier's costs.[29]
- **Bulk movement of materials:** can any of your raw materials or finished products be transported in bulk to reduce the need for extra packaging? Can you also employ reusable containers or packaging, with final packing being undertaken in markets nearer the customers? Unilever's work on 'rethinking plastic packaging' illustrates their approach to using 'less, better or no plastic', and might provide inspiration.[30]
- **Partnerships:** consult your current suppliers of packaging and distributors of packaging and packaged products. Information sharing and knowledge from such partnerships can support greater efficiency, as the weight and size of packaged products can be reduced, with benefits for vehicle efficiency and space optimisation too.

Finally, it would be good to think about circular economy considerations, for your product range and its packaging. If you take on board the messages linked to the CE, you should be facilitating the recovery and return/re-distribution of resources and packaging at their end of life. Your organisation will probably need to think about innovations, perhaps creating value from waste or eliminating waste at the start of the design process. This may require agreements and commitments with other stakeholders, to ensure materials are handled or returned in certain ways. This hopefully means that potential challenges, related to control, residual value, product and packaging complexity for example are addressed as early as possible, and the business case is clear.[31] This may be a stretch when it comes to your current processes and approach, but there should be definite procurement and supply chain benefits.

Wherever you are based, it is worth looking at the TerraCycle website[32] to see what the options are. TerraCyle recognises that even when something is recyclable, it does not always make economic sense. Their mission is 'Eliminating the Idea of Waste'®, and they work with lots of different organisations to reduce the materials going to incineration or landfill.

Procurement and supply – how can action be initiated and facilitated?

CDP suggests that, aside from a few trailblazers, the majority of organisations are not cascading climate or wider environmental action through their supply chains, with only 38% of its members disclosing in 2021 that they actively engaged their suppliers in climate change and GHG emissions action.[33]

To help you, CDP has produced its sustainable procurement pathway, the stages of which reflect their significance and priority. This provides a clear framework for action, which will support reductions in GHG emissions from your procurement and supply work.[34]

- **Foundation:** if you don't have one already, develop a procurement, supply and logistics strategy and ensure it's supported by senior management, and reflects the organisation's overall strategy. This will be the foundation for your work in this important area and will help raise awareness and educate your suppliers.
- **Practice:** it will be a waste of time producing the above strategy if it is not implemented internally within your organisation, and externally with suppliers. A focus may be on ZE vehicles, specifically medium and heavy-duty ones, and other priority areas such as packaging, to ensure you gain Quick Wins.
- **Embed:** you will need to ensure the strategy is embedded within the organisation and through procurement processes into the wider supply and value chains. You won't be able to target all external suppliers at once, so prioritisation will be necessary.
- **Enhance:** check your plans against industry 'best practice' via benchmarking. This will support dialogue between your own organisation and others, but also a wider field of experts with experience and insights. This may also benefit your organisation and its brand positioning.

- **Lead**: to achieve a 1.5°C future, ensure a longer-term focus is adopted and maintained via reviews and performance assessment, while learning from the organisation's own experience, and that of others.

It will be essential, and grounded in your procurement process and its management, for the organisation to assure the quality of data and information used to support GHG emissions accounting and supplier performance. The GHGP value chain accounting and reporting standard,[35] and GHGP supplier engagement guidance,[36] both set out the importance of assurance supported by audits and supplier engagement and the value of clear dialogue with suppliers to benefit all parties.

Another great resource launched at the time of COP26 is the Exponential Roadmap Initiative (ERI) 1.5°C Supplier Engagement Guide (SEG),[37] and we have picked up some of their recommendations in answering the next question.

Awareness raising and training – will engagement and dialogue be important?

It will be important to work closely with your suppliers and other stakeholders, and this fits the bigger picture of driving sustainability activity by using the 'lever' of procurement and supply to accelerate action. BCG highlights that many consumer product organisations already use this 'lever', for example L'Oréal, a company that chooses 80% of its suppliers based on their environmental and social performance.[38] Also Unilever, who worked with the biotech company Evonik, to develop a biodegradable and renewable surfactant, used as a global first in its Quix brand in Chile.[39]

The added benefit of the provision of information and training is that your current model of supply does not need to be fundamentally changed, unless, of course, your business model changes or other high-impact actions necessitate this. You could also offer incentives and reward improvements, to encourage individual and collective learning. This may be particularly useful when you are seeking to embed and sustain knowledge within your procurement and supply processes.

The aforementioned ERI 1.5°C Supplier Engagement Guide (ERI SEG) provides detailed insight into how you can take action to engage your suppliers. Key here will be:

- Two-way communications and dialogue
- Breaking down barriers to knowledge, information-sharing and learning
- Addressing any data deficiencies
- Close working relationships, which facilitate further creativity and innovation.

It may be necessary to target some of your suppliers with different forms of support at different times. This will enable the rolling out and sustaining of activity in this area. The decisions about whom to target and engage first are likely to be informed by the importance of a supplier within a chain, or their importance to an organisation or customer. Those needing to act sooner or faster than others should be engaged as soon as possible, and the reasons and logic for action should be established and clearly articulated. In the 'Further Resources' section below, you will find links where you can locate template letters, for example, to help engage suppliers.

Case study

We will now look at how an organisation can support the transition to ZE vehicles through its procurement activities, with a focus on its employees. This helps the organisation to reduce its own GHG emissions, whilst enhancing the employee benefit package.

Climate solutions can be business opportunities

By Hannah-Louise Kirkpatrick (Founder, Harmoto: https://www.harmoto.co.uk/)

Do you need to own everything? Would it not be beneficial for organisations to share machinery and equipment if they only rarely use it? Could there be a different model in procurement, where organisations did not buy everything, but 'owned' things temporarily, through a leasing arranging for example? This is a common practice for fleet vehicles but could become standard for other items. With these questions in mind, the new start-up harmoto, based in Derbyshire (United Kingdom), saw a business opportunity and developed a scheme that combines the potential for the reduction of GHG emissions with benefits for employees. Although harmoto operates nationwide, its HQ is in a fairly rural location, with a greater need for personal vehicles than urban areas where schemes such as car clubs are more common, and it is also a county often affected by inclement weather that affects public transport.

Background

It is evident that there is a need to transition to zero emission (ZE) supply and logistics solutions and support the achievement of this transition. Work has started, and the UK government has announced phasing out the sale of new diesel, petrol and hybrid cars and vans from 2030. From late 2020, the government also committed to ensuring that electric and hydrogen ZE vehicle alternatives would be a cheaper, more cost-effective option for individuals and organisations by the mid-2020s. This addresses concerns associated with climate change and GHG emissions from the vehicles, along with overall air pollution and air quality challenges in many towns and cities. As part of the government's plan, the development of replacement ZE vehicles and the associated infrastructure will underpin 'levelling up', enabling growth and prosperity across the country, evidenced by direct investment and an increase in jobs and opportunities. This has already been evidenced by strategic investments in Nissan for example, who have committed to produce ZE vehicles in the United Kingdom.[40]

Manifestos and reports by organisations such as Logistics UK ('Route to Net Zero') and WEF/McKinsey ('Road Freight Zero')[41] identify the importance of policy and strategy frameworks to frame the transition to ZE cars, vans and heavier goods vehicles, with the associated reduction in and removal of GHG emissions. Organisations either have direct or indirect control over these emissions, as they emanate from their vehicles, the suppliers they contract or their employees. To support this, the UK government, and the manifestos and reports mentioned above, identify the following:

- the importance of the network and infrastructure for fuel distribution and vehicle battery charging
- the need for investment in the networks and infrastructure
- the influential role of investment and funding of pilot and test projects that illustrate ZE benefits
- the role of incentives through taxes to support the transition to ZE vehicles (cars, vans and trucks)
- the impact of alternative funding models and approaches to support the pace of transition to ZE vehicles.

The UK government not only recognises its important and pivotal role here, but also that of industry and organisations and the need for new and innovative solutions in this area. This will include models for funding and enabling the finance of ZE vehicles by organisations to support their own activities and those of their suppliers. It also includes new models and approaches, for example, the procurement of contracts to support employees with their transition to ZE vehicles – with employee travel an important element in an organisation's emissions inventory and its wider commitment to provide attractive employment packages to employees.

Harmoto saw this as a business opportunity and created such a scheme. Through this they aim to help organisations and their employees to transition to electric vehicles through what is termed 'salary sacrifice' in the United Kingdom, similar to the scheme already in place in the UK to encourage cycling to work. In simple terms, the employer leases the car and the employee 'rents' it from the employer. The employee pays for the car each month out of their gross pay (i.e. before tax and other contributions are deducted). This means that employees who are keen to switch to electric cars, but feel that the upfront investment is too great, can do so in a financially efficient way. Such approaches are relevant for businesses large and small – including those which would not usually operate a vehicle fleet.

The current UK government incentives are making this particularly attractive for businesses, employees and the climate. Some of the *current* attractions include:

- A government grant (in 2022 – up to £5,000)
- Potentially lower recharging costs
- The low Benefit in Kind (BIK) tax charge for the employee *(and the UK government has committed to maintaining the low charging structure until at least 2024/25).*

Currently, this scheme only allows organisations to lease cars, not vans, but that would seem an obvious extension of the scheme for the UK government in the future.

Signing up to such a scheme means that individuals and organisations can continue to operate as before, but with a significant reduction in, or removal of, GHG emissions. Given that existing and prospective employees are increasingly considering the social and environmental impact of their own work and of their employers,[42] this brings benefits, not least the funding of a car package from gross pay (i.e. before taxes) rather than net.

Such schemes are primarily focused on facilitating the transition to ZE vehicles by employees of organisations, but by using such a scheme, the employer can support the pace of transition and provide employee and climate benefit too. So it's a real win-win result.

Hannah-Louise Kirkpatrick has a background in corporate banking and finance. Having worked with SMEs and corporate businesses in this field for 14 years, she founded harmoto to fill a gap in the market to help businesses to transition their fleets to electric and emerging powertrains, and to offer vehicle salary sacrifice options for this segment's employees.

Quick Wins

1. Understand where your biggest impacts are in relation to emissions, prioritise these 'hot spots' and establish clear outcomes and targets for your work.
2. Speak to your suppliers – it is likely they will have ideas about how to make changes and support reductions of emissions.
3. Work with suppliers as partners and assure assessments of performance and the quality of data and information provided by all parties.
4. Minimise the use of packaging and adopt reusable or recycled materials where possible, with the overall aim to minimise the GHG emissions impacts of any packaging.
5. Source and produce closer to your production facilities and customers if feasible.
6. Optimise the use of resources and space – only move items over a long distance if you must, and move in bulk if possible, making maximum use of space.
7. Update your contracts now, or as soon as possible, to ensure they support your ambitions to reduce emissions.
8. Make the most of your networks beyond your suppliers – chambers of commerce, professional bodies or sector groups, and local universities (their staff and students).

Outlook

Procurement and supply are areas that generate significant GHG emissions and therefore affect most businesses, their products and services. Organisations large and small have started the process and their first point of call has been to collect the best available data, information and climate solutions. Equipped with this information they have made a plan, and this is what we recommend as the first action too. You could for example make an implementation plan following our example in Figure 8.3. The next step is to ensure you are ready to communicate with your suppliers, and the resources and templates available via the 1.5°C Supplier Engagement Guide mentioned above would help you to do so.

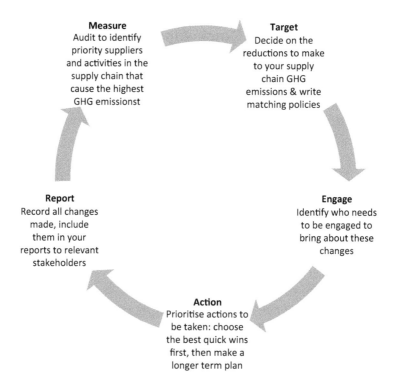

Figure 8.3 Implementation plan for procurement and supply-related GHG emissions.

The 'best' solutions will see the elimination of GHG emissions, and their causes. Moving in bulk and packing or producing locally will directly benefit emissions. Ensuring you eliminate packaging where possible and reusing packaging will further benefit. Short- to mid-term solutions will include the use of new technologies and zero emission vehicles. All of these will support your organisation's overall work, now and in the future.

Further Resources

On the companion website to this book, you can find further material to help you plan and implement this work.

HSBC –Seven steps to tackle a USD50 trillion challenge
https://www.hsbc.com/insight/topics/seven-steps-to-tackle-a-usd50-trillion-challenge
Located within the HSBC site is a report, **'Delivering Net Zero Supply Chains'** (Oct. 2021), written with BCG. In addition to identifying the scale of the opportunity and investments required, it provides insights and gives examples of sectors illustrating where the largest emissions are likely to be within the supply chain, supporting prioritisation.

Transform to Net Zero (TONZ): Buyer-supplier engagement to reduce Scope 3 emissions
https://transformtonetzero.org/resources/buyer-supplier-engagement-to-reduce-upstream-scope-3-emissions/
This guide, led by organisations such as Microsoft, Unilever and Nike, addresses how companies should prioritise suppliers for engagement, the incentives that can be offered, how to work within multiple layers of the supply chain, and how to enable measurement. Examples of work by organisations is provided to facilitate action.

Exponential roadmap initiative (ERI): 1.5°C business playbook
https://exponentialroadmap.org/business-playbook/
This provides insights and a layered approach to the implementation of strategy related to climate change and the 1.5°C commitment and transition. The second pillar of the playbook focuses specifically on work within the supply and value chains to drive the strategy forward. Key actions and measures for assessing reductions are provided.

Exponential roadmap initiative (ERI): 1.5°C Supplier Engagement Guide (SEG)

https://exponentialroadmap.org/supplier-engagement-guide/

Reference has been made in the main part of the chapter to the SEG and the work with suppliers contained within. It is mentioned again here as there are really good supplier engagement sections. Within the elements focused on 'dialogue' and 'support', you will find policy examples and templates for letters, supplier booklets, presentations, etc. that are tried and tested. Also check out the elements on 'recognition' that provide insight into how organisations have recognised the work of their suppliers and how this can motivate changes and the transition needed.

Route to Net Zero

https://logistics.org.uk/environment/netzero

This campaign was launched following COP26 in November 2021. It is a manifesto for future logistics and sets out steps that organisations, policy makers and governments can take to lead to the decarbonisation of logistics. It links in well with 'Road Freight Zero' mentioned in High-impact solutions, above.

GLEC Framework

https://www.smartfreightcentre.org/en/how-to-implement-items/what-is-glec-framework/58/

This is the only globally recognised methodology for harmonised calculation and reporting of the logistics footprint. It was developed by the GLEC, which is led by the Smart Freight Centre and large industry partners. The framework is aligned to the GHG Protocol standard and will support work related to new ISO standards produced for this area.

Notes

1. CIPS: https://www.cips.org/cips-for-individuals/what-is-procurement/
2. CDP, *CDP Global Supply Chain Report 2021*: https://cdn.cdp.net/cdp-production/cms/reports/documents/000/006/106/original/CDP_SC_Report_2021.pdf
3. GHG Protocol, *Technical Guidance for Calculating Scope 3 Emissions*: https://ghgprotocol.org/sites/default/files/ghgp/Scope3_Calculation_Guidance.pdf

4. GHG Protocol, WRI & WBCSD (2004) *The GHGP Corporate Accounting and Reporting Standard*. WRI and WBCSD, March, p. 26: https://ghgprotocol.org/corporate-standard

5. Ellen MacArthur Foundation, *Circular Economy Procurement Framework*: https://emf.gitbook.io/circular-procurement/-MB3yM1RMC1i8iNc-VYj/overview

6. WEF, *Circular Economy and Material Value Chains*: https://www.weforum.org/projects/circular-economy

7. Ellen MacArthur Foundation, *Overview*: https://ellenmacarthurfoundation.org/topics/circular-economy-introduction/overview

8. Hasanbeigi A, Becque R and Springer C (2019) *Curbing Carbon from Consumption: The role of Green Public Procurement*. San Francisco CA: Global Efficiency Intelligence

9. Scottish Government (2021) *Advice and Guidance*: https://www.gov.scot/publications/taking-account-of-climate-and-circular-economy-considerations-in-public-procurement-sppn-1–2021/

10. The Carbon Trust: https://www.carbontrust.com/what-we-do/measure-and-evaluate/value-chain-and-supply-chain-sustainability

11. Deloitte, *Scope 1, 2 and 3 emissions*: https://www2.deloitte.com/uk/en/focus/climate-change/zero-in-on-scope-1–2-and-3-emissions.html

12. Boston Consulting Group (2021) *Supply chains as a game-changer*: https://www.bcg.com/en-gb/publications/2021/fighting-climate-change-with-supply-chain-decarbonization

13. Based on the following paper: Marinello S, Balugani E & Gamberini R (2021) Coffee capsule impacts and recovery techniques: A literature review. *Packaging Technology and Science*, 34(11–12), pp. 665–682

14. McKinsey & Company (2021) *Making supply-chain decarbonization happen*: https://www.mckinsey.com/business-functions/operations/our-insights/making-supply-chain-decarbonization-happen

15. Böge (1993) *Registration and evaluation of transportation by means of product-related transportation analysis*: http://www.stefanie-boege.de/texte/yogurtengl.pdf

16. European Commission, *Reducing CO_2 emissions from heavy duty vehicles*: https://ec.europa.eu/clima/eu-action/transport-emissions/road-transport-reducing-co2-emissions-vehicles/reducing-co2-emissions-heavy-duty-vehicles_en

17. European Commission, *Reducing CO₂ emissions from aviation:* https://ec. europa.eu/clima/eu-action/transport-emissions/reducing-emissions-aviation_en
18. BCG (2020) *Your Supply Chain Needs a Sustainability Strategy*: https:// www.bcg.com/publications/2020/supply-chain-needs-sustainability-strategy
19. Ellen MacArthur Foundation, *Closing the look on single-use food packaging*: https://ellenmacarthurfoundation.org/circular-examples/closing-the-loop-on-single-use-food-packaging
20. Mackie's: https://www.mackies.co.uk/about-mackies/environment/
21. EC, *Reducing CO₂ Emissions from Heavy Duty Vehicles*: https://ec.europa.eu/ clima/eu-action/transport-emissions/road-transport-reducing-co2-emissions-vehicles/reducing-co2-emissions-heavy-duty-vehicles_en
22. WEF/McKinsey (2021) *Road Freight Zero*: https://www3.weforum.org/ docs/WEF_RFZ_Pathways_to_faster_adoption_of_zero_emission_trucks_2021.pdf
23. The Exponential Climate Action Roadmap (2018): https:// exponentialroadmap.org/wp-content/uploads/2018/09/Exponential-Climate-Action-Roadmap-September-2018.pdf
24. Edie (2022) *Tesco fits HGV refrigeration trailers with solar panels*: https://www. edie.net/tesco-fits-hgvs-refrigeration-trailers-with-solar-panels/
25. WEF/McKinsey (2021) *Road Freight Zero*: https://www3.weforum.org/ docs/WEF_RFZ_Pathways_to_faster_adoption_of_zero_emission_trucks_2021.pdf
26. BCG, *Supply Chains as a Game-Changer in the Fight Against Climate Change*: https://www.bcg.com/publications/2021/fighting-climate-change-with-supply-chain-decarbonization
27. WEF, *7 Ways Packaging is Changing to Reduce Plastics Waste*: https://www. weforum.org/agenda/2020/12/sustainable-packaging-reduce-plastic-waste/
28. Plastics Pollution Cooalition, *Eight Solutions for the Earthshot Prize 2022*: https://www.plasticpollutioncoalition.org/blog/2022-earthshot-prize-nominees
29. NTU: https://www.ntu.ac.uk/about-us/sustainability/sustainability-in-action/food
30. Unilever, *Rethinking plastic packaging*: https://www.unilever.com/planet-and-society/waste-free-world/rethinking-plastic-packaging/

31. CIPS (2021) *Four supply chain barriers to the circular economy*: https://www.cips.org/supply-management/news/2021/april/four-supply-chain-barriers-to-the-circular-economy/

32. TerraCycle: https://www.terracycle.com/en-US/select-country

33. CDP (2021) *Engaging the chain*: https://www.cdp.net/en/research/global-reports/engaging-the-chain

34. CDP (2020) *Transparency to Transformation – a chain reaction*: https://www.cdp.net/en/research/global-reports/transparency-to-transformation

35. GHGP, Value Chain Accounting and Reporting Standard: https://ghgprotocol.org/sites/default/files/standards/Corporate-Value-Chain-Accounting-Reporing-Standard_041613_2.pdf

36. GHGP, Supplier Engagement Guidance: https://ghgprotocol.org/sites/default/files/standards_supporting/Supplier%20Engagement%20Guidance.pdf

37. ERI, *1.5°C Supplier Engagement Guide*: https://exponentialroadmap.org/supplier-engagement-guide/

38. BCG (2020) *Your supply chain needs a sustainability strategy*: https://www.bcg.com/publications/2020/supply-chain-needs-sustainability-strategy

39. Unilever, *Working with Suppliers to Beat Climate Change*: https://www.unilever.com/news/news-search/2021/working-with-suppliers-to-beat-the-clock-on-climate-change/

40. Gov.UK, *Transitioning to Zero Emissions Cars and Vans*: https://www.gov.uk/government/publications/transitioning-to-zero-emission-cars-and-vans-2035-delivery-plan

41. Logistics UK: https://logistics.org.uk/environment/netzero and WEF and McKinsey: https://www3.weforum.org/docs/WEF_RFZ_Pathways_to_faster_adoption_of_zero_emission_trucks_2021.pdf

42. Forbes (2021): https://www.forbes.com/sites/adigaskell/2021/10/31/employees-demand-that-we-become-more-sustainable/?sh=6eaae2c73f80

9

MARKETING FOR A BETTER CLIMATE

Richard Howarth and Fiona Winfield

Climate change and marketing are closely related, not least because of the greenhouse gas (GHG) emissions from the production and consumption of products and services, throughout their use and life cycle. It is also fair to say that while organisations and customers are expressing interest in the effects of climate change, action to address related concerns has not always been evident and some businesses have been accused of 'greenwashing'. Hence, ways to ensure climate action is embedded will be explored, alongside core considerations in this important area for marketers.

This chapter is for you if:

- You work in marketing or are interested in marketing's role with respect to climate change
- You want to take action related to climate change, but are unsure where to start

DOI: 10.4324/9781003274049-11

- You are seeking to connect elements of the marketing mix to climate change
- You want more guidance and examples to support decision-making in this area.

It will cover:

- Core definitions and marketing tools, and their links to climate change
- The role of customers
- The importance of 'value' for customers and wider society in relation to climate change
- Action beyond the core products and services and the potential climate benefits.

Supporting Net Zero plans

McKinsey identifies that organisations and brands are building climate change action into their marketing strategies and committing to Net Zero or Net Positive plans.[1] This is not surprising given that according to Deloitte more than 200 of the world's largest companies predict climate change will cost each of them US$1 trillion in the years to come.[2]

In addition to the reduction in production-related GHG emissions, potential benefits arise when climate action is built into organisational and marketing strategies including:

- Improved product and packaging solutions, which reduce or eliminate the climate-harming materials
- Better designed products and packaging, with potential cost savings due to associated reductions in resources, energy use and consequently fewer GHG emissions
- Reductions in waste from supply through to use, and beyond
- Innovations in the form of new products, packaging and production as well as sourcing processes
- Communicating with customers in a more climate-friendly way.

Such changes lead to the creation and delivery of value to customers in a wider sense, supporting:

- A reduction in climate, societal and business risks which can build resilience
- Product solutions that effectively address customer requirements and desire to reduce their own climate impact
- Progress towards the business' targets, plans and purpose-driven strategies
- A brand's ethical or sustainable positioning and the associated advantages
- Improved engagement with employees and attraction of new talent
- Wider benefits that flow from the activities of 'first movers' and trail blazers, who motivate others – organisations and customers – to prioritise action in this area.

Action cannot come soon enough for many organisations as research in 2021 identified that within a year, 3 in 5 customers would start boycotting brands that failed to address climate change.[3] Gen Z customers are of particular importance due to their awareness and commitment to action. For many, the availability of social media will continue to be a driving force in awareness and change, and it is a prime means for 'calling out' organisations and holding them to account.

Sadly, some businesses are guilty of 'greenwashing', by hiding or mis-representing information, or making unsubstantiated claims about the extent to which they are sustainable, which if found to be untrue are likely to contravene existing consumer law in some parts of the world. In the United Kingdom, the Competition and Markets Authority (CMA) issued guidance in 2021 in the form of its Green Claims Code,[4] which followed similar activity in Australia and the EU. The CMA's associated campaign[5] includes a quiz to help businesses understand whether they are within the law or not, and during 2022, the CMA is carrying out a full review and states that it is ready to take action against offending firms.

Using the Chartered Institute of Marketing (CIM) definition as the basis, we know that *satisfying* customers' needs and *identifying* and *anticipating* their *requirements* are key issues for marketers.[6] Added to this, the emphasis of the American Marketing Association (AMA) is that benefits and solutions associated with products and services on offer must have *value for customers, clients, partners and society at large.*[7]

Building on the above, definitions of *sustainable* marketing recognise the importance of value for customers and their situation in a wider context. They also mention *consumption behaviour and business practices* and the management of *environmental harm, quality of life* (QOL) and the *well-being* of stakeholders, now and in the future.[8] This last point recognises the importance of 'value', within the broader global context, which may well change over time.

There is a clear role here for organisations, not only through their operations and practices, but through their engagement and assessment of the fairness and equity evident in the 'value' that is exchanged and how that happens. A range of opportunities and outcomes will also result from customer concerns about climate change; see Figure 9.1 for more detail.

The field of social marketing is important to climate too, as it links to communications and is designed to influence behaviour change and support more positive actions. These might include not leaving devices on stand-by, or turning down a thermostat to reduce GHG emissions and costs.

Any concerns that customers and society may have about climate change will influence their understanding of the wider context and their own personal situation. This in turn influences perceptions of the likely benefits to be gained from different products or brands, and the solutions provided. Customers may be led to make certain consumption-related sacrifices, with people forgoing options perceived to be less climate-friendly. Alternatively, they may simply consume less, considering this to be more climate-conscious.[9] The key message for any marketer is to bear the above in mind, and ensure it is easy for your customers to understand options and take appropriate action.[10]

The next section is organised around the traditional 4Ps of the marketing mix, as this provides a useful framework for marketing decisions. It is also central to understanding the *creation of value* (via Product and Price) and the *delivery of value* (via Place and Promotion). As all marketers will know, it is essential to recognise that value is not something simply embedded within a product or service, it is based on the customer's perception; it is personal, depends on the context and can vary over time or through experience.[11]

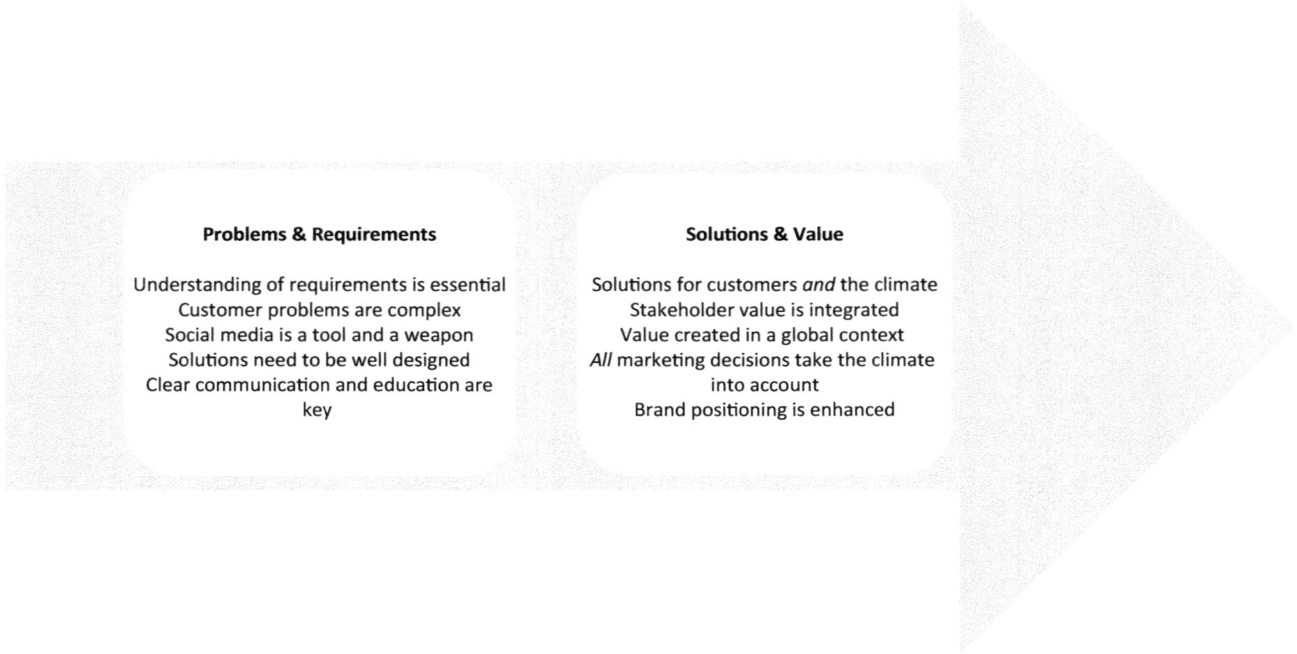

Problems & Requirements

Understanding of requirements is essential
Customer problems are complex
Social media is a tool and a weapon
Solutions need to be well designed
Clear communication and education are key

Solutions & Value

Solutions for customers *and* the climate
Stakeholder value is integrated
Value created in a global context
All marketing decisions take the climate into account
Brand positioning is enhanced

Figure 9.1 Solving customers' climate problems through better marketing.

Creating value: product design and price setting, with the climate in mind

Whatever the **Product**, there will be climate-related impacts from its production, the supply and value chain, the consumption of the product and, ultimately, its treatment at the end of life.

As noted on the Ellen MacArthur Foundation website,[12] *[i]n our current economy, we take materials from the Earth, make products from them, and eventually throw them away as waste — the process is linear. In a circular economy, by contrast, we stop waste being produced in the first place.*

The circular economy is based on three principles, driven by design:

- *Eliminate waste and pollution*
- *Circulate products and materials (at their highest value)*
- *Regenerate nature.*

As an example, the Fashion Task Force, part of the Sustainable Markets Initiative (SMI), promotes a manifesto for regenerative fashion which embraces the three principles mentioned above. It seeks to ensure fashion is closed-loop and directly reduces the climate impacts through its life cycle.[13]

Linked to the product element of the mix, any packaging used performs an important role (whether it is for protection or presentation). Packaging is often essential, but it is important not to send mixed or muddled messages. For example, an organic or Fair Trade product wrapped in layers of packaging composed of different materials probably won't be easy to separate, compost or recycle. From the customer perspective, the packaging may be judged as unnecessary or inappropriate. Solutions will need thinking through carefully to ensure value is created, but not then being reduced through poor design and choices. There can also be confusion in the minds of customers with a proliferation of environmental labels on products, more than 450 worldwide.[14] Product labels are important for communication, noted in chapter 3 (Communication & Reporting) and packaging considerations are covered in more depth in chapter 8 (Procurement & Supply).

Price is an important aspect of value for the customer and how the product or service is perceived. It is much more than just the cost of the product itself. The effective use of price is a way to communicate value to customers in a market, and the organisation must first identify and understand its customers and their priorities. Without this, it will be hard to establish what is important to them, and what influences their choices related to climate change and mismatches may occur as a result.

To pull these two aspects of the marketing mix together, we will look at the example of Boots (the British health and beauty retailer and pharmacy chain) and their wet wipes.[15] The company has made commitments and taken clear action when it comes to the development of their products vis-à-vis climate change and have pledged to be completely Carbon Neutral by 2040.[16] Boots has maintained its value price point whilst removing plastic from its baby wipes (replacing them with FSC certified viscose) and focusing on the reuse and refilling of products and extending product life spans. It is also rolling out its toiletry packaging recycling initiative.[17]

Delivering value: place and promotion – forces for climate solutions?

How products are made available relates to **Place** (location and distribution) and the consideration of convenience – a major driver in many markets for a lot of people and companies, and it may influence their purchases. Even if there is no pressure from customers, some organisations may still seek to minimise their GHG emissions as they realise it's the right thing to do.

Of relevance will be decisions relating to how products and services are delivered – via physical stores (bricks and mortar) or online, or a combination of the two. Although internet shopping may be seen as more convenient and may appear to be more climate-friendly (it reduces the need for a physical presence and for customers and employees to travel, thereby reducing GHG emissions[18]), this may not in reality be the case.

For example, because products are more widely available through the internet, and customers more aware of what's on offer, selling online might actually:

- Create extra demand from customers not reached before
- Lead to products being moved over longer distances (global not local)
- Fuel consumerism, with people simply purchasing more.

While this is great for a business, the extra GHG emissions may be problematic from a customer, wider society and stakeholder perspective.

A specific challenge related to shopping online and distribution is the 'last mile' – the delivery or transportation from the last 'hub' to its final destination.[19] Consumers are increasingly wanting more control over when their parcels are delivered, and some suppliers are seeking innovative solutions through the use of drones and automated vehicles, or a subscription model for next day delivery.[20] Many efficiencies achieved further up the chain of supply (such as through bulk movement of goods) can be lost if the number of small local trips potentially increases.

Issues relating to other aspects of 'Place', including transportation and location of production, proximity to the market, routing and logistics in general, are important. These are also covered in chapter 8 (Procurement & Supply).

If carried out effectively, **Promotion** facilitates the connection between target customers and suppliers of relevant solutions, through raising awareness and facilitating action. This also links to chapter 3 (Communication & Reporting).

For all organisations, promotion and associated communications should:

- **Emphasise the benefits**: if customers are unaware of the climate benefits of a product, they might be less likely to consider buying it.
- **Differentiate through positioning**: climate impacts might be part of the selection and choice criteria, conscious or sub-conscious, perhaps wrapped up in quality and price evaluations and how the product is perceived. Recognition of these can ensure there are appropriately tailored and targeted communications.
- **Reinforce**: customers receive many messages through different channels – there's a lot of 'noise' as a result and the potential for an organisation's core message to be undermined. Reinforcement can come through eco-labelling, pricing strategy, messaging on packaging and other communications. It's important to note here that communication methods have different GHG emissions too. For example, in the United Kingdom, a small catalogue printed and posted to every household is calculated as 2 kg CO_2e emissions per item, versus 17 g CO_2e for one long email.[21] It will be important to recognise such impacts in the selection of the communication channel.

- **Persuade the audience to respond and behave in a certain way**: it will be important to ensure stakeholders are aware of the global importance of climate change and the benefits of your products offered, the solutions they provide, and so on. Messages about GHG emissions and the climate are no different from other communications – they must reflect an understanding of customer requirements and what they value, and should be targeted at specific customer segments.

It is evident that promotion and communication facilitate awareness, and support education and learning. This is particularly important when linked to climate change and GHG emissions, and the attempt to influence. Noise (too many different or conflicting messages, for example) should be avoided, as it can be a barrier, and the messaging should not undermine what the organisation is seeking to communicate, about themselves or the products and services they offer.

WANT TO DIG DEEPER?

Sustainable Brands: https://sustainablebrands.com/
Edie: https://www.edie.net/
Two examples of news and information services which provide free and regular updates on legislation and organisations taking action related to climate change. Useful for understanding, direction and inspiration when it comes to current and upcoming topics.

Sustainable Marketing: How to Drive Profits with Purpose – book by Michelle Carvill, Gemma Butler and Geraint Evans (2021)
A very practitioner-oriented book that has been written by practitioners. It provides contemporary industry insights into sustainable marketing practice and each chapter offers viable action points for improving an organisation's work related to sustainability.

Chartered Institute of Marketing (CIM) – Content Hub
https://www.cim.co.uk/content-hub/
The CIM is the leading professional body for marketing and marketers. It has a strong focus on sustainability and the content hub contains useful materials and updates. The CIM runs webinars and training, and

offers professional recognition in a range of areas relevant to marketers, including sustainable marketing.

Accenture and World Economic Forum: Shaping the Sustainable Organization
https://www.accenture.com/gb-en/insights/sustainability/sustainable-organization
This report, a collaboration between Accenture and the WEF's Young Global Leaders and Global Shapers communities, looks at the overall role of responsible leaders in creating lasting value and equitable impact for all stakeholders.

High-impact solutions

This may seem obvious, but it is important to recognise that climate change requires most organisations to re-think marketing and their customer requirements, not least because of the global context and the fact that we are facing an emergency. The products and services you produce help customers solve their problems, so as always in marketing, it is imperative that you focus on identifying your customers and understanding their current and future problems, and as a result, their requirements.

Choosing the best high-impact climate solutions to be integrated into your marketing strategy, and ultimately your marketing mix, will depend on the sector you're in and your type of organisation. So our first question is: **what should be our marketing strategy for climate action?**

Only then will it be possible to break down your plan into the different elements of the marketing mix and consider how the value you create may be impacted or enhanced by your Products and Services and their Price. The second question is therefore: **are we creating value through a climate-responsible product offer?** Followed by the third question: **what is the impact on price for products that are more climate-friendly?**

The last two questions relate to the delivery of value created via Place and Promotion, with the fourth being: **how do we offer the benefits of online shopping while minimising harm to the climate?** And finally: **are we maximising the climate benefits of our communications?**

What should be our marketing strategy for climate action?

A key element of your marketing strategy will be identifying and understanding your customers, their behaviour, their problems and consequently their requirements. When these are clearly understood, it is possible to align them to the benefits offered by your organisation and its product and service offerings.

However, even if you have a good understanding of your customer base already, it might not yet include climate change attitudes, perceptions and behaviours. With COP27 in November 2022, increased discussion around Net Zero, and public awareness of climate-related disasters over the last few years, it is likely that many more people are starting to think more deeply about the whole topic. This may in turn affect their decision-making, but even though your customers may have good intentions, these will not always result in an immediate change in behaviour.

In respect of climate change and associated customer motivations and behaviour, there are resources available to help you understand your customer segmentation. While customers can be grouped in many different ways, and traditionally demographics have featured heavily in both business and consumer marketing, recent work identifies the predominance of behaviour as the prime means of segmentation in relation to climate change.[22] However, with behaviour being only one dimension, you will probably also require insights into exactly 'who' your customers are, and 'why' they do what they do, based on psychographics.

Back in 2008, the UK government (via DEFRA) published work exploring customer attitudes and pro-environmental behaviour.[23] Although it was written some years ago and is UK-based, it is still a useful resource to understand how the research was undertaken and the insights gained. This included the underpinning behaviours and strategies, and the interventions considered relevant for different segments; it may therefore provide some useful pointers.

The Yale Programme on Climate Change Communication also produces a range of publications and insights.[24] Again territory specific, it offers detailed insight into climate opinions and consumer activism on global warming, and what drives and informs this. It also integrates segmentation based on the 'Six Americas', which illustrates current and likely responses to climate change for different groups. As with DEFRA's work, this can be useful to prompt your thinking, and it is likely to provide new insights and could be a vehicle for reviewing current approaches and understanding.

Specialist organisations like Crobox[25] can also support. This comes as a result of their discussion of the role of psychographic segmentation and examples of its use. Please also see the Smart Insights website. While the latter relates to digital marketing strategy, it has some useful free tools and templates.[26] These sources alone are unlikely to provide a ready-made solution for your organisation, but they will hopefully give you inspiration, support improvements to your understanding of what your customers want, and assist you in selecting your approach to segmentation, targeting and your organisation's positioning.

By way of an example, Unilever has developed its climate action strategy and goals.[27] The strategy sets the scene for how the organisation is addressing the climate, environmental and wider sustainability impacts of its products and processes. It puts in place priorities, plans and targets for the management of its GHG emissions, and the associated roadmap articulates clear outcomes. These climate action goals include commitments to:

- Achieve Net Zero emissions by 2039 (relating to Scopes 1, 2 and 3)
- Reduce Scope 1 and 2 emissions by 100% by 2030, compared to a baseline of 2015 (interim goal to reduce by 70% by 2025)
- Halve the full value chain emissions of its products by 2030, against a 2010 baseline.

These targets are supported by innovation and redesign of products, their packaging and the use of concentrated liquids to reduce transport emissions, supported by clear messaging and further marketing impacts. If any of the terms used above, such as Scopes, are unclear, please refer to chapter 12 (Carbon Accounting) for more information.

For some organisations, depending on their existing priorities and those of their customers, climate and GHG impacts may not currently be high on the agenda. In which case, insights developed above will be essential in helping prioritise and forming future marketing strategy. Having decided on priorities as an organisation and having defined a clear marketing strategy (based on research and evidence) it will be essential to review your current tactical and marketing mix approaches, which leads us into the next four questions.

Are we creating value through a climate-responsible product offer?

In analysing what your customers *really* value and need, and creating your overall strategy and climate action goals, there are various options open to you.

As stated earlier, awareness of climate change may affect people's attitudes and alter their behaviour, leading to lower consumption rates, alternative product choices or even boycotting certain brands.

As a result, you could decide to:

- **Stop** offering certain products and services altogether, if their emissions are too difficult to reduce or eliminate
- **Change** your product offering, so it emits fewer greenhouse gases
- **Encourage** your customers to buy less.

The first option might seem extreme, but it's happening already in the United Kingdom in respect of new petrol and diesel cars/vans (the sale of which will be ended by 2030, with all new ones being fully zero emission ZE by 2035).[28] Organisations in sectors impacted by these changes are therefore having to come up with innovations. These include the use of zero or lower emissions technologies, innovations in terms of materials employed, and the effectiveness of the batteries available and used. Some vehicles, such as the VW ID. Buzz van have bidirectional charging, for example. This means the battery is used as a power source when travelling, and when back at base, energy from the battery can be fed into the owner's home.[29] Wider customer requirements are recognised and solved through a more integrated product solution, with climate benefits.

It may be more feasible to encourage your customers to buy fewer, better quality products with lower GHG emissions. Or encourage your customers to use their products for longer, have them repaired or return them to be repurposed. For example, clothing companies such as Finisterre UK provide product repair and end of life returns services linked to the wider Reskinned initiative, where the company *repurposes old gear for new adventures.*[30] Turtle Doves is another British company, which *specialises in using post-consumer [cashmere] waste to create beautiful new garments and accessories.*[31] These extra services and benefits extend the life of products or reuse, upcycle or recycle them, ensuring material use is maximised. Depending on the scheme, customers either pay a fixed cost for repairs, receive a set fee or a free product.

Another option is to introduce an alternative more climate-friendly product such as the plant-based burgers marketed by Beyond Meat, whose vision is to 'feed a better future'. Their burgers have been calculated to emit 90% fewer GHG emissions than the traditional US quarter-pounder, using significantly less water, land and energy.[32]

Finally, your organisation may simply continue to produce in the same quantity, while eliminating, reducing and managing the GHG emissions through your products' life cycles. This may be possible by changing processes or using alternative or recycled materials. Whether this results, for example, in actions such as the use of recycled plastic water bottles in the production of underwear, fleeces, carpets and lampshades, recycled stainless steel to make new water bottles, old fishing nets to make skateboards, or plant-based materials such as potato starch instead of traditional plastic, the choice will be yours. See 'Further Resources' below for more inspiration.

What is the impact on price for products that are more climate-friendly?

When it comes to climate change, setting an appropriate price is not straightforward because, as in any situation, price is a key element in your *creation of value*. It is core to the perception of value in your market by your customers, and is not just the amount for money paid for a product or service.

There needs to be clarity and consistency in what you do in relation to your product offer and pricing, so customers are neither confused nor misled. Your positioning must recognise and reflect:

- Your customer expectations
- Their sensitivity to changes in your pricing and to any different benefits offered
- The willingness of your customers to pay more for these, or the expectation to pay less.

Sensitivity related to your pricing decisions will reflect the nature and category of your product. It also reflects the loyalty shown, and therefore the strategies you deploy to maintain and enhance relationships.

With respect to climate change, the perception of the value created will be grounded in an understanding of how 'fair' your price is. This might reflect your customers' awareness of the costs involved in making GHG emission improvements, along with their expectations of what a product costs to produce and how much it is worth to them. There is unlikely to be a simple, straightforward answer, so research and insights into their opinions will be necessary.

Aside from understanding what your customers are willing to pay, and recognising the importance of your costs and expected margins, you may also consider what your competitors charge for a comparable product. You may decide to match your competitors' prices, even though your costs have been reduced due to a reduction in your carbon footprint, thereby maximising your profit margin. Or, if your costs have increased overall, you may decide to increase your prices. The 'right' decision will depend on your customers and their likely behaviour, as well as your brand's positioning, informed by appropriate insights and your strategy.

If you change your price because of the different costs associated with GHG emission reductions, it would be good to provide information to your stakeholders related to the benefits associated with lower emissions. This will either reassure your customers that your product solution is of greater value, or that it will still meet their requirements and is of a comparable quality, if it costs less.

You may also consider other price-based approaches that reduce climate impacts and provide benefits for customers too. For example, Zipcar provides many of the benefits associated with car ownership, but on a 'pay per use' basis. A clear understanding of the likely response from customers would be needed. It is worth noting that despite not using a product for the majority of the time, the perceived benefits of ownership may outweigh any cost savings. Please also see the case study relating to electric vehicles (EV) and salary sacrifice in chapter 8 (Procurement & Supply).

How do we offer the benefits of online shopping while minimising harm to the climate?

We take a focused look in this section at both place and climate impacts related to online shopping. We recognise this may not be relevant to all organisations, but it's a large challenge in different markets, so is used as an example. As with any element of the marketing mix, you will need to think through the implications of your decisions, not only on your operations and the climate, but also on your targeted customers.

With respect to online shopping, in addition to the impacts from packaging, as mentioned earlier, there will be 'last mile' and other logistics impacts linked to consumer behaviour. These may be as a result of:

- **Missed deliveries**: perhaps due to issues of flexibility, delivery slots and tracking
- **Increased levels of purchase**: customers may initially buy more to try on items at home or buy products speculatively, as it's convenient to return unwanted items, possibly without cost
- **A higher level of returns**: these are estimated to be double to quadruple that of physical stores.[33]

There may be opportunities for your organisation when it comes to operating online, but there will be clear challenges related to GHG emissions for the reasons listed above. These are exacerbated if your customers prioritise convenience over your own organisation's route and space optimisation plans, for example. It is therefore important to understand the conflicting priorities of the different parties involved.

Various options are available, and it is best to focus on what you currently do and your customers' requirements, but also think about how changes can support reductions or the elimination of emissions and impacts. Given the need to balance all of these, it will be appropriate for you to explore options that may include:

- **Interconnectedness of freight activities across providers**: data and insights will be key and will also benefit your GHG accounting and reporting. It makes sense to optimise the vehicle space available to you, or you are able to make available to others. You should also consider reverse logistics; in other words, what happens when products are returned, and whether they are recycled, repaired or re-distributed.[34]

- **Flexibility and transparency of delivery**: this should be a win-win situation, as it should address the number of failed or missed deliveries, thereby providing greater value to customers *and* reducing GHG emissions.
- **Transparent delivery costs via pricing**: you could signal the true level (and therefore cost) of greenhouse gases and other impacts linked to the delivery timings, methods and returns. You may wish to encourage slower delivery time scales and methods, with lower GHG levels. These should encourage customers to appreciate and acknowledge the impacts at the point of purchase, which may reduce speculative ordering, unnecessary extra purchases and returns. However, this will probably only work if all operators follow suit, otherwise competitors may appear to have an advantage through price, which will doubtless be valued by some customers over climate and GHG emissions benefits. Your organisation could potentially collaborate with others, perhaps creating temporary or mobile hubs within hubs for example. The key thing is that it's best to ensure customers are aware of the extent of the impacts of the deliveries in the first place.
- **Local fulfilment and inventory**: you may be able to gain advantage alone or by working with others by sharing spaces and technologies. Perhaps organisations that are not close competitors have physical resources closer to your customers which could be used. This might include another organisation's store as a micro hub.
- **Embracing new technologies**: there is clear potential here including zero emissions (ZE) vans or e-bikes, or even drones for your deliveries. At the very least, you could investigate using climate-friendly transportation such as bikes and scooters. The 'last mile' delivery report cited above suggests there is progress to be made in this area as, in the case of food deliveries for example, only 5% from 54 million miles travelled were by pedal bike. Other technologies available may include local manufacturing and supply, perhaps supported by local 3D printing.

- **Adoption of the latest refrigeration and vehicle technologies**: this may be a challenge for your organisation, depending on your size and where you are within the supply chain. Many operators in the 'last mile' space work on very low margins, hence, limited resources to invest in newer technologies. This may therefore need to be a longer-term consideration.

A single solution is unlikely to suit all organisations, all products or all customers. It will be important to explore the options, and to understand the climate and customer implications, in order to make appropriate choices.

Are we maximising the climate benefits of our communications?

Until recently the GHG emissions of different channels and media had not been fully considered or even recognised by many organisations. It is now increasingly understood that such choices have different impacts, and action is needed to address the direct and wider GHG emissions of the decisions you make. In the United Kingdom, for example, you can gain support from organisations such as the Advertising Association (AA). Working with the IPA (Institute of Practitioners in Advertising) and ISBA (the Incorporated Society of British Advertisers), the AA has established Ad Net Zero. The aim is to raise awareness, provide education and training, and offer tools to support advertising campaigns in relation to their climate impacts.[35] Even if you are not UK-based, there are useful suggestions that could be applied elsewhere.

In your selection and use of different channels and media, you will need to challenge the status quo and current behaviour in your organisation, and perhaps in the wider industry. Take for example, the work to re-cognise the climate and wider impacts of the different Fashion Weeks (which are core to fashion brand promotions, both B2B and B2C). If current habits regarding seasons and the desire to have the latest designs and colours are not challenged, and the impacts are not understood, then little progress will be achieved.[36]

The role of communication in awareness raising and behaviour change will also affect the messages you develop and how they are communicated.

Chapter 3 (Communication & Reporting) looks specifically at internal and external climate change communications, the impacts from the narrative you weave, the various tools you employ and the role of social media. With focus again on your target customers and your positioning, and the purpose of your communications, clear decisions will need to be made.

Some companies, for example Patagonia in 2011, have actively encouraged customers through their advertisements and communications to consume less. They intentionally timed their 'Don't Buy This Jacket' campaign to coincide with Black Friday.[37] This highlighted the impacts of clothing on the climate and the environment, with the need for consumers to take steps to consume less (or at least make more thoughtful choices). The timing was deliberate, to highlight the excessive consumption encouraged by events such as Black Friday, and this could apply to other public holidays and celebrations.

The key thing to remember here is that customers may be overloaded and feel bombarded by the messages they receive about the climate from a variety of organisations, whether suitably crafted and targeted or not. Feeling overwhelmed, they may judge messages from some organisations to be excessive. While sending out fewer messages may be perceived as better for the climate, your product's climate benefits may then be overlooked. We return to the fact that you need a good understanding of your customers, their product and communication requirements and their commitment and loyalty to your organisation. Finding the right balance will be crucial.

Case study

The case study below provides some insights into how an organisation, in this case a hotel, has used the improvements they have made with respect to their GHG emissions as an intrinsic part of their offer. It focuses on the marketing practices of an eco-conscious boutique hotel located in Bournemouth, England, known as one of the most 'sustainable in the UK'. We explore the marketing methods used by the Green House Hotel to tell their story and show potential customers the beauty and the integrity that they have in the practice of their hospitality.

Green is the colour of hospitality! The marketing of the Green House Hotel[38]

By Tammi Sinha (IT Continuous Improvement Lead, University of Southampton)

According to the Green House Hotel's General Manager: *on the face of it, [it] is simply a beautifully restored, 32-room Grade II Victorian villa in the heart of Bournemouth, perfectly nestled between Dorset's finest blue-flag golden beaches and the ancient mysteries of the New Forest. Dig a little deeper, however, and you'll discover that we eat, sleep and breathe sustainability. So much so that we've been recognised as one of the world's top eco-hotels. After a painstaking 18-month refurbishment during which we considered the environmental impact of every single decision we made, we opened in April 2010 to rave reviews. The awards have been rolling in ever since.*

Marketing has changed. Consumers have changed. The practices of telling the story of product, place and purpose have moved online. Digital marketing is pivotal in getting the stories, branding and messages out to potential customers and retaining them.

Digital marketing

Digital marketing is the use of multiple digital strategies and tactics, using multiple channels to connect with customers, in the multiverse, where they spend a large amount of time. TikTok, Instagram, LinkedIn, Facebook, Twitter, web pages and targeted emails all have a part to play.

What is sustainable digital marketing? As consumers we are expecting a great deal more from our suppliers of goods and services. Survey results vary, but a consensus has emerged that internet users have moved their product loyalties based on their ethical and sustainability views. Being Good and Green makes business sense. Yelling about it through your storytelling and marketing makes even better sense. In this respect it is a win-win.

Sustainable digital marketing

If we go back to basics, sustainable development, as defined by the Brundtland Commission in 1987, is *development that meets the needs of the present without compromising the ability of future generations to meet their own needs.* In essence how does the Green House Hotel attract, convert and retain its customers in the real world and the digital world in a way that does not compromise future generations and the planet.

Tactics and strategies for marketing the Eco credentials of the Green House Hotel

As an eco-hotel, they have chosen the following for their marketing phases:

ATTRACT

The website has been designed to be beautiful, calming and easy to navigate. Highlighting their eco credentials, starting with food! A great place to show carbon literacy and carbon reduction strategies. It is easy to click and book, and details are available for calls and emails. The link to an event catches your attention and hooks you in. The tag line of '**Serious about luxury, passionate about sustainability**' embeds this approach.

The general manager adds: *essentially, we are taking a responsible attitude to our carbon footprint by making decisions that are the best we can at the present time to mitigate our effect on the environment. Our marketing is a subtle message that says to customers that it is possible to have a boutique hotel experience that is environmentally conscious. We always do our best when it comes to sustainability, and there's always more we can do, we're not saying we're perfect, and we don't want to lecture our guests on what we are doing or ask them to compare our green credentials to other hotels either. What we do want is for our guests to sleep easy knowing that we are constantly thinking about how we can do this even better, how we can be even more sustainable. As far as marketing is concerned, we try to do as much as we can online and social media is a strong focus of ours going forward.*

CONVERT

This then leads to 'convert'. You can book online or via platforms such as booking.com, increasing 'footfall'. Online platforms enable data analytics about what works and what doesn't. The top link is environment, enabling potential customers to uncover the headline of 'the greenest hotel in the UK' telling the story of energy efficiency, free EV charging, reuse of towels and the nature of the built environment, for example.

RETAIN

Reviews are a key element of marketing. Checking out feedback on TripAdvisor, the hotel is rated (at the time of writing) 7th out of 66 hotels in their locality, with an average of 4.5/5. The credentials described in marketing need to be experienced to retain customers.

The Green House Hotel focuses on telling the story, sharing its credentials and finding the 'hook' to attract customers, and to bring them back.

Source locally: Reduce, Reuse, Re-cycle: Consider what comes in and what goes out: Insist on high welfare standards: Be transparent, open and honest: Sustainable marketing
According to marketing guru Philip Kotler, *the concept of sustainable marketing holds that an organization should meet the needs of its present consumers without compromising the ability of future generations to fulfil their own needs.*[39] This presents a tension, marketers craft messages and content to attract, convert and retain customers. The changing nature of customers and their expectations for sustainable solutions may be key. When organisations want to sing about their eco credentials they need to link people, planet and profit together to serve those customers who are interested and passionate in supporting businesses in this space.

Dr. Tammi Sinha is IT Continuous Improvement Lead at University of Southampton, working to facilitate principles of lean and the circular economy within professional services. Tammi was previously a senior lecturer in operations and project management at Solent University, and the Director for Climate Action at the University of Winchester. She has worked in higher education (HE) for over 20 years and her PhD is in operations strategy. Her aim is to weave continuous improvement and sustainability into the operational excellence area of work within HE and leads external CI and Sustainability communities of practice. She is involved in the Carbon Literacy Project, the Help to Grow programme for businesses, and serves on Hampshire County Council's expert panel for climate.

Quick Wins

1. Prioritise your activity based on insights – specifically those relating to your customers and their requirements and use these to inform your marketing strategy.
2. Customer attitudes and opinions do not always lead to behaviour and purchase – understand your customers and their behaviour and use this to support your decision-making.

3. Products and services and their pricing are at the core of what you do – ensure any changes maintain or enhance the value created.
4. Avoid mixed messages – for example, via poor packaging decisions or decisions about pricing.
5. Convenience and speed are likely to be customer priorities – recognise and account for the climate impacts and help them make informed decisions as a result.
6. Your communications have impacts too – make choices about the channels you use, taking into account emissions data.
7. Consider working with local universities, by connecting with Marketing course teams to generate new ideas and provide the students with work-like experience that is mutually beneficial.

Outlook

It is vital to understand the importance of climate change and climate impacts to your customers and to their motivation and satisfaction, both now and in the future. Your marketing strategy and your understanding of your customers' behaviour and requirements must be linked to your marketing mix. It will be important to use feedback based on your marketing decisions to inform future work. This should all feed into your understanding of your brand's reputation and the overall company strategy and positioning.

Any work related to the reduction of emissions in respect of your product offering will hopefully be seen as a benefit to your customers, and it is through an appropriate marketing mix that value will be created and delivered. This is likely to be an ongoing task, with the arrival of new materials for products and packaging (which may well be recycled) and options for how your products and services are made available to the market continuing to develop. It will be important to be aware of innovations in all these areas, and to understand how they can add value to your organisation and your customer base, without negatively affecting society. (See Figure 9.2 for further guidance on implementation.)

Measure
Understand your customers, their requirements and behaviour, use segmentation theory to support

Target
Ensure your marketing strategy recognises customer requirements, and sets the direction for work related to climate change and the impacts from all your marketing activity

Report
Feed reviews and insights into your future marketing strategy; report on progress via your marketing communcations

Engage
Develop the elements of the marketing mix to ensure value is created and distributed, and the mix supports efficiency and effectiveness

Action
Implement selected marketing mix; review as necessary

Figure 9.2 Implementation plan for the reduction of marketing-related GHG emissions.

Further Resources

On the companion website to this book you can find further material to help you plan and implement this work.

The materials below should complement the resources and links referenced throughout the chapter. There are also suggestions in the Dig Deeper box above.

B Corp movement

https://www.bcorporation.net/en-us

Potentially very important for your purpose driven marketing strategy, and brand positioning, the B Corp movement was established following the recognition that organisations could lead the way towards a new, stakeholder-driven business model. The movement challenges and seeks to change the current economic system, through changing the rules of the game. B Corps collectively act to address society's most critical challenges, and organisations large and small across diverse sectors have joined this movement as part of how they see their organisation, its strategies and work progressing over time.

The Circular Economy – Ellen MacArthur Foundation
https://ellenmacarthurfoundation.org/topics/circular-economy-introduction/overview
Launched in 2010, with the intent of accelerating the transition to a circular economy, the website contains resources to explain the concept itself and how it supports climate change. It also includes general and sector specific information, guidance and resources.

TerraCycle Recycled products: https://www.terracycle.com/en-GB/pages/recycled-products and **Wired: our 27 favourite products made of recycled and upcycled material:** https://www.wired.com/gallery/our-favorite-upcycled-and-recycled-products/
These might provide inspiration when evaluating your product offering and how you could redesign your product.

Carbon Trust – Product Carbon Labelling
https://www.carbontrust.com/resources/the-resurgence-of-product-carbon-footprint-labelling
Discusses and identifies the demand for product carbon labelling and how that supports the quantification of the carbon footprint of products and services. Further links within the Carbon Trust and to different footprint standards are also provided.

Dentsu and Microsoft, The Rise of Sustainable Media
https://sustainablemedia.dentsu.com/home1/home
This provides a deeper insight into customer behaviour related to climate change, and likely customer responses. The work specifically considers media and communications solutions, which may be applicable to a range of organisations.

Sustainable Brands for Good:
https://sbbrandsforgood.com
This organisation's mission is to help brands make sustainable living easier and more rewarding. It is grounded in the recognition that brands have a role to play in informing and supporting customer behaviour change, and ensuring this becomes mainstream.

Notes

1. McKinsey, *The net-zero transition: What it would cost, what it could bring*: https://www.mckinsey.com/business-functions/sustainability/our-insights/cop26-made-net-zero-a-core-principle-for-business-heres-how-leaders-can-act

2. Deloitte, *Communications for a changing climate*: https://www2.deloitte.com/global/en/blog/responsible-business-blog/2021/communications-for-a-changing-climate.html

3. The Drum (2021) *Customers Say They'll Boycott Bands*: https://www.thedrum.com/news/2021/12/07/59-consumers-say-they-ll-boycott-brands-don-t-address-climate-emergency

4. CMA, *Guidance – making environmental claims on goods and services*: https://www.gov.uk/government/publications/green-claims-code-making-environmental-claims/environmental-claims-on-goods-and-services

5. Gov.UK, *Green Claims Code*: https://greenclaims.campaign.gov.uk/

6. CIM, *Marketing Expert – Glossary*: https://marketingexpert.cim.co.uk/glossary/

7. AMA, *Definition of Marketing*: https://www.ama.org/the-definition-of-marketing-what-is-marketing/

8. Lunde M (2018) *Sustainability in marketing*: https://www.researchgate.net/publication/326448765_Sustainability_in_marketing_a_systematic_review_unifying_20_years_of_theoretical_and_substantive_contributions_1997-2016

9. Helm *et al* (2018) *Materialist Values, Financial and Pro-environmental Behaviors, and Well-being*: https://www.emerald.com/insight/content/doi/10.1108/YC-10-2018-0867/full/html

10. Thøgersen (2021) *Consumer Behavior and Climate Change*: https://www.sciencedirect.com/science/article/pii/S2352154621000309

11. Woodall T (2003) *Conceptualising Value for the Customer*: https://www.researchgate.net/publication/228576532_Conceptualising_'Value_for_the_Customer'_An_Attributional_Structural_and_Dispositional_Analysis

12. Ellen MacArthur Foundation, What is a circular economy?: https://ellenmacarthurfoundation.org/topics/circular-economy-introduction/overview

13. SMI, *Manifesto for Regenerative Fashion*: https://www.circularonline.co.uk/news/fashion-task-force-announces-manifesto-for-regenerative-fashion/

14. European Commission, *Initiative on substantiating green claims*: https://ec.europa.eu/environment/eussd/smgp/initiative_on_green_claims.htm

15. Clarke J (2022) Boots to stop selling all plastic-based wet wipes ..., *The Independent* (19 April): https://www.independent.co.uk/business/boots-to-stop-selling-all-plasticbased-wet-wipes-by-end-of-the-year-b2060428.html?r=30434
16. Boots has signed up to the BRC Climate Action Roadmap: https://www.walgreensbootsalliance.com/news-media/our-stories/boots-uk-has-signed-brc-climate-action-roadmap
17. Recycle at Boots: https://www.boots.com/shopping/boots-recycling-scheme
18. Ensia, *In Store or Online*: https://ensia.com/features/environmental-cost-online-shopping-delivery/
19. Worthy F (2021) *Last Mile Delivery in Scotland*: https://www.climatexchange.org.uk/media/4893/cxc-last-mile-delivery-in-scotland-july-21.pdf
20. PwC, *The Last Mile*: https://www.pwc.co.uk/services/consulting/operations/the-last-mile.html
21. Berners-Lee M (2020) *How bad are bananas?* The carbon footprint of everything, pp. 6, 49
22. Black I and Eiseman D (2019) *Climate Change Behaviours-Segmentation Study*: https://www.climatexchange.org.uk/research/projects/climate-change-behaviours-segmentation-study/
23. DEFRA (2008): https://assets.publishing.service.gov.uk/government/uploads/system/uploads/attachment_data/file/69277/pb13574-behaviours-report-080110.pdf
24. Yale Programme on Climate Change Communication: https://climatecommunication.yale.edu/
25. Crobox, *Psychographic Segmentation*: https://blog.crobox.com/article/psychographic-segmentation
26. SmartInsights.com: https://www.smartinsights.com/digital-marketing-strategy/customer-segmentation-targeting/segmentation-targeting-and-positioning/
27. Unilever, *Climate Action Strategy and Goals*: https://www.unilever.com/planet-and-society/climate-action/strategy-and-goals/
28. GOV.UK (2021) Outcome and response to ending the sale of new petrol, diesel and hybrid cars and vans: https://www.gov.uk/government/consultations/consulting-on-ending-the-sale-of-new-petrol-diesel-and-hybrid-cars-and-vans

29. electric & hybrid (2022) *ID. Buzz Volkswagen:* vehicletechnology.com/news/oem-news/id-buzz-volkswagen-launches-classic-camper-reborn-with-electric-power.html

30. Finisterre UK: https://takeback.reskinned.clothing/finisterre

31. Turtle Doves, *A potted history*: https://www.turtle-doves.co.uk/pages/turtle-doves-story

32. Beyond Meat: https://www.beyondmeat.com/en-GB/mission/

33. Tian X and Sarkis J (2022) Emission Burden Concerns for Online Shopping Returns, *Nature*: https://www.nature.com/articles/s41558-021-01246-9

34. Clearcycle, A guide to reverse logistics and how it works: https://clearcycle.co.uk/guide-to-reverse-logistics-and-how-it-works/

35. WARC (2021) *Ad Net Zero*: https://www.warc.com/newsandopinion/opinion/ad-net-zero--the-advertising-industrys-climate-action-plan/en-gb/4473

36. OneGreenPlanet (2021) *Fashion Week's Impact on the Planet*: https://www.onegreenplanet.org/environment/fashion-weeks-impact-on-the-planet/

37. Marketing Week (2013) *Case study: Patagonia's ... campaign*: https://www.marketingweek.com/case-study-patagonias-dont-buy-this-jacket-campaign/

38. The Green House Hotel, Bournemouth, England: https://www.thegreenhousehotel.co.uk/

39. Network for Business Sustainability (2021) *What is Sustainable Marketing*: https://nbs.net/other/what-is-sustainable-marketing/

10

PENSION FUNDS, ACCOUNTS AND OTHER INVESTMENTS FOR A GOOD FUTURE

Petra Molthan-Hill and Fiona Winfield

Every organisation, every manager and indeed every employee can influence the transition to a low-carbon future by selecting investment strategies that focus on climate solutions and the reduction of greenhouse gas emissions. A similar lever is available by choosing the best providers and banks for handling all the organisation's financial transactions, pension schemes, loans, mortgages and insurance, and/ or influencing the employees to do so.

This chapter is for you if:

- You oversee the accounts and payment cards used in your organisation
- You run the pension scheme for your organisation
- You are a pension fund manager or a financial adviser
- You work in investment management, a bank, or an insurance company
- You want to do something in your private life about choosing the right bank account and investing in high-impact climate solutions via your pension scheme, for example

DOI: 10.4324/9781003274049-12

- You want to lobby for a transition of the banking and insurance sectors.

It will cover:

- Definitions of key concepts such as ESG investing
- Networks and initiatives such as the Impact Management Project
- Key investment strategies to support climate solutions
- Criteria for selecting a bank based on your values
- Green bonds and 'green pensions'
- Cryptocurrencies
- A case study, Quick Wins and Further Resources to start your journey.

Investing in a good future for all

Mark Carney, previous governor of the Bank of England (2013–2020) and governor of the Bank of Canada (2008–2013) highlights in his book 'Value(s) – Building a better world for all': [t]he effects of climate change are beginning to impact assets which have a market price, making the scale of the looming calamity more tangible. Climate change is setting in train a vicious cycle in which rising sea levels and more extreme weather are damaging property, forcing migration, impairing assets and reducing the productivity of work. [...] As society awakes to these risks, it is beginning to place greater value on sustainability - the precondition to solving the climate crisis. To solve the climate crisis, Carney suggests that [t]he objective is a financial system in which climate change is as much a determinant of value as creditworthiness, interest rates or technology, where the impact of an activity on climate change is a new vector, a new determinant, of value.[1]

In his book, Mark Carney goes on to outline the changes required for the financial systems, which we recommend as further reading in this chapter's 'Want to Dig Deeper' box. However, in this chapter here, we will just focus on investments, as every company, organisation and in fact every employee can make their own climate-friendly investment choices by carefully selecting their current account provider, choosing a 'green' pension scheme, having a 'good' credit card and so on. Sir David Attenborough observed: it is crazy that our banks and our pensions are investing in fossil fuels, when these are the very things that are jeopardising the future we are saving for.[2] So let's find out how we can invest in a way that safeguards our future.

The International Energy Agency estimates that US$3.5 trillion in energy sector investments alone are needed every year for decades to come, in order to achieve the required low-carbon transition; in addition, climate-resilient infrastructure investments could reach US$90 trillion by 2030. As Carney points out *smart decisions now can ensure that investment is both financially rewarding and environmentally sustainable.*[3]

Socially Responsible Investing (SRI) has a long-standing history reaching back to the 18th century, when Quakers decided not to work with those involved in the slave trade; single investors and whole congregations chose not to buy 'sin' stocks in companies involved in gambling, alcohol production, prostitution or tobacco. SRI really took off in 1970 when the first shareholder resolutions were filed against companies investing or working under the apartheid regime in South Africa; by the 1980s, billions of dollars had been divested from South African–related companies such as Johnson & Johnson.[4] Over the decades leading up to the present day, so-called 'ESG' investing has gained in popularity. **ESG** stands for **E**nvironmental Impacts, such as climate change and GHG emissions; **S**ocial Contributions, such as Human Rights and Labour Standards; and last, but not least, **G**overnance and Management, such as board composition and lobbying.

Many investment companies are keen to label their products as ESG investing to benefit from the trend. However, this labelling might be misleading or even greenwashing, a term used when companies or fund managers claim their products are more environmentally-friendly than they really are. Some financial advisers and investors worry that investment firms are launching new products to try and ride the recent wave of interest without putting too much thought into them. The fact that ESG labelling is currently so confusing for investors makes it even easier to greenwash. For example, the so-called 'best in class' ESG investment strategy might define a fossil fuel company that invests minimally into renewable energy as the 'best in their class' as compared to their fossil fuel peers. *A 2019 report from market researcher Cicero found that 97 out of 100 financial advisers were either very or fairly concerned about the possible mis-selling of products marketed as having strong ESG credentials as consumer interest in the responsible investment sector surged.*[5]

The **Principles For Responsible Investment (PRI)** were initiated in 2005 by the then United Nations Secretary-General Kofi Annan, who invited a group of the world's largest institutional investors to develop them.

The aim is to support signatories in integrating ESG issues into investment and ownership decisions. The six Principles, developed by those investors and supported by the United Nations, had in 2021 more than 4,000 signatories from over 60 countries, representing over US$120 trillion of assets.[6]

Another important initiative to mention in this context is the **Task Force on Climate-related Financial Disclosures (TCFD)**, which we discuss in more detail in chapter 3 (Communication & Reporting). The TCFD, established by the Financial Stability Board, develops recommendations for more effective climate-related disclosures that could promote more informed investment, credit and insurance underwriting decisions, and in turn enables stakeholders to understand better the concentrations of carbon-related assets in the financial sector, and the financial system's exposures to climate-related risks.[7]

SRI and ESG investing include many approaches, for example **Responsible Shareholding**. This includes voting at AGMs, filing resolutions and engaging as a shareholder with companies to improve their practices. A fund manager for example, holding a substantial share in a company, might ask for annual meetings to discuss issues of concern. An institutional investor, such as a bank or a fund manager, can also decide to apply positive or negative screening, such as excluding tobacco industries or fossil fuels from their portfolio. Impact investment has especially gained in popularity, and we will discuss this approach now in more detail.

Impact investment: choices and strategies for investors

The **Global Impact Investing Network (GIIN)**, a non-profit organisation dedicated to increasing the scale and effectiveness of impact investing, defines 'Impact investments' as those *made with the intention to generate positive, measurable social and environmental impact alongside a financial return*.[8] The **European Venture Philanthropy Association (EVPA)** has gone a step further, focusing on the concept of *additionality* and introducing the distinction between investing for impact and investing with impact.

As highlighted in Figure 10.1, the two strategies are placed between traditional grant-making and SRI. On the left-hand side of the diagram, investing for impact builds on the concept of venture philanthropy (VP) and refers to organisations that deploy long-term and high-risk capital,

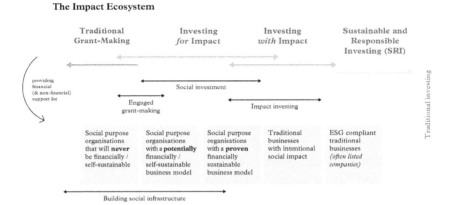

Figure 10.1 The Impact Ecosystem Spectrum – reprinted with permission of the EVPA.

which have impact embedded at the core of their strategies and seek an impact that is *additional*. EVPA co-developed the **Charter of Investing for Impact**[9] with its community, which includes a wide range of capital providers, such as grant making foundations, impact funds, banks and crowdfunding platforms, as well as other market builders like incubators and accelerators, philanthropy advisers and business schools. The Charter highlights the ten principles that represent the DNA of investing for impact and distinguish it from other investment strategies. Towards the right-hand side of the diagram, investing with impact refers to capital providers that usually have access to larger pools of resources, but need to guarantee a certain financial return on their investment alongside the intended positive impact they aim to achieve.

Investing for impact and investing with impact are both needed and offer complementary approaches to ensure a well-functioning impact ecosystem, where ventures access the right type of financial and non-financial support throughout their life cycle, enabling them to grow and deliver impact at scale. Recognising the differences however is important to enhance transparency on intentions, manage expectations towards stakeholders and create the right setting to foster collaboration among different types of investors.

It is one thing having the intention to effect change through one's investment activity, it is however also important to measure and manage the resultant impact. Given the relevance of the topic, in recent years there has been a proliferation of 'impact measurement and management' (IMM) initiatives aimed at supporting practitioners. EVPA recently investigated the complementarities among the most relevant IMM initiatives, including the EVPA five-step process,[10] the **Impact Management Project's (IMP)** five dimensions of impact,[11] the SDG Impact Standards,[12] the Operating Principles for Impact Management[13] and the Principles of Social Value,[14] and clarified the connections throughout the investment journey from the investors' perspective.[15]

Among all those initiatives, the IMP has been the most visible and acknowledged. It was started in 2016, to build global consensus on how to measure, assess and report impacts on people and the natural environment. As a result, there is now a set of resources available to organisations to improve their sustainability impact. Guidance is provided on how enterprises can classify these, focusing on three principles: Act to Avoid Harm, Benefit Stakeholders and Contribute to Solutions. The IMP recommends using this classification as a communication, market segmentation and portfolio management device for investors.

The above-mentioned IMP's **five dimensions of impact** are:

- **WHAT**: understanding the outcomes to which the enterprise is contributing and how important the outcomes are to stakeholders
- **WHO**: understanding which stakeholders experienced the effect, and how underserved they were previously
- **HOW MUCH**: understanding how many stakeholders experienced the outcome, what degree of change they experienced, and for how long they experienced it
- **CONTRIBUTION**: assessing whether an enterprise's and/or investor's efforts resulted in outcomes that were likely to have been better than would have occurred otherwise
- **RISK**: assessing the likelihood that the impact will be different from the one expected.

These five dimensions of impact are for example recommended by the **Global Impact Investing Network (GIIN)**, mentioned at the start of this section. The GIIN is the global champion of impact investing, dedicated to increasing its scale and effectiveness around the world, as the way forward to become the new norm.[16] The GIIN builds critical market infrastructure and supports activities, education and research, which help accelerate the development of a coherent impact investing industry.

What about the financial returns?

George Serafeim, based at Harvard and one of the leading researchers on the performance of companies, found that those organisations which focus on material social and environmental factors outperform the market, relative to a market median ('alpha'), by 3 to 6% annually.[17] The financial data provider Morningstar found that over ten years, 75% of sustainable funds available to investors survived, compared to only 46% of traditional funds.[18] In a meta study from 2018, researchers from the University of Hamburg and DWS, a German asset manager, concluded that all studies undertaken since 1970 show that ESG and Corporate Financial Performance are positively correlated; a company performs better if it does not focus on revenue for the shareholders alone, but underpins its reputation and its operational activities with ESG criteria.[19] This trend is likely to increase as the values of society are shifting towards a Net Zero future and the transition to a low-carbon society. Mark Carney suggests that in theory, the more that society values the transition to Net Zero, the more valuable companies that are part of the solution will be, because of greater demand for their products as well as because of developments in regulation and carbon pricing that support society's objectives.[20]

In practice, many investors are now asking for this information to select appropriate companies for their portfolios. In chapter 3 (Communication & Reporting) is a detailed case study of 'ESG Book', which helps companies to prepare their information according to different ESG frameworks, in order to provide the right information to investors. Investors can easily find the information they need to fulfil their own criteria, for example if they have decided only to invest in companies that work towards science-based targets.

From the perspective of an owner of a small company, a manager, or even any employee or citizen, a basic understanding of the different approaches taken by pension providers or banks is important to make an informed decision, allowing investment of their money according to their values as well as their financial needs. We will discuss this in more detail in the next section. We will also discuss the new trend of investing in cryptocurrencies, as this has such a high negative carbon impact. In chapter 5 (Digital Footprint) we provide detailed information and the technological changes which could reduce the carbon emissions of cryptocurrencies, here we will focus on them as an investment.

WANT TO DIG DEEPER?

Value(s) – Building a better world for all – book by Mark Carney
Based on his experience as governor of the Banks of England and Canada, and a long career at Goldman Sachs, Mark Carney offers a handbook on how to combine profit with purpose. Chapter 11, 'The Climate Crisis', is especially worthy of note as he explains why inactivity would be very costly and could threaten assets worth 20% of global GDP. Chapter 12, 'Breaking the Tragedy of the Horizon', then details how *every* financial decision should take climate change into account.

Sustainable Investing. A Path to a New Horizon – edited by Herman Bril, Georg Kell and Andreas Rasche
This book tells the story of how the convergence between corporate sustainability and sustainable investing is now becoming a major force, driving systemic market changes. The idea and practice of corporate sustainability is no longer a niche movement; investors are increasingly paying attention to sustainability factors in their analysis and decision-making, thus reinforcing market transformation.
Aimed at both investment professionals and academics, this book gives the reader access to more practitioner-relevant information, and it also discusses implementation issues. The reader will gain insights into how 'mainstream' financial actors relate to sustainable investing.

High-impact solutions

In this chapter, we have organised our three questions according to the relevance for every organisation and every manager, so the first question will be relevant to every reader of this book as most people have a bank account of some sort, and therefore everyone could contribute (to a smaller or larger degree) by choosing a bank that invests exclusively into a low-carbon future. Organisations should handle all their transactions through the best providers of sustainable finance. Our first question is, therefore: **current and savings accounts - how can you select the most appropriate providers?**

Many readers of this book will be investing in a retirement pension, and their employer will doubtless be making a lot of the necessary decisions on their behalf. So, whether an organisation is small or large, choosing a climate-friendly pension fund is another high-impact solution that every reader and every organisation can select and, hence, our second question is: **pension funds - how do you invest in a good future for you and your employees?**

Cryptocurrencies are gaining in popularity; some football clubs are starting to use Bitcoins to pay their players, issuing fans tokens with associated perks, such as votes on small decisions about which song to play over the stadium tannoy after a goal, and some players are promoting non-fungible tokens (NFT) – the controversial digital art form. This is despite the risks, as stated by football finance expert Kieran Maguire: *it's unregulated, it's volatile and it's subject to manipulation by people who own large amounts of the asset.*[21] In chapter 5 (Digital Footprint) we have highlighted that the use of cryptocurrencies and other blockchains could in the coming years outweigh any reductions made in other areas and *bitcoin emissions alone could push global warming above 2°C.*[22] Our third question is, therefore: **cryptocurrencies - what do they add to a portfolio, and should they be developed?**

Other topics could be covered here such as ethical mortgages or insurance. For example, the insurance companies have to invest their premiums somewhere, and can also can make a difference depending on how and where they invest.[23] The checklist given below for choosing the best bank based on your own values could equally be applied to screening insurance or (business) mortgage providers.

Current and savings accounts – how can you select the most appropriate providers?

Choosing the right bank is an important decision for any organisation, and to a certain extent every person. Any investment made in a bank (or via a bank), whether through savings accounts, stock options or loans, provides the bank with the finance which is subsequently loaned to other companies, and therefore supports the transition to a low-carbon economy, or otherwise. It is therefore important to understand the objectives of the bank and to whom they lend. Do they make high returns by lending money to organisations involved with fossil fuels or gold mining for example?

In order to choose the right bank for you, based on your personal values, the following five questions can guide you:

1. **Is the whole bank ethically focused?**
   You will often find that a bank offers some ethical options in an otherwise diverse portfolio. There are only a few banks that take a clear stance; an example would be **Triodos**.[24] Founded in 1980 in the Netherlands, Triodos now operates in several European countries with a clear focus on reducing energy demand, using energy as efficiently as possible, and investing significantly in renewable energy systems. It also clearly excludes investing in fossil fuels with regards to extraction and generation. In 2009, Triodos Bank co-founded the **Global Alliance for Banking on Values**,[25] an independent network of banks that use finance to deliver sustainable economic, social and environmental development.

2. **Who owns the bank – are they ethically focused?**
   If you want to invest your money according to your values you need to know who owns the bank and what their approach is. For example, a bank's subsidiary might offer a fantastic high-scoring ethical fund. However, the parent company might actually invest heavily in fossil fuels. Without further research this might not be apparent, so it is advisable to use guides such as Ethical Consumer for more information on the credentials of different organisations.[26]

3. **What stance is the bank taking with regards to fossil fuels?**
   You might want to choose a bank that takes a clear stance against fossil fuel extraction and generation such as Triodos, or you might want the option to exclude these companies for yourself, so the bank needs to allow you to make such a choice easily on their platform. Alternatively, you might want to invest in fossil fuel companies that have a transition plan in place – again, is your bank transparent about this and does it provide you with enough information to make the right choice? Some institutions have started to pledge to reduce thermal coal, but perhaps they have not addressed the other fossil fuels that also need reducing.

4. **Is the bank transparent about its criteria and methodology?**

    All banks should publish all their selection criteria, for example whether they are excluding companies (such as fossil fuels) or specifically selecting companies for inclusion e.g. those which improve the energy efficiency of buildings. This is even more important for specific products such as Green Bonds. These *enable capital-raising and investment for new and existing projects with environmental benefits. The Green Bond Principles (GBP) seek to support issuers in financing environmentally sound and sustainable projects that foster a Net Zero emissions economy and protect the environment. ... GBP promote a step change in transparency that facilitates the tracking of funds to environmental projects, while simultaneously aiming to improve insight into their estimated impact. ... The GBP emphasise the required transparency, accuracy and integrity of the information that will be disclosed and reported by issuers to stakeholders through core components and key recommendations.*[27]

5. **Is the bank transparent about any investments you make, prior to purchase?**

    In addition to describing the criteria for inclusion or exclusion, it is also important that banks provide the information on the companies and industries in which they are investing. In some cases, you will only see a selection of companies, such as the top ten holdings in the portfolio, or you may receive scant information about the savings fund at all, so it is worth insisting on receiving this information *before* investing or choosing a bank.

These five questions can also be used to choose a specific investment. For example, which stocks and shares to hold. Obviously, it is also important to make sure your money is invested in a bank that is secure, and is transparent about the risks it is taking.

With regards to bank accounts, besides the issues raised above regarding how your bank invests your money,[28] any company owner might ask themselves the question, does my choice of bank reflect the general objectives and ethos of my company? Customers and suppliers will necessarily be aware of the identity of your banker, and if that bank is involved in a major scandal, it could put account holders in a bad light, which might contradict the sustainable objectives you have declared in your own marketing communications, for example.

Pension funds – how do you invest in a good future for you and your employees?

We all want to experience a secure retirement, however most pension providers tend to focus mainly on the financial return to ensure a good future. Increasingly, people are realising that a good future also means being in an environment that provides a good quality of life (including a liveable environment!). We might want to be able to buy a good quality coffee in a nice café each day when we retire, but besides the money to pay for the drink, we need appropriate climate conditions that are suitable for coffee production. We might want to sit in the garden, on the beach or in the countryside without this being flooded, too hot or destroyed by frequent storms. If we really want a 'good future' in both senses of the expression, we need to combine financial returns with positive living conditions for all human beings including ourselves.

Richard Curtis, film producer and '**Make My Money Matter**' co-founder said during the launch of the COP26 Private Finance Agenda in February 2020: [it] *really is time for people to make their money matter. It's time for green pensions. It's time to be proud of our pensions. It's time for pensions to help create a world that we all want to retire into and that we want our children to grown [sic] up into. And businesses are the necessary heroes in this journey. The public needs you to be brave and take the lead.*[29]

In Europe, one good place to start to check the credentials of a pension provider is the **Novethic** website, where there is an overview of the different sustainable finance labels used by providers.[30] For UK-based organisations and individuals, 'Make My Money Matter' has issued a Green Pensions Guide with the aim to use the power of pensions – for example the £2.6 trillion invested alone in UK pensions – to help deliver the Paris Climate Goals, fund critical green infrastructure or ensure our economy 'builds back greener' post-Covid. This could also be a good starting point, along with applying the questions outlined above for selecting a pension fund based on your values. 'Make My Money Matter' has also produced a Net Zero Pensions Guide for SMEs, and points out that not only is this good for the planet, it can enhance the company's reputation and could attract and retain employees.[31]

In the United Kingdom, an example of a 'green' pension fund would be 'The PensionBee Fossil Fuel Free plan', created and managed by Legal & General, one of the UK's first mainstream private pension plans to completely exclude companies with proven or probable reserves in oil, gas or coal. It also excludes tobacco companies, manufacturers of controversial weapons, nuclear weapons and persistent violators of the UN Global Compact. Alongside this, it invests in companies that are aligned with the Paris Climate Change Agreement.[32]

While some companies have taken a proactive stance, it may be the employees who lobby their organisation to think more carefully about where their pension funds are invested. Shareholders may play a part too, so overall pensions could be invested into providing a better future for all.

Cryptocurrencies – what do they add to a portfolio, and should they be developed?

Cryptocurrencies have gained in popularity over the last decade; in chapter 5 (Digital Footprint), we outline the high carbon impact associated with their use and discuss technological improvements on how the carbon emissions could be reduced. Here in this chapter, we will explore non-technical climate solutions around cryptocurrencies. However, we will only be scratching the surface, as this topic alone deserves its own book.

Given the high carbon impact, an important question should be: what do we gain by using cryptocurrencies and would this outweigh the environmental and societal damage they will cause through more carbon consumption? Mark Carney highlights in the aforementioned book several other, not climate-related, reasons why using cryptocurrencies might not be advisable.

Cryptocurrencies are token-based digital assets rather than currencies and it is debatable whether they can or will fulfil the functions of money. Advocates of a decentralised cryptocurrency such as bitcoin claim that it is more trustworthy than centralised fiat money because its supply is fixed, its use is free from risky private banks and those who hold it can remain anonymous and therefore free from the ravenous eyes of tax authorities or law enforcement. Mark Carney argues that the latter raises a host of issues around consumer and investor protection, market integrity, money laundering, terrorism financing, tax evasion and the circumvention of capital controls and international sanctions.

Mark Carney also outlines that cryptocurrencies are proving volatile short-term stores of value, exhibiting price fluctuations that can lead to gains or losses of 50% within months. Over the past five years, the daily standard deviation of bitcoin was ten times that of sterling. And bitcoin is one of the more stable cryptocurrencies. This extreme volatility reflects in parts the fact that cryptocurrencies have neither intrinsic value nor any external backing. Their worth rests on beliefs regarding their future supply and demand – ultimately whether they will be successful as money or as a hedge against the debasement of other forms of money.[33]

However, supporters of cryptocurrencies argue that they might even contribute to a more sustainable future. Stephen Stonberg, CEO, Bittrex Global for example argues in an article published by the World Economic Forum that *traditional finance and gold mining account for a significantly larger share of greenhouse gas emissions than crypto*, however his calculations would need some scrutiny.[34] It also poses the question whether cryptocurrencies would replace traditional finance and gold mining or be added to them, if it is the latter, any energy used (even if powered by renewables), would increase carbon emissions not decrease them.

Case study

In the case study for this chapter, Silke Stremlau, board member at Hannoversche Kassen, explains how her company, which runs pension funds for several small and medium enterprises, chooses investment strategies that combine environmental, social and financial factors. Although based in the German context, many of the principles will apply to other countries.

Sustainable investment of a German pension fund

By Silke Stremlau (Chief Investment Officer, Hannoversche Kassen, Germany and Chairperson of the Sustainable Finance Advisory Committee of the Federal Government of Germany)

Most people avoid thinking about their financial security in their retirement. They might perceive the topic as too dry and frustrating, especially when they read in the media that there may not be enough money to support everyone in the future, and we may need to work much longer before reaching retirement age. At the same time, surveys undertaken with younger people show they are mostly concerned about climate change and their financial security, two topics that might destroy their hope for a comfortable future.

Is it possible to address these two concerns simultaneously?

Yes, it is. The Hannoversche Kassen, a German pension funds provider, is one of the sustainability pioneers in the sector. Supported and encouraged by our members, we have for quite some time included ESG criteria in our investment strategies to reduce risks and to optimise the investment in relation to the values and aspirations of our beneficiaries.

The Hannoversche Kassen was founded in 1985 by 'Waldorfschulen' (Rudolf Steiner Schools) and other charities, to develop their own pension funds. Today, more than 500 charities are members and over 13,000 clients are insured with us, within a legal structure (Versicherungsverein auf Gegenseitigkeit – VVaG) that includes many democratic voting rights for the insured and the members. Many of the clients are teachers in the Rudolf Steiner Schools and employees of charities or enterprises with a sustainable focus, and they deal with sustainability-related topics in their daily work and therefore want a pension fund that reflects their values. With such a base, we have very strong support to focus on ESG criteria.

Powerful leverage

The Hannoversche Kassen is not dealing in billions of euros in the market. However, as a middle-sized pension fund our biggest leverage to achieve a sustainable and future-proofed economy is the investments we make. Obviously, we already have internal sustainability guidelines for daily activities, such as taking the train for work-related travel, not having company cars and having family-friendly working conditions, but is this enough? Our biggest leverage is very clearly the way we invest, where we can integrate social, ecological and economic criteria.

How does this work in practice?

Since 2013, the Hannoversche Kassen has designed ESG criteria for all investments, which everyone is required to follow. We constantly work on improving our criteria, so that we add new topics such as climate solutions for example, or we take a more stringent stance on how we deal with fossil fuels.

When investing in companies, we screen them using our established and transparent exclusion criteria, for example we would not invest in companies that violate human rights, construct or own nuclear power stations, are accused of corruption or make their profits in relation to fossil fuels. With regards to countries or states, we would investigate whether they support democracy, how they deal with corruption and whether they still have the death penalty. All exclusion criteria and their detailed descriptions can be found on our website (www.hannoversche-kassen.de) and in an annually published transparency and investments report, which we introduced in 2019 for the first time; the first pension fund in Germany ever to do so!

However, exclusion criteria can only be the first step. The second step has to be an exploration of companies, projects and innovative ideas that are essential to future-proof our world and to analyse in detail those which support a socio-ecological transformation. During this analysis, and to choose the best investment instruments, we use the expertise of sustainability rating agencies. These agencies constantly rate the environmental performance of companies, how they deal with human rights and/or how they work towards Net Zero targets. Before buying bonds and shares, an external sustainability rating is required, this is our internal quality standard!

For us, the impact of climate change has to be the overarching factor in deciding whether to invest in a company or not. In June 2020, the Hannoversche Kassen signed a self-declaration together with 16 other financial institutions representing €5.5 billion and over 46 million customers in Germany (www.klima-selbstverpflichtung-finanzsektor.de) to align all our investment portfolios with the Paris agreement.

To be more specific, in the last 12 months, the Hannoversche Kassen has made direct investments in renewable energy in Europe, bought shares in companies that are sustainability pioneers and built student accommodation in north Germany with Kf W40-Standard (a building that requires a maximum of 40% of the annual primary energy requirement permitted by the Energy Saving Ordinance). Additionally, the Hannoversche Kassen has bought properties to donate to social-ecological residency projects, thereby reducing real estate speculation.

Our sustainability council: benefitting from external expertise
Since 2014, a very important building block in the organisational structure of the Hannoversche Kassen is the collaboration with our Sustainability Council. The Council consists of four external experts representing sustainable finance, sustainable construction and member organisations. In regular meetings, the Council together with our CIO and our investment team, reflect on the appropriateness of the investment criteria and debate changes to be made, as well as strategic priorities and conflicts. This is, for both sides, a good and constructive learning process.

Do we need more than a sustainable business model?
The coming year will be challenging for pension funds and sustainable investors. The pandemic has increased national debt in every country considerably, and we need to see how interest rates will develop.

A sustainable business model forms the basis of future financial, social and ecological prosperity. It needs to respect the planetary boundaries, to take stakeholder interests seriously, to design products that are functional and make sense, and to contribute clearly to the Sustainable Development Goals.

But it also needs a transformative culture in organisations and companies, otherwise positive initiatives will just fall through and not go beyond the initial investment. These cannot just be exciting concepts developed by consultants to which we pay lip service, these transformative initiatives require hard work. A transformative organisational culture starts with employees who feel empowered and take responsibility, it must be more bottom-up than top-down oriented, it builds on cooperation and collaboration instead of competition, and it is inspired by 'New Work' or 'Reinventing Organisations'.

The Hannoversche Kassen started such a transformative process four years ago and were slowed down by the pandemic. To move a pension fund regulated by the 'Bundesanstalt für Finanzdienstleistungsaufsicht' (the German Finance Authority) to a self-regulated and empowered organisation requires strength and determination, but it is worth it! Last but not least, more than ever before, we need colleagues who question established structures and procedures, and develop them further, so that we have future-proofed pension funds that secure a sustainable future for us all.

Silke Stremlau has been on the board of Hannoversche Kassen, a sustainable pension fund, since 2018 being responsible for the areas of capital investment, sustainability and human resources. Previously she was the general representative at BANK IM BISTUM ESSEN eG. Between 2000 and 2015, she built up and managed the ESG division at imug rating, where she developed extensive expertise in the area of sustainable investment. She is also the Chairperson of the Sustainable Finance Advisory Committee of the Federal Government of Germany and a member of the Supervisory Board of UmweltBank AG in Nuernberg.

Quick Wins

1. Familiarise yourself with different investment options, and for your next investment decision choose one which will positively affect the future.
2. Move your account/s to a bank dedicated to the transition to a low-carbon economy.
3. Choose a climate-friendly pension fund for yourself and your employees.
4. Do not start to use cryptocurrencies. If you *do* use them, make sure you have considered all technological carbon reductions that can be

made, see chapter 5 (Digital Footprint). Or consider whether you want to keep them, or maybe invest in something else that develops a climate solution for the future and promises a good return too.

Outlook

As shown in this chapter, you can decide to invest in climate solutions that would help you to reduce greenhouse gas emissions, by choosing for example to move your bank account, invest in green bonds or opt for impact investment. We recommend that you draw up an implementation plan like the one suggested in Figure 10.2 for all your finance-related possibilities. As a next step, you could review each element, such as your pension plan, analyse the options available to you using the criteria outlined above and choose the most appropriate options.

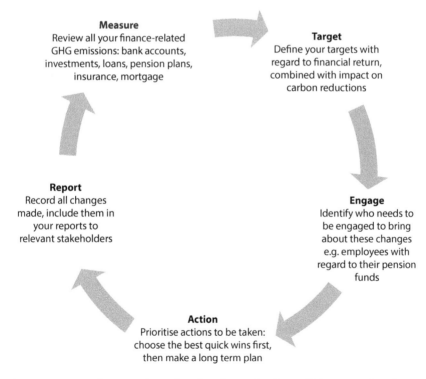

Measure
Review all your finance-related GHG emissions: bank accounts, investments, loans, pension plans, insurance, mortgage

Target
Define your targets with regard to financial return, combined with impact on carbon reductions

Engage
Identify who needs to be engaged to bring about these changes e.g. employees with regard to their pension funds

Action
Prioritise actions to be taken: choose the best quick wins first, then make a long term plan

Report
Record all changes made, include them in your reports to relevant stakeholders

Figure 10.2 Implementation plan for the reduction of finance-related GHG emissions.

Further Resources

On the companion website to this book, you can find further material to help you plan and implement this work. Below you can find links that go into more detail on the topics above, in addition to the sources mentioned in the endnotes. We have also added recommendations for online courses and modules if you want to go into more detail.

General

Article in the Financial Times: Pilita Clark, 'Banks risk becoming new fossil fuel villains in 2022', 07.01.2022

Alice Ross (2020) *Investing To Save The Planet: How Your Money Can Make a* **Difference, London: Penguin Business**
In this book, Alice Ross, the editor of FT Trade Secrets at the *Financial Times*, editor of FT *Wealth* and the deputy editor of FT *Money*, draws upon 14 years of experience reporting on investment, to explain to her readers how to make sure their money is making a positive difference, whatever the level of investment.

Bank.Green, Introducing the Fossil Free Banking Alliance:
https://bank.green/blog/introducing-the-fossil-free-banking-alliance

Good-with-money.com:
Credit cards: https://good-with-money.com/2022/01/26/top-4-ethical-credit-cards/
Mortgages: https://good-with-money.com/2022/01/26/top-4-responsible-mortgage-providers/
Loans: https://good-with-money.com/2019/01/03/top-5-responsible-personal-loan-choices/
An independent website and private limited company that provides a good starting point to think about all your financial transactions, for example how to choose an ethical credit card.

A Blueprint for Responsible Investment (PRI)
https://www.unpri.org/download?ac=5330
To mark their 10th anniversary in 2016, the PRI undertook a series of initiatives to review progress so far and to create an ambitious and

achievable vision for how the PRI and the wider responsible investment community should progress over the next decade. This included global signatory and stakeholder surveys, an independent impact evaluation and major signatory consultations. These activities culminated in the launch of a Blueprint for Responsible Investment in 2017, setting the direction of their work for the ten years ahead.

Webinar

The Transparency Task Force

This was founded in May 2015 with the mission: [to] *promote ongoing reform of the financial sector, so that it serves society better.* As part of their strategy for driving change, which they describe as *bringing together the thinking of those with a sense of passion and purpose for the change we want to see; with those with the power and position to make change possible,* they organise regular (virtual) events: https://www.transparencytaskforce.org/upcoming-events/.

Course/module

Understanding Responsible Investment

https://cdn.shopify.com/s/files/1/0013/2153/3539/files/PRI_Academy_Understanding_RI.pdf

This course, offered by the PRI Academy, covers the following: Define responsible investment | Recognise ESG issues, trends and themes | Compare traditional analysis versus ESG analysis and how this relates to investment decision making | Recognise the key material impacts of corporate governance | Identify the role and outcomes of engagement.

What is impact investing?

https://www.impactinvest.org.uk/modules/introduction-to-impact-investing/

This provides the answer, and places impact investing in the context of traditional, responsible and sustainable investing. The module also introduces the 'spectrum of capital', a vital aid in explaining impact investing to others, and gives a briefing on the development of impact investing over time and the key global frameworks and standards that govern the market.

It also acknowledges some of the challenges that impact investing is addressing, along with the opportunities.

EVPA Training Academy
https://evpa.eu.com/knowledge-centre/training-academy
As a learning and capacity-building hub, EVPA Training Academy offers a range of learning opportunities for investors for impact. Whether participants work in a foundation, a social impact fund, a financial institution or a corporation, EVPA has designed its training courses to help them become more effective and maximise their impact.

Notes

1. Carney M (2021) *Value(s) –Building a better world for all*, London: William Collins, pp. 264 and 316
2. Green Pensions Guide: https://makemymoneymatter.co.uk/wp-content/uploads/2021/10/Green-Pensions-Guide.pdf, p. 4
3. Carney M (2021) *Value(s) –Building a better world for all*, London: William Collins, p. 317
4. More detailed information about the history and early approaches of SRI can be found in: Molthan P (2003) Introduction in D Broadhurst, J Watson and J Marshall, eds., *Ethical and socially responsible investment: a reference guide for researchers,* München: KG Saur
5. Ross A (2020) *Investing to Save The Planet: How Your Money Can Make a Difference*, London: Penguin Business, pp. 10 and 12
6. PRI: https://www.unpri.org/download?ac=10948
7. Task Force on Climate-related Financial Disclosures: https://assets.bbhub.io/company/sites/60/2020/10/TCFD_Booklet_FNL_Digital_March-2020.pdf
8. GIIN: https://thegiin.org/impact-investing/need-to-know/#what-is-impact-investing
9. EVPA: https://evpa.eu.com/knowledge-centre/publications/charter-of-investors-for-impact
10. Hehenberger L, Harling A-M, and Scholten P (2015) *A Practical Guide to Measuring and Managing Impact* – 2nd ed., EVPA: https://evpa.eu.com/knowledge-centre/publications/measuring-and-managing-impact-a-practical-guide

11. Impact Management Project (IMP): https://impactmanagementproject.com/

12. SDG Impact Standards: https://sdgimpact.undp.org/practice-standards.html

13. Operating Principles for Impact Management: https://www.impactprinciples.org/9-principles and https://www.impactprinciples.org/signatories-reporting

14. Principles of Social Value. For more information, please consult: https://www.socialvalueint.org/principles and https://www.socialvalueint.org/standards-and-guidance

15. Picón Martínez A, Gaggiotti G and Gianoncelli A (2021) *Navigating impact measurement and management – How to integrate impact throughout the investment journey.* EVPA: https://evpa.eu.com/knowledge-centre/publications/navigating-impact-measurement-and-management

16. IRIS+ and the five dimensions of impact: https://s3.amazonaws.com/giin-web-assets/iris/assets/files/guidance/IRIS-five-dimensions_June-2020

17. Khan M, Serafeim G and Yoon A (2016) 'Corporate Sustainability: First Evidence on Materiality' (9 Nov) *The Accounting Review*, Vol. 91, No. 6, pp. 1697–1724. Available at SSRN: https://ssrn.com/abstract=2575912 or http://dx.doi.org/10.2139/ssrn.2575912

18. Morningstar: https://www.morningstar.co.uk/uk/news/203214/do-sustainable-funds-beat-their-rivals.aspx

19. Busch T *et al* (2018) *ESG - Faktoren und Unternehmensentwicklung –die 2018-Meta-Studie von DWS und Universität Hamburg*, Frankfurt: DWS Investment GmbH

20. Carney M (2021) *Value(s) –Building a better world for all*, London: William Collins, p. 425

21. Guardian article (2022): https://www.theguardian.com/technology/2022/jan/22/dangerous-game-football-clubs-look-to-mine-fans-cash-with-crypto-offerings

22. Nature article (2018): https://www.nature.com/articles/s41558-018-0321-8

23. Insurance Business (2021): https://www.insurancebusinessmag.com/uk/news/breaking-news/how-can-insurers-kick-start-their-esg-investment-journey-250786.aspx

24. The description is cited from https://www.triodos.co.uk/about-us

25. You can find all member banks worldwide on the map here: https://www.gabv.org/

26. Ethical Consumer: https://www.ethicalconsumer.org/money-finance and Banking on Climate Chaos: https://www.bankingonclimatechaos.org/

27. International Capital Market Association (ICMA): https://www.icmagroup.org/sustainable-finance/the-principles-guidelines-and-handbooks/green-bond-principles-gbp/

28. Good with Money: https://good-with-money.com/2022/01/05/top-6-ethical-current-accounts/

29. The Green Pensions Guide: https://makemymoneymatter.co.uk/wp-content/uploads/2021/10/Green-Pensions-Guide.pdf

30. Novethic, *Overview of European sustainable finance labels 2020*: https://www.novethic.com/sustainable-finance-trends/detail/overview-of-european-sustainable-finance-labels-2020.html

31. Net Zero Pension Guide for SMEs: https://makemymoneymatter.co.uk/organisations/sme-pensions-guide/

32. Selected as one of the top ethical funds by Good-with-money.com: https://good-with-money.com/2022/01/13/top-6-ethical-pension-funds/

33. Carney M (2021) *Value(s) –Building a better world for all*, London: William Collins, pp. 110–115

34. World Economic Forum (WEF): https://www.weforum.org/agenda/2021/06/how-blockchain-and-cryptocurrencies-can-help-build-a-greener-future. The webinar 'Towards Sustainable Cryptocurrencies' organised by the WEF also provides more detail: https://www.linkedin.com/video/live/urn:li:ugcPost:6846808192651931648/

PART III

CARBON FOOTPRINTING: INTRODUCING GREENHOUSE GAS MANAGEMENT FOR THE WHOLE ORGANISATION

Shaping the journey: guidance for Chapters 11–14

In this section of the book, we want to guide anyone who is responsible for the greenhouse gas management in their organisation through the steps they need to take. These chapters will also be interesting for those who want to understand the wider efforts undertaken by organisations to address carbon and other greenhouse gas emissions. Also for anyone who reads about Scope 1, Scope 2, Scope 3 and science-based targets in newspapers or journals and wonders what is meant there. In some ways, these chapters set the wider context and could have been presented at the beginning of the book, however we know that not everyone in an organisation needs to understand the wider picture, as long as they know what they can achieve in their sphere of influence, which we have covered in the previous chapters.

While writing these chapters, we chose many examples that are relevant for SMEs, as such organisations will not always have the resources to hire

DOI: 10.4324/9781003274049-13

someone to do the greenhouse gas (GHG) management for them. SMEs will however often be required to show their approach when they tender for a contract. In Chapter 12 'Carbon Accounting' we have chosen for example a van as an illustration on how to do carbon accounting, as many SMEs will have at least one such vehicle, so this will be a useful calculation for most organisations.

Especially helpful for SMEs will be Chapter 3 'Communication and Reporting' where we have included a case study about ESG book: a new tool, where SMEs and other organisations can upload their emissions data to fulfil the needs of different stakeholders and frameworks, free of charge.

The topics covered in this final section of the book are:

* Chapter 11 – Scope 1, 2 and 3 (defining the scopes and setting Organisational and Operational Boundaries)
* Chapter 12 – Carbon Accounting (calculating GHG emissions and developing an emissions inventory)
* Chapter 13 – Science-based targets (setting targets for the reduction of GHG emissions)
* Chapter 14 – Strategies, policies and practices (goal setting and embedding good practice)

In Figure 11–14.1 we show how these chapters interconnect.

Measure
Chapter 11 - understanding
the Scopes and the need to
set Boundaries - *leads* to
Chapter 12 - collecting data
and information and compiling
the inventory. *Answers* where are
we now and where are we going?

Target
Chapter 13 - the role and importance
of (science-based) targets - *leads* to
the definition of where next and why?

Report
Follows through on the targets and
assesses progress - grounded by the
accounting/ inventory principles and
approach to reporting/ disclosure
(links to **Chapter 3** - Communication &
Reporting)

Engage
Chapter 14 - supporting and guiding
action through defining strategies,
policies and the supporting programmes
- *addresses* where do we want to be
and how do we get there?

Action
Taking action and implementing
the policies and programmes
- includes monitoring,
collecting data, learning and
communicating

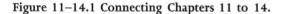

Figure 11–14.1 Connecting Chapters 11 to 14.

11

UNDERSTANDING GREENHOUSE GAS MANAGEMENT: SCOPES AND BOUNDARIES FOR CARBON FOOTPRINTING

Muhammad Mazhar

This chapter gives an overview of the different scopes (Scopes 1, 2, 3) as defined by the Greenhouse Gas (GHG) Protocol Corporate Accounting and Reporting Standard. It guides managers on how they can set up a GHG management plan in their own organisation by setting Organisational and Operational Boundaries (OOB). It discusses the need to engage stakeholders of business organisations for data management and to achieve a holistic approach to measure and manage all three scopes of GHG emissions.

This chapter is for you if:

- You are a manager responsible for environment, sustainability, energy, carbon emissions or corporate social responsibility (CSR) matters in an organisation
- You are the company owner

DOI: 10.4324/9781003274049-14

- You are interested in understanding the language of different scopes for Operational Boundaries used worldwide in all types of organisations.

It will cover:

- An introduction to the Greenhouse Gas (GHG) Protocol used worldwide to understand scopes, Organisational and Operational Boundaries
- A definition of the scopes of GHG emissions within an organisation
- GHG emissions associated with business activities of an organisation categorised into the three scopes (Scopes 1, 2 and 3)
- Setting up an Organisational and Operational Boundary for an organisation to calculate GHG emissions (carbon footprint)
- The data required in relation to different scopes of emissions and the need to engage stakeholders.

What are the different scopes of greenhouse gas emissions?

The Paris Climate Agreement (which came into force in 2016), commits countries to reduce their greenhouse gas emissions, to keep the global temperature rise below 1.5°C, compared to the pre-industrial levels, in order to avoid the catastrophic impacts of climate change.[1] To ensure this reduction actually happens, it is necessary for all organisations to play their part. An understanding of emissions and their provenance is therefore required, and all organisations should be setting up their own Greenhouse Gas Management Plan.

Way back in 1998, the Greenhouse Gas Protocol (GHGP) was developed by the World Resources Institute (WRI) and the World Business Council for Sustainable Development (WBCSD), to address the need to help countries and organisations in accounting, reporting and mitigating GHG emissions.[2] The main aim was to reduce the harmful impacts of global climate change through standardised measurement of GHG emissions, by categorising those gases into three main scopes: Scope 1, 2 and 3, based on their sources. The term 'scope' first appeared in the GHGP in 2001 and it is now a widely used global standard to measure, manage and report GHG emissions, with 90% of the Fortune 500 companies using it for their re-porting to the Carbon Disclosure Project (CDP). CDP is one of the global disclosure systems for companies looking to manage their environmental impacts using a standardised framework.[2] The GHGP offers a range of resources that are accessible to all types of business organisations looking to reduce their GHG emissions and to help achieve the objectives set out in the 2016 Paris Climate Agreement.

In this chapter, we have mainly used the term 'carbon emissions', which means carbon dioxide equivalent emissions (CO_2e) and incorporates other greenhouse gases. This is discussed and explained in chapter 1: Finding Your Best Decarbonisation Pathway (see 'What is the Greenhouse Gas Effect' section). *A carbon dioxide equivalent or CO_2 equivalent, abbreviated as CO_2e is a metric measure used to compare the emissions from various greenhouse gases on the basis of their global-warming potential (GWP), by converting amounts of other gases to the equivalent amount of carbon dioxide with the same global warming potential.*[3] Therefore, the term 'carbon emissions' is considered interchangeable with carbon dioxide equivalent and greenhouse gas emissions.

How are scopes defined?

Scopes 1, 2 and 3 categorise different types of greenhouse gas emissions that an organisation creates in its operations and value chain. The scopes are based on the control and influence of an organisation over its emissions. Scopes 1 and 2 are mostly within an organisation's direct control, however organisations have less control over their Scope 3 emissions. Committing to reach Net Zero involves tackling all three scopes of emissions, including the indirect ones classed as Scope 3.[4] This ensures that carbon management is comprehensive and has a bigger impact beyond the boundary of an organisation itself. Each organisation therefore needs to address *all* carbon emissions, both direct and indirect, to achieve impactful carbon management, involving *all* relevant stakeholders within and outside its boundaries.

Using the resource produced by Deloitte, it is explained that the GHGP defines Scopes 1, 2 and 3 as follows:[4]

Scope 1 (Direct Emissions) are those that occur from sources owned or controlled by the organisation

Scope 2 (Indirect Emissions) accounts for those that occur from the generation of purchased electricity, heat, steam or cooling

Scope 3 (All Other Indirect Emissions) are those from various organisational activities from external sources, not owned or controlled by the organisation. These are referred to as 'value chain emissions' and can be both upstream and downstream of an organisation's activities. Figure 11.1 from the GHGP shows the three scopes of carbon emissions and highlights how they link to the key activity areas in an organisation.

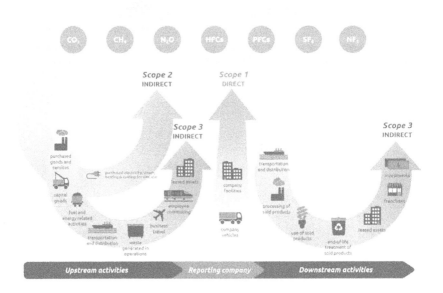

Figure 11.1 Overview of the GHG Protocol scopes and GHG emissions across the value chain. [5]

The scopes of carbon emissions encompass all sizes and types of businesses and organisations across all sectors. They can be applied to the public and private sector and include government agencies, not-for-profit organisations, universities, assurers and verifiers. [5] One organisation's indirect emissions are another organisation's direct emissions, whilst some Scope 3 emissions for one organisation are the Scope 1 and 2 emissions of another. So, every organisation taking responsibility for their own carbon footprint can make a significant difference, whilst ensuring there is cooperation in reducing the carbon emissions in a joined-up effort. This means that organisations need to work collaboratively and ensure emissions are tackled through appropriate stakeholder engagement.

In total, there are 15 categories of Scope 3 emissions including those which are upstream and downstream of the organisation's activities. However, not every Scope 3 category will be relevant to every organisation. Table 11.1 originally produced by the Carbon Trust categorises different scopes that organisations should be managing.

Table 11.1 Scopes of carbon emissions[6]

Scope 1	Scope 2	Scope 3
Fuel combustion Company-owned vehicles Fugitive emissions	Purchased electricity, heat and steam	Purchased goods and services Business travel Employee commutes Waste disposal Use of sold products Transportation and distribution (both upstream and downstream) Investments Leased assets and franchises

According to the GHGP, all organisations should quantify Scope 1 and 2 emissions when reporting, but there is currently no mandatory requirement to report Scope 3 emissions. Having said that, increasing numbers of organisations are reaching into their value chain to understand the full impact of their operations. Scope 3 often offers carbon emission reduction opportunities, as these may be a significant part of an organisation's total carbon footprint. Although they are not under the organisation's own control, it may be possible to have an impact on the activities that cause them. This also represents an opportunity for the organisation to influence and engage its suppliers.[7]

Consider all three scopes in a holistic way

It is relatively easy for organisations to reduce their Scope 1 and 2 emissions due to the direct influence or control, and they may already have the required data and information to measure and manage their carbon footprint. However, many organisations have realised that their highest impact falls under indirect Scope 3, particularly the supply chain, with some organisations reporting that as much as 80% of their emissions are in this category, and a few stating that these account for up to 97% of their total carbon footprint.[8] This therefore makes Scope 3 emissions accounting and management very important. Undertaking this activity can strengthen a company's understanding of its value chain, as a step towards effectively managing emissions-related risks and opportunities. If an organisation is not including Scope 3 in its carbon management, it means a significant portion of emissions is neglected. However, Scope 3 emissions are the toughest for many organisations to measure and reduce. When evaluating specific measures to reduce emissions, the carbon management action plan must consider the impact of both direct and indirect emissions (i.e, Scope 1, 2 and 3).

Countries such as the United Kingdom, the United States of America and those in the EU are predominantly focused on Scopes 1 and 2. However, in the United Kingdom, under the Streamlined Energy and Carbon Reporting (SECR) legislation, certain entities must report on Scope 3, and the rules relating to which size and type of organisation and the types of emissions have been tightened up since their introduction in 2019, and it is believed they may get tighter still as the country approaches its Net Zero deadline.[9] Under Scope 3, certain companies must currently disclose energy use and related carbon emissions from business travel in rented or employee-owned vehicles where the organisation purchases the fuel.[10] Reporting on Scope 1 and 2 emissions is mandatory for all companies in SECR: quoted companies need to report on global emissions and large unquoted companies/LLPs must report on their UK emissions.[9] Countries such as the United Kingdom, the United States of America, Australia and Canada have developed carbon accounting and reporting tools to support organisations, as covered in chapter 12 (Carbon Accounting).

Key steps for managers in their carbon management journey

With regards to measuring and managing the three scopes of emissions, the following are the key steps for managers:

1. **Understand your carbon emissions impact** based on the three scopes to have a clear picture of your organisation's emissions (baseline).
2. **Treat carbon management as a journey**, starting with Scopes 1 and 2, and those elements in Scope 3 where you have data/information and control.
3. **Report (and reduce) those emissions that fall into Scopes 1 and 2**. This is already mandatory for many organisations across the world (Scope 3 emissions remain mostly voluntary to report at present).
4. **Develop the Organisational and Operational Boundary (OOB) for the whole organisation** based on business operations and the value chain (Scopes 1, 2 and 3). Your organisation's Net Zero journey cannot be achieved without measuring and reducing Scope 3 impacts.
5. **Review the data required** for the different scopes that will enable the calculation of your organisation's carbon footprint (see chapter 12); to develop carbon reduction targets (chapter 13) and strategy, policies, and practices for carbon management (chapter 14).
6. **High impact will only be achieved if organisations address Scope 3 emissions in a holistic way** alongside Scopes 1 and 2. Companies should work with their suppliers and other stakeholders to achieve reductions along the supply chain. See chapter 8 (Procurement & Supply) in this book for inspiration on how this can be done.

Carbon management is about making gradual progress, not perfection. Every step an organisation can take, such as securing more accurate data, is a step forward in their continuous improvement journey.

WANT TO DIG DEEPER?

Doing Business in a New Climate: A Guide to Measuring, Reducing, and Offsetting Greenhouse Gas Emissions – book by Paul Lingl, Deborah Carlson and the David Suzuki Foundation
This guide presents a step-by-step approach for greenhouse gas/carbon management with real-life examples to illustrate the options available to organisations to reduce their emissions and climate impact, as well as improve their bottom line. It provides insights into scopes, boundaries and collecting data for carbon footprinting.

A Corporate Accounting and Reporting Standard
The Greenhouse Gas Protocol https://ghgprotocol.org/corporate-standard
This explains the requirements and provides guidance for organisations preparing a corporate-level GHG emissions inventory. It includes the greenhouse gases covered by the Kyoto Protocol. Updated in 2015, it allows organisations to measure and report carbon emissions. This is a comprehensive document that managers can follow whether at the early stages or more advanced.

Carbon Footprinting Introductory Guide
Carbon Trust https://www.carbontrust.com/resources/a-guide-carbon-footprinting-for-businesses
This guide introduces two types of carbon footprinting within organisations: one that measures the overall activities, and another that examines the life cycle of products/services (beyond the scope of this book). It also explains how organisations can measure and communicate their carbon footprint and the related commercial benefits to their stakeholders. This is particularly helpful for managers at the early stage, with a step-by-step approach for carbon accounting.

What are Organisational and Operational Boundaries?

To develop an Operational Boundary, organisations should first define their Organisational Boundary. That will detail any branches or subsidiaries to be included in their carbon footprinting. It will also help determine which parts of the business organisation need to be involved in its carbon management, through the measurement of its carbon emissions.

The Organisational Boundary is used to develop an Operational Boundary based on the scopes of emissions. Establishing the Organisational Boundary ensures the carbon footprint is a representation of emissions based on the ownership or control of activities and appropriate actions can then follow. Operational Boundary decisions lead to the identification of direct and indirect emissions, thus the different 'scopes', and help identify which are included, which are not, and why. One way to determine this for an organisation is to draw up a simple map of all its sites and related carbon emission sources, and to determine whether they are Scope 1, 2 or 3.[11]

Mapping the Operational Boundary

The following are the steps an organisation can take to identify its carbon emission sources, categorise them as Scope 1, 2 and 3 and draw up an Operational Boundary.[11] These are then used in the organisation's carbon accounting (demonstrated in chapter 12).

1. Identify the physical sites within the Organisational Boundary
2. Map electricity and gas use, as well as any other fuels used for all the business sites
3. Map other sources of carbon emissions:
    a. all types of travel and transportation activities
    b. other on-site emission sources, such as the fugitive emissions of chemicals used in refrigeration or manufacturing processes within the organisation
    c. material inputs (e.g. packaging, paper and other supplies) sourced externally
    d. outsourced services such as cleaning
    e. products sold by the business (their end-use will produce emissions during the life of the product)
    f. waste produced by the organisation (this will produce emissions when sent to landfill)
    g. external events such as conferences or meetings hosted by the organisation.

Once the carbon emission sources are identified and categorised by scope, and an Operational Boundary is mapped, the next step is to gather emissions activity/resource data for all the sources that have been included in the Boundary.

Figure 11.2 shows the carbon emission sources for an example business organisation, showing how emissions are categorised and form part of an Operational Boundary. In the figure, **Electricity** used at the Head Office, the Branch Office and the Processing Plant is **Scope 2**, whereas for the Warehouse, as a leased space, it is categorised as **Scope 3**. On the other hand, **Heat** (natural gas) used in the Head Office, the Branch Office and the Processing Plant, is **Scope 1**, whereas for the leased Warehouse, the Heat (natural gas) is once again **Scope 3** (as with the Electricity).

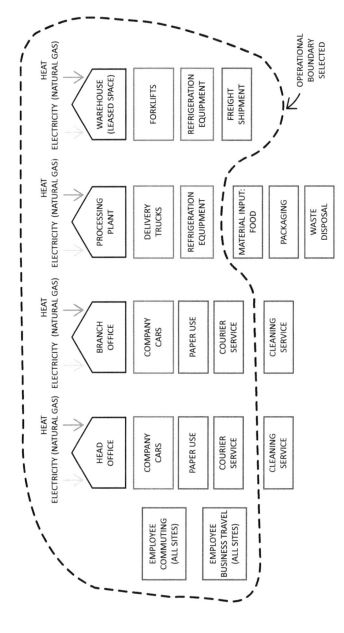

Figure 11.2 Emission sources and Operational Boundary for an example business organisation used with permission of the David Suzuki Foundation.

Likewise, **Company Cars** at Head and Branch Offices, and **Delivery Trucks** and **Refrigeration Equipment** at the Processing Plant will be **Scope 1,** as are the **Forklifts and Refrigeration Equipment** in the Warehouse (even though it is leased space) – this is due to the direct control the company has over fuel consumption and associated emissions for all of these. All are shown inside the Operational Boundary (the dotted line in the figure) for this example business organisation. All other sources of emissions presented in the boxes both inside and outside the Boundary will be Scope 3. (For clarity, those inside the Boundary include all Employee Commuting and all Business Travel, Paper Use and Courier Services, and finally Warehouse Freight Shipments.)

It must be noted that organisations need to avoid double counting. By clearly defining their approach to the Organisational Boundary, stating what is included, and why, and how the decisions were made, along with consistent application, double counting should be avoided. This should ensure that organisational emissions are not included in the inventories of two different companies during carbon footprinting. Double counting is likely to be more of a problem for national greenhouse gas accounting if the Organisational Boundaries are not clearly identified.

Measuring and reducing carbon emissions

How do I measure and reduce Scope 1?

Scope 1 is the starting point when it comes to measuring and managing carbon emissions. These occur from sources that are owned or controlled by the organisation, and the data related to the resources such as gas, boiler fuel, furnaces and vehicles should be readily available. With the help of carbon conversion factors, these emissions can therefore be measured relatively easily. After the calculations, organisations need to decide what actions they can take to reduce their Scope 1 emissions. You can find some inspiration in chapter 7 (Estates & Facilities) and chapter 14 (Policies & Practices) for developing your plan to reduce these direct carbon emissions.

How do I measure and reduce Scope 2?

Scope 2 is also not difficult to measure as these are indirect emissions associated with the purchase of electricity, heat, steam or cooling. These occur at the facility where they are generated and are accounted for in the reporting organisation's carbon inventory, as they are a result of that organisation's energy use. After the calculations, organisations need to decide what actions they can take to reduce Scope 2 emissions. As with Scope 1, we recommend chapters 7 and 14 for emission reduction suggestions related to the use of energy (electricity) in estates, buildings and other facilities within your organisation. Scopes 1 and 2 are areas where organisations can act fast and make an impact very quickly.

How do I measure and reduce Scope 3?

By contrast, Scope 3 presents organisations with a challenge in terms of both measurement and management. These are all other indirect emissions, for example, business travel, employee commuting, waste, water and emissions from the organisation's value chain. These carbon emissions are often hard to track, especially in a long and complex chain. It can be difficult to obtain necessary information or data as the reporting organisation is not producing these emissions directly and does not have control over them. At the same time, the organisation has less influence on reducing these emissions.

Start by engaging your internal stakeholders (employees) and external stakeholders (suppliers) where you do not have the necessary data. This can make a real difference and you can share knowledge and support each other to help minimise impact, as well as securing all the required information in a transparent way. The goal is to account for all Scope 3 elements in your defined Operational Boundary so that you can have a comprehensive picture of your carbon footprint that will help you to plan to achieve a Net Zero future.

See chapter 4 for understanding how your organisation can reduce Scope 3 emissions associated with travel and transport, and chapter 8 for those associated with procurement and the supply chain. Chapter 6 deals with reducing food waste and gives insights into various measures to reduce this as part of your carbon management strategy.

Data requirements and stakeholder engagement

Once the Operational Boundary is mapped out for your organisation, the next step is to gather the relevant information about each emission source.

This is also referred to as resource or activity data and it is simply the measurement of the activities that generate carbon emissions, in standard units such as kilometres driven, litres of fuel used, and kilowatt hours of electricity consumed.[11] Collecting the required data is often the most challenging and time-consuming part, because it might not have been captured in a systematic way. The accuracy of the carbon footprint is based on the quality of data and it is therefore important to collect these carefully. Your organisation may not have all the data for emission sources, so you should make a start and work on what you *do* have already. Where details are unavailable, you may need to make estimates and sensible judgments, particularly in your first year.

To simplify and standardise the process, many organisations develop an information management system. This will involve identifying which data need to be gathered, from which sources, who will be responsible, and how the data will be managed and stored.

The following are all likely to be needed, and in most cases will be readily available:

- Energy consumption (electricity, gas, heat, diesel, liquefied petroleum gas (LPG) and other fuel)
- Travel and transport (related to business travel, distribution of goods and employee commuting)
- Water consumption
- Waste generation
- Refrigerant consumption, for example in air conditioning or refrigeration units.

Further details can be seen in Table 11.2 where emission sources and related data requirements are presented with their respective units. That is reprinted with permission from the book: **Doing Business in a New Climate**, by Lingl, Carlson and the David Suzuki Foundation, which we recommend to support you in setting up a Greenhouse Gas Management Plan.

As discussed earlier, stakeholder engagement is very important for carbon accounting and management. You would need to engage different departments in your own organisation to gather the required information, for example, the Finance department for your energy bills and fuel

Table 11.2 Common emission sources and where to find activity resource data reprinted with permission of the David Suzuki Foundation

Emission Source	Where to Find Activity Data	Typical Units/Data Type
Purchased electricity	Utility bills; online customer accounts.	kWh, MWh
Purchased heat (e.g. district heating)	Utility bills; online customer accounts.	GJ, BTUs, therms, MWh, lbs of steam
On-site heat generation (e.g., furnaces)	Utility bills; fuel purchase records and invoices; storage tank logs; online customer accounts.	Litres, gallons, GJ, m^3, cubic ft, kg, lbs, BTUs
Company-owned vehicles	Fuel purchase records; fuel receipts; fuel tank logs. If fuel consumption data are not available, kilometres travelled (trip records, odometer readings, maintenance records) and vehicle make and model year are a second-best option when used with online vehicle emission calculators.	fuel type and amount (litres/gallons), or km/miles travelled and vehicle make/model year
Business travel (vehicle)	Accounting receipts; expense claims.	fuel type and amount (litres/gallons), or km/miles travelled and vehicle make/model year
Business travel (air)	Online calculators can be used to find distances for flights.	km/miles flown, or possibly fuel used (in the case of charter flights)

SCOPES & BOUNDARIES   279

Employee commuting	Many employers use surveys to collect data about this – free online survey providers can be useful.	km/miles travelled and mode of transportation, or fuel type and amount consumed
Freight transport	Shipping invoices; delivery invoices. Shipping and delivery companies may need to be contacted to obtain the information required, i.e. the weight shipped and the distance travelled.	kg/lbs/tonnes and km/miles transported, and mode of transport (truck, rail, air, ship)
Leased space	Lessees might not receive bills for electricity or heating/cooling charges. In this case, average calculations can be done based on the size of the space and the length of time it is used.	m^2 or sq. ft and number of days
Material inputs	Receipts for purchases; suppliers; life-cycle analysis calculators.	Varies
Fugitive emissions (air conditioning/refrigeration equipment, pipelines, etc.)	Industry and government publications; equipment specifications.	Varies
Outsourced services	Request this information from contractors or suppliers, or work with them to obtain it.	Varies

purchase records. External stakeholders will need to be engaged in collecting the necessary Scope 3 activity data, such as information from suppliers and contractors regarding the products you purchase for your organisation.

Various online tools can be used to secure travel-related data, such as distances for business travel. It is probably easiest to start with the relevant departments within your organisation and then go to external stakeholders for comprehensive data collection. Table 11.2 highlights where to find different types of data and who might be the relevant stakeholders to engage in this process.

Other considerations such as deciding on your base year and how to calculate each scope, are covered in chapter 12 (Carbon Accounting).

Case study

In order to help you understand how a small company could attempt to measure its carbon footprint, the case study below explains how a small Nottingham-based design company used the services of its local university to start the process. The benefits to the organisation are also outlined.

Carbon footprint calculations for an SME – Red Peak Design

By Jane Bannister (BA (Hons) International Business 2022 Graduate)

Red Peak Design Ltd. is an SME located in The Creative Quarter of Nottingham, England. Its primary business activity is the creation of exhibitions, interiors and design. At present, the company is owned and operated by a single proprietor, with plans for expansion in the next 12 months.

Wanting to safeguard the company against increasing utility bills and keen to learn more about carbon reduction strategies, Red Peak engaged the services of Nottingham Business School, Nottingham Trent University's Student Carbon Consultants on the Sustainability in Enterprise Project (SiEP) module. SiEP is part of the Sustainability in Enterprise Programme, partly funded by the European Regional Development Fund (ERDF).[12] Red Peak has taken a proactive approach to sustainable development by early engagement with the SiEP and exploring business practices that could potentially reduce its carbon footprint. The company is at the early stage of its sustainability journey, and like many SMEs has limited resources.

The House of Commons Library reported that in 2021 there were over 5.6 million SMEs in the United Kingdom, and the British Business Bank revealed that these organisations accounted for *nearly 50% of all greenhouse gas emissions emitted.*[13] This means that SMEs have the opportunity to make significant reductions in their carbon footprints through sustainable business practices.

Risks and opportunities

Through the SiEP consultancy work, three main drivers for action on climate change for Red Peak were identified: water usage, electricity usage and reputation. Each issue was assessed for its potential risks and opportunities.

Addressing water and electricity usage may present opportunities for Red Peak to improve operational efficiencies and lead to cost savings. For example, expenditure on water in 2020 was twice as much as in 2019. Inadequate management and monitoring of this resource would continue to expose the company to rising costs.

By taking action, it would demonstrate to stakeholders that the organisation is moving towards being more sustainable. This also connects with the issue of Red Peak's reputation. Inaction against climate change may see Red Peak lose business to other more sustainable design companies, and it also inhibits innovative design prospects. On the other hand, taking a proactive approach to sustainable development is an opportunity for Red Peak to generate positive publicity for the organisation and expand its customer base. This could also be highlighted throughout its communications as a USP for the company.

Methodology/approach for scopes and operational boundary setting

In order to conduct the carbon emissions assessment, primary data were collected and supplied by the proprietor. The data related to electricity and water usage for 2019 and 2020 and were supplied in the form of utility bills. Electricity is measured in kilowatt hours (kWh) and water is measured in cubic metres (m^3).

The earliest, most comprehensive and complete data were provided for 2019. This was therefore taken as the base year, using the corresponding conversion factors. This is an important decision as incomplete or missing data would skew the carbon calculations and would not be representative of actual emissions.

Following the data collection, Red Peak's business activities were identified, categorised into appropriate scopes, and the Operational Boundary was defined to ensure all sources of emissions were accounted for and to avoid double counting.

Figure 11.3 shows the scopes and Operational Boundary for Red Peak Design. The company operates out of a single office space in a shared building with a single employee. A company vehicle was the single Scope 1 emission source. As explained earlier, Scope 2 activities were included within the Operational Boundary with Scope 3 water use, as data were available for these items. Other Scope 3 activities included end use of products by clients, outsourced printing and design, paper use, packaging, waste disposal, business travel and employee commuting, where relevant.

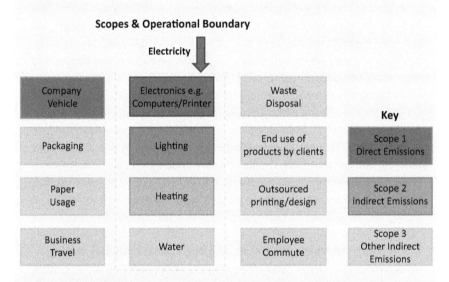

Scope 1: Company Vehicle
Scope 2: Electricity - Electronics equipment, e.g., computers/printer, Lighting, Heating
Scope 3: Water, Waste Disposal, End use of products by clients, Outsourced printing/design, Employee Commute, Business Travel, Paper Usage, Packaging

Figure 11.3 Scopes and operational boundary for Red Peak Design.

The proprietor acknowledged that greater impacts could be made with regards to carbon emission reductions via supplier analysis, however, without the appropriate data, these activities could not be analysed. Suppliers and procurement fall under Scope 3 emissions and usually form the greatest share of an organisation's carbon footprint. These are notoriously difficult to calculate as they are based on third-party data, which is not always available.

Recommendations

Following the data analysis, and in order to reduce Red Peak's carbon emission levels, the student consultants gave recommendations, such as switching to LED lighting. The installation of LED lights is aimed at reducing electricity wastage leading to energy bill savings. LEDs consume less energy, create fewer carbon emissions and last up to 25 times longer than traditional bulbs. Combined, these factors make LED lights the more sustainable choice.

The second recommendation was to install Amazon Smart Plugs, also aimed at saving energy. These enable users to control electronic device settings via a compatible app (Alexa) on their mobile phone. Controls such as timer settings and the capability to turn devices off remotely means users can save on energy costs and wastage. It is simple to set up and does not require a smart home hub, only the Alexa app.

If adopted, switching to LED lights and using Amazon Smart Plugs could see Red Peak Designs reduce their carbon emissions from electricity use by 6% in 2023, alone.

Jane Bannister is a 2022 BA (Hons) International Business graduate from Nottingham Business School, NTU, England. Jane has a keen interest in sustainability, demonstrated through her involvement in the SiEP module (when she was part of the student consultancy team to Red Peak Designs), Eco Ambassador and Enactus roles and achievement of the Gold Sustainability Award. Jane plans to incorporate her skills and knowledge into her food gifting business.

Quick Wins

1. Focus on Scope 1 and Scope 2 first to measure and reduce carbon emissions and start to collect the necessary data.
2. Choose the elements of Scope 3 where you have data available and start gathering data related to the difficult parts of Scope 3, so you can measure and manage these indirect emissions in future.
3. Engage with your internal and external stakeholders.
4. Ensure that you are improving your data management systems for accurate carbon accounting and expanding your Operational Boundary to include all three scopes.
5. Check whether local organisations, such as a university, local authority, chamber of commerce or trade association, offer any relevant support or resources.

Outlook

As shown in this chapter, having established the Organisational Boundary, there are three scopes of emissions which an organisation needs to understand within its defined Operational Boundary. This will facilitate the measurement of carbon emissions so that actions can be taken to reduce them, and to deploy high-impact climate solutions for reaching Net Zero.

We recommend that you start by drawing up an implementation plan like the one suggested in Figure 11.4 for all your scopes. Following that, you would need to develop your boundaries and collect the relevant data to calculate your actual carbon footprint.

It is then worth reading some of the other chapters, such as chapter 13, to help you to set science-based targets, along with chapters 4, 5, 6, 7 and 8

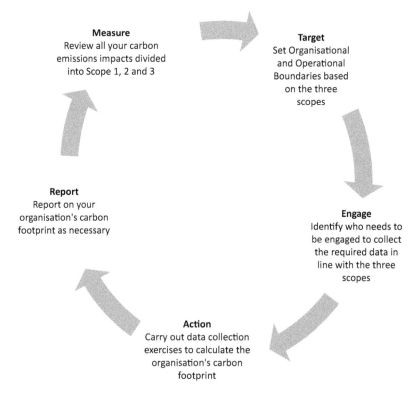

Measure
Review all your carbon emissions impacts divided into Scope 1, 2 and 3

Target
Set Organisational and Operational Boundaries based on the three scopes

Engage
Identify who needs to be engaged to collect the required data in line with the three scopes

Action
Carry out data collection exercises to calculate the organisation's carbon footprint

Report
Report on your organisation's carbon footprint as necessary

Figure 11.4 Implementation plan for developing scopes for calculating your organisation's carbon footprint.

where specific carbon reduction measures are suggested which affect all three scope areas. These are potential ideas for your organisation to borrow and adapt in your own context as part of the carbon management process. Chapter 12 will assist you in carrying out the calculations involved, and chapter 14 will help you set the policies and strategy to support your work.

Further Resources

On the companion website to this book you can find further materials to help you plan and implement this work.

Below you can find some links that go into more detail on the above or suggest further insights and support that might be of interest in addition to the ones mentioned already.

General

The GHG Protocol Corporate Value Chain (Scope 3) Accounting and Reporting Standard:
https://ghgprotocol.org/standards/scope-3-standard
This is a global standard that allows organisations to assess their value chain emissions impact and identify areas of focus in carbon emission reduction.

GHG Protocol Scope 3 Calculation Guidance:
https://ghgprotocol.org/scope-3-technical-calculation-guidance
This international Scope 3 guidance helps organisations in their corporate value chain Scope 3 accounting. By accounting for your value chain emissions, you can start to manage them.

Small business user guide –Guidance on how to measure and report your greenhouse gas emissions:
https://www.gov.uk/government/publications/small-business-user-guide-guidance-on-how-to-measure-and-report-your-greenhouse-gas-emissions
This guidance aims to explain how UK organisations can measure and report their greenhouse gas emissions and set reduction targets.

Courses

How to Measure, Reduce and Offset your Company's Carbon Footprint:
https://www.futurelearn.com/courses/how-to-measure-reduce-and-offset-your-companys-carbon-footprint
This six-week online course (three hours per week) can guide you to measure your carbon footprint and develop carbon management strategies for your organisation.

Corporate Value Chain (Scope 3) Standard:
https://ghgprotocol.org/scope3-standard-online-course
This online course can help you in carbon accounting for Scope 3 value chain emissions. It can guide you to identify and categorise Scope 3 emissions, collect the required data based on your scopes and Operational Boundary, calculate your emissions and set your Scope 3 targets.

Notes

1. UNFCCC, *The Paris Agreement*: https://unfccc.int/process-and-meetings/the-paris-agreement/the-paris-agreement
2. World Resources Institute, *Greenhouse Gas Protocol*: https://www.wri.org/initiatives/greenhouse-gas-protocol
3. European Commission, *Glossary: Carbon dioxide equivalent*: https://ec.europa.eu/eurostat/statistics-explained/index.php?title=Glossary:Carbon_dioxide_equivalent
4. Deloitte, *Zero in on Scope 1, 2 and 3 emissions*: https://www2.deloitte.com/uk/en/focus/climate-change/zero-in-on-scope-1-2-and-3-emissions.html
5. GHG Protocol, WRI & WBCSD (2004) *The GHGP Corporate Accounting and Reporting Standard*. WRI and WBCSD, March, p. 26: https://ghgprotocol.org/corporate-standard
6. The Carbon Trust, *Scope 3 emissions*: https://www.carbontrust.com/resources/briefing-what-are-scope-3-emissions
7. United States Environmental Protection Agency, *Scope 3 Inventory Guidance*: https://www.epa.gov/climateleadership/scope-3-inventory-guidance
8. Edie, *Scope 3 and the supply chain*: https://www.edie.net/scope-3-and-the-supply-chain-how-businesses-are-taking-sustainability-leadership-to-a-new-frontier/

9. SECR FAQS: https://secrhub.co.uk/scope-3-emissions-your-frequently-asked-questions/

10. Inspired Energy, *SECR reporting*: https://inspiredenergy.co.uk/secr-reporting-including-scope-3/

11. Lingl P, Carlson D and the David Suzuki Foundation, *Doing Business in a New Climate:* https://davidsuzuki.org/wp-content/uploads/2021/03/Doing_Business_2010.pdf

12. Sustainability in Enterprise 2022: more information about this project https://www.ntu.ac.uk/business-and-employers/financial-and-funded-support/sustainability-in-enterprise

13. Mavrokefalidis D (2021) SMEs are to blame for nearly half of UK firms' emissions, *United Kingdom: Energy Live News*: https://www.energylivenews.com/2021/10/21/smes-are-to-blame-for-nearly-half-of-all-uk-firms-emissions/

12

CARBON ACCOUNTING: WHY WHAT YOU MEASURE MATTERS!

Richard Howarth and Fiona Winfield

In this chapter, we seek to keep carbon accounting simple and adopt a step-by-step approach which provides insights to key issues and considerations. We have primarily used information and guidance from the World Resources Institute (WRI), which publishes the Greenhouse Gas Protocol (GHGP) – the global standards for measuring and managing GHG emissions.

Moving through the chapter, we set out and define principles in carbon accounting using examples to support action. We will look at important elements such as: where do you start, what data and information do you need, how do you support accuracy of the GHG emissions inventory and what else do you need to do to ensure action and improvements in the future.

This chapter is for you if:

- You are an owner of a company
- You do the accounting for any organisation

DOI: 10.4324/9781003274049-15

- You are interested in how the carbon footprint of products, processes and entire organisations can be calculated
- You want to make a Greenhouse Gas Emissions Inventory for an organisation.

It will cover:

- Definitions of key terms such as base year and carbon intensity
- A step-by-step approach to compile a Greenhouse Gas Emissions Inventory
- A quick and basic inventory
- Detailed calculations, for example activities or GHG sources, in each of the scopes (1, 2 and 3)
- A case study on how to read GHG accounts.

Measure to reduce!

The starting point for the chapter is – why is it important to account for carbon emissions? The simple answer is that it's for the same reason as we account for anything related to an organisation's activities – to support decision-making, including the assessment and improvement of performance and effectiveness. Carbon 'footprinting' (see also chapter 1) and accounting for GHG emissions enable you to identify the availability of data and information, to set and evaluate objectives, and to manage risks and results over time. Increasingly, various stakeholders, investors for example, demand carbon accounting along with reporting and disclosure, and these are discussed in chapter 3 (Communication & Reporting) and chapter 10 (Pensions & Investments). If we want to report effectively, to improve our performance and to reduce our GHG emissions, we need to start by measuring them, so we therefore need to do carbon accounting!

This chapter is relevant for individuals, micro and smaller businesses, as well as larger corporate organisations. For some, carbon auditing and reporting may be a requirement; normally larger, quoted or permitted organisations are legally bound to undertake this, and some have to report when bidding for contracts. Or there may simply be a desire to take action in this important area reflecting the organisation's values and priorities. Whatever the starting point, carbon accounting is fundamental to the assessment of countries, industries and organisations, and the effective tracking and benchmarking of results. Ultimately, this facilitates the achievement of global, national and organisational commitments and also reflects the requirements of society, customers and investors.

There is a raft of information and guidance available from many different sources: governments and agencies, professional bodies and representative groups, charities and interested parties, consultancies and so on. In this chapter, we will adopt a step-by-step approach, which provides insights to key issues and considerations. As mentioned above, we will draw on the resources of the GHG Protocol as it is relevant for organisations of all sizes, across diverse industries and territories. This supports consistency, when used correctly. For many years, the term 'carbon accounting' has been used – see for example the 'Handbook of Carbon Accounting' recommended in our 'Dig Deeper' section in this chapter – and that is the term we will use here. Others however are tending to use the term 'greenhouse gas (GHG) accounting' and that may well eventually replace 'carbon accounting', particularly as the United Nations' work related to climate change signals the importance of 'GHG accounting' and the harmonisation of work and standards in this area.[1]

Carbon accounting – key approaches and definitions

Whichever specifications or guidelines are followed, the approach to carbon accounting is nearly always the same and will address:

- **Planning** – selecting and identifying the approach to be taken and planning the GHG emissions inventory. This includes establishing the Organisational and Operational Boundaries – these are further defined and explained in chapter 11 (Scopes & Boundaries) – and a data time frame.
- **Measurement** – collating the relevant data and information to facilitate calculations. This process must produce a true and fair account of emissions and account for the significance and importance of related activities and sources.
- **GHG emissions management** – using a base year and setting objectives and targets to support the tracking of trends and progress, for example

towards Net Zero (defined in the introductory chapter 1), and finally reviewing progress. This also includes accounting for GHG reductions, reporting and disclosure, and ongoing inventory management and quality.

The following should underpin your approach when starting the process:

- **Relevance** – as an important first step, you must define your Organisational and Operational Boundaries carefully as this affects all the decisions you need to make. Ensure the boundaries selected effectively capture the organisation's GHG emissions. If they do not, ensure this is recognised and the reasons are acknowledged.
- **Completeness** – having defined the boundaries, make sure you include the full extent of GHG emissions from identified sources and activities within them.
- **Consistency** – ensure you always use the same approach to collect, collate and use data and information. Keep notes of the definitions used and explanations to support, as necessary.
- **Accuracy** – without accurate data, or acknowledgement of uncertainties (which should ideally be avoided), judgements and decisions about performance and the next steps will be undermined.
- **Transparency** – ensure you explain the processes, data sources and calculations used in a way that can be understood easily by others to support comparison.

Some useful terms and explanations used to develop a GHG Emissions Inventory are described in chapter 11 (Scopes & Boundaries). We therefore recommend reading that chapter before this one, to understand the different scopes and how to establish boundaries. We have highlighted some key considerations again below, as they are especially relevant for good carbon accounting.

The **'accounting and reporting' timeframe** identifies and establishes the period covered by the inventory. This is normally 12 months to account for seasonal differences. Only GHG emissions relating to the specified time period and from the specified boundaries should be included.

Setting a suitable **base year** is fundamental to allow comparisons and effective performance tracking over time. Relevance is the best criterion for establishing this at an organisational level. Some choose 1990 as it matches the year of the Kyoto Protocol. However, this only works if you have the associated data readily available. We therefore recommend that you select the earliest *relevant* year, maybe the first year a GHG emissions assessment is undertaken. If the approach to calculations is changed in subsequent years, it will be necessary to go back to the base year and re-calculate that in the same way, to support consistency, accuracy and comparisons.

A ratio indicator/benchmarking metric also needs to be agreed upon, this is a performance metric relevant to the organisation which, along with the base year, provides a means for interpretation and realistic comparisons internally and externally. In the Campbell's case study later in this chapter, the ratio indicator is 'tonnes of food'. This ratio is then used to offer assessment and comparisons based on energy used and GHG emissions produced for the company in question.

Calculating GHG emissions and related matters

GHG emissions are measured either directly or through the use of activity data and conversion factors, which are very important in this context as there is more than one greenhouse gas. The GHGs regulated by the Kyoto Protocol are carbon dioxide (CO_2), methane (CH_4), nitrous oxide (N_2O), hydrofluorocarbons (HFC), perfluorocarbons (PFC) and sulphur hexa-fluoride (SF_6).[2] These all have very different global warming potentials (GWP), which means they may contribute to faster rises in temperature than CO_2 – the benchmark gas – as they retain more heat or remain in the atmosphere for longer.

The use of different fuels, direct and indirect, leads to GHG emissions, but so do other activities and sources, such as landfills for waste man-agement, which release methane. To compare the carbon impact, the GWP of different fuels, activities and gases, a 'standardised' emission measure-ment is needed, which is CO_2 equivalent: CO_2e. The GHGP Corporate Standard defines CO_2e as *the universal unit of measurement to indicate the global warming potential (GWP) of each of the six greenhouse gases, expressed in terms of the GWP of one unit of carbon dioxide.*[3] It is used to evaluate the impact of different GHGs against a common basis.

'Carbon Intensity' is another important unit to both suppliers and users of power. According to the British National Grid ESO (Electricity System Operator), [w]hen we talk about the carbon intensity of electricity, we are referring to the number of grams of carbon dioxide (CO_2) that it takes to make one unit of electricity a kilowatt per hour (kW/hour). When electricity is generated using coal power stations, the carbon intensity value is high as CO_2 is produced as part of the power generation process. Renewable forms of generation such as hydro or solar produce almost no emissions, so their carbon intensity is very low. The lower the carbon intensity, the greener the electricity.[4]

Awareness of carbon intensity, which can change from day to day and hour to hour, can be used to manage an organisation's emissions.[5] Carbon Intensity UK, a collaboration between partners including Environmental Defense Fund Europe and Oxford University, produces a forecast of the carbon intensity of UK electricity generation 96+ hours ahead.[6] This can be used to help schedule certain activities which demand higher electricity usage, and links to GHG emissions management, associated plans and practices.

Despite the benefits of understanding carbon intensity to support plans and practices, your organisation's carbon accounting must be based on your GHG emissions and their impacts.[7] Total GHG emissions and removals will, therefore, be the focus of your inventory and the calculations used in its production. A focus on carbon intensity and performance based on this 'metric' alone will not support the transparency of your work related to GHG emissions and removals, and does not facilitate effective comparisons across years and organisations. This leads to misunderstanding, or even misrepresentation, of performance by organisations and interested parties.[8]

Due to the cost and complexity of direct measurement, most organisations calculate the GHG emissions from the different scopes based on activity information and data. In chapter 11, we discussed the various sources of emissions from each scope (see Table 11.1 in that chapter). Here in Table 12.1 we examine the types of activity data that might need assembling.

As indicated in the Table 12.1, the availability of data and information for Scope 3 calculations, and the format of units and data type, may be

Table 12.1 Scopes of carbon emissions[9]

Scopes	Includes	Activity Data Examples
Scope 1	Fuel combustion Company-owned vehicles Fugitive emissions	Fuel usage data for gas or oil used for heating or production
Scope 2	Purchased electricity, heat & steam	Usage data for electricity
Scope 3	Purchased goods & services Business travel/employee commutes Waste disposal/use of sold products Transportation & distribution (up & downstream) Investments/leased assets & franchises	Varies depending on the activity: fuel used, distance travelled, tonnes of waste etc.

more of a challenge to source. The activity information probably won't be stored by the organisation, for example if it relates to transport services provided by others or to raw materials and ingredients. Waste management data on the other hand should be more readily available, as will fuel purchased for a leased vehicle. Although Scope 3 data present a much greater challenge, those emissions will be a core focus for carbon accounting in the next 3–5 years for all organisations due to the high proportion of total emissions that they represent.

The calculation tools available through the GHG Protocol (https://ghgprotocol.org/calculation-tools) are likely to be the most appropriate for an organisation in any country, as this is a central resource and is regularly updated. However, other tools may be more accurate and less generic, therefore more relevant to a specific industry, country, activity or indeed source (such as fugitive emissions – those from leaks or mining activity for example). In the United Kingdom, for example, the Department for Business, Energy and Industrial Strategy (BEIS) produces annual conversion factors for GHG emissions and these are used in this chapter to calculate our examples. If you are based outside of the United Kingdom, it's worth checking if your government advises any specific resources; some suggestions are shown in Box 12.1.

Box 12.1   GHG calculation tools

GHG calculation tools (as at November 2022)

Universal
GHG Protocol:
https://ghgprotocol.org/calculation-tools

Australia
National Greenhouse and Energy Reporting:
http://www.cleanenergyregulator.gov.au/NGER/Forms-and-resources/
Calculators

Canada
Natural Resources Canada:
https://oee.nrcan.gc.ca/corporate/statistics/neud/dpa/calculator/
refs.cfm

European Union (EU)
European Environment Agency:
http://efdb.apps.eea.europa.eu/

United Kingdom
Dept for Business, Energy and Industrial Strategy (BEIS):
https://www.gov.uk/government/collections/government-conversion-
factors-for-company-reporting

United States of America
United States Environmental Protection Agency (EPA):
https://www.epa.gov/energy/greenhouse-gas-equivalencies-calculator

The tools used and the factors underpinning the calculations should be documented so that changes are easily identified. To support consistency, transparency and the creation of GHG inventories, a range of organisations produce and provide inventory or 'footprinting' tools, for example the SME Climate Hub's Business Carbon Calculator.[10] These often consist of a website where activity data can be input, allowing calculation of the equivalent GHG emissions. Whilst clearly useful, do check the credibility of the tool and the underpinning conversion factors before using.

GHG emissions accounting

Estimates may be necessary where data and information are incomplete, unavailable or where accuracy cannot be assured. Signalling clearly that these *are* estimates facilitates transparency and will ensure effective tracking and comparisons over time.

It is most likely that estimates will be needed when undertaking an assessment for the first year or when compiling *indirect* Scope 3 activity data (remember, Scope 3 emissions are from up and down the value chain, buying products from suppliers and the business' own products when its customers use them).

Whether working at organisation or country level, the recognition of reductions in GHG emissions is fundamental. The 'rolling up' approach recommended by the GHGP means working systematically through all sources of emissions, and it supports the recognition of change within the organisation and its operations. For any reductions claimed, it must be possible to identify how and why this happened: the location, cause and effect and the reasons. All this must be clearly articulated, lessons should be learnt, and the results fed into ongoing action and future targets. Being accurate and transparent will also add credibility to any claims made and will underpin the integrity of reports and disclosures.

The outcomes of your carbon accounting activity should be *formally* documented to permit reviewing, assessments and comparisons. Reports are a core element and are essential for communicating and disclosing your ambitions and achievements to relevant stakeholders, internally and externally. If mandated to report externally, there will be specific information and guidance available on what to provide, when and how. The GHGP can also be a source of support, and we have covered that further in chapter 3 (Communication & Reporting). In the following section, we focus on accounting, i.e. the actual bookkeeping, as this needs to be done before any reporting can be undertaken.

GHG emissions disclosure essentially supports transparency and assessment of organisations and, if necessary, industries. It may help organisations to be ahead of changes to policy, and can lead to competitive advantage and promote a positive brand image. Initiatives, such as the Carbon Disclosure Project (CDP)[11] have been developed to support the process, and specific work such as the Task Force on Climate-related Financial Disclosures (TCFD) further facilitates, guides and leads on this topic.

When it comes to carbon accounting and disclosure the question of materiality is also relevant. As mentioned in chapter 3 (Communication & Reporting), this term has traditionally been used in accounting and other contexts but has more recently extended to include wider sustainability and climate-related impacts of, and on, a company. As further explained in chapter 3, materiality can either relate to impact or financial issues (and there is also double materiality).

WANT TO DIG DEEPER?

GHG Protocol: https://ghgprotocol.org/companies-and-organizations
The information and links contained support more detailed insights to GHG emissions' accounting and reporting. There is overall 'corporate' guidance available here and also specific information related to accounting in relation to Scope 1, 2 and 3.

SME Climate Hub: https://smeclimatehub.org/
A global initiative that seeks to empower SMEs to take action related to climate change and GHG emissions, supporting the achievement of targets and resilience. It is complemented by a range of other initiatives and programmes, and has a free business carbon calculator developed with Normative and Google.[12] It is a particularly useful resource for SMEs, but also larger organisations who may wish to signpost it to their suppliers and other partners.

The Handbook of Carbon Accounting
Written by Dr Arnaud Brohé, the CEO of an international carbon reduction and offset firm, and published by Routledge, this is a practical guide for any organisation to help them calculate, reduce, offset and report on their greenhouse gas emissions. It also covers carbon taxation, carbon markets and voluntary offsetting.

Developing a greenhouse gas emission inventory

Creating or updating a GHG emissions inventory is a key component in carbon accounting, management and reporting and is linked to organisational strategy, objectives and result indicators. In this section, we provide details of how to calculate each of the scopes as well as addressing some broader questions.

Whether or not you are *required* to undertake a GHG inventory, without one you will not know the extent of your current GHG emissions. Even if this is not a legal requirement for your organisation at this juncture, a responsible business would normally be keen to act and calculate the effect of its emissions on the bottom line. Our first question is, therefore: **where do I start when developing my GHG emissions inventory?**

A key element of the inventory will be identifying the different types of direct and indirect emissions and carrying out the necessary conversions and calculations, so our second question is: **how do I identify and calculate GHG emissions within the inventory?**

Finally, having sorted your inventory, you might be wondering about the links between accounting, reporting and disclosure. So, our third question is: **what else do I need to consider at this stage?**

Where do I start when developing my GHG emissions inventory?

The starting point for any GHG inventory is to ensure its *relevance*, so your selection and identification of 'boundaries' will be key. That must permit the effective capture of the organisation's GHG emissions and should ensure *completeness*. Start with the identification of the Operational Boundaries and decisions on which scopes to cover. The selection of these must also reflect the Organisational Boundaries selected, that is the parts of the organisation that will be included and those excluded, taking care to avoid any double counting of GHG emissions.

When it comes to the Operational Boundaries, many organisations choose to focus only on Scope 1 and 2 emissions and shy away from Scope 3. But as discussed in chapter 11 (Scopes & Boundaries) and chapter 8 (Procurement & Supply), Scope 3 emissions contribute a large proportion of total GHG emissions for most organisations. To address *relevance* and *completeness*, Scope 3 emissions *should* be included. For clarification on the boundaries, please refer back to chapter 11.

The choices related to the above, what to include and what to exclude, must be documented, along with any reasoning and assumptions. This responds to the principles of *accuracy* and *transparency* and will ground *consistency* over time.

It is recognised that not all organisations want to follow a formalised approach and some might prefer to review more basic relevant information, in order to achieve *Quick Wins*. Although there are downsides to this approach, a simple calculation *can* be undertaken. In Box 12.2, we suggest key points you need to consider for a basic inventory.

Box 12.2   Making a quick and basic inventory

Identify a relevant time period

- Normally 12 months to allow for seasonal differences
- Can be a calendar or financial year

Describe the organisation (or unit) and the approach taken

- Description of organisation (unit) and main GHG sources and fuels – plan what you want to collect (see suggestions below)
- Set the starting point (baseline). Taking electricity as one example: check your usage – if you don't have accurate data, make an estimate, but do keep track from now on
- List metering or monitoring devices used (if applicable)
- List sources used to calculate the activity data – this could include: purchase receipts, utility bills, delivery receipts, contract purchases, on-site metered fuel documentation, stock inventory documentation and heat content documentation from suppliers
- Description of methods applied to estimate emissions for each activity, source and unit
- Description of quality management procedures implemented
- Summary of any changes that may have affected the accuracy, consistency or completeness of calculations

Collect 12 months' worth of data/evidence (in appropriate unit for conversion) as relevant

1. Use of natural gas – for example, for space heating or in production processes (normally kWh)
2. Use of LPG – for example, for space heating or in production processes (normally kWh)
3. Use of coal (normally long or short tons or kg)
4. Use of heating oil (litres or gallons)
5. Top ups to refrigerants (normally litres)

---

6. Petrol or diesel used by company vehicles for business purposes (ideally in litres used)
7. Use of LPG by vehicles for business purposes (ideally in litres used)
8. Electricity use (normally in kWh)

Not all the above will apply, include only those relevant. Activities 1–7 relate to Scope 1 (direct) GHG emissions, while Activity 8 is Scope 2 (indirect) emissions.

To support the creation of the inventory, you can then use the calculators below:

• https://www.carbontrust.com/resources/sme-carbon-footprint-calculator (UK data is used)
• https://www.eia.gov/energyexplained/units-and-calculators/energy-conversion-calculators.php (uses data from the USA)

When using the above calculators, please note they provide an overall assessment of the specific activities, which is only a part of your overall inventory. They also use data from a few years ago, so the conversion factors will not be the most up to date. They are country specific, and this will not be relevant for all territories.

As mentioned elsewhere, you can also use the SME Climate Hub's Business Carbon Calculator, which provides a more detailed assessment: https://smeclimatehub.org/start-measuring/.

How do I identify and calculate GHG emissions within the inventory?

We will now provide a more complete assessment to support the development of a GHG inventory by looking at each scope. Remember, these are only examples, and you need to apply these calculations to all the other sources of emissions that you have identified as relevant to your organisation (see chapter 11 Scopes & Boundaries).

To guide you through the steps to be taken, please refer to Figure 12.1, which is adapted from the GHG protocol's guidance.[13] Once you have mapped the Organisational and Operational Boundaries as advised in chapter 11, and set the time frame, you need to decide which activity resource data to collect. Most data and calculations will be based on 'usage' linked to a suitable metric and associated resource or activity data, such as electricity or oil used, or distance travelled. The calculation approach and tools must then be applied, and the subsequent outcomes mapped against the scopes within the different business areas.

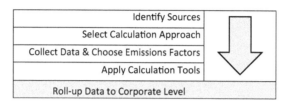

Figure 12.1 GHGP's steps in identifying & calculating GHG emissions adapted from the GHG Protocol.

Using worked examples, we will now guide you through how to carry out the necessary calculations. In these, we assume we are doing an inventory of a small business and have chosen examples which might apply to any such organisation that owns a van (Scope 1), uses electricity (Scope 2) and produces waste (Scope 3). We are basing the calculations on the United Kingdom and the source used was highlighted earlier and comes from: https://www.gov.uk/government/collections/government-conversion-factors-for-company-reporting. The whole process must be suitable to provide as accurate a snapshot as possible, and should allow sufficient insight to support analysis, assessment, judgement and decision-making.

How do I calculate Scope 1?

As noted in chapter 11, Scope 1 emissions are 'direct' and occur from sources owned or controlled by the organisation itself. They are based on the activities and emissions outlined in Figure 12.2.

For our worked example (see Table 12.2), we will use a medium-sized van. According to data from the Society of Motor Manufacturers and Traders (SMMT)[14] in the United Kingdom about 65% of new vehicles are company vehicles. After fleet cars, vans make up the largest proportion of registrations and the segment, based on registrations, has grown about 30% since 2010. The SMMT states that 3.4 million people use or depend on vans for their work, supporting 10% of the UK workforce and delivering a combined wage bill of £56 billion (11% of the United Kingdom's GDP). Important for GHG emissions too!

Scope 1	Scope 2	Scope 3
Fuel combustion **Company vehicles** Fugitive emissions	Purchased electricity, heat, and steam	Purchased goods and services Business travel Employee commuting Waste disposal Use of sold products Transportation and distribution (up-and downstream) Investments Leased assets and franchises

Figure 12.2 Scopes of carbon emissions – highlighting Scope 1.

Table 12.2 Calculating Scope 1 emissions [15]

Applying GHGP's steps in identifying and calculating Scope 1 GHG emissions	
Identify Sources	Company van
Select Calculation Approach	The company does not directly measure the van's GHG emissions, so must gather usage data and use BEIS conversion factors
Collect Data and Choose Emission Factors	The company has details of the number of litres of fuel used in the reporting period
Apply Calculation Tools	The calculation for the vehicle is undertaken using a suitable tool
Roll-up Data to Corporate level	If the company has more than one vehicle, the data for all would be needed
Calculations	
Source	**Diesel van (in 1.7 to 3.5 tonne group)**
Calculation approach	BEIS 2021 conversions - suitable for organisations operating in the United Kingdom
Usage data available	**2,750 litres** used in 2021 (the chosen reporting period) Convert litres to kg of CO_2e as per BEIS guidance Factor to convert litres of fuel to kg CO_2e: 2.51233
Apply calculation	2,750 litres x 2.51233 = 6,908.9075 kg CO_2e = **6.909 tonnes CO_2e**

Calculation comments – Scope 1

The example is relatively straightforward as the conversion factors are available, up to date and are published by a known reputable source – BEIS UK – they are therefore trusted to be used by UK organisations. The activity data can also be cross-checked against the van mileage.

Different cars and travel options could be calculated to decide the best solution to reduce GHG emissions. Fuel consumption could also be reduced by travelling shorter distances, and other solutions are outlined in chapter 4 (Meetings & Transport).[16]

How do I calculate Scope 2?

As noted in chapter 11, Scope 2 emissions are 'indirect' and relate to emissions from the generation of purchased electricity, heat or steam (see Figure 12.3).

Scope 1	Scope 2	Scope 3
Fuel combustion Company vehicles Fugitive emissions	**Purchased electricity, heat, and steam**	Purchased goods and services Business travel Employee commuting Waste disposal Use of sold products Transportation and distribution (up-and downstream) Investments Leased assets and franchises

Figure 12.3 Scopes of carbon emissions – highlighting Scope 2.

Electricity is used in our example (see Table 12.3), as we assume that most UK small businesses use this for lighting and office equipment.

Calculation comments – Scope 2

At face value, this is a relatively basic calculation and is quite straightforward. For most organisations, the availability of bills and meters will mean it is possible to check activity data to support accuracy. It will be important to check both sources, in case of discrepancies. Organisations may have

Table 12.3 Calculating Scope 2 emissions

Applying the GHGP's steps in identifying and calculating Scope 2 GHG emissions	
Identify Sources	Electricity use
Select Calculation Approach	GHG emissions are indirect, so usage data are employed with the current BEIS conversion data
Collect Data and Choose Emission Factors	Energy bills and meter readings are available – it has been possible to undertake a kWh calculation
Apply Calculation Tools	The calculation for electricity use is undertaken using a suitable tool
Roll-up Data to Corporate level	Rolling up the emissions to support corporate level data and insights with connection to activities etc.
Calculations	
Source	Electricity from the grid used in the office
Calculation approach	BEIS 2021 conversions – suitable for organisations operating in the United Kingdom
Usage data available	**6,000 kWh** used 2021 (chosen reporting period) from UK generation kWh must be converted to kg CO_2e as per BEIS guidance Factor to convert kWh of electricity to kg CO_2e is 0.21233
Apply calculation	6,000 kWh x 0.21233 = 1,273.98 kg CO_2e = **1.273 tonnes CO_2e**

sub-metering, 'smart' meters or more complex systems for monitoring and collecting usage data from electricity – the ability to link this use to different activities will be very useful.

If the company used PV solar panels to generate the equivalent amount of electricity this would produce 0 kg CO_2e; please check also chapter 7 (Estates & Facilities) for further ideas on how to reduce the energy consumed or how to use more renewables.

How do I calculate Scope 3?

As noted in chapter 11, Scope 3 emissions are 'indirect' and relate to those from the upstream and downstream activities, use of fuels and sources (see Figure 12.4). As can be seen elsewhere in the book, emissions range from the purchase of goods and services for the 'production' process, and from employee commuting and transport and distribution of goods produced, to the treatment of products at the end of life, waste disposal and recycling.

Scope 1	Scope 2	Scope 3
Fuel combustion Company vehicles Fugitive emissions	Purchased electricity, heat, and steam	Purchased goods and services Business travel Employee commuting **Waste disposal** Use of sold products Transportation and distribution (up-and downstream) Investments Leased assets and franchises

Figure 12.4 Scopes of carbon emissions – highlighting Scope 3.

For this example (see Table 12.4), we use waste produced by the organisation. This is for illustrative purposes but, as DEFRA identifies,[17] about 19% of all UK waste comes from commercial and industrial premises; the vast majority, 69% of all UK waste coming from construction, demolition and excavation activities. As a result, it can be assumed that our UK business in these calculations will, in addition to a van and the use of electricity, also produce some waste.

Calculation comments – Scope 3

The selection of waste disposal was intentional as it's something that most organisations undertake as an activity. The disposal of the waste is not the only Scope 3 emission however, and further calculations would be necessary based on the Operational and Organisational Boundaries.

Concluding comments – calculating GHG emissions from scopes

These worked examples relate to a relatively simple business, so the identification of what needs to be included in the boundaries and the

Table 12.4 Calculating Scope 3 emissions

Applying the GHGP's steps in identifying and calculating Scope 3 GHG emissions	
Identify Sources	Waste disposal
Select Calculation Approach	The company does not directly measure GHG emissions from waste or the types of waste – it will need activity data and the current BEIS conversion data
Collect Data and Choose Emission Factors	The business does not calculate the amount or type of waste produced – estimates are required and must be declared
Apply Calculation Tools	The calculation and notes are below
Roll-up Data to Corporate level	Overall GHG emissions from these sources can be rolled up to the corporate level through different activities etc.
Calculations	
Source	Waste disposal from office and related office activities
Calculation approach	BEIS 2021 conversions – suitable for organisations operating in the United Kingdom
Usage data available	No specific data is available, so an estimate is needed The business has a standard UK wheelie bin (240 litres) collected weekly and the business operates 46 weeks a year There is no hazardous waste and currently no recycling of any waste A month of waste was monitored and weighed: on average, two bin bags were disposed of weekly, containing a total of 10 kg of waste This 'benchmark' was used to identify an average estimated total waste: 10 kg x 46 weeks = **460 kg i.e. 0.46 tonnes** (based on the month's estimate) The weight of waste must be converted to kg CO_2e as per the BEIS guidance: Tonne of commercial waste to landfill converted into kg CO_2e is 467.046
Apply calculation	0.46 tonnes x 467.046 = 214.84116 kg CO_2e = **0. 215 tonnes CO_2e**

associated calculations is straightforward. Any estimates and assumptions used to produce the calculations (such as those related to waste disposal) should be clearly stated and steps should be taken to improve the collection of more accurate data in subsequent years.

It should be recalled that all the calculations need to be *complete* and they must offer an *accurate* assessment of GHG emissions related to the activities and sources captured by the inventory boundaries. The *consistency* of this work should be checked over time to ensure it reflects current guidance and requirements for the organisation and externally. The outcomes should, through their *relevance* and *transparency*, support effective evaluation, comparisons and reviews and, ultimately, decisions.

The example organisation, and these calculations, can be taken forward through work related to chapters 13 and 14, which look at Science-based Targets (SBTs) and Strategy, Policies & Practices, respectively. This will support the illustration of the approach to managing GHG emissions based on the GHG inventory.

What else do I need to consider at this stage?

You may be wondering at this point about the links between ac-counting, reporting and disclosure, in which case, please refer to chapter 3 (Communication & Reporting) where this is discussed in more depth.

It may be relevant for you to gain external recognition or verification of your organisation's GHG inventory, perhaps for reporting and disclosure purposes. There are several standards and specifications available to recognise the quality of the GHG inventory and associated claims. The Greenhouse Gas Protocol (GHGP) is one of these standards.

It should also be noted that the different elements can be measured in different ways, but it is important to ensure that the *right* things are being measured from the perspective of the outputs and the outcomes, while using appropriate ratios and benchmarking metrics. Materiality is key here, in other words, deciding what should be reported alongside the financial information. This should include accounting for, and reporting of, the carbon impacts and any changes.

Within chapters 13 and 14 that follow, we will look at how the GHG emissions from different sources and activities can be removed or managed. In this work, you will need to attend to 'hot spots' – which demand prioritisation due to their impacts and/or importance for your organisation and its products and services, or for your customers. Attention should also be paid to improvements and the removal of GHG emissions. Attention should also be paid to improvements and the removal of GHG emissions and (via SBTs, policies and practices) why, what and how those emissions are removed. The assessment of GHG emissions impact gained via the respective calculations will be important. Your work in supporting the transition to Net Zero will necessitate recognition of both your assessed GHG emissions impacts and insight to the carbon intensity of, for example the energy and fuel used. The focus should be the removal of GHG emissions through climate effective and efficient solutions, this could include for example, the use of renewables.

Case study

With the following case study, we now change the perspective and look at how an accountant would make sense of a published report presented by another company. It also highlights that we need to be very careful which measurements we are using in our accounts and to make sure that we are not 'comparing apple with pears'. Last but not least, it might sensitise you to look very carefully into the claims made by companies, in both ways good and bad.

Making sense of GHG accounting: the devil is in the details

By Professor Ian Thomson (Centre for Responsible Business, University of Birmingham) and Ewan Thomson (Sustainable Finance Analyst, Climate Bonds Initiative)

We are all familiar with the old joke when an accountant was asked what does 2+2 make, they reply – what would you like it to make? The essence of the joke can be applied to GHG reporting too. For example, when is a 579% increase in greenhouse gas not an increase in greenhouse gas? When a business tries to comprehensively measure and report its carbon footprint, rather than comply with misleading listing requirements or corporate reporting guidelines.

So rather than criticising the company responsible for this 'increase' we should reflect on the massive under-reporting of GHGs by almost all businesses.

The apparent 'carbon culprit' reporting a 579% increase was Campbell's in FY2019 (see Table 12.5). Looking at the figures in more detail reveals a whopping 56,501% increase in their Scope 3 emissions, which was slightly offset by reductions in their Scopes 1 and 2.

Table 12.5 Campbell's GHG disclosures for financial years 2016–2020; all figures in tonnes CO_2e[18]

	2016	2017	2018	2019	2020
Scope 1	403,057	427,564	443,186	434,869	469,912
Scope 2	321,939	259,856	250,690	214,265	252,288
Scope 3	8,443	9,742	7,262	4,110,382	5,575,612
Total	733,439	697,162	701,138	4,759,516	6,297,812

Table 12.6 presents the year-on-year percentage change for each scope and for total reported emissions, again the increase seems to be immense.

Table 12.6 Campbell's year-on-year percentage change in GHG emissions by scope for financial years 2016–2020[18]

	16–17	17–18	18–19	19–20
Scope 1	6%	4%	−2%	8%
Scope 2	−19%	−4%	−15%	18%
Scope 3	15%	−25%	56,501%	36%
Total	−5%	1%	579%	32%

But the story beneath the figures, from a GHG inventory and accounting perspective, is a positive one – Campbell's are, quite rightly, refining their approach to the calculation and disclosure of Scope 3 emissions. The result of the changes can be seen in the third row of Tables 12.5 and 12.6 (Scope 3); whilst this suggests a 'problem' – emissions jump between FY2018 and FY2019 from 7,262 to 4,110,382 CO_2e (a 56,501% increase) – the differences here are explained in the supporting notes:

In prior years, Scope 3 emissions included only employee business travel by car, plane and train. In FY2019, Purchased Goods and Services, Capital Goods, Fuel and Energy Related Activities, Waste Generated in Operations, Business Travel, Employee Commuting, Upstream Leased Assets, Downstream Transportation and Distribution, and End of Life Treatment of Sold Products were also included. We have also corrected a unit error from kg to metric tons, removed divestitures and included acquisitions.

With further changes in FY2020 too: *[i]n partnership with an external consultant, we have improved our Scope 3 calculation methodology to be more detailed and accurate and have restated our FY2020 Scope 3 emissions using this methodology.* In other words, they have substantively expanded the categories included in their reported Scope 3 emissions and are now one of the most complete Scope 3 reporters (see Table 12.7) in the S&P 500. Remember that currently in the United Kingdom, corporations are only required to report their Scope 1 and 2 emissions. However, this does suggest that Campbell's Scope 3 emissions in FY2016, 2017, 2018 are not suitable for any meaningful trend or performance analysis.

Table 12.7 Campbell's FY2019/2020 GHG emissions related to the UN GHG Protocol (shaded cells)

Scope 3 upstream	Scope 2 purchase of energy	Scope 1 direct operational emissions	Scope 3 Downstream (after sale)
Purchased goods & services	Purchased electricity	Company facilities	Transportation & distribution
Capital goods	Purchased gas	Company vehicles	Processing of product
Fuel & energy	Purchased heating	Fugitive emissions	Use of product
Transportation & distribution	Purchased steam		End-of-life disposal
Waste from operations	Purchased cooling		Leased assets
Business travel			Franchises
Employees commuting			Investments
Leased assets			Sale of renewable energy

Putting Campbell Soup's emissions in some context

It would be reasonable to assume that given mounting political, scientific and public concern over climate change you would expect an increase in the number of companies disclosing more comprehensive measures of their GHG emissions. Table 12.8 illustrates that the percentage of S&P 500 corporations reporting *any* form of GHG emission in any one year never exceeded 63%. The equivalent percentage for firms reporting any Scope 3 emissions was 43%.

Table 12.8 The number of S&P 500 companies reporting GHG emissions 2015–2019

Scope reported	2015	2016	2017	2018	2019
Scope 1	245	270	298	315	267
Scope 2	238	262	294	309	264
Scope 3	167	183	201	214	196
Percentage reporting any GHG emission data	49%	54%	60%	63%	53%

Externally tracking trends across the years and Scopes benchmarking is at best difficult. Campbell's definition of Scope 3 GHG emissions is substantively different from the definition used by most data providers, listing requirements of most Stock Exchanges or national disclosure requirements.

In our sample of S&P 500 companies disclosing Scope 1, 2 and 3 emissions, on average Scope 1 and 2 emissions only represented 23% of total GHG emissions disclosed by S&P 500 firms in the period 2015–19. However, there was considerable sectoral variation.

Table 12.9 Scope 3 as percentage of voluntary reported emissions by sector for period 2015–2019; S&P 500 companies who voluntarily reported Scope 1, Scope 2 and Scope 3 emissions

Category	2015	2016	2017	2018	2019
Basic Materials	24%	23%	24%	50%	52%
Consumer Discretionary	75%	79%	80%	80%	83%
Consumer Staples	81%	85%	85%	80%	80%

(continued)

Table 12.9 (Continued)

Energy	86%	85%	86%	85%	87%
Financials	47%	55%	68%	74%	69%
Health Care	64%	87%	86%	86%	88%
Industrials	80%	94%	94%	93%	95%
Real Estate	31%	38%	37%	62%	67%
Technology	90%	85%	85%	87%	89%
Telecomms	18%	22%	29%	41%	86%
Utilities	42%	44%	41%	42%	61%
Average for sample	**71%**	**78%**	**78%**	**76%**	**84%**

As Table 12.9 illustrates, Scope 1 and 2 ranged from 82% in Telecomms (where Scope 3 was only 18% in 2015), to as little as 5% in Industrials (where Scope 3 was 95% in 2019). These results confirm prior research that relying on Scope 1 and 2 as a meaningful proxy for climate change impact is highly problematic. It is important to note that this analysis only includes the voluntary disclosure of some Scope 3 emissions, which means these figures are a conservative estimate.

GHG accounting choices matters

If we were to measure GHG performance based on the UK Government's disclosure standard (which is limited to Scope 1 and 2), then we could conclude that in this five-year period the S&P 500 firms had reduced their collective GHG emissions by 26%. Using a similar metric, 61% of the companies could be classified as reducing their annual GHG emissions.

However, if we were to use their self-reported GHG emissions (which include non-standardised inclusion of some Scope 3) we would come to a very different conclusion. Aggregate GHG emissions for this same sample in the same period had increased by 16%, with only 54% of businesses classified as reducing their GHG emissions. And this only relates to *some* Scope 3 emissions!

Top 10 Tips when interpreting GHG accounts

1. Never take GHG emissions disclosed in corporate reports at face value!
2. Confirm how the company has calculated the disclosed GHG emissions, look for a breakdown by UN GHG protocol categories. This detail is normally found in the assurance statement or in notes to

the figures. A breakdown by scope is not granular enough to undertake any meaningful analysis.

3. If you cannot identify which categories are included in disclosed GHG emissions, you cannot use these figures in any reliable evaluation of trends or benchmarking.

4. Look for discrepancies in GHG emissions given in different reports, e.g. Annual Reports, regulatory returns, voluntary CSR reports (i.e. Integrated Reports, Sustainability Reports), corporate websites or other sources, such as the Carbon Disclosure Project. In the case of multiple figures use the most comprehensive measures.

5. Look for discrepancies between corporate climate change strategies, aspirations, targets and how the GHGs are reported. For example, some companies have set Net Zero targets (based on Scope 1 and 2 emissions) yet report Scope 1, 2 and selected Scope 3 emissions. You cannot assume that reported GHGs are appropriate measures of progress against targets.

6. Confirm the reporting entity for the GHG emissions. You cannot assume that the GHG data relates to the consolidated accounting corporate entity for which financial data is available. We have identified cases where the GHG data relates to different accounting entities, particularly if these figures were disclosed in voluntary reports.

7. Do not normalise Scope 1 and 2 emissions by sales, as most GHG emissions associated with sales are excluded.

8. Undertake any analysis at GHG protocol category level, not at an aggregate level if you want to make any sense of the data.

9. Contact businesses to get as much additional detail on their GHG emissions before starting your analysis, and lobby using whatever means at your disposal, to get companies to disclose their full carbon footprint.

10. Always qualify any analysis of GHG performance with an assessment of the quality of data available and clearly disclose what information is missing.

Ian Thomson is professor of accounting and sustainability at Birmingham Business School and has been researching and teaching different dimensions of sustainability, including carbon accountability and climate finance, for over 30 years. He has worked with governments, international development agencies, major corporations and civil society organisations. He is the co-author of Urgent Business: Five myths business needs to overcome to save

itself and the planet, lead author of Net Zero Accounting for a Net Zero UK and an editor of the Routledge Handbook on Environmental Accounting.

Ewan Thomson is a sustainable finance analyst working in the sustainable debt sector on establishing and identifying standards for credible transition finance in the agri-food sector. Previously supported programme development at UNEP's climate finance unit, and as an economic research assistant at the University of Stirling. Graduated with a Master's in Climate Change Finance and Investment from the University of Edinburgh.

Outlook

As mentioned in our overview for chapters 11 to 14, this one, Carbon Accounting, needs to be read in conjunction with chapter 11 (Scopes & Boundaries), chapter 13 (Science-based Targets) and chapter 14 (Policies & Practices). We recommend that you now read the next chapter to understand whether your company would like to set science-based targets. Having set such targets, you would need to ensure you could achieve them by putting the right policies and practices in place. Chapters 4–10 can give you inspiration on how these reductions could be achieved in different parts of the business.

Further Resources

On the companion website to this book you can find further material to help you plan and implement this work. Here we have chosen a few resources which you might find inspiring.

Manufacturing Resilience: Driving Recovery Towards Net Zero
https://www.policyconnect.org.uk/research/manufacturing-resilience-driving-recovery-towards-net-zero
This offers insight and a clear connection between the recovery post– Covid-19 and the transition to Net Zero. It seeks to encourage all organisations to strive to be more efficient and effective. The sorts of challenges and performance improvements mentioned are relevant to manufacturing organisations, but as Scope 3 has a potential impact on all organisations (e.g. through purchased products and services), it should be a useful resource for any organisation.

HBR Article – Accounting for Climate Change

https://hbr.org/2021/11/accounting-for-climate-change

This article offers a useful discussion about accounting for climate change and specifically how emissions are tracked across the supply and value chain (upstream and downstream). Whilst it does not adhere specifically to the guidelines, it offers insight to some of the challenges which may be addressed through more effective inventories and engaging Scope 3 emissions accounting. This will, as noted above, be a necessity in most territories.

Task Force on Climate-related Financial Disclosures – Guidance on Metrics and Targets

https://assets.bbhub.io/company/sites/60/2021/07/2021-Metrics_Targets_Guidance-1.pdf

This resource from the TCFD looks specifically at metrics, targets and transition plans. It offers clear comment and guidance on taking forward the work described earlier in this chapter, and discusses the associated challenges and opportunities. The TCFD's work focuses specifically on effectiveness, which is important when seeking change and ensuring performance is appropriately directed and ultimately assessed.

Notes

1. UNFCCC, *Harmonization of Standards for GHG Accounting*: https://unfccc.int/climate-action/sectoral-engagement/ifis-harmonization-of-standards-for-ghg-accounting

2. Water vapour, ozone and CFCs are other GHGs not covered by the Kyoto protocol, for more information see: Brohe, A (2016) *The Handbook of Carbon Accounting*, London & New York: Routledge, p. 183

3. GHG Protocol, WRI and WBCSD (2004) *The GHGP Corporate Accounting and Reporting Standard*, WRI and WBCSD, March 2004, p. 99: https://ghgprotocol.org/corporate-standard

4. National Grid ESO: https://www.nationalgrideso.com/future-energy/net-zero-explained/what-carbon-intensity

5. Fortune, *Reducing Carbon Emissions is Important*: https://fortune.com/2021/06/25/carbon-intensity-emissions-climate-change-paris-agreement/

6. Carbon Intensity UK: https://carbonintensity.org.uk/

7. GHG Protocol, WRI and WBCSD (2004) *The GHGP Corporate Accounting and Reporting Standard,* WRI and WBCSD, March 2004: https://ghgprotocol.org/corporate-standard

8. TCFD, *Guidance on Metrics, Targets, and Transition Plans*: https://assets.bbhub.io/company/sites/60/2021/07/2021-Metrics_Targets_Guidance-1.pdf

9. GHG Protocol, WRI and WBCSD (2004) *The GHGP Corporate Accounting and Reporting Standard*. WRI and WBCSD, March 2004, p. 26: https://ghgprotocol.org/corporate-standard

10. SME Climate Hub, *Business Carbon Calculator*: https://smeclimatehub.org/start-measuring/?utm_medium=referral&utm_source=partner&utm_campaign=BCC_press_release

11. CDP - https://www.cdp.net/en

12. SME Climate Hub, *Business Carbon Calculator*: https://smeclimatehub.org/normative-launches-carbon-calculator-sme-climate-hub/

13. GHG Protocol, *Corporate Value Chain (Scope 3) Accounting and Reporting Standard*: https://ghgprotocol.org/sites/default/files/standards/Corporate-Value-Chain-Accounting-Reporing-Standard_041613_2.pdf

14. SMMT, vehicle data: https://www.smmt.co.uk/vehicle-data/

15. GHG Protocol, WRI and WBCSD (2004) *The GHGP Corporate Accounting and Reporting Standard*, WRI and WBCSD, March 2004, p. 41: https://ghgprotocol.org/corporate-standard

16. Scope 1 calculations: if the mileage were the only activity data available, the calculation would have been more complex and less accurate. The BEIS conversion tool does explain the process for this, while commenting on its shortcomings. You could use a spreadsheet with the relevant conversion factors applied to the sources/activities, and this would support tracking year on year. It is important to read the notes in the conversion tool to ensure the correct conversion factor and the correct fuel is selected.

17. DEFRA, *Waste and recycling data*: https://www.gov.uk/government/collections/waste-and-recycling-statistics

18. Campbell's Scorecard: https://www.campbellcsr.com/cr-at-campbell/performance-scorecard.html

13

SETTING SCIENCE-BASED TARGETS: THE RIGHT APPROACH FOR YOUR BUSINESS ORGANISATION?

Muhammad Mazhar

This chapter introduces the concept of science-based targets (SBTs) and gives an overview of a step-by-step approach and process to be followed as per the criteria set by the Science-Based Target Initiative (SBTi). It highlights why setting SBTs can be the right approach for reducing carbon emissions in organisations. It will share a good practice case study from an SME already involved in this approach to inspire others.

This chapter is for you if you are:

- Interested in understanding SBTs and how they can be set
- Keen to help organisations reach Net Zero (or even Net Positive) and achieve a 1.5°C future
- An environmental, sustainability, energy or carbon manager, or are involved in corporate social responsibility within an organisation
- A member of senior management or the executive team.

DOI: 10.4324/9781003274049-16

It will cover:

- The concept of SBTs and the Science-Based Target initiative (SBTi)
- The case for setting SBTs for organisations and the associated benefits
- An overview of a step-by-step approach and process to be followed, highlighting sector-specific guidance
- A case study of an SME involved in setting SBTs, whilst exploring whether this is the right approach.

What are science-based targets (SBTs)?

Organisations have been setting carbon reduction targets for several years now. These usually involve committing to a reduction in carbon emissions intensity, for example, by revenue, or aiming to reduce a percentage of their absolute emissions by setting a science-based target (SBT), with the aim of achieving Net Zero by 2050, or even earlier. More recently, the focus has been on setting SBTs for a reduction in greenhouse gas (GHG) emissions in the corporate landscape, and many larger businesses are setting out their own vision and ambitions, while engaging with their supply chain on this subject. *Targets are considered 'science-based' if they are in line with what the latest climate science deems necessary to meet the goals of the Paris Agreement – limiting global warming to well-below 2°C above pre-industrial levels and pursuing efforts to limit warming to 1.5°C.*[1] Using science-based targets demonstrates best practice in setting goals to reduce carbon emissions.

The Science-Based Targets initiative (SBTi) was founded in 2015 through a partnership between the Carbon Disclosure Project (CDP), the UN Global Compact (UNGC), the World Resources Institute (WRI) and the World Wildlife Fund (WWF) to support business organisations in setting appropriate carbon reduction targets. These organisations are leading authorities in driving ambitious climate action. This chapter is mainly based on the resources and guidance provided by the SBTi through their website and publicly available documents, and your organisation should make use of these resources while setting targets and gaining validation. In different sections of this chapter, we have signposted relevant resources, as appropriate. The SBTi is especially keen to encourage businesses in the high-emitting sectors to set targets.

To translate the overall Paris Climate Agreement ambitions into individual targets, organisations have a key role, and three methods exist to translate high level targets to organisational ones. Each method has application to multiple sectors, but not all are applicable to every business sector. *The key components of an SBT method are the carbon budget (defining the overall amount of GHGs that can be emitted to limit warming to within well-below 2°C or 1.5°C), emissions scenario (defining the magnitude and timing of emissions reductions), and allocation approach (defining how the budget is allocated to companies). It is recommended that companies use either the Sectoral Decarbonization Approach (SDA) or the absolute emissions contraction approach. For Scope 1 and 2 emissions, economic intensity targets should only be set if they lead to absolute reductions in line with climate science.*[2]

The SDA allocates the carbon budget to different sectors and this method uses data from the International Energy Agency's 2°C Scenario model. Organisations' own targets then contribute to the sectoral carbon budget in line with climate science.[3] The absolute emission contraction approach assumes that all organisations reduce absolute carbon emissions at the same rate irrespective of their initial carbon performance, whereas the economic intensity contraction method is used for setting economic intensity targets based on the unit of value added.[2] Tables 13.2 and 13.4 in this chapter provide details of these methods. To explore and understand the methods available for target setting to deliver 1.5°C, you are encouraged to follow the guidance in the Science-Based Target Setting Manual available from the SBTi.[2] The SDA method is also useful and offers different case studies to provide an in-depth understanding of setting SBTs across different sectors.[3] Both resources can be accessed via our endnotes to help start your journey.

Why set SBTs?

SBTs have gained momentum in the corporate business world across multiple sectors. They support setting Net Zero carbon targets in line with the climate science and a 1.5°C future. These targets offer a clearly defined pathway for businesses to reduce carbon emissions which can add credibility to their strategy and objectives. By setting ambitious SBTs, organisations can lead the way to a zero-carbon economy, increase innovation and drive sustainable economic growth.[1] This allows businesses to demonstrate how much and how quickly they need to reduce their emissions to avoid the catastrophic impacts of global climate change. There are various benefits for your business in setting SBTs apart from climate change mitigation, which include: cost savings, increased profitability, enhanced brand reputation, improved employee engagement, improved investor confidence and resilience against regulations.[4] SBTs can also support supply chain engagement by offering an opportunity to cooperate with your suppliers to address carbon emissions for an effective carbon management programme. According to the SBTi (as at spring 2022), over 1,400 companies have set SBTs so far and over a thousand have made Net Zero commitments (see Figure 13.1).[5] To assist business organisations, the SBTi has developed a Net Zero Corporate Standard that provides guidance and tools that businesses can deploy. Please check out the 'Dig Deeper' section in this chapter to locate these.

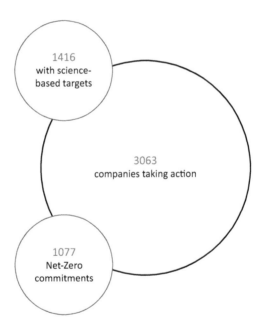

Figure 13.1 Companies taking climate action with SBTs by spring 2022 (SBTi 2022).[5]

What are the steps involved to set targets?

The SBTi website outlines the five stages necessary to set your targets.[6] These are: **Commit, Develop, Submit, Communicate** and **Disclose**. The steps are now explained in more detail.

1. **Commit**

This is the starting point for your journey.

- Register your business organisation online using the SBTi standard commitment application process. SMEs are allowed to skip this step and they can use the streamlined route instead.
- Submit the standard commitment letter to the SBTi. Business organisations are encouraged to commit to Net Zero and by default join the Business Ambition for 1.5°C and the Race to Zero campaign. The first is a call to action from a coalition of UN agencies, business organisations and industry leaders and is linked to the Race to Zero campaign, which involves a commitment to achieve Net Zero emissions by 2050.[7]
- All businesses that undertake this are recognised as 'Committed' on the official SBTi and other partner organisations' websites. These include the Carbon Disclosure Project (CDP) (a not-for-profit organisation that runs the disclosure system for companies globally to manage their environmental impact)[8] and the We Mean Business Coalition, a global non-profit coalition working with business for climate action.[9]

2. **Develop**

Once your organisation has signed the commitment letter, there is a maximum of two years to:

- Develop your targets following the criteria set by the SBTi. These include for example being at the parent or group-level (Organisational Boundary) and covering all relevant organisation-wide Scope 1 and 2 GHG emissions, as per the GHG Corporate Protocol. A full list of criteria is available on the SBTi website.
- The SBTi has attempted to make target-setting an easy process by providing a range of resources and tools. Start with their 'How-To Guide',[10] followed by reviewing the requirements in the 'Criteria and Recommendations' section[11] or the Net-Zero Standard Criteria (see 'Dig Deeper' in this chapter). These documents not only provide you with the criteria, they also give suggestions for implementation.
- There is some sector-specific guidance, which should be followed if you are part of one of those sectors. That is discussed again later in this chapter to provide more insights.

- Review the Target Validation Protocol to have an in-depth understanding of the SBTi's validation requirements and recommendations.[12] Then use the SBTi's ready-made target setting tools which help you develop your own SBTs. These are Excel spreadsheets that require input of data into different sections, such as the SDA (Sector Decarbonization Approach) scenario, the SDA sector, the base year and the target year. To access these tools, see the SBTi 'Develop a Target Resource' section of their website.

3. **Submit**

Once the targets are ready, submit to the SBTi team for validation. Again, guidance is available on the SBTi Step-by-Step area of their website, along with a template letter.

- Use the SBTi's checklist to help ensure the target has been developed as per the required standard. There is a submission form to complete.
- A team of experts will review the submission and communicate the decision to your organisation with feedback.
- Please note there is a fee attached and the latest details are outlined on the SBTi website.

4. **Communicate**

It is important to inform your stakeholders (internal and external) of your commitments. Unilever for example has approved SBTs for all three scopes (including emissions from suppliers and consumers). These inform the company's wider sustainability strategy and are made public on its website.[13] Auchan the French-headquartered international retailer is another example of a larger organisation which explains its targets and commitments via its website.[14]

- Organisations are required to make their targets publicly available within six months of approval.
- Approved targets will also be published on the SBTi website.

5. **Disclose**

This is all about formally reporting your progress.

- You must report on your organisation's carbon emissions reduction annually and your improvements.
- Disclosure should be via the CDP's global disclosure system (their website has detailed advice)[15] and also (as applicable) via annual report, sustainability report and the organisation's website.

As indicated throughout, there are lots of useful resources on the SBTi website, and in the 'Dig Deeper' section below and the endnote resources. There are also sector-specific requirements and guidance which you might find helpful.

WANT TO DIG DEEPER?

Science-based targets guide
https://www.carbontrust.com/resources/science-based-targets-guide
This guide gives insights into the need for setting SBTs, how to make the internal business case and implications for your business organisation.

Net Zero Standard https://sciencebasedtargets.org/developing-the-net-zero-standard
In 2019, the SBTi started an inclusive and stakeholder-informed process to develop a framework to support organisations in setting robust and credible Net Zero targets. This standard provides more details about methodologies and criteria to be used. It is useful for any organisation to understand the key elements of SBTs.

How can your organisation get started?

Getting started is a key step once you have commitment to setting targets. Using the SBTi's 'How-to Guide for Setting Near-Term Targets' (version 2.0) is a good starting place. SBTi has provided a systematic and engaging flowchart, and pages 2 and 3 of the guide clarify what organisations need to do. The flowchart begins with key questions that you might have in your mind as you start the journey. You are guided step-by-step on each leg of the journey, and it walks you through the process and signposts as necessary. We would propose you use this flowchart to find your own approach.

Organisations are recommended to submit their targets at parent company or group level rather than subsidiary level. The SBTi distinguishes between organisations based on their number of employees. With 500+ employees, you would need to look at the GHG inventory or the carbon footprint across all three scopes (1, 2 and 3), which are covered in detail in chapter 11 (Scopes & Boundaries). SMEs with fewer employees can follow the streamlined approach and this is covered later in this chapter.[16]

In the SBTi's 'How-to Guide' there is in-depth insight into the requirements in relation to Scope 1, 2 and 3 and whether Scope 3 targets are required.[17] You can also access other resources and links as mentioned above within the five-step process approach. Where companies need to complete a Scope 3 inventory, this might also include offsets, avoided emissions, bioenergy, optional Scope 3 and exclusion of relevant Scope 3 activities. In this case, they must follow the instructions as there can be different requirements for the 'Target Submission Form' and 'Target Validation Protocol'. If these are not included in the inventory, your company can model targets using the SBTi Tool with the SBTi criteria and submit targets for validation using SBTi's Target Submission Form.

Currently, the SBTi does not assess targets for cities, local governments, educational institutions, public sector institutions and non-profit organisations.[2]

What can different business sectors do to set SBTs?

The SBTi would like all companies in all sectors to set science-based targets, because every sector has an important role to deliver carbon reductions due to the nature of their operations and value chain. Apart from the resources available, there is now sector-specific guidance, and associated business organisations can use that to access specific criteria while setting their own SBTs. Where tailored guidance is still under development, organisations should follow the SBTi's generic guidance.

The sectors covered so far and those in development are shown alphabetically in Table 13.1 (as at November 2022).

Table 13.1 Sector guidance for setting science-based targets (November 2022)

Sector	Status
Aluminium	Scoping Phase
Apparel and footwear	Finalised
Aviation	In Development
Buildings	In Development

Chemicals	In Development
Cement	Finalised
Financial institutions	Finalised
Forest, Land and Agriculture (FLAG)	Finalised
Information and Communication Technology (ICT)	Finalised
Oil and Gas	In Development
Power	Finalised
Steel	In Development
Transport	In Development

Spotlight 1: the apparel and footwear sector

The global apparel and footwear sector produces more carbon emissions than the shipping and aviation sectors combined. In view of this, the World Resources Institute (WRI) has developed sector-specific guidance to support associated companies. The aim of this guidance is to provide clarity on credible approaches for setting SBTs, increase consistency in the sector, help address sector-specific barriers for setting the targets and share examples of good practice.[18] This sector example explains how SBTi guidance can support companies to reduce the fashion industry's carbon footprint. The SBTi aims to encourage companies across the value chain to set ambitious carbon reduction targets. The guidance is aimed at retailers, brands, finished goods manufacturers, mills and companies engaged in the production and sale of all types of clothing and footwear.

Scope 1 and 2 emissions are the starting point as per any such exercise. While these are usually higher for apparel and footwear manufacturers and upstream suppliers than for brands and retailers, all companies are required to set Scope 1 and 2 targets. These should be aligned with a 2°C goal as a minimum, although organisations are encouraged to aim higher and align with 1.5°C.

For the eligibility and target validation, companies need to complete their carbon accounting following the GHG Protocol Corporate Standard,

GHG Protocol Scope 2 Guidance, and the GHG Protocol Corporate Value Chain (Scope 3) Standard.[18] Please also refer to chapter 12 (Carbon Accounting) for further guidance. The criteria and recommendations for the GHG Emissions Inventory & Science-based Target Boundary, time frame, ambition with regards to the targets, Scope 2 emissions and

Table 13.2 Methods for Scope 1 and 2 target-setting in the apparel and footwear sector[18]

Method & Description	Examples of Approved Targets
Absolute Contraction Assumes all companies reduce absolute carbon emissions at the same rate: • Well below 2°C – min 2.5% annual linear reduction • 1.5°C – min 4.2% annual linear reduction	Levi Strauss & Co. commits to reduce absolute Scope 1 and 2 emissions by 90% by 2025 (2016 base year). Walmart commits to reduce absolute Scope 1 and 2 emissions by 18% by 2025 (2015 base year).
Physical Intensity **Option 1**: physical intensity targets with indicators representative of the company's overall product portfolio that result in a minimum of 2.5% annual linear carbon reduction in absolute emissions, linked to well below 2°C targets (and 4.2% for 1.5°C targets) **Option 2**: physical intensity targets modelled using the most relevant (SDA) pathways. SDA for power generation may be used to set Scope 2 targets if emissions from purchased electricity are significant. (This option is more relevant to suppliers and manufacturers.)	There are currently no approved examples of this category from the apparel and footwear sector for either option 1 or 2. As an example from another sector, AB InBev commits to reduce emissions across the value chain (Scope 1, 2 and 3) by 25% per beverage by 2025 (2017 base year).
Economic Intensity These are indicators representative of the company's overall product portfolio that result in a minimum of 2.5% annual linear reduction in absolute emissions for well below 2°C targets (and 4.2% for 1.5°C targets).	Kering commits to reduce Scope 1, 2 and 3 emissions from upstream transportation and distribution, business air travel, and fuel and energy-related emissions 50% per unit of value added by 2025 (2015 base year). Kering commits to reduce Scope 3 emissions from purchased goods and services by 40% per unit of value added within the same time frame.

Reporting & Recalculation, as well as sector-specific advice, are detailed in the apparel and footwear guidance document. There are three methods available to set Scope 1 and 2 targets as described in Table 13.2 and SBTi tools also incorporate these methods. This table is adapted from the SBTi's footwear and apparel sector guidance.

The SBTi apparel and footwear sector guidance offers the criteria applied to all Scope 3 targets submitted to the SBTi with recommendations and best practice. For most brands and retailers, and some suppliers, Scope 3 emissions are significant and complicated to measure and manage, mainly due to issues such as data availability (see chapter 11 'Scopes & Boundaries'). Apart from SBTi's sector guide, there is also the Corporate Value Chain (Scope 3) Accounting and Reporting Standard, as covered in chapter 11 (Scopes & Boundaries) and chapter 12 (Carbon Accounting).

For Scope 3, Table 13.3 summarises the 15 categories of upstream and downstream emissions based on the GHG Protocol.[19] Although setting these targets requires a full Scope 3 GHG emissions inventory to calculate the carbon footprint, in general Category 1, 'Purchased goods and services', is the most significant portion. More information on the use of sold products (Category 11) is also provided in the SBTi guidance.

Table 13.3 Scope 3 emissions categories (GHG Protocol)[20]

Upstream Scope 3 Emission Categories	Downstream Scope 3 Emission Categories
1. Purchased goods and services 2. Capital goods 3. Fuel- and energy-related activities (not included in Scope 1 or Scope 2) 4. Upstream transportation and distribution 5. Waste generated in operations 6. Business travel 7. Employee commuting 8. Upstream leased assets	9. Downstream transportation and distribution 10. Processing of sold products 11. Use of sold products 12. End-of-life treatment of sold products 13. Downstream leased assets 14. Franchises 15. Investments

As per the SBTi sector guidance, companies have three options to meet criterion 19 (level of ambition for Scope 3 targets). These options can be used to set one or more Scope 3 targets on at least two-thirds of total Scope 3 emissions, except for 'indirect use-phase' emissions. Ambitious reductions in Scope 3 emissions, can be difficult to achieve, as they are often outside of the company's direct control as explained elsewhere. Unlike the current requirement for Scope 1 and 2 targets, absolute or intensity Scope 3 targets are required to align with a 2°C scenario *as a minimum*. Therefore, you should focus on this, and more ambitious well-below 2°C and 1.5°C targets are encouraged.

Table 13.4 outlines methods to set targets that are applicable to apparel and footwear companies and for brands and retailers, Scope 3 are largely the Scope 1 and 2 emissions for their suppliers, often from purchased goods and services. Therefore, brands and retailers need to have carbon emission reductions upstream in the supply chain.

In addition to methods outlined in Table 13.4, brands and retailers need to set supplier engagement targets for the adoption of SBT setting for suppliers' carbon emissions. The four methods are described in Table 13.4 with examples of approved targets by the SBTi. This table is an adaptation of the SBTi's footwear and apparel sector guidance.

Table 13.4 Summary of Scope 3 target-setting methods in apparel and footwear sector[18]

Method & Description	Examples of Approved Targets
Absolute Contraction This method requires companies to reduce absolute emissions at the same rate: • 2°C: Minimum 1.23% annual linear reduction • Well below 2°C: Minimum 2.5% annual linear reduction • 1.5°C: Minimum 4.2% annual linear reduction	Levi Strauss & Co. commits to reduce absolute Scope 3 emissions from purchased goods and services by 40% by 2025 (2016 base year).
Physical Intensity (PI) **Option 1**: targets with indicators most representative of the company's overall product portfolio that, translated into absolute terms, are in line with absolute contraction.	**Option 1**: H&M Group commits to reduce Scope 3 GHG emissions from purchased raw materials, fabric and garments by 59% per piece by 2030 (2017 base year).

Option 2: targets modelled using the most relevant SDA pathways, in line with the 'well below 2°C' and the '1.5°C' targets. For brands and retailers to set targets for their suppliers, the SDA power generation pathway may be relevant for purchased electricity emissions. An SDA transportation tool is available for transportation emissions.	**Option 2**: No approved examples in the apparel and footwear sector.
Economics Intensity (EI) The GHG emissions per unit of value added (GEVA) method is available for companies to set these targets. Under GEVA, companies must achieve a minimum year-on-year reduction of 7% in $tCO_2e/\$$ of value added.	Kering commits to reduce Scope 3 emissions from purchased goods and services by 40% per unit of value added by 2025 (2015 base year).
Other Companies drive ambitious PI reduction to maintain Scope 3 at baseline year level over the target period. Targets must meet the minimum requirement for PI reduction of 2% in annual linear terms. E.g. if a company commits to reduce emissions per pair of shoes by 30% by 2030 from a 2017 base year, this is a 30/13=2.31% intensity reduction in annual linear terms, and meets the minimum PI improvement requirement.	ASICS commits to reduce Scope 3 from purchased goods and services and end-of-life treatment of sold products by 55% per product manufactured by 2030 (2015 base year).

Spotlight 2: streamlined route for small and medium-sized enterprises (SMEs)

A streamlined route for SMEs has been developed by the SBTi. This enables smaller organisations to avoid the initial step of committing to set targets and the regular target validation process. This will help SMEs to set SBTs for Scope 1 and 2 emissions by choosing from one of several predefined target options. SMEs also have fewer intensive requirements to fulfil around

Scope 3 emissions. Committing to reduce carbon emissions from the value chain is important. However, setting targets to reduce Scope 3 emissions and monitoring the progress against them requires huge data collection and analysis that goes beyond the resources available to smaller companies.[2]

The above can be very resource intensive for SMEs and managers may not have the necessary skills and technical knowledge. Therefore, the new pathway has been developed under which SMEs will be required to commit to measure and reduce their emissions, without a strict requirement to set quantified targets.[20] SMEs submit their targets using the Target Setting Letter and will be automatically approved and posted to the SBTi website after the review and payment. For further information, we would suggest you access the SBTi website where you can review the 'Frequently Asked Questions for SMEs' to help you answer any queries you might have. The website addresses the key issues such as SME route requirements, target options for SMEs (near-term science-based targets, Scope 1 and 2 and Net Zero targets, Scope 1, 2, 3) and the target validation process.[21]

Case study

This case study of a company already involved in setting science-based targets is presented here to inspire you and help you see that it is not such a difficult process. The anonymised company 'V' is based on a long-term client of greenhouse gas inventory tool 'Compare Your Footprint', which is part of the environmental services group, Green Element. It shows how 'Compare your Footprint' helped the company to submit its SBTs for validation and develop a carbon reduction strategy.

How to set science-based targets for real climate action
By Emma Littlewood (Strategy Director Green Element) and Liberty Bollen (Marketing Director, Green Element)

Company V is a large, limited company operating within the food and household goods retail, e-commerce, and home delivery sectors. It provides organic and largely locally grown produce across the United Kingdom, so sustainability has always been at the heart of its agenda. The business needed to turn its attention to auditing the environmental impact of its business operations to continue to achieve high sustain-ability standards, meet growing pressure from eco-conscious customers and comply with increasing environmental regulation required for larger companies.

Science-based targets show organisations how much and how quickly they need to reduce their greenhouse gas (GHG) emissions to prevent the worst effects of climate change.

Near-term targets outline what companies will do now, and over the next 5–10 years, to reduce emissions in line with what's needed to get on track for net-zero and the 1.5°C limit on global heating.

Long-term targets indicate the degree of decarbonisation needed to ultimately achieve net-zero. Companies are expected to make emissions reductions of at least 90% of baseline.

A company will be considered as reaching net-zero under the SBTi Net-Zero Standard when it has achieved its long-term science-based target. A company cannot balance its emissions with removals ahead of that and claim to be net-zero. While companies may reach a balance between emissions and removals before they reach the depth of decarbonisation required to limit warming to 1.5°C, this is only a transient state on the journey to net-zero emissions.

In other words, a company's net-zero target date may not come before its long-term science-based target.

Company V's steps to set its targets

Step 1. Conducted a full value chain GHG emissions inventory to measure the company's carbon footprint in 2019 – a 'business as usual' pre-Covid year. A list of the activities that Company V measured is featured in Table 13.5.

Step 2. Highlighted carbon 'hot spots' within the company's operations and supply chain emissions, and recommendations for reduction strategies:

Food and drink: particularly meat and dairy

• Replace 50% of total weight of meat with more pulses, beans and bean curd to reduce *Company V's* footprint by 2,300 tCO_2e pa.

- Increase the proportion of organic plant-based spreads in the product range by 50% to reduce the related footprint by up to 37%, saving more than 250 tonnes of emissions pa.

Transport and distribution: fleet emissions, energy and paper
- Introduce driver phone app to replace paper, eliminating 8 tonnes of emissions pa.
- A shift to electric vehicles (EVs) fleet could make a big impact on the Scope 1 target (see Table 13.6).
- Conduct Energy Savings Trust fleet audit to obtain optimal fleet decarbonisation strategy and incorporate free 'eco' driver training.
- Further promote to customers and source local seasonal produce to reduce transport emissions.
- Install radiative heating for warehouses to replace gas (Scope 1), thus decarbonising heat provision.

Packaging: plastic and cardboard
- Sourcing paper and plastic with a higher recycled content where available
- Emissions from wool insulation food packaging are circa 14kg CO_2e per tonne. Switch to flock recycled clothing to replace this. Hemp (4.05kg CO_2e/tonne*), cotton (5.9kg CO_2e/tonne*) and denim off-cuts or recycled polyester can be used to make insulation for food, leading to a reduction of c12kg CO_2e per tonne.

Step 3. Developed a science-based net-zero strategy including a carbon reduction route map and forecast model incorporating the projected growth of the company combined with the projected carbon reduction impacts of the strategies outlined in Step 3.
Step 4. Selected the most ambitious level of target-setting available at the time by committing to targets through **Business Ambition for 1.5C**,[22] which incorporates a near-term science-based target, and science-based net-zero by 2050 latest.

For the SBTi, Company V qualifies as a 'larger' company (500+ employees). Thus, its science-based targets route required committing to set their targets across Scope 1, 2 and 3* through completion of the commitment letter. The commitment was then published on the SBTi website.

*Refer to Table 13.5 for an explanation of the different scopes

Step 5. Had the targets validated through SBTi. After submitting their commitment form, Company V had up to two years before they were required to set their targets and have them officially validated by the SBTi. If you are not using a climate partner to help you through the process, you can use the SBTi tools to help calculate targets.

Company V had already calculated its targets and only needed sign off by its board.

How company V measured Its baseline carbon footprint
The scopes and boundaries of the project were identified to establish the categories and business activities that should be included in the baseline carbon footprint in accordance with the GHG Protocol principles. To have its targets validated by SBTi, Company V adhered to the GHG Protocol Corporate Standard for its GHG inventory calculation, and the SBTi Criteria and Recommendations to calculate its targets.

Table 13.5 Categories and activities measured for SBTi targets validation

Scope 1	**Alldirect emissions from the activities of an organisation or under their control.** Including fuel combustion on site such as gas boilers, other fuels combustion, fleet vehicles, and air-conditioning leaks of refrigerant gases
Scope 2	**Indirect emissions from electricity, heat and steam purchased and used by the organisation.** Emissions are created during the production of energy and eventually used by the organisation. SBTi requires companies to select whether to report their location-based (average fuel mix of grid based on location) or market-based emissions (fuel mix specific to energy supplier). The GHG Protocol requires 'dual reporting' – calculating both market-based and location-based emissions.
Scope 3	All other indirect emissions from activities of the organisation, occurring from sources they do not own or control. Company V included all 15 categories, of which the following were relevant: • Purchased goods and services (includes all food which is the largest proportion of *Company V's* Scope 3 emissions) as well as office and warehouse goods and services • Capital goods (delivery vans purchased) • Fuel and energy-related activities • Upstream transportation and distribution • Waste generated in operations

	• Use of sold products (energy used to cook foods bought by the consumer – optional) • End-of-life treatment of sold products (consumer disposal of food waste and packaging)
Life Cycle Analysis (LCA) of product	**Method to measure the environmental impact of a product through its life cycle –extraction and processing of the raw materials, manufacturing, distribution, use, recycling and final disposal.** LCA of three UK-grown fruit and veg boxes (products). The analysis complies with ISO 14064 standard that provides governments, businesses, regions, and other organisations with tools to measure, monitor, report, and verify greenhouse gas emissions. We used supplier-specific and industry averages (UK organic farming metrics from DEFRA and scientific bodies). This will be more accurate when specific grower metrics are supplied by the individual fruit and vegetable farms. The boxes had a lower impact than similar boxes due to local sourcing, warehouses being closer to customers, and 100% organic farmers generating lower GHGs.
Excluded	The following Scope 3 categories were not applicable, so evidence was provided to SBTi for their exclusion from the validation process: • Upstream leased assets (no assets leased) • Downstream transportation & distribution (no downstream freight as goods are delivered directly to customers) • Processing of sold products (not relevant) • Downstream emissions from fossil fuels distributed but not by company n/a • Downstream leased assets n/a • Franchises n/a • Investments (negligible) – pensions emissions calculated but less than 5% of total Scope 3
Bioenergy accounting	No biofuels and/or biomass feedstocks or carbon dioxide removals associated to report on.

Table 13.5 has been taken from the SBTi validation form to present Company V's near-term science-based targets.

Table 13.6 Science-based targets validated with SBTi – Company V

Target	Scope	Time frame ambition: targeted % change from base year	Forward looking ambition: targeted % from most recent year	For intensity target(s) only:				Base year	Target year
				Activity amount in base year*	Activity amount in most recent year	Activity amount in the target year	% change in absolute emissions/ Scope		
Absolute (reduction in total emissions)	1 & 2	42%	42%					2020	2030
Intensity (emissions reductions /tonne of food)	3	53%	53%	18,520	18,520	39,686	0%	2020	2030

Note

* e.g. tonnes of steel

Emma Littlewood and Liberty Bollen are Strategy and Marketing Directors for Green Element (https://www.greenelement.co.uk/) and Compare Your Footprint

Emma created the online Greenhouse Gas accounting tool Compare Your Footprint and is a science-based net-zero specialist, an ESOS Lead Energy Assessor, and develops analytical models in nascent areas such as digital emissions and scenario analyses. She is an advocate for climate justice and an expert in climate risk.

Liberty is a senior marketing specialist who has worked across a variety of sectors including environmental services, private equity, impact invest-ment, ethical property, and human rights. She helped to develop and bring to market Green Element Group's carbon calculation software, Compare Your Footprint and is now responsible for raising the profile of the Group. Liberty also supported the launches of Abode Impact, and Pineapple Sustainable Partnerships (now a board member) and worked for Survival International to support the rights of tribal peoples. She volunteered behind the scenes for Extinction Rebellion to create Rebellion Academy, a training platform for volunteers and other related movements.

Quick Wins

1. Make a strategic commitment to set science-based targets.
2. Access the SBTi website for guidance and updates.
3. If sector-specific guidance has been developed for your area, use that to guide you.
4. Explore good practice examples of businesses within your sector for inspiration, approach your own networks.
5. If your supply chains include supermarkets or other retailers, check their websites, many are trying to support their suppliers.
6. Start the SBTi target-setting process and follow the guidance and tools to be validated.
7. Engage with the relevant resources provided by the SBTi and seek advice where needed, as setting science-based targets can be complex and might need some time and resources to understand the requirements and process.
8. Communicate targets to all your stakeholders and develop an action plan for delivery.
9. Track your performance against the targets for your Net Zero ambition.
10. You might want to get support from a consultancy company to help you through the process.

Outlook

As shown in this chapter, science-based targets can help you to reduce the greenhouse gas (GHG) emissions linked to your organisation. We recommend that you develop SBTs as suggested above, using the resources signposted. Alternatively, you could review your GHG emissions in more detail by conducting a Greenhouse Gas Emissions Inventory as shown in chapter 12 (Carbon Accounting), then set your own targets and draw up a specific implementation plan to reduce carbon emissions and meet the targets.

To support your work, draw up a plan such as the one shown in Figure 13.2. As part of this, your organisation needs to develop a carbon management strategy and policies to help meet your objectives. Chapter 14 (Policies & Practices) provides guidance on developing a strategy and carbon management-related policies. You might also want to read other chapters to get inspiration on how you can implement specific measures to

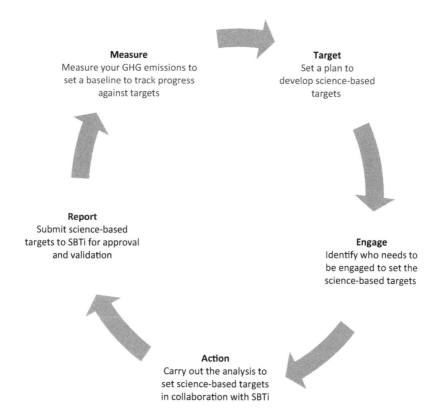

Figure 13.2 Implementation plan for setting SBTs for your organisation.

reduce GHG emissions to help meet your targets in different parts of your organisation (Marketing, Procurement, HR etc). As always, targets must be supported by relevant action.

Further Resources

On the companion website to this book you can find further materials to help you plan and implement this work.

Below you can find some links that go into more detail on the above or suggest further insights or support that might be of interest in addition to the ones mentioned in the notes.

Guides

Adopt a science-based emissions reduction target
https://www.wemeanbusinesscoalition.org/wp-content/uploads/2017/
08/Commitment_SBTs.pdf

This resource details how companies can engage with SBT setting.
Major international retailer **Walmart** provides information to their suppliers
via their own website. **Walmart Sustainability Hub**, *Setting an Emissions Target*:
https://www.walmartsustainabilityhub.com/climate/project-gigaton/
emissions-targets

Case studies

SBTI Companies Taking Action – numerous company case studies are
available from the SBTi and we list here just four from different sectors to
whet your appetite and offer inspiration.
P&G – the multinational consumer goods company:
https://sciencebasedtargets.org/companies-taking-action/case-studies/
procter-gamble
IPC (International Post Corporation) a cooperative of 24 postal operators
based worldwide:
https://sciencebasedtargets.org/companies-taking-action/case-studies/
international-post-corporation
Tesco (International retailer):
https://sciencebasedtargets.org/companies-taking-action/case-studies/
tesco
JLL – a real estate services company, based in the United States and EMEA:
https://sciencebasedtargets.org/companies-taking-action/case-studies/
net-zero-case-study-jll

Videos

SBTi Science-based Target-setting tool: demo video
https://www.youtube.com/watch?v=-XLjbyAOt-M
This demonstrates how to use the tool (SBT Tool v 1.2.1) developed by the
SBTi to help companies model science-based emission reduction targets.

How to Set Science-Based Targets Aligning with 1.5°C Pathways
https://www.youtube.com/watch?v=sxZjmX1Upzo&t=3178s
In this UN Global Compact Academy webinar session, experts from the SBTi and corporate leaders present guidance to help companies raise ambition in practice and also on how Scope 3 targets are affected by the new climate science.

eLearning course

How to Set a Science-Based Target to Achieve Net-Zero course is available for you to develop knowledge and skills: https://www. unglobalcompact.org/take-action/events/1726-how-to-set-a-science-based-target-to-achieve-net-zero

Notes

1. SBTi, *Lead the Way to a Low-Carbon Future*: https://sciencebasedtargets.org/how-it-works
2. SBTi, *Science-Based Target Setting Manual*: https://sciencebasedtargets.org/resources/legacy/2017/04/SBTi-manual.pdf
3. SBTi, *Sectoral Decarbonisation Approach (SDA)*: https://sciencebased-targets.org/resources/files/Sectoral-Decarbonization-Approach-Report.pdf
4. SBTi, *Six business benefits of setting science-based targets*: https://sciencebasedtargets.org/blog/six-business-benefits-of-setting-science-based-targets
5. SBTi, *Ambitious Corporate Climate Action*: https://sciencebasedtargets.org/
6. SBTi, *Step-by-Step Process*: https://sciencebasedtargets.org/step-by-step-process
7. UNGC, *Business Ambition for 1.5°C*: https://www.unglobalcompact.org/take-action/events/climate-action-summit-2019/business-ambition
8. Carbon Disclosure Project: https://www.cdp.net/en
9. We Mean Business Coalition: https://www.wemeanbusinesscoalition.org/about
10. SBTi, *Sector Guidance*: https://sciencebasedtargets.org/sectors
11. SBTi, *Criteria and Recommendations*: https://sciencebasedtargets.org/resources/files/SBTi-criteria.pdf

12. SBTi, *Target Validation Protocol for Near-Term Target*: https://sciencebased-targets.org/resources/files/Target-Validation-Protocol.pdf

13. Unilever, *What are science-based targets and why do we use them?*: https://www.unilever.com/news/news-search/2018/what-are-science-based-targets-and-why-do-we-use-them/

14. Auchan, *Our Commitments* (translated): https://www.auchan-retail.com/fr/nos-engagements/

15. CDP, *How to disclose as a company*: https://www.cdp.net/en/companies-discloser/how-to-disclose-as-a-company/faqs-for-companies#1-cycle

16. SBTi, *Small and medium-sized Enterprises (SMEs) FAQS* (v4, April 2022): https://sciencebasedtargets.org/resources/files/FAQs-for-SMEs.pdf

17. SBTi, *How-to Guide for Setting Near-Term Targets*: https://sciencebased-targets.org/resources/files/SBTi-How-To-Guide.pdf

18. SBTi, *Apparel and Footwear Sector*: https://sciencebasedtargets.org/resources/legacy/2019/06/SBT_App_Guide_final_0718.pdf

19. GHG Protocol, Corporate Value Chain (Scope 3) Accounting and Reporting Standard: https://ghgprotocol.org/sites/default/files/standards/Corporate-Value-Chain-Accounting-Reporing-Standard_041613_2.pdf

20. SBTi, *Smoothing the way for small and medium-sized businesses to set science-based climate targets*: https://sciencebasedtargets.org/blog/smoothing-the-way-for-small-and-medium-sized-businesses-to-set-science-based-climate-targets

21. SBTi, *Small and Medium-Sized Enterprises (SMEs) FAQs*: https://sciencebasedtargets.org/resources/files/FAQs-for-SMEs.pdf

22. https://sciencebasedtargets.org/business-ambition-for-1-5c

14

STRATEGY, POLICIES AND PRACTICES FOR CARBON MANAGEMENT

Muhammad Mazhar and Petra Molthan-Hill

This chapter guides managers to develop a strategy and policies for the implementation of greenhouse gas (GHG) management in any organisation, and shows how they can be linked to the practices and climate actions already suggested in other chapters of this book.

This chapter is for you if:

- You are part of the senior management/executive team of an organisation
- You are an environment, sustainability, carbon, energy or Corporate Social Responsibility manager
- You are designing a GHG management strategy, policies and practices related to any part of an organisation.

It will cover:

- The role of strategy and policies to reduce GHG emissions in organisations

DOI: 10.4324/9781003274049-17

- Strategy and policies for different topics, such as energy and waste management, offering structured guidance with examples from different sectors
- How to adopt a planned approach by utilising the Institute of Environmental Management and Assessment's (IEMA's) greenhouse gas (GHG) management hierarchy – from 'elimination' to 'compensation' – to reduce GHG emissions
- An introduction to, and an evaluation of, carbon offsetting as a concept.

Choosing the right strategy, policies and practices for your organisation

In the previous chapters, we discussed individual actions that managers can take in their teams or departments. However, if we want to move our actions from a departmental to an organisational level, we need to introduce policies that communicate to all colleagues how we deal with certain issues such as energy, food waste, sourcing of materials or employee travel. All these policies should then feed into an overarching strategy and set of objectives, for example that the organisation wants to reduce greenhouse gas (GHG) emissions by 10% in the coming year. This would be a bottom-up approach, but clearly a top-down approach is also necessary. In that case, the owner or board of executives would set a strategy and then develop associated policies to be implemented in each department or function.

Organisations develop strategy and policies to demonstrate their commitment to the environment, carbon reduction and climate change mitigation. Carbon or GHG management strategy and policies establish the strategic direction of the organisation: *[a]n environmental policy is a written statement, usually signed by senior management, which outlines a business' aims and principles in relation to managing the environmental effects and aspects of its operations.*[1]

An environmental policy can include overarching environmental impacts from core organisational activities. It can also help address the impact of GHG emissions from energy use, waste, water, travel and transport, procurement and the supply chain. In chapter 11, we discussed the different scopes associated with GHG management, in chapter 12, we calculated the current GHG emissions by scope, and in chapter 13, we discussed setting targets for each of the scopes. The next step is to design environmental and other related policies to address Scope 1, 2 and 3, in order to implement

GHG management processes effectively. These policies form the basis of an organisation's GHG or carbon management strategy and plans for implementation, and therefore underpin the strategy and actions of an organisation to reduce GHG emissions. Policies are a mechanism through which organisations can demonstrate to customers and other stakeholders that they are committed to managing GHG emissions as part of their sustainability journey.

GHG management-related policies can offer significant benefits to organisations and businesses, which include:[1]

- Compliance with relevant government policies and regulations
- Financial savings
- Management of risk
- Improved brand image
- Competitive advantage in the market
- Conservation of raw materials and energy, and improvement of resource efficiency
- Improved efficiency of organisational processes
- Positive relations with external stakeholders such as investors, customers, suppliers, local authorities, government, regulatory bodies and communities.

This chapter helps you to design policies for all sources of emissions in an organisational context. To implement these and the overall strategy, specific practices will need introducing or enhancing, to achieve the planned GHG reductions. Previous chapters provide ideas and climate solutions to help achieve this, so it is worth returning to earlier parts of the book, to ensure that policies are written which lead to the actions proposed in each function.

Alternatively, you could turn to any of the chapters, choose the best practices for your organisation and write the matching policies. Some examples are:

Chapter 4 (Meetings & Transport) – running meetings in a more carbon-friendly way; online recruitment, as part of an organisation's travel and transport policy; innovative solutions to incentivise others to choose low-carbon transport options.

Chapter 5 (Digital Footprint) – green or low-carbon information and communication technology (ICT) practices; calculations for datacentres, cryptocurrencies, social media and different technologies, such as artificial intelligence; suggestions to reduce emissions, focusing on behavioural change, improvements to information systems and website energy efficiency.
Chapter 6 (Food Waste & Food) – guidance for ordering catering/hospitality; evaluating food and drink provision; improving meal planning to reduce carbon impact and minimise food waste.
Chapter 7 (Estates & Facilities) – managing carbon emissions in building operations and new constructions; suggestions for practices to reduce energy, water, waste and carbon.
Chapter 8 (Procurement & Supply) – sustainable procurement and emissions reduction strategy for the supply chain.

Finally, another route would be to prioritise one area, such as your organisation's digital footprint, if for example you suspected this was your highest emissions source. In this case, turn to chapter 5 first and design a Green ICT policy.

IEMA GHG management hierarchy

A useful tool for organisations to provide a systematic and structured approach to reduce GHG emissions is the IEMA GHG Management Hierarchy (see Figure 14.1) which was developed by The Institute of Environmental Management and Assessment, the largest professional body for environmental management practitioners in the United Kingdom and globally. In 2020, they updated their GHG Management Hierarchy in their 'Pathways to Net Zero' report to take account of the need to transition to Net Zero. A survey cited in there found out that over half of the respondents have used the hierarchy to help manage their carbon emissions in an organised manner.[2]

The hierarchy aims to help an organisation become Net Zero by presenting a planned approach, from 'Eliminate' to 'Compensate'. It is a reminder for organisations to focus 'up the hierarchy' and search for both direct and significant GHG emissions savings within and across the organisation, project or other business entity. Whilst the context of an organisation or sector may vary, the low-carbon transition actions are not limited by any particular sequential approach.[2] The GHG Management Hierarchy offers significant flexibility in terms of which level and what actions to select first. Low-hanging fruit and low/no cost measures can be the starting point, with overarching and strategic guidance for organisations also offered.

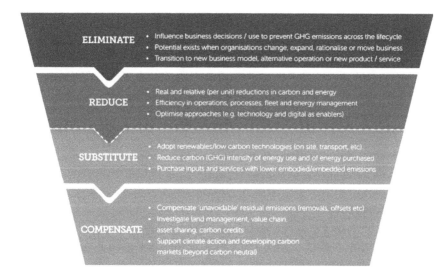

Figure 14.1 GHG Management Hierarchy reprinted with permission from IEMA.[2]

In the four levels of the GHG Management Hierarchy:

- **'Eliminate'** suggests starting by influencing decisions to prevent GHG emissions across the life cycle. Organisations may need to transition to new business models to offer products and services with minimal GHG emissions impact.
- **'Reduce'** is aimed at reducing energy and resources for GHG management. Managers need to follow the 'efficiency first' principle in their business operations and processes.
- **'Substitute'** suggests adopting renewable and low-carbon technologies on site and in transportation to reduce intensity of carbon emissions. Inputs, materials and services should be selected with lower embodied carbon.

- **'Compensate'** involves selecting reliable and high-quality carbon offsets, where there are residual GHG emissions that are difficult to remove. Some offset schemes can support climate change mitigation and have multiple benefits in communities from a social and economic perspective.

Carbon offsetting

A carbon offset is a credit an organisation can purchase to use against its own carbon emissions. *Carbon offsetting is a way of paying for others to reduce emissions or absorb CO_2 to compensate for your own emissions. For example, by planting trees to suck carbon out of the atmosphere as they grow, or by delivering energy-efficient cooking stoves to communities in developing countries.*[3]

The concept has been popular for several decades. However, there has been critique in the corporate world, as it is argued that it can be problematic in terms of seriously tackling the issue of carbon reduction and climate change mitigation, and has been referred to as 'dangerous distraction'. Organisations really need to stop carbon emissions from entering the atmosphere in the first place. It is suggested that planting trees alone may not reduce *absolute* carbon emissions if they are used to make up for flying, for example, which causes more GHG emissions in the first instance. Carbon offsetting can distract organisations from taking *meaningful* actions to reduce their carbon emissions.[3] Many companies shout about their achievements, but their offsetting could be classified as greenwashing as highlighted by Bloomberg in the following extract:

> At first glance, big corporations appear to be protecting great swaths of U.S. forests in the fight against climate change. JPMorgan Chase & Co. has paid almost $1 million to preserve forestland in eastern Pennsylvania. Forty miles away, Walt Disney Co. has spent hundreds of thousands to keep the city of Bethlehem, Pa., from aggressively harvesting a forest that surrounds its reservoirs. Across the state line in New York, investment giant BlackRock Inc. has paid thousands to the city of Albany to refrain from cutting trees around its reservoirs. JPMorgan, Disney, and BlackRock tout these projects as an important mechanism for slashing their own large carbon footprints. By funding the preservation of carbon-absorbing forests, the companies say, they're offsetting the carbon-producing impact of their global operations. But in all of those cases, the land was never threatened; the trees were already part of well-preserved forests.

Rather than dramatically change their operations—JPMorgan executives continue to jet around the globe, Disney's cruise ships still burn oil, and BlackRock's office buildings gobble up electricity - the corporations are working with the Nature Conservancy, the world's largest environmental group, to employ far-fetched logic to help absolve them of their climate sins. By taking credit for saving well-protected land, these companies are reducing nowhere near the pollution that they claim.[4]

So, while the carbon-offsetting market is rapidly developing globally, organisations are sometimes being misled by the concept of carbon off-setting. There can be an issue of trust when it comes to offset providers, and some schemes are operated by companies with their own motives and vested interests. It has also been found that some of the projects are being run by logging companies.[5] There are positives however: *[m]any of the carbon offsetting projects also provide additional benefits such as biodiversity, education, jobs, food security, clean drinking water and heath & well-being in developing countries.*[6]

The main message here is that GHG management strategy and policy need to focus on reducing GHG emissions as a priority following the IEMA GHG Management Hierarchy (Figure 14.1). If necessary to achieve Net Zero, carbon offsets should only be used as a last option, to address residual carbon emissions which might be hard or impossible to reduce or eliminate.

WANT TO DIG DEEPER?

How to Write an Environmental Policy:
https://www.haringey.gov.uk/sites/haringeygovuk/files/environmental_policy_fact-sheet_o.pdf
This provides a policy framework for setting objectives and targets to improve your environmental and GHG management performance.

Carbon Management Plan – Zero Waste Scotland:
https://www.zerowastescotland.org.uk/save-energy-reduce-waste/carbon-management-plans
This resource can help organisations as it offers a template for a carbon management plan and guides managers on the different elements required for delivery. It also offers a Climate Change Assessment Tool (CCAT), targeted especially at the public sector.

Developing carbon management strategy and policies for your own organisation

Organisations wanting to make a commitment and implement climate actions need an overarching strategy, plan and integrated policies in all areas where GHG emissions are caused in the context of the organisation. It is important to understand the strategic direction of the organisation to become Net Zero. Therefore, our first question to answer is:**how can I design a good carbon management strategy for my organisation?**

This strategy then needs to be broken down into several policies in order to achieve the targets set. Our second question is, therefore: **which policies do I need to write for my organisation?**

Policies need to be effective and implemented if they are to make a difference in terms of GHG emission reductions, and not just documents which sit on the shelf. Therefore, our third question to support managers responsible for developing policies is: **how do I write good policies?**

Engaging stakeholders such as employees is important for organisations, to ensure buy-in from all colleagues, who will then do their bit. Therefore, our fourth question is: **how can I use an exciting approach to engage employees in my organisation?**

Carbon offsetting may be needed to address residual emissions which an organisation cannot reduce, due to the nature of its operations. Therefore, carbon offsetting can help transition to Net Zero once all measures have been implemented to make actual carbon reductions. The final question to answer is therefore: **when and how do I offset my remaining carbon emissions?**

How can I design a good carbon management strategy for my organisation?

Your organisation needs to develop a carbon management strategy using the four-pillar approach (see Figure 14.2). The four pillars are inspired by the 1.5°C Business Playbook developed by the Exponential Roadmap Initiative (ERI).[7] In this approach, each pillar has key carbon reduction actions which you need to consider for implementation in your own organisation. These are very specific actions, which you will find useful considering the urgency of the climate change agenda and the role of business.

Figure 14.2 Four pillars of a carbon management strategy reprinted with permission from the ERI.

- **Pillar 1** focuses on an organisation's activities to reduce its own carbon emissions aligned with the 1.5°C climate science. These are reductions with regards to Scope 1 and 2 emissions (explained in chapter 11).
- **Pillar 2** focuses on an organisation's indirect activities to reduce its value chain carbon emissions (Scope 3) with the same 1.5°C climate goal. As per chapter 11, Scope 3 is a complex area and businesses which have not yet addressed this will need to make a start in the second pillar.
- **Pillar 3** integrates carbon management into business strategy. It addresses the alignment of the organisation's vision, strategy, value proposition, products and services with the 1.5°C climate goal. It may include core activities such as prioritising products and services that enable reduction and removal of customers' and wider society's carbon emissions, enabling a resource-efficient lifestyle and consumption patterns.
- **Pillar 4** describes how to contribute beyond your own organisational activities, through cooperation and networks and involves influencing climate action in society. This includes sharing good practice or supporting behavioural change in a variety of groups: customers, employees, suppliers, industry, government bodies, research institutes and not-for-profit organisations. This suggests to become a climate leader by facilitating low-carbon practices and funding projects outside your company's value chain.

According to the ERI, these four pillars must be integrated into an organisation's iterative planning cycle, starting by measuring and analysing the current situation as a baseline, setting carbon reduction targets and priorities, then moving to the implementation phase.

The four pillars are not strictly ordered in terms of timeline and sequential implementation, which may differ by organisation. However, there is a logic to their order. Pillars 1 and 2 link to the need for all organisations to start by reducing their own carbon emissions. Pillar 3 addresses aligning the vision, strategies and portfolios with the 1.5°C climate goal to become Net Zero carbon. Finally, Pillar 4 builds on the others and considers the organisation as a societal actor with the opportunity to make a positive impact on society.[7]

SMEs are key to low-carbon transition and need to develop a carbon management strategy which works for them. As with any organisation, they should start with reducing their own carbon emissions (Scopes 1 and 2 – Pillar 1), and then their value chain emissions (Scope 3 – Pillar 2) if the latter are significant in terms of their total carbon footprint (assuming data are available to measure and manage them). SMEs usually have relatively limited impact on their suppliers but can have an impact through their selection of suppliers, the design of products and by reducing the use of goods and services with high GHG emission impacts. SMEs with their core business in the area of climate change solutions should build their carbon management strategy from Pillar 3 and are encouraged to communicate their contribution through Pillar 4. SMEs having sustainable innovation at the heart of their business model should also aim to embed Pillars 3 and 4, to have a bigger impact beyond their own boundaries.

Which policies do I need to write for my organisation?

After you have designed your overall strategy, you should decide which specific policies you need, given the purpose, products and processes of your organisation. These could include the following topics:

1. Environmental
2. Carbon Management
3. Energy
4. Waste and Recycling
5. Water
6. Travel and Transport
7. Sustainable Procurement

8. Sustainable Food and Drink
9. Sustainable Construction
10. Green ICT
11. Biodiversity
12. Fair Trade
13. Ethical Investment.

How do I write good policies?

Organisational policies need to have the right format and content which is interactive and engaging for stakeholders. This will ensure they are implemented effectively and make a real impact. All the policies need to be updated on a regular basis, so they are dynamic documents rather than static. There is no standard format for a policy, but to achieve maximum impact and the best outcomes, it should have certain features.[8]

Inspired by Haringey Council[8] and Info Entrepreneurs, we present below ideas to try and ensure maximum impact, along with the key ingredients for effective environmental and GHG management policies.

• Secure senior management/executive-level support
• Co-create policies with stakeholders where possible
• Review good practice examples for structure and format
• Tailor policies to your context
• Be concise – one page maximum is ideal
• Use peer review and feedback mechanisms when developing policies
• Ensure there are clear roles and responsibilities, and have the policy signed, dated and endorsed by a senior colleague
• Make the policy publicly available on your website
• Design measures and targets for your policies and show results
• Communicate annual progress against the policy and targets, as well as related actions, to internal and external stakeholders
• Review the policies on a regular basis and update as necessary.

Examples of policies

Organisations need to consider all the above-mentioned issues in the design and development of any GHG management-related policies. Examples of some publicly available policies are presented in this section as mini case studies for inspiration. These provide insights into well-developed policies which can be used to draw up associated policies as necessary (see above list). The examples below are chosen as they are quite comprehensive and address most areas of GHG management.

An example from the public sector is presented in Box 14.1 to inspire other organisations, both public and private, large and small. This provides insight into the areas and content that an environmental policy needs. As one of the United Kingdom's largest universities, Nottingham Trent University (NTU) actively promotes environmental sustainability in all its activities, in line with its strategic plan.[9] The publicly available policy (example below dated 2022, but usually updated annually) is underpinned by the university's aim to engage all staff and students, inspiring and embedding environmental principles for the future of NTU. Your organisation can follow this good practice guide and develop a similar environmental policy.

Box 14.1   Extract from NTU's 2022 environmental policy

NTU is committed to:

- *Developing and embedding environmental awareness and principles with colleagues and students; encouraging university-wide participation in environmental activities, training and programmes. Promoting Education for Sustainable Development for all, via a formal curriculum-based approach, coupled with informal initiatives.*
- *Protecting the environment and preventing pollution ... through a life cycle perspective in pursuance of high standards of environmental management across the NTU estate.*
- *Minimising significant environmental impacts and enhancing environmental performance including the maintenance of an environmental management system... [to ensure] that NTU fulfils its compliance obligations.*
- *Setting environmental objectives and targets and reporting performance annually on the NTU website.*

- *Communicating the Environmental Policy to employees and all interested parties.*
- *Delivering Net Zero Carbon by 2040, across all three scopes … and reporting on progress annually.*
- *Minimising waste through effective management, focusing on avoidance, reuse, and recycling.*
- *Minimising water wastage and optimising the use of water saving and harvesting technologies.*
- *Protecting the environment by enhancing biodiversity within the management of the existing estate as well as with any new developments, where appropriate, including the appropriate management of protected and invasive species.*
- *Promoting and enhancing our Sustainable Procurement Policy.*
- *Managing a proactive travel plan to reduce staff and students' carbon footprint.*
- *Implementing the Sustainable Construction Policy, including committing to BREEAM Excellent for all new builds and SKA Rating for major building refurbishments as a minimum.*

The Policy is fully supported by the University Executive Team. We appreciate that colleagues and student education, engagement and ultimately their acceptance of the Environmental Policy, are key to its success. As such, this will provide an ongoing focus to create a sense of ownership, responsibility and a constantly relevant strategy to improve our environment.

Signed: Professor Edward Peck, Vice-Chancellor

Next, an example of an organisation-wide energy policy is shared from the retail sector. Marks & Spencer (M&S) is a multinational headquartered in London (UK), selling clothing, food and home products, renowned for its (2008) 'Plan A, as there is no Plan B [for our planet]' campaign.[10] The example in Box 14.2 was published in 2018 and was signed by both the Plan A Director and the Property Director, who will be key to ensuring this policy is implemented. Your organisation could follow this example, to develop your own energy policy, as it addresses both energy and water.

Box 14.2   M&S Energy Policy

Marks & Spencer is committed to ensuring that its global stores, offices and distribution centres are constructed and operated in a way which considers economic, comfort, environmental and energy whole life impacts.[11] *As part of this commitment we will:*

- *Consider energy and water efficiency and carbon emissions when designing, developing, and refurbishing properties for the life of M&S's use of these assets*
- *Seek to use renewable energy where technically and commercially feasible to reduce emissions*
- *Work in partnership with others to develop renewable energy generation capacity and, where feasible, M&S will purchase the energy output*
- *Maintain and further develop active automatic metering systems to give visibility of energy and water consumption data to users of all our worldwide locations*
- *Aim to achieve year-on-year consumption savings in energy and water*
- *Promote practical ways to conserve energy and water to both M&S colleagues and third parties*
- *Measure and report on annual energy consumption and resultant carbon emissions*
- *Comply with legislation and regulation.*

We will achieve these aims by:

- *Including building designers in energy management processes and sharing performance data*
- *Ensuring that renewable energy is considered as an option when making procurement decisions*
- *Regularly benchmarking stores against internal profiles and expected performance figures to identify opportunities for improvement*
- *Periodically delivering energy conservation awareness campaigns to widen the knowledge base of our employees and contractors and encourage them to highlight energy-saving opportunities.*
- *Publishing independently audited energy consumption and carbon emissions data annually as part of our Plan A reporting governance*
- *Working in partnership with third parties to identify best practice and innovation*

- *Regularly reviewing energy and water performance at Director level through Plan A reporting*
- *Including legal compliance in all contract requirements.*

Signed by Property Director and Plan A Director

Example waste management policy

Finally, we present a sample Environmental waste management policy. This needs to comply with existing waste legislation and improve business practices, thereby reducing waste produced by business activities and processes. Here we have chosen an example for a full-service law firm, Shoosmiths. This is an organisation that recognises the importance of adopting best practice for the business to move towards a zero-waste future, through its waste management policy (version below dated 2021).[12] Your organisation could use Box 14.3 as inspiration to develop their own policy.

Box 14.3   Shoosmiths' waste management policy

Shoosmiths is committed to protecting the environment by demonstrating high standards of environmental responsibility in all our operations and minimising the environmental impacts associated with our activities, products and services. In particular we recognise the importance of adopting best practice in the way we move towards a zero-waste future.[12]
    Our documented approach is based on:

- *Legislative compliance and demonstration of best management practice using registered contractors*
- *Adoption of waste hierarchical approach to the elimination of waste by focusing on prevention, re-use, recycling, other recovery or, as a last resort, disposal*
- *Encouragement of a circular economy approach that keeps resources in use for as long as possible, extracting the maximum value from them whilst in use, then facilitating the recovery and regeneration of products and materials at the end of their Shoosmiths' life*

- *Approach to waste elimination that supports our Net Zero emissions strategy*
- *Understanding of strategic decisions and operational practices that impact on waste generation and the design, implementation and review of procedures and programmes to address them*
- *Measurement, monitoring, analysis and reporting of waste generation*
- *Establishment and regular review of objectives and targets*
- *Investment of appropriate resources to minimise waste, based on best available techniques*
- *Donating unwanted items that have benefit to registered charities or community organisation*
- *Working with our supply chain to minimise waste associated with products and services*
- *Implementing, maintaining and communicating policy across the firm and interested parties*
- *Training and communication for staff to increase awareness, understanding and technical knowledge to reduce and manage waste*
- *Publishing our approach and progress against performance.*

Signed by Chief Executive

While all examples given here are strong from a content perspective, they could be more engaging in their presentation, perhaps using an infographic style. An example would be the '24 Menus of Change Principles' (see Figure 14.3) a food policy developed for the foodservice industry by The Culinary Institute of America, a private, not-for-profit culinary college to provide guidance and direction as issues of health, sustainability, and food ethics arise.[13]

How can I use an exciting approach to engage employees in my organisation?

Employees are important stakeholders and need to be engaged right at the beginning when it comes to implementing a successful GHG management programme within an organisation. Too often GHG management stays within the environmental sustainability function, whereas it really needs to go beyond that. Employees in all functions need to be engaged in GHG reduction and ensure that personal and business decisions are made by

Figure 14.3 24 Menus of Change Principles graphic reprinted with the permission of The Culinary Institute of America.

considering the emissions of their activities. Training is one way to engage employees and in the United Kingdom, the John Lewis Partnership[14] is working with the Energy Institute to ensure their Partners become 'EnergyAware' by undertaking a 30-minute immersive online course. This is part of the organisation's pledge to be Net Zero by 2035.

Other tools to engage employees include Green Rewards, which is gaining popularity in public and private sector organisations. It is a platform to engage employees in sustainability and GHG management through their day-to-day activities. Green Rewards aims to motivate participants to take part in gamified challenges and competitions which can add up to a significant impact in terms of GHG emissions reduction.[15] Various public and private sector organisations are now using Green Rewards as a bottom-up strategy for GHG management. Beyond that, the county of Nottinghamshire (England) has been leading the way as nine local councils have joined the two local universities (NTU and the University of Nottingham) and Jump (the developers of Green Rewards) to build a partnership for local residents. This is to help them reduce their GHG emissions in their day-to-day activities to tackle climate change. Participants receive incentives and vouchers in return for positive environmental actions.[16] The platform is worth checking out as you might also want to introduce this or a similar scheme.

In chapter 3 (Communication & Reporting), we explore other possibilities for employee engagement and in several other chapters, we share ideas as well.

When and how do I offset my remaining GHG emissions?

In the first instance, as many GHG reductions as possible should be made, by implementing appropriate measures and practices, as per the IEMA's GHG Management Hierarchy. However, there will always be some residual emissions. For those, carbon offsetting can help you to be a Net Zero or Carbon Neutral organisation. It should be reiterated that offsetting needs to be the *last option* in your carbon management journey. Organisations cannot keep producing GHG emissions through a business-as-usual approach and then offset, as explained earlier.

Carbon offsetting is an immediate, measurable and cost-effective method for your organisation to reduce emissions by investing in external conservation and renewable energy projects. There are different types of projects available, such as those connected with forestry and conservation, sustainable and renewable energy, and converting waste to energy. However, quality and reliability must be considered before any purchasing decision is made. Once the organisation's carbon footprint has been calculated, the percentage reduction in emissions must be decided upon. At that point, an accredited high-quality provider should be selected for the purchase of the carbon offsets. There are now many providers selling carbon offsets or carbon credits, and the projects may be in your home country or abroad. Projects can be verified by international standards such as the Verified Carbon Standard (VCS), Gold Standard and Certified Emission Reductions.[17]

Carbon offsetting – Lewis & Graves Partnership Limited

This case study is adapted from Carbon Footprint Ltd[18] and illustrates how organisations can offset carbon emissions. Lewis and Graves Partnership is a cleaning company based in London (England). The business provides environmentally friendly cleaning services to its clients.

Lewis and Graves provides their facility management, consulting and training services for corporate, educational and governmental clients in the United Kingdom. The company wanted to achieve PAS 2060 standard which is the internationally recognised standard for carbon neutrality. To do this Lewis and Graves used carbon offsetting for the remainder of their carbon emissions by supporting a variety of Quality Assurance Standard (QAS) certified carbon reduction projects. In addition to carbon emissions reduction, these projects supported the local communities by providing social and environmental benefits.

Lewis and Graves invested to support a range of carbon offsetting projects which include the following.

- UK tree planting – over 100 trees in schools in the United Kingdom
- Wind energy projects in the Philippines and India
- A landfill gas project in Tanzania
- Preventing deforestation projects in Brazil.

It needs to be noted that an organisation can invest in one carbon offsetting project or multiple, based on their residual emissions. Prices are normally based on each tonne of carbon emissions. The cost for carbon offsetting can be expensive if enacted in the United Kingdom, and relatively cheaper abroad in a developing country.

Quick Wins

1. Develop an environmental policy for your business, most organisations have waste and use energy, so start here as these should be the easiest ones.
2. Find a good template or practical example like those shared above and select the points that also apply to your organisation.
3. Develop a policy for an emissions hot spot (where your actions would achieve the greatest impact), don't reinvent the wheel – search for existing good policies in your chosen area.
4. Engage your stakeholders and co-create policies and strategy for GHG management with them (design, develop and implement).
5. Adopt the GHG Management Hierarchy in your strategy as per the needs of your organisation.

6. Make your policies and strategy dynamic and adaptable to future changes in your organisation; consider using infographics to motivate your employees and other stakeholders.
7. Regularly monitor and review progress to report and continuously improve.
8. Consider carbon offsetting, but only as a last resort, to address residual emissions.

Outlook

As shown in this chapter, there are various policies and practices that can help you reduce the GHG emissions in your organisation. We recommend that you develop an implementation plan such as the one suggested in Figure 14.4 for all your emissions to ensure a comprehensive strategy. As a

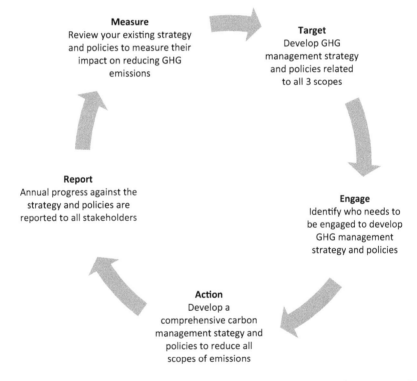

Measure
Review your existing strategy and policies to measure their impact on reducing GHG emissions

Target
Develop GHG management strategy and policies related to all 3 scopes

Report
Annual progress against the strategy and policies are reported to all stakeholders

Engage
Identify who needs to be engaged to develop GHG management strategy and policies

Action
Develop a comprehensive carbon management stategy and policies to reduce all scopes of emissions

Figure 14.4 Implementation plan for developing policies and practices for GHG management.

first step, you could review the state of your current GHG management strategy and policies, then start the development or redevelopment process as part of your GHG management journey. You may have some policies already, or you may have none, whatever your situation, this chapter should get you started. It will then allow you to implement GHG management practices using the other chapters in this book.

Further Resources

On the companion website to this book you can find further material to help you plan and implement this work.

Below you can find links which go into more detail or suggest further insights or support that might be of interest in addition to the ones mentioned in the endnotes.

Good practice policies:
https://www.ntu.ac.uk/about-us/strategy/sustainability/policies-and-reports
Here you will find other examples of NTU's sustainability and GHG management-related policies for inspiration.

Carbon management practices and carbon offsetting case studies:
https://cityswitch.net.au/Resources/CitySwitch-Resources/Respond-with-Renewables2/Renewable-Energy-Article/category/case-studies-for-carbon-offsetting
This resource offers various case studies with measures to reduce GHG emissions in businesses, including carbon offsetting.

A guide to Net Zero for businesses:
https://www.carbontrust.com/resources/a-guide-to-net-zero-for-businesses
This is an introductory guide designed to help businesses understand Net Zero. It looks at the importance of planning Net Zero targets and how to get started on your journey.

Julie's Bicycle (2017) Environmental Policy and Action Plan Guidelines and Environmental Policy and Action Plan Creation – Template:
https://juliesbicycle.com/wp-content/uploads/2022/01/Environmental_Policy_and_Action_Plan_Creation_template_-_no_branding.pdf

This template guides you through the process of designing your own environmental policy and an environmental action plan. While Julie's Bicycle is dedicated to improving climate action in arts and culture, the template can be used in any sector.

For the music industry, this guide might also be interesting: https://juliesbicycle.com/resource/music-top-tips-guide/

Notes

1. Info Entrepreneurs, *How to write an Environmental Policy*: https://www.infoentrepreneurs.org/en/guides/how-to-write-an-environmental-policy/
2. The Institute of Environmental Management and Assessment (IEMA), *Pathways to Net Zero: Using the IEMA GHG Management Hierarchy*: https://www.iema.net/resources/reading-room/2020/11/26/pathways-to-net-zero-using-the-iema-ghg-management-hierarchy-november-2020
3. Greenpeace, *The biggest problem with carbon offsetting is that it doesn't really work*: https://www.greenpeace.org.uk/news/the-biggest-problem-with-carbon-offsetting-is-that-it-doesnt-really-work/
4. Bloomberg (2020) *These Trees Are Not What They Seem*: https://www.bloomberg.com/features/2020-nature-conservancy-carbon-offsets-trees/
5. Greenpeace, *Airlines are selling carbon offsets as the solution to climate change*: https://www.greenpeace.org.uk/news/airlines-carbon-offsets-solution-climate-change-wrong/
6. Carbon Footprint, *Carbon Offset Projects*: https://www.carbonfootprint.com/carbonoffsetprojects.html
7. ERI, *The 1.5°C Business Playbook*: https://exponentialroadmap.org/wp-content/uploads/2020/11/1.5C-Business-Playbook-v1.1.1pdf.pdf
8. Haringey Council, *How to write an Environmental Policy*: https://www.haringey.gov.uk/sites/haringeygovuk/files/environmental_policy_fact-sheet_0.pdf
9. Nottingham Trent University (2022) *Environmental Policy*: https://www.ntu.ac.uk/__data/assets/pdf_file/0039/1693758/Environmental-Policy-2022.pdf
10. M&S (2007) *Plan A*: https://corporate.marksandspencer.com/sustainability/plan-a-our-planet

11. M&S, *Marks & Spencer Group Energy Policy*: https://corporate. marksandspencer.com/documents/plan-a-our-approach/m-and-s-group-energy-policy.pdf

12. Shoosmiths, *Shoosmiths waste management policy*: https://www.shoosmiths.co.uk/our-responsibility/corporate-responsibility/cr-policies/waste-management-policy

13. Menus of Change (2022), *24 Menus of Change Principles:* https://www.ciaprochef.com/MOC/Principles.pdf/

14. John Lewis Energy Aware courses for staff: https://www.edie.net/john-lewis-partnership-launches-online-training-in-energy-efficiency-for-all-staff-amid-energy-price-crisis/

15. Jump, *Create a culture of sustainability and wellness in your workplace*: https://teamjump.co.uk/about/

16. Carbon Copy, *Notts Green Rewards*: https://carboncopy.eco/initiatives/notts-green-rewards

17. Carbon Footprint, *Carbon Offsetting*: https://www.carbonfootprint.com/carbonoffset.html

18. Lewis and Graves LLP Case Study, *How Lewis And Graves Became A Carbon Neutral Organisation*: https://www.carbonfootprint.com/lewis_and_graves_case_study.html

PART IV

THE ROAD TO NET ZERO: MAKING IT A REALITY

15

TEAM HUMANITY ON THE ROAD TO NET ZERO: WILL YOU MAKE IT HAPPEN?

Richard Howarth, Petra Molthan-Hill and Fiona Winfield

Team Humanity is on the journey to a low-carbon future, but we need to keep global warming to below 1.5°C. This chapter will support you further by highlighting key insights and building blocks in the various chapters of this book and by signposting you to support networks, awards, incentives and strategies which could inspire you further on your own journey to a positive future for all!

This chapter is for you if you want to:

- Collaborate with others and find suitable networks
- Connect the dots for your team, department or organisation
- Apply for a climate-related award or other form of recognition
- Achieve systemic changes and help Team Humanity save the planet.

DOI: 10.4324/9781003274049-19

It will cover:

- Key insights from this book
- The role and benefits of partnerships and collaboration, giving examples from various countries with high greenhouse gas emissions
- Planning and developing an integrated approach
- Awards, accreditations and other incentives
- Strategies used by the fossil fuel industry and others to disengage citizens
- How to spot fake news
- Positive strategies to achieve the systemic changes required
- Education, training and the competences required
- Key message   IT'S REAL. IT'S US. EXPERTS AGREE. IT'S BAD. THERE'S HOPE.[41]

Where are we now, and where do we need to go?

We have to act fast! As outlined in chapter 1, the EARTH INDEX 2022 (developed by the research division of Corporate Knights with other experts in the field and contributions from CEOs of the 100 most sustainable corporations) shows that countries and sectors are not on target. *For the G20 in total, GHG emissions increased in 2019, resulting in an EARTH INDEX score of -15%. The power sector had a score of 5%, indicating that while there was a slight decline in emissions, the pace of reductions would have to be 20 times higher than in 2019 to be on track for meeting the aggregate G20 target. Emissions increased in all the other sectors, yielding negative EARTH INDEX scores and revealing the extent to which outcomes and aspirations are not yet aligned, at least at the level of the entire G20.*[1]

We also highlighted in chapter 1 that Net Zero means that **we must halve our GHG emissions by 2030!** This is strongly advised by the IPCC alongside their assertion that we have to make **deep reductions in non-CO_2 emissions across the economy.**[2]

So how do we get on target?

We have shown in chapter 1 that it is possible to keep global warming to 1.5°C compared to pre-industrial levels, and that we might be able to draw down the temperature after the peak at 1.5°C as suggested by Project Drawdown. However, we need to act fast, and we need to embed high-impact solutions into everything we do. Into our organisations, into our daily habits and last, but not least, into our policies, in whichever country we are based. We should be accelerating this change by investing our money in the right industries as shown in chapter 10 and choosing the right pensions. Having money and a pension is pointless if there is no-where on the planet where we can survive, let alone live comfortably within our means!

In chapter 1 we also recommended that every climate solution should be evaluated against whether it addresses other problems such as pov-erty, inequality or job creation, using the FLOWER framework. If you have not done this already, we would definitely recommend that you return to Tables 1.1 and 1.2, and carry out the En-ROADS and FLOWER activities. The German comedian and physician, Dr. Eckart von Hirschhausen, highlighted on the cover of his climate book[3] that we are getting three crises for the price of two! Yes, if Climate Action (SDG 13) is not addressed, we will experience even more crises than that: loss of biodiversity, more poverty, more hunger, more inequality. The opposite is true too: the more we invest in reducing GHG emissions and em-bedding climate solutions, the more we will improve working condi-tions for everyone, create new jobs, reduce hunger, improve health and so on.

This book offers plenty of solutions to choose from. For example, we make the point in chapter 2 that one person choosing to eat less meat might not seem to make a big difference. However, if 60 million people took the same decision, we would suddenly be talking about tonnes of GHG emissions saved, as lots of small changes add up.

In this book, we have given you many examples of how these solutions could be embedded into different functions within your organisation. It starts with convincing your colleagues and all your stakeholders as to how they could also make changes. In chapter 2, we highlight why everyone needs to have a basic knowledge of the best options available through training, and we offer insights into good communications and reporting in chapter 3. We also address meetings and transport (chapter 4) and how every employee can reduce their emissions through thoughtful travel options. In chapter 5, we discuss the digital footprint of the organisation, and how much can be achieved through sustainable web design, reductions in GHG emissions in data centres and other ICT-related activities, such as cryptocurrencies. Catering and your food waste are covered in chapter 6, estates and facilities in chapter 7, and actions and strategies for procurement and marketing in chapters 8 and 9 and your pension/investments in chapter 10. We encourage everyone in an organisation to read the relevant chapters so they can choose the best high-impact solutions for their team, department and the whole organisation.

In this final chapter, we provide some hints and tips to ensure you secure support, and we offer insights into how the way forward might look, and what might facilitate change. Later in this chapter, we will also return to the wider context of the whole organisation, which we cover in chapters 11–14, and to some extent in chapter 10 (Pensions and Investments) and chapter 3 (Communication & Reporting). If you want to set up a greenhouse gas management plan for the whole organisation or influence senior management, you might want to read the section 'Transforming action: connecting the dots' in this chapter.

Start with a plan

If you are leading a company, department or team, we encourage you to start by assessing the current situation. We give recommendations for this in chapter 1 when we discuss the Five Practices for Climate Leaders, and we would encourage you to go through the practices for yourself. If you are leading a company, we would recommend you revisit chapters 11–14 to set up appropriate GHG management systems for your whole organisation. We would then recommend that you draw up a summary for your company (or department or team), so everyone can understand the sources of your greenhouse gas emissions and where you could potentially reduce them. For this we have provided ideas in each chapter, especially 4–10. If you lead a catering team you might decide to focus on chapter 6 'Food'; if you work in a web design team, you could read chapter 5 'Digital Footprint'. Choose the chapter that relates most closely to your area of responsibility and influence. You might want to go for the 'Quick Wins' first, included in each chapter, but we would encourage you to start to draw up a longer-term plan as soon as possible, so you can also focus on the bigger wins – addressing the question: 'What would really reduce GHG emissions in our team, department and/or organisation'?

It is worth using a step-by-step approach – you could follow the guidance in the 'implementation planning cycle' provided in the 'Outlook' section of most chapters. See for example the one included in chapter 4, Meetings & Transport (Figure 4.3). In chapter 4 we also provide the Transport Report Card from Ethical Consumer (Figure 4.1) which gives an overview of the targets to be achieved, where we are currently, and what individuals, companies and governments have to do, in order to reach the targets. You could decide to create a similar report card for other areas in your organisation. The Ethical Consumer has made such report cards for food, heating and selected consumer goods, along with an overall Summary Report Card 2021. This shows that 75% of total consumer emissions could be addressed if the actions suggested on the different cards were achieved.[4]

To support the development of your plans and strategies, we would recommend that you re-visit chapter 2 'Climate Literacy Training'. You might also find it beneficial to take such a training course or even organise one for your colleagues. Please contact Petra Molthan-Hill (petra.molthan-hill@ntu.ac.uk) if you would like to do this, so we can put you in contact with trainers worldwide from diverse backgrounds, to deliver this for you and your organisation.

Support: organisations, sources of inspiration and mentors

We hope that you are inspired after reading this book and that you will put many of the ideas suggested into practice. However, you might like some further support to sustain you. You will not have all the answers, either at the start or as your work progresses; collaborating with others, from inside or outside your organisation, would be beneficial. According to EY[5] and Accenture,[6] collective problem solving and working together to lead action are very valuable and powerful tools in climate action, and the act of collaborating can create more innovative and effective solutions. According to the World Economic Forum (WEF),[7] this is rooted in Sustainable Development Goal 17 (Partnerships for the Goals[8]) which is about mutual support, co-production and co-creation to facilitate cohesion and leadership. This is why in the Climate Literacy Training we have used interactive sessions, where managers from various industries work together on shared issues and challenges (such as the television industry, as covered in our chapter 2 case study). This embraces the sharing of best practice and the creation of new ideas, both within and beyond one's sphere of influence.

Working with others also helps organisations and managers to realise that they are not alone; it is an opportunity to spur one another on to achieve results as a consequence. Collaboration and the sharing of ideas and solutions across organisations, sectors and territories is a key element in the work of organisations such as the **Carbon Disclosure Project (CDP)**, which we introduce in chapter 3 (Communication & Reporting). The CDP facilitates organisations to support their work on disclosure, which benefits both the organisations and other stakeholders (e.g. investors). The CDP supports others via its global disclosure system and enables collaboration and action within an organisation's supply chain.

Whether focused on facilitating action, lobbying for change or recognising and rewarding good practice, there are many options available to you. Depending on the size of your organisation, working with sector-wide groups may help, these include for example:

- **Exponential Roadmap Initiative (ERI)**[9] – collaboration is at the core of the ERI's work and they have identified 36 solutions with exponential scaling potential to halve GHG emissions by 2030. That is in addition to providing a platform for sharing best practice in the supply chain (which we highlighted in chapter 8), suggestions for the transformation of cities and much more. We recommend this report in our 'Further Resources' section in chapter 8, where we provide more information.
- **SME Climate Hub (SCH)**[10] – focuses on specific support for SMEs recognising the benefits from working together and the provision of shared solutions and tools developed at scale. The SCH is also highlighted in chapters 3, 8 and 12.

Your organisation may want to build on your commitments and join forces with others in appropriate initiatives. There are many to choose from, and at a global scale you might want to engage with the work of the **Global Compact (GC)**.[11] Over 12,000 organisations are already involved across 160 different countries; they represent almost all sectors and sizes of organisation, so you will not feel alone. The GC supports and inspires action related to the SDGs and their focus on partnerships is at the core of their work. You can find local networks and partners through the GC website.[12] Through its programmes such as 'Caring for the Climate', there are clear opportunities to commit to action and work with others.[13]

Engaging with the GC may not be for you however, as the commitments and the scale at which it operates may seem daunting. It may be better to focus on where you are now and the next steps to take – in this case in relation to any collaborations. There is every chance you will find national, or even local, alliances, groups and networks which engage a range of organisations and activities. These may be supported by specific business organisations, industry bodies or other stakeholders. The key is to have an idea of what you are looking for, and the scale and nature of the work you want to do. Get involved, either to share your own challenges and solutions or to gain insights and inspiration from others. The opportunity to mentor others, or to gain mentoring input yourself may also be an option, and a valuable one too!

Many groups can be found by simple internet searches, in addition to more traditional networking and 'asking around'. **Climate ADAPT**[14] is a good place to start online, as it lists a range of organisations and co-operative programs that operate on global, European (both EU and non-EU) and transnational levels. There is also the **Chambers Climate Coalition**,[15] a global grassroots movement to provide an insightful international network of chambers of commerce. This supports business needs through sharing best practice and actionable guidance, with a focus primarily on SMEs.

In addition to global networks, groups and organisations, in Table 15.1 we have provided examples of organisations operating nationally, some of these also have a global reach and connections. This list is by no means exhaustive, nor is it a complete listing for each territory identified. However, the table offers examples of the types of organisation you could research in your own country, their focus and the support offered. It is also worth checking whether there is a local **Climate Action Network** in your country or region. It claims to be the *largest environmental network of over 1,500 non-governmental organisations in over 130 countries fighting the climate crisis.* Some of the CA Networks are mentioned below and the full details are here: https://climatenetwork.org/.

Table 15.1 Examples of groups, organisations and networks in various countries and territories

Country/ Region	Group, Organisation or Network	Weblink
Australia	Climate Action Australia and **Cool Australia** work directly with citizens and communities.	**Climate Action Australia**: https://climateactionaustralia.net.au/ **Cool Australia**: https://www.coolaustralia.org/
	WWF Australia works with businesses and groups to support and direct action/ change.	**WWF Australia**: https://www.wwf.org.au/
	Australian Conservation Foundation promotes benefits of climate-related action; supports organisations through the promotion of renewable energy (runs events/ webinars).	**ACF**: https://www.acf.org.au/
	Networks with reach beyond Australia: **Beyond Zero Emissions Australia** and the **Investor Group on Climate Change** (also in New Zealand).	**Beyond Zero Australia**: https://bze.org.au/ **IGCC**: https://igcc.org.au/
	The **Climate Council** is an impactful leading climate change communications organisation.	**Climate Council**: www.climatecouncil.org.au
Canada	**Canada Climate Action Network** supports multi-stakeholder/ themed action.	**CAN-RAC**: https://climateactionnetwork.ca/
	The **David Suzuki** Foundation works to help create a sustainable Canada, through evidence-based research, education and policy analysis.	**The David Suzuki Foundation**: https://davidsuzuki.org/
	Future Earth seeks to advance transformations to sustainability via local projects, private and public partner institutions, and the broader community.	**Future Earth**: https://montreal.futureearth.org/
	The **Chartered Professional Accountants Canada** (CPA) supports transitions to remove climate impacts (workshops & campaigns).	**CPA Canada**: https://www.cpacanada.ca/
	Organisations such as **Maple Leaf Foods, CN** and **Celestica Inc** work via coalitions to guide organisations towards Net Zero.	**Maple Leaf Foods, Alliance**: https://www.mapleleaffoods.com/ **CAN Europe**: https://caneurope.org/
Eastern Europe & Central Asia	**CAN-EECCA** – the Climate Action Network for Eastern Europe, the Caucasus and Central Asia.	https://climatenetwork.org/region/eastern-europe-caucasus-and-central-asia/

Europe	**Climate Action Network Europe** *promotes sustainable climate, energy and development policies* – active in 38 countries.	**CAN Europe:** https://caneurope.org/
	GreenEcoNet supports SMEs in the EU.	**GreenEcoNet**: https://www.econet-project.eu/
Qatar	The **Qatar Foundation** organises biennial World Innovation Summit for Health (WISH) and climate-focused events.	**Qatar Foundation:** https://www.qf.org.qa/
	The **Qatar Green Building Council (QGBC)** encourages collaboration and change.	**QGBC:** https://www.earthna.qa/
United Kingdom	**Business in the Community (BITC)** and the **Sustainable Markets Initiative (SMI)** promote collaborative action and run events/ awards.	**BiTC:** https://www.bitc.org.uk/ **SMI**: https://www.sustainable-markets.org/
	Sector-specific groups include **Logistics UK** and its **Route to Net Zero** initiative, plus **NetZeroNow** for accounting profession.	**Logistics UK**: https://logistics.org.uk/environment/netzero **NetZeroNow**: https://netzeronow.org/accountants
	Local groups and networks such as **Carbon Neutral Nottingham**.	**Carbon Neutral Nottingham**: https://www.nottinghamcity.gov.uk/cn2028
	Investors in the Environment (iiE): national accreditation scheme which runs events, shares case studies and provides resources: posters | questionnaire templates | audit guides.	**iiE**: https://www.iie.uk.com/
USA	The **Business Environmental Leadership Council (BELC)** is supported by global brands from many sectors and is the largest group of corporations focused on climate change in the USA.	**BELC**: https://www.c2es.org/our-work/belc/ *part of The Center for Climate and Energy Solutions (C2ES)*
	Carbon 180 works with policymakers, enterprises and organisations across USA.	**Carbon 180**: https://carbon180.org/
	The **Climate Adaptation and Knowledge Exchange (CAKE)** and the **Georgetown Climate Center (GCC)** support action through dialogue and partnerships, and inform policy and action.	**CAKE**: https://www.cakex.org/ **GCC**: https://www.georgetownclimate.org/
	Organisations focused on specific themes/ industries include: **Association of Climate Change Officers**, **National Association of Environmental Professionals (NAEP)** and the **Sierra Club**.	**ACCO**: https://climateofficers.org **NAEP**: https://www.naep.org **Sierra Club**: https://www.sierraclub.org/

Networks and groups whether global, local or industry/sector-specific all promote partnership, collaboration and support through lobbying, guidance, events and training. There are many organisations and groups out there, and their relevance will depend on your focus, whether at the organisational level or related to a specific activity or function. For the latter, marketing, HR, procurement or finance for example, we recommend your professional body as the first port of call, and we have made suggestions in relevant chapters. You could also investigate the Institute of Environmental Management & Assessment (IEMA)[16] – a professional body providing training, sharing best practice, and engaging in thought leadership and advocacy. Its 16,000 members are sustainability experts from the public and private sectors in 116 countries.

There are also public sector networks, such as the **C40 CITIES**,[17] a global network of mayors, taking action against climate change. You may, on the other hand, be interested in specific GHG emission sources (from transport or data for example) or perhaps you simply want to encourage or lobby others to take action. Whatever your motivation, use that as your starting point to determine which groups are the most relevant for you.

Collaboration means that solutions to specific and wider problems can be identified and worked through collectively. This may simplify the decision-making processes of others and can speed up action as a result – it is possible for example that someone else has already made a plan that could be adapted and implemented straight away; there is no need to keep reinventing the wheel! Much of the hard work may have been done already, allowing you to follow the guidance provided by others. Alternatively, you may decide that you want to work through the issues yourself, alone or with other interested parties, and then produce and share guidance for others.

Collaboration and partnerships are relevant within an organisation too; working with others in and across departments, functions and business areas can often prove beneficial. Look also to work externally, with your supply and value chains, as discussed in chapter 8 (Procurement & Supply). This can lead to similar benefits and outcomes as a result of collectively solving problems and sharing information.

You could also sign up to a variety of news organisations to receive their updates and guidance on climate change (either international or local). A comprehensive list would be far too long to include here, but the sort of sites we suggest in Table 15.2 would include the ones below (in no

Table 15.2 Examples of news sources providing climate change updates

News sources	Weblink
54 Sources for climate change news (George Washington University)	https://onlinepublichealth.gwu.edu/resources/sources-for-climate-news/
UK-based newspapers such as The Financial Times and The Guardian	https://www.ft.com/climate-capital https://www.theguardian.com/environment/climate-crisis
Magazines such as The Economist and Le Point (French – subscription required)	https://www.economist.com/climate-change https://www.lepoint.fr/dossiers/sciences/climat-rechauffement-transition-ecologique-cop26/
News channels such as the BBC, CNN and ABC News, and news agencies such as Reuters	https://www.bbc.co.uk/news/science-environment-56837908 https://edition.cnn.com/specials/world/cnn-climate https://www.abc.net.au/news/topic/climate-change https://www.reuters.com/subjects/focus-climate-change
SciDev.Net – *Bringing science & development together through news & analysis*	https://www.scidev.net/asia-pacific/environment/climate-change/
Google News – then choose topic, such as 'Climate Change' or 'Climate Change News'	https://news.google.com/

specific order), and you may wish to seek out some which are more local or relevant to you.

News organisations regularly share insights into climate change and action by businesses. They usually have online resources and may also host events; it is worth checking them out and signing up for updates. Other organisations, already mentioned elsewhere in the book, that provide information and updates include: **Edie**, which runs courses and provides regular updates, insights and guides[18] and **Sustainable Brands**, which offers a twice weekly update.[19]

Awards and accreditations: recognition and benchmarking

BELC and **C2ES** offer awards[20] and these can validate action achieved and provide the chance to communicate how progress has been made, in the hope of inspiring others to follow suit. The chance to receive recognition via an award might also be the trigger for work in the first place. For example, in order to submit for an award you usually have to evidence what has been done; the potential award is thus the motivator for action. In the case of the global **Earthshot Prize**, which incentivises change and repair to the planet over the next ten years, submissions must focus on the development of innovative solutions to the challenges posed by climate change and wider sustainability.

Table 15.3 shows just some of the climate-related prizes and awards, which is by no means exhaustive for all territories and sectors, but may provide a starting point.

Table 15.3 Examples of climate change prizes and awards

Prize/Award	Weblink
Green Matters A curated list of climate change awards to reward those doing incredible things in the climate space (covers many different sectors)	https://www.greenmatters.com/p/climate-change-awards
UN Global Climate Action Awards Recognise innovative and transformative solutions that address both climate change and wider economic, social and environmental challenges	https://unfccc.int/climate-action/un-global-climate-action-awards
Climate Breakthrough Project Awards Global award seeking novel and game-changing strategies to reduce GHG emissions and limit global warming	https://www.climatebreakthroughproject.org/
Prince William's Earthshot Prize Prestigious global environment prize that aims to turn current pessimism surrounding environmental issues into optimism	https://earthshotprize.org/
Global Good Awards Recognises businesses, NGOs, charities and social enterprises around the world which are driving social and environmental change	https://globalgoodawards.co.uk/
Global Change Awards Fashion industry awards aimed at scaling disruptive ideas to lead transformation in the industry	https://hmfoundation.com/gca/about-global-change-award/

The Green Gown Awards Recognise exceptional sustainability initiatives undertaken by universities and colleges across the world	https://www.greengownawards.org/
The Sustainability Awards Encompasses start-ups and global brands, and relates to the international packaging value chain; judges are from leading brands and retailers, sustainability organisations, waste management, academia and industry	http://thesustainabilityawards.com/
The Good Housekeeping Sustainable Innovation Awards GH's scientists and industry experts evaluate c200 contenders to choose winning home, beauty, apparel, toy and food brands	https://www.goodhousekeeping.com/institute/a37728461/sustainable-innovation-awards-2021/

Recognition and opportunities to collaborate and work in partnership, not only develop via networking groups and awards, but also from organisations such as **ISO (International Standards Organisation)**.[21] This is an independent organisation made up of 167 national bodies which engage experts in their respective fields to support the development of their international standards. These influence how organisations approach and solve global challenges. ISO's approach simplifies processes and provides access to others, with whom to share internationally benchmarked tools. ISO's commitment to combat climate change, through its work with carbon footprinting and emissions standards, gives credibility to how organisations approach work in this area, and the outcomes they achieve.[22] Individuals and organisations can work with ISO on technical committees, both broad and specific, which support and lead standardisation work. They include, for example, ISO/TC 322,[23] which is focused on sustainable finance.

Gaining recognition via an ISO standard is also important as it demonstrates to others who have the same standard, and a wider audience, that you have followed a recognised approach to your work, which has been undertaken at the appropriate level. This can generate interest to collaborate from others with the same recognition. It might also mean that your work is held up as good practice for action in certain areas and can inspire others.

Specific to climate change-related action, ISO standards and guidance include, for example:

- ISO14021 – environmental labels and declarations
- ISO14064 – the quantification and reporting of GHG emissions
- ISO14090 – adaptation to climate change.

Transforming action: setting the scene

Often collaboration will start within your own team or organisation, in which case, it will be essential to understand your colleagues' and managers' current positions. Start by asking:

- Do we have policies or strategies that cover the topic in question, and what structures support these?
- Who else is interested in taking and supporting action within this area of work and in the wider organisation?
- Is anyone already taking action in this area, and what have they achieved so far?
- Who are the relevant stakeholders and what role do they play in taking and supporting action?
- Does the organisation have current systems for collaboration and sharing information?
- What information is already available, and what further information is needed?

The answers to these questions will help you establish a sense of the structures, systems and processes you need to put in place, and the people you might want to ask for support. It could be that the organisation has already started work in this area, and perhaps has a climate change policy or a wider sustainability policy? If not, and depending on your role and your sphere of influence, use insights from chapters 2–10 to help guide your understanding of the priorities for action and identify how these relate to your organisational structures and systems. You might want to suggest relevant policies, if none exists (see chapter 14).

The ERI (Exponential Roadmap Initiative) suggests that it's best to focus internally to start with, and then move to work with suppliers (see also chapter 8) – so if you were thinking about energy use and raw materials, you might want to ask questions such as:

- How is our energy produced?
- How is our energy-use monitored and who holds this information?
- Are the data and information available to us?
- How are the materials for our products and services sourced?

- What guides our choice, and who is responsible for any standards?
- Can we support changes and developments to specifications?

With the answers to these questions, you can start to influence change. This might need a shift in the overall strategy of the organisation, and if you are at a fairly junior level, you may only be able to put forward ideas via the organisation's 'suggestion box'.

If, on the other hand, you are more senior, or even responsible for the whole organisation, the work might either be more straightforward or an even greater challenge. Straightforward, because you will have oversight of the structures, systems and processes and will have authority over who takes action, how and when. But challenging, as your task may be much larger, involve more elements and be a lot more complex. No matter which level you are working at, breaking down the tasks and phasing your work is key. This involves recognising what supports action, and what constrains it. Along with how such factors will affect the project as your work progresses, and what should be the different phases. Finally, what will need to happen in order to move on to the next level.

WANT TO DIG DEEPER?

Exponential Roadmap Initiative – Scaling 36 Solutions to Halve Emissions by 2030
https://exponentialroadmap.org/exponential-roadmap/
This report is an excellent overview of how to transform the sectors with the highest emissions, but also how to transform cities and how to set efficient policies. The report was co-designed by a *multidisciplinary team representing academia, business and NGOs – from energy specialists, data modellers, ICT analysts and urban researchers to exponential strategists, journalists, editors, designers and data visualisers*. It provides 36 solutions to halve emissions by 2030. These are evidence-based and each relates to a specific theme or area, with associated information and guidance to facilitate action planning and outcomes.

The Climate Communications Handbook 2022
https://www.edie.net/the-edie-communications-handbook-2022/
Edie, like other publishers, identifies the important role of communications and, with a focus on ensuring key terms are defined and understood,

their handbook supports the communication around climate change and related action, and how this connects to wider work in this area, reporting and disclosure.

Michael E Mann – The New Climate War
We have summarised some of the key insights from this book here in this chapter at the end, but would recommend reading the book in full, to understand some of the vested interests at play.

Transforming action: connecting the dots for your organisation

At whichever level you are operating, you might be able to influence policies in your organisation. Even if you are looking at minor changes to your daily habits, or those of a small department, it will ultimately connect you to work at a more strategic level, either because the strategic direction of your organisation guides what you are doing in the first place, or because what you decide to do will hopefully become part of future overall strategy. If you are interested in influencing the policies of your organisation, we recommend that you read chapter 14. You might also consider working with other departments, as the changes you are implementing in your team or department might benefit from this collaboration. Furthermore, you might want to influence organisations and/or stakeholders connected to your place of work, such as suppliers.

If you are leading an organisation, you might want to consider whom to engage, in order to reduce GHG emissions. As mentioned before, chapters 4–10 embrace a number of core business functions (including transport, procurement and supply, marketing and the management of your estate) and other aspects (including your organisation's digital footprint, how you operate meetings and what food you serve). You might want to identify the employees in your organisation who could take the lead in one of these functions, such as the Head of Purchasing, who might benefit not only from chapter 8 (Procurement & Supply), but also chapter 6 (Food Waste & Food) in order to include criteria for 'low-carbon food procurement'. However, it is also important to design a GHG management plan (chapters 11–14) to give direction and to connect the dots for your employees, who might also benefit if you communicate your vision and associated actions (chapter 3). Last but not least, you might decide that you, your employees and colleagues would benefit from climate literacy training (chapter 2).

Chapters 4–10 conclude with a phased plan of action in the form of a circular implementation plan, which informs the development of strategy in the respective area, and Quick Wins. Within each chapter, there is an assessment of where to start and, via the contents of the chapter and the suggested action planning, we guide you towards making commitments, setting objectives and targets. This culminates in putting your ideas into action and reviewing afterwards. These should all inform your work and its ongoing progress and impacts. As mentioned earlier, chapters 10–14 ultimately ground your work in a recognised approach, which should give it structure and add credibility and therefore connect it to your organisation's strategy.

PwC[24] highlights the importance of progression and building blocks for climate change-related work, and consequently the implementation of strategies and how these flow up and down within the organisation. PwC stresses the importance of identifying impacts and setting baselines and calculating the organisation's (or the department's) carbon footprint. Having agreed on the baseline, PwC recommends setting targets and developing strategies. The extent of the overall transformation of the organisation will depend on the type of business, its operations, the sector and its overall business model. All these activities support both transparency and reporting, which is PwC's final building block.

Transforming action: getting going and accelerating change

An important point when talking about transformation is noted by Accenture in their 2021 report.[25] When they interviewed leaders across a wide range of organisations, they found that just over a third had not yet started the transition to Net Zero. Of the 65% who had started, 45% described their organisation's progress towards Net Zero as 'basic'. In other words, most had either not started or were in the very early stages of transformation. Only about 25% of CEOs suggested their organisational maturity regarding transition was 'advanced'. So, if you are only just getting started or feel you are behind others – take heart, this is not the case. BUT, please start to act NOW, as your work and that of others is crucial as part of the process here!

So where should you start in trying to connect the dots and how do you set off on the apparently elusive journey towards Net Zero?

As identified elsewhere, the **ERI Playbook**[26] is a good place to start, as it provides useful guidance in designing an organisation's strategy. The initiative is underpinned by a wealth of knowledge, experience and resources and its playbook lays out four 'pillars' as the foundation for action:

1. Reduce your own emissions
2. Reduce your supply and value chain emissions
3. Integrate climate into your business strategy
4. Influence climate action in society.

While working through each of the above, the ERI also advocates that you:

- First halve your own emissions, and then halve your supply and value chain's emissions
- Prioritise by creating and using available insights, paying attention first to the highest impact areas
- Assess, Analyse and Disclose: what emissions, where from, what done, what achieved and what next?

This is a relatively simple but effective process to follow, and should support you and your organisation with the journey. Also, based on the ERI's pillars, attention to the following will be influential:

- **Energy:** eliminate, reduce and manage your energy emissions (favour renewables, shift to lower emitting energy sources, manage requirements)
- **Materials**: eliminate or reduce where possible (consider reuse and recycling, and the use of alternative materials, perhaps recycled content, to reduce emissions).

As you progress through the different areas of your GHG reduction plan, internally and externally, use appropriate data to guide you. This might identify 'hot spots' – areas which require urgent action, especially if they are important to the business. We strongly recommend at this point to access the aforementioned 'Exponential Roadmap Initiative' highlighting 36 solutions to halve emissions by 2030, and to choose some of them and the associated actions to support the transition required.[27]

Whilst these may not all be applicable to all organisations, most will have some relevance and will help you to set priorities and move forwards. Accenture identifies that technology will play a large role in supporting the transition to Net Zero.[28] It is easy to see how this might be the case when developing the electrification of the power source for vehicles and other equipment, but technology and the application of scientific knowledge can also assist in introducing 'better' systems and processes in any organisation. This might include the business model that frames your work, or the frameworks used, shaping what gets done and why it's done that way. Reviewing the life cycle of products and services could be helpful here to understand the impacts throughout: from materials and ingredients at the start, via the products and services you purchase and the energy used, to what happens at the end of life.

The concept of the circular economy (CE) and its role as a solution, are discussed in a number of chapters (such as numbers 8 and 9: Procurement & Supply and Marketing). CE's attention to the removal of waste and the decoupling of economic activity from the consumption of finite resources will be as important as other factors in supporting progress.[29,30] Various examples of the circular economy in action are available, but we recommend especially looking at the work of the **Ellen MacArthur Foundation**,[31] set up to lead CE solutions. One such example provided by the foundation is how the multinational clothing company H&M is working towards being 100% circular.[32] This started back in 2015, when H&M was already addressing its sustainability and climate impacts. While the company's development at that time had been important, it wanted a major shift to a CE approach since its practices could not support material and energy sustainability into the future. As a result, the company focused on the design of the product, including its end of life, the use of materials, and the supply chains, with the latter supporting garment production, remaking and re-cycling.

Transforming action: 'sticks', 'carrots' and behaviour change

We recommend making an action plan for your organisation, your department or your team. Consider including references in your plan to the 'sticks' and 'carrots' used in your country of operation. Sticks for example could include the introduction or development of regulations around the reporting and disclosure of GHG emissions and consequent action, as seen recently following decisions by the SEC (Securities and Exchange Commission) in the USA.[33] Carrots could include funding available to you to support your work. In Canada for example, as elsewhere, there are incentives to support the purchase and lease of electric vehicles.[34] Both sticks and carrots can also add weight to your arguments as to why action is needed and may shape the action you take. They could also help you build the associated business case for work in specific parts of the organisation.

The discussion provided earlier in this chapter (and elsewhere in the book) contains reference to levers, pillars, platforms or rules, which can help frame the stages of your work. The levers traditionally employed to support implementation include:

- **Awareness, guidance and encouragement**: to underpin recognition of need and encourage action
- **Incentivisation**: to sweeten the pill and ensure there is follow-through
- **Requirements and penalties**: laws or regulations, and maybe fines, for non-compliance.

The best levers or pillars for you to use will depend on how far the organisation has travelled, the type of work undertaken, and the nature and scale of change involved. It will probably also be based on your sense of likely resistance, and your previous experiences, especially in relation to earlier stages of the plan, while collecting evidence. We should also recognise that not everyone will move at the same pace, with the same priorities or interests; as with management of any sort of change, it's a good idea to work out who your allies are, and to get them on board early on.

As covered in chapter 3 (Communication & Reporting) and chapter 9 (Marketing), when it comes to climate change and removing GHG emissions, attitudes and espoused commitments do not always lead to action. It is important to use approaches that make the necessary changes to do the right thing seem appealing. Unless you are a trained social scientist, using such approaches drawn from behavioural science may sound a bit scary, but it actually makes a lot of sense and is based on straightforward, easy-to-follow logic.

The **UNEP**[35] for example advocates five core principles which should prove helpful. Some of this is about how you present options, and others are simply about removing options, making it inevitable that people will select the best solutions for the climate.

- **Make the default the better option**: ensure that what is seen as the norm is the option that's more effective in reducing GHG emissions. Use your previous analysis and evidence collected to inform the choice of default option.
- **Change how choices are presented to favour sustainable behaviour**: this could relate externally to your pricing strategy, or how you present choices to staff internally. For the latter, it could relate to your meetings, the food served at work, pension options etc. You may be interested to know that the ideas here are grounded in what is termed 'choice architecture' coined by Professors Thaler and Sunstein, which became more widely known through their book 'Nudge'.[36] Examples include 'opt out' (an often-used example is enrolling employees automatically in the pension scheme, rather than giving the choice to opt in). This can be a really powerful tool for your work, and it's an interesting book too, so worthy of further exploration.
- **Remove the 'unsustainable' option altogether**: this may link to regulation and the banning or removal of certain options. Again, this should be based on your previous analysis and may include the removal of certain packaging materials, because of their negative impact. It could also relate to the day-to-day activities in your organisations, such as providing everyone with a high-quality mug and no longer offering drinks in take-away cups.
- **Remove the hassle factor**: make it as easy as possible to achieve the 'best outcome'. In some cases, current habits actually involve more hassle, but the routine itself sometimes perpetuates behaviour. Recognise this,

and make things simple, so that the most GHG-efficient options are selected.

- **Go small, make it personal**: tailoring the message internally and externally is key. Try to get the right tone for your audience - the narrator and the narrative is central (as discussed in chapter 3). Allies were mentioned above, and maybe reach out firstly to motivated individuals and groups, to support your wider action. Targeting difficult to change individuals might also result in them assisting you, by advocating change in the future. 'One size fits all' is probably not the best solution, so you will need to think about whom to target, why and how, and learn from your experiences to support others.

While it will be important for you to understand the problem by analysing and assessing your GHG emissions and developing your strategy and plan, your overall assessment of the current situation and your organisation's setup will help inform you on the implementation of your strategy. That aspect is sure to be the key to success and any future transformation, but it will probably be the hardest part. You need to recognise and use any sticks and carrots available to support and guide you, identify the priorities and build a sound business case. Your assessments and insights into your GHG 'hot spots' will support, but colleagues and others outside of the organisation will not act just because it seems like a 'good idea'. You will need to think about structures and processes, current and new, and how attention to behaviour will ensure your plans are brought to life, progress is made, and the transition required to reach Net Zero is achieved.

Climate wars: check your sources and information

One of the most famous and reputable climate change scientists Professor Michael Mann has written a fascinating, but also frustrating, book about the new climate strategies used by the fossil fuel industry and others, designed to discourage any sort of action by society. Instead of denial, which they used in the last decades, they now use other strategies. Michael Mann suggests to call them *inactivists*, which includes *deceivers and dissemblers, namely, downplayers, deflectors, dividers, delayers and doomers* — willing participants in a multipronged strategy seeking to deflect blame, divide the public, delay action by promoting 'alternative' solutions that don't solve the problem, or insist we simply accept our fate — it is too late to do anything, so we might as well keep the oil flowing.[37] We have highlighted here three of the key strategies he describes in detail:

Strategy 1: It is your fault! Corporations individualise the actions to be taken to distract from the actions they should take!

Strategy 2: Make climate change so threatening that everyone thinks it is too late and that no action can reverse it, resulting in inaction being acceptable.

Strategy 3: Propose solutions that are non-solutions! This is illustrated by Michael Mann with regards to geoengineering: A price on carbon, or incentives for renewable energy? Too difficult and risky! Engaging in a massive, uncontrolled experiment in a desperate effort to somehow offset the effects of global warming? Perfect![38]

We would strongly recommend reading his book, as he explains why geoengineering might not be the best solution, and he describes very well the different actors and their interests at play, especially in the American context.

We therefore need to be very mindful of the sources of our information and we need to be able to judge whether something is factually correct or is 'fake news'. For example, the innocent sounding 'Creative Society' is in fact a vehicle for climate denial, or more specifically denies that climate change is caused by humans, and uses its conferences to spread unscientific opinions. The BBC climate disinformation reporters Marco Silva and Merlyn Thomas analyse the 'Creative Society' in a very informative article, explaining how it operates and how several high-profile scientists felt tricked by the organisation.[39] Maybe it is useful to remind ourselves at this point that 99% of scientists agree that climate change is human induced[40] and that we have the chance to do something about it.

John Cook from George Mason University (USA), Geoffrey Supran from Harvard University (USA) and others have also analysed how the fossil fuel industry has misled the American public for decades, along with the strategies they have used to do this.[41] They have summarised the essential truth about climate change in ten words: **IT'S REAL. IT'S US. EXPERTS AGREE. IT'S BAD. THERE'S HOPE.**

Positive strategies to turn this around

Michael Mann highlights the following strategies if we want to be successful and build a better future for ourselves, future generations and all other living species.

Positive strategy 1: Disregard the doomsayers.[42] It's not too late and we can turn this around. Let us focus on the solutions we have and make sure we embed them ASAP!

Positive strategy 2: A child shall lead them. As Michael Mann points out: [t]*he youngest generation is fighting tooth and nail to save their planet, and there is a moral authority and clarity in their message that none but the most jaded ears can fail to hear. They are the game-changers that climate advocates have been waiting for. We should model our actions after theirs and learn from their methods and their idealism.*

In this context, we would like to recommend listening to Greta Thunberg's famous speech to world leaders at the UN Climate Action Summit in 2019[43] and the book from the millennial Solomon Goldstein-Rose – **The 100% Solution: A Framework for Solving Climate Change** and also his TED talk.[44] We would however add a caveat – not to rely on the future generations to solve our problems. Try to research a variety of solutions, whether they are provided by young people or older generations. Choose the most appropriate and implement them now, whatever your age! This is especially important if you are a corporate leader or a politician, or in any sort of position where you can bring about major changes.

But now back to the positive strategies suggested by Michael Mann.

Positive strategy 3: Educate, educate, educate. Michael Mann highlights that there are many, many people out there who are willing to learn and want to know the best high-impact solutions they could implement in their work and life. Our book aims to do exactly this and help as many people as possible to select the best climate solutions for their own benefit and our all futures. We have also highlighted in chapter 2 how everyone needs to be climate literate and that a form of Climate Literacy Training should be integrated into every school curriculum, at universities, in further education and also offered to citizens everywhere.

Michael Mann has recommended a few resources in his book if you want to keep on top of the newest insights; one of his personal favourites is

Skeptical Science (skepticalscience.com), which rebuts all the major climate-change-denier talking points and provides responses that you can link to online or via email.[45]

Apart from the ideas above, we would like to add a few other recommendations here, and more can be found in the upcoming third edition of 'The Business Student's Guide to Sustainable Management. Principles and Practice',[46] updated to include climate change mitigation education in every chapter. This will be useful for training in companies, but also in business schools. A recent article in the *Harvard Business Review* argues that business schools have a crucial role to play here in influencing current and future leaders, and by providing a curriculum that has climate change at its heart.[47]

In 2022, the EU released the European sustainability competence framework **GreenComp**,[48] which outlines the competences every citizen in Europe needs to acquire, be it in primary, secondary or tertiary education or as part of anyone's lifelong learning. In Figure 15.1 we share the visual image of the GreenComp created by the EU — lots of busy bees achieving the European Green Deal! In 2021, the UK education secretary also announced new measures that would put climate change at the heart of education, including the new Climate Leaders Award and an annual national awards ceremony for children and young people.[49] Organisations such as **eduCCate** are also doing their bit to

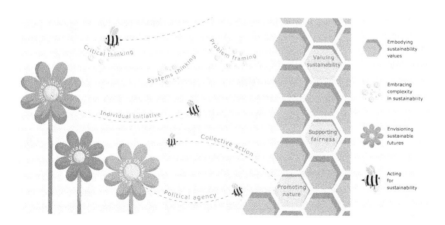

Figure 15.1 EU GreenComp (Green Competences) image reprinted with permission from EU.

ensure teachers worldwide are prepared; between 2019 and early 2022, 429k teachers in 43 countries undertook their climate action training.[50] In the United Kingdom, Nottingham Trent University (NTU) and Manchester Metropolitan University (MMU) have both created courses and toolkits available free of charge to eligible organisations (via the Carbon Literacy Project) including many public organisations such as universities or local councils.[51] Also, as a PRME Champion, Nottingham Business School, NTU led the design of the Carbon Literacy Training for Business Schools (CLT4BS) available worldwide, in collaboration with other PRME champions, oikos International and the Carbon Literacy Project.[52] The latter also makes resources and courses available to a wide variety of audiences (see chapter 2).

Changing the system requires systemic change

We need policies that will incentivise the needed shift away from fossil fuel burning towards a clean, green global economy. Throughout this book, we have outlined the changes that could be made on every level. We have recognised that an understanding of the systems and the associated levers is required. We hope that after reading this book, whatever your role in an organisation, you will know what is at stake and how you could have an impact. We feel that everyone needs to use their sphere of influence to make these changes in every part of our society.

If we are going to transition to Net Zero and ensure global warming is kept to a maximum of 1.5°C compared to pre-industrial times, we need to **think big** and we need to **act now**.

As many people as possible, from every part of the globe, need to be on board. Everyone should understand the part they can play and should be encouraged to do their bit. This requires:

- Access to high-quality climate education for all
- Appropriate systems in place at all levels
- Levers and appropriate tailored communications
- The right policies, processes and regulation to support throughout.

In this book we have outlined the changes we believe are necessary at every level. We all have our own sphere of influence, and we all have an important role to play. **Collectively, we can create a positive future for everyone. It's now over to you to help make it happen!**

Notes

1. Corporate Knights (2022) *Earth Index: Tracking the G20 response to the climate emergency*: https://www.corporateknights.com/wp-content/uploads/2022/04/2022-Earth-Index-Report.pdf p. 12

2. IPCC (2022) Climate Change 2022. Impacts, Adaptation and Vulnerability - Summary for Policy Makers: https://report.ipcc.ch/ar6wg2/pdf/IPCC_AR6_WGII_SummaryForPolicymakers.pdf

3. Dr. Eckart von Hirschhausen (2021) *Mensch, Erde! Wir koennten es so schoen haben*, dtv https://www.dtv.de/buch/mensch-erde-wir-koennten-es-so-schoen-haben-28276

4. *Ethical Consumer* 193 Nov/Dec 2021. A summary can be found here: https://www.ethicalconsumer.org/climate-gap-report

5. EY, *Why collaboration is key to tackling climate change:* https://www.ey.com/en_uk/sustainability/cbf/why-collaboration-is-key-to-tackling-climate-change

6. Accenture, *Climate Leadership Eleventh Hour*: https://www.accenture.com/_acnmedia/PDF-166/Accenture-UNGC-CEO-Study-Sustainability-2021.pdf

7. WEF, *How cross-sector collaboration is driving the global climate agenda*: https://www.weforum.org/agenda/2020/01/how-cross-sector-collaboration-is-driving-the-global-climate-agenda/

8. WEF, *SDG17–Partnership for the Goals*: https://intelligence.weforum.org/topics/a1G0X0000057N05UAE/key-issues/a1Gb00000015QfqEAE

9. ERI: https://exponentialroadmap.org/

10. SME Climate Hub: https://smeclimatehub.org/

11. UN Global Compact: https://www.unglobalcompact.org/

12. UNGC, *Engage Locally*: https://www.unglobalcompact.org/engage-locally

13. UNGC, Caring for Climate: https://www.unglobalcompact.org/what-is-gc/our-work/environment/climate

14. Climate ADAPT: https://climate-adapt.eea.europa.eu/network/organisations

15. Chambers Climate Coalition: https://www.chambers4climate.iccwbo.org/

16. IEMA: https://www.iema.net/

17. C40CITIES: https://www.c40.org/

18. Edie: https://www.edie.net

19. Sustainable Brands: https://sustainablebrands.com/

20. C2ES, Climate Leadership Conference and Awards: https://www.c2es.org/our-work/climate-leadership-conference-and-awards/

21. ISO: https://www.iso.org/about-us.html

22. ISO, *Climate Collaboration in a Changing World*: https://www.iso.org/news/ref2776.html

23. ISO, *TC 322*: https://www.iso.org/committee/7203746.html

24. PwC, *Accelerating the Journey to Net Zero*: https://www.pwc.co.uk/services/sustainability-climate-change/insights/accelerating-the-journey-to-net-zero.html

25. Accenture, *Climate Leadership Eleventh Hour*: https://www.accenture.com/_acnmedia/PDF-166/Accenture-UNGC-CEO-Study-Sustainability-2021.pdf

26. ERI, *Playbook*: https://exponentialroadmap.org/wp-content/uploads/2020/11/1.5C-Business-Playbook-v1.1.1pdf.pdf

27. ERI, *Scaling 36 Solutions to Halve Emissions by 2030*: https://exponential-roadmap.org/wp-content/uploads/2020/03/ExponentialRoadmap_1.5.1_216x279_08_AW_Download_Singles_Small.pdf

28. Accenture, *Climate Leadership Eleventh Hour*: https://www.accenture.com/_acnmedia/PDF-166/Accenture-UNGC-CEO-Study-Sustainability-2021.pdf

29. WEF, *Circular Economy and Material Value Chains*: https://www.weforum.org/projects/circular-economy

30. Ellen MacArthur Foundation, *Overview*: https://ellenmacarthurfoundation.org/topics/circular-economy-introduction/overview

31. Ellen MacArthur Foundation: https://ellenmacarthurfoundation.org/

32. Ellen MacArthur Foundation, *H&M Example*: https://ellenmacarthur-foundation.org/circular-examples/hm-group

33. SEC, *Rules to Enhance and Standardise Climate Related Disclosures*: https://www.sec.gov/news/press-release/2022-46

34. Government of Canada, *Zero-emission Vehicles*: https://tc.canada.ca/en/road-transportation/innovative-technologies/zero-emission-vehicles

35. UNEP, *Five Ways Behaviour Science Can Transform Climate Change Action*: https://www.unep.org/news-and-stories/story/five-ways-behavioural-science-can-transform-climate-change-action

36. Thaler and Sunstein, *Nudge*: https://yalebooks.yale.edu/book/9780300122237/nudge/

37. Mann ME (2021) *The New Climate War – the fight to take back our planet*, London: Scribe Publications, p. 45

38. Mann ME (2021) *The New Climate War – the fight to take back our planet*, London: Scribe Publications, p. 160

39. BBC News (April 2022) *How high-profile scientists felt tricked by group denying climate change*: https://www.bbc.co.uk/news/blogs-trending-61166339

40. Environmental Research Letters (2021) *Greater than 99% consensus on human caused climate change in the peer-reviewed scientific literature.*

41. Cook J et al (2019) *America Misled: How the fossil fuel industry deliberately misled Americans about climate change.* Fairfax, VA: George Mason University Center for Climate Change Communication: https://www.climatechangecommunication.org/america-misled/

42. These and the other quotes are taken from Mann ME (2021) *The New Climate War – the fight to take back our planet*, London: Scribe Publications, p. 6

43. Greta Thunberg's full speech to world leaders at UN Climate Action Summit: https://www.youtube.com/watch?v=KAJsdgTPJpU

44. You can find more info about the book and the link to the TED talk on his webpage: https://www.solomongr.com/

45. Mann ME (2021) *The New Climate War – the fight to take back our planet*, London: Scribe Publications, p. 161

46. Molthan-Hill, P (Ed) *The Business Students Guide to Sustainable-Management*, London: Routledge https://www.routledge.com/The-Business-Students-Guide-to-Sustainable-Management-Principles-and-Practice/Molthan-Hill-Molthan-Hill/p/book/9781783533190?gclid=CjwKCAjwo4mIBhBsEiwAKgzXOJQpuHITVUvssowuV3YRj4WcfjoPaalrUNl7BVv7pyV9u657qHpulhoCZKMQ-AvD_BwE

47. HBR (2022) *Business schools must do more to address the climate crisis*: https://hbr.org/2022/02/business-schools-must-do-more-to-address-the-climate-crisis

48. EU (2022) The European sustainability competence framework: https://green-comp.eu/wp-content/uploads/2022/02/jrc128040_greencomp_f2.pdf

49. Gov.UK, *Education Secretary puts climate change at the heart of education*: https://www.gov.uk/government/news/education-secretary-puts-climate-change-at-the-heart-of-education--2

50. eduCCate: https://educcateglobal.org/
51. The Carbon Literacy Project: https://carbonliteracy.com/toolkits/universities-colleges/
52. NTU, PRME: https://www.ntu.ac.uk/study-and-courses/academic-schools/nottingham-business-school/about-nbs/prme

ACKNOWLEDGEMENTS

This book was a team effort, and we are thankful that we had so many supporters encouraging us to keep working on this book as they thought this is so much needed. We were also inspired by many books and articles, and some of them found their way into this book. While we cannot mention everyone who has sent us a good article or link, we would like to name a few who dedicated their time and expertise to this book.

Firstly, we would like to thank everyone who wrote a case study to inspire our readers:

Chapter 2 – Dan Jackson and Lee Rayner; Chapter 3 – Herman Bril and Parul Gupta; Chapter 4 – Ani Raiden; Chapter 5 – Claire Miller and Max Wakelin; Chapter 6 – Kirsty Hunter and Sat Bains; Chapter 7 – Helen Taylor and Becky Valentine; Chapter 8 – Hannah-Louise Kirkpatrick; Chapter 9 – Tammi Sinha; Chapter 10 – Silke Stremlau; Chapter 11 – Jane Bannister; Chapter 12 – Ian Thomson and Ewan Thomson; Chapter 13 – Emma Littlewood and

Liberty Bollen; Chapter 14 – Lewis & Graves Partnership Limited, adapted from Carbon Footprint Ltd.

We would also like to thank several people who carried out research and gave us inputs for one or more chapters: Richard Brattle, Alex Mifsud and Eric Molthan-Hill.

And last but not least, we would like to thank our peer reviewers: Caroline Aggestam Pontopiddan, Ahmed Hassan Ahmed, Rae André, Roberta Bosurgi, Tim Breitbarth, Karen Cripps, Claire Fargeot, Frank Goedekke, Helen Goworek, Chris Harwood, Melanie Harwood, Barbara Henchey, Klemens Hoeppner, Richard Holmes, Kirsty Hunter, Lavinia-Cristina Iosif-Lazar, Ellie Johnston, Jennifer Leigh, Ian Thomson and Myriam Weiss. Sincere apologies if we missed anyone, so many people have been so generous with their time.

GLOSSARY

Term	Definition
5-tonne lifestyle	A measurement used by carbon calculation expert Mike Berners-Lee as a way of expressing how much impact one's personal activity might have on the carbon equivalent emissions we cause each year. Berners-Lee suggests that countries should aim for every citizen to have no more than a 5-tonne lifestyle, which would represent an important reduction in the emissions per capita experienced currently in many developed countries.
15-minute city	Where everything is in close vicinity so that people can live, go to school, work, shop and spend their leisure time within a fifteen-minute walking or cycling radius of their home.
Base year	The year selected as the one against which future emissions data will be compared. Fundamental to comparisons and effective GHG emissions tracking and performance over time.
Bidirectional charging	Electric vehicle (EV) charging that sees electricity flowing from the electricity grid to the EV battery, and from the EV battery to the home or the grid.

(continued)

Term	Definition
Carbon accounting	The process of identifying and measuring the quantity of greenhouse gases (GHG) emitted by an organisation. It should follow consistent and transparent processes, based for example on the GHG Protocol – GHGP (from the World Resources Institute - WRI). (See also Carbon footprint).
Carbon budget	The overall quantity of GHG that can be emitted to limit warming to 2.0°, or even even 1.5° (c.f. SBTi or IPCC).
Carbon dioxide equivalent/CO_2 equivalent (CO_2e)	The GHGP Corporate Standard defines CO_2e as the universal unit of measurement to indicate the global warming potential (GWP) of each of the six greenhouse gases, expressed in terms of the GWP of one unit of carbon dioxide.
Carbon footprint	According to youmatter, this corresponds to the whole amount of greenhouse gases (GHG) produced, directly and indirectly, to support a person's lifestyle and activities. This is usually measured in equivalent tonnes of CO_2, during the period of a year. A carbon footprint can be calculated for an individual, an organisation, a product or an event, etc.
Carbon footprint calculator	Online tool (usually in the form of a quiz) that helps you to calculate your own carbon, or environmental, footprint.
Carbon impact	The contribution to climate change resulting from greenhouse gas (GHG) emissions, assessed using carbon dioxide equivalent (CO_2e) and GWP (Global Warming Potential).
Carbon intensity	According to the GHG Protocol, the carbon intensity of electricity (for example) refers to the number of grams of carbon dioxide (CO_2) that it takes to make one unit of electricity – a kilowatt – per hour (kW/hour). A low-carbon intensity indicates that the energy source in question (e.g. renewable energy) contributes less to global warming.
Carbon negative	When an organisation produces more energy than it consumes for the running of its operations.
Carbon Neutral	When an organisation releases no more carbon emissions than it consumes. Some organisations may achieve this via carbon offsetting, so being Carbon Neutral does not necessarily mean that the organisation's emissions have been reduced.
Carbon offsetting	Where an organisation or person purchases credits to use against their own carbon emissions. It is a way of paying others to reduce one's emissions or absorb CO_2, in order to compensate for your own emissions.
Carbon sink	Defined by the environmental charity ClientEarth as anything that absorbs more carbon from the atmosphere than it releases – for example, plants, the ocean and soil.

Carbon storage	This is a means of storing or absorbing carbon from the atmosphere which could be based on a natural or a technical solution. (See also Carbon sink, Natural carbon storage and Technical carbon storage.)
Circular Economy (CE)	According to the Ellen MacArthur Foundation, this is *based on three principles, driven by design: elimination of waste and pollution; circulation of products and materials (at their highest value); regeneration of nature. It is underpinned by a transition to renewable energy and materials which decouples economic activity from the consumption of finite resources.*
Climate change	According to the United Nations, this *refers to long-term shifts in temperatures and weather patterns. These shifts may be natural, such as through variations in the solar cycle. But since the 1800s, human activities have been the main driver of climate change, primarily due to burning fossil fuels like coal, oil and gas.*
Climate or Carbon disclosure	The act of making available to others: information, data and a 'report' about an organisation's performance related to its GHG emissions and associated performance.
Climate justice	This is based on the knowledge that many countries that emit the least greenhouse gases (GHGs) are the most vulnerable to changes in the climate, and they have to bear the consequences caused by the actions of others. According to the United Nations, this therefore *looks at the climate crisis through a human rights lens and in the belief that by working together we can create a better future for present and future generations.*
Climate literate/ literacy	This includes a basic understanding of climate change science and the ability to identify and calculate climate solutions, which will reduce greenhouse gas (GHG) emissions and therefore reduce global warming.
Climate Risk Country Profiles	Reports compiled by The World Bank Group. They are based on a formal analysis of the likelihood and consequences of climate change, and are used to compare different countries. (See also Climate justice.)
COP	Conference of the parties – a UN Climate change conference. The first was in Berlin, Germany in 1995, with COP27 being in Egypt in 2022. See also Paris Agreement (adopted at COP21 in 2015).
COP26	A UN climate change conference of the parties held in Glasgow from 31 Oct – 13 Nov 2021, with the aim to accelerate action towards the goals of the Paris Agreement (COP21 2015) and the UN Framework Convention on Climate Change. (See also Paris Agreement.)
Decarbonisation	The act of reducing an organisation's carbon footprint by reducing its greenhouse gas (GHG) emissions.

(continued)

Term	Definition
Decarbonisation of the grid	Relates to reducing the emissions per unit of electricity generated.
Earth Index	According to Corporate Knights, *this is a measurement of the speed at which countries (by sector) are reducing greenhouse gas (GHG) emissions relative to the speed required to deliver on their commitments. Its objective is to create global awareness of whether annual GHG emissions are being reduced fast enough to meet the long-term targets countries have set for themselves. The focus is on G20 countries, which account for about 80% of global GHG emissions.*
Eco-labelling	The use of labels and stickers to communicate information to customers regarding the environmental, energy and/or climate performance of products and services. This is currently voluntary and encourages organisations to seek recognition by adopting higher standards of performance.
Electrification	The process through which equipment and appliances that currently use fossil fuels switch to using electricity as their source of energy. If the latter is generated from renewable sources, it can potentially mean a reduction in greenhouse gas emissions.
Embodied carbon	This is the CO_2 emitted in the process of making a product such as a car. This includes the energy used to extract and transport the raw materials, as well as the emissions from manufacturing processes. The embodied carbon of a building would include all the emissions from the construction materials, the building process, the internal fixtures and fittings, as well as the demolition and disposal of the building materials at the end of its life.
Emissions	See greenhouse gas (GHG) emissions
Emissions – upstream and downstream	The sources of upstream emissions include those from business travel for example (in vehicles not owned or controlled by the reporting organisation), the disposal of waste, and from goods and services purchased. The sources of downstream emissions relate for example to products sold by the organisation, their usage and their consequent disposal. (See also Scope 3.)
Energy efficiency first principle	According to the European Commission, this means placing emphasis on *cost-efficient energy efficiency measures in shaping energy policy and making relevant investment decisions.* This has been at the heart of European climate and energy policies for many years.
En-ROADS	According to Climate Interactive, *En-ROADS is a global climate simulator that allows users to explore the impact of roughly 30 policies - such as*

electrifying transport, pricing carbon, and improving agricultural practices - on hundreds of factors like energy prices, temperature, air quality, and sea level rise. [It] runs on an ordinary laptop in a fraction of a second, is freely available online, offers an intuitive user-friendly interface, and is available in over a dozen languages.

Environmental policy This is a written statement outlining how the organisation will manage different aspect of its operations in respect of the environment and related activities. It is usually signed by a senior manager.

ESG Environmental, Social and Governance.

ESG investing In terms of investing, ESG relates to products that take into account: **E**nvironmental Impacts, such as climate change and GHG emissions; **S**ocial contributions, such as Human Rights and Labour Standards; and **G**overnance and management, such as board composition and lobbying.

EU Taxonomy A classification system of the European Commission, which entered into force in July 2020, detailing environmentally sustainable economic activities.
It sets out four overarching conditions for an economic activity to qualify as 'environmentally sustainable', and it establishes six objectives in relation to:

1. *Climate change mitigation*
2. *Climate change adaptation*
3. *The sustainable use and protection of water and marine resources*
4. *The transition to a circular economy*
5. *Pollution prevention and control*
6. *The protection and restoration of biodiversity and ecosystems.*

Farm to fork The whole life cycle of food products on offer. This includes agriculture, transportation and refrigeration of ingredients/produce, food processing, retail logistics, food and drink offered across the hospitality sector, food preparation, meal and menu planning, food and drink packaging, and finally the consumption or disposal of food and drink.

Financial Stability Board (FSB) According to their website, the FSB *promotes international financial stability … by coordinating national financial authorities and international standard-setting bodies as they work toward developing strong regulatory, supervisory and other financial sector policies. It fosters a level playing field by encouraging coherent implementation of these policies across sectors and jurisdictions.*

Fugitive emissions Those which escape for a variety of reasons, maybe due to leaks in the equipment, evaporation or the weather.

Geoengineering The deliberate large-scale intervention in the Earth's natural systems to counteract climate change.

(continued)

Term	Definition
GHG	Abbreviation for greenhouse gas.
GHG emissions – conversion factors	These factors are used when reporting GHG emissions associated with an organisation's activities. They enable activity data, such as distance travelled, litres of fuel used and tonnes of waste disposed, to be converted to carbon dioxide equivalents or GHG-specific quantities, through the use of identified and standardised factors.
GHG Emissions Inventory	A list of GHG emission sources and the associated quantification of GHG emissions using standardised methods such as GHG emissions – conversion factors.
GHGP Corporate Standard	A standard and guidance for companies and other types of organisations to prepare a GHG Emissions Inventory to cover the accounting and reporting of the GHGs chosen in the Kyoto Protocol.
GHG Protocol/GHGP	The GHG Protocol was published in 1998 by the World Resources Institute (WRI) and the World Business Council for Sustainable Development (WBCSD), to help countries and organisations in accounting, reporting and mitigating GHG emissions. It was the first such framework and is still used as a benchmark.
Global Reporting Initiative (GRI)	According to the GRI website, it is the independent, international organization that helps businesses and other organizations take responsibility for their impacts, by providing them with the global common language to communicate those impacts. [It provides] the world's most widely used standards for sustainability reporting – the GRI Standards.
Global warming	Refers to the heating of the Earth and changes to the climate over a period of time. (See also greenhouse gas effect.)
Global Warming Potential (GWP)	Means that certain greenhouse gases (GHGs) may contribute to faster rises in temperature (as they retain more heat than the benchmark gas – carbon dioxide, CO_2) and/or they remain in the atmosphere longer, trapping more heat over a given period. GWP relates to how much energy the emissions of 1 tonne of a gas will absorb over a given period of time, relative to the emissions of 1 tonne of CO_2 and therefore provides a common unit of measurement. This allows quantification and analysis of GHG emissions to support the development of inventories and comparisons, benchmarking and tracking of performance.
Green Claims Code	This is guidance from the UK Competition and Markets Authority (CMA) and affects claims made by businesses in the United Kingdom in relation to their sustainability credentials. According to the CMA, the underpinning principles are that claims must be truthful, accurate, clear and unambiguous. They must not omit or hide important

relevant information, comparisons must be fair and meaningful and claims must consider the full life cycle of the product or service, and must be substantiated.

Greenhouse gas effect
This describes the process of global warming. GHGs ensure the rays from the sun are kept in the atmosphere to provide a warm climate for the planet, similar to the walls of a greenhouse. However, since the Industrial Revolution we have been adding more and more of these gases to the atmosphere, leading to a rise in the average temperature on Earth.

Greenhouse gas (GHG) emissions
The term covers the seven gases under the Kyoto Protocol: Carbon dioxide (CO_2); methane (CH_4); nitrous oxide (N_2O); hydrofluorocarbons (HFCs); perfluorocarbons (PFCs); sulphur hexafluoride (SF_6); nitrogen trifluoride (NF_3). All of them contribute to global warming.

Greenhouse Gas Protocol (GHGP)
See GHG Protocol.

'Green' Procurement Policies (GPP)
An approach led by public authorities who use their purchasing power to choose environmentally-friendly goods, services and works. This makes an important contribution to sustainable consumption and production.

Greenwashing
The provision of false or misleading information or impressions about the environmental or climate credentials of a product or organisation without clear evidence to substantiate.

GWP
An abbreviation for Global Warming Potential explained above.

Impact investments
The GIIN (Global Impact Investing Network) defines such investments as those *made with the intention to generate positive, measurable social and environmental impact alongside a financial return.*

Intergovernmental Panel on Climate Change (IPCC)
An intergovernmental body of the United Nations *created to provide policymakers with regular scientific assessments on climate change, its implications and potential future risks, as well as to put forward adaptation and mitigation options.*

ISO (International Organization for Standardization)
An independent organisation made up of 167 national bodies that engage experts in their respective fields to support the development of their international standards.
An example is ISO 14064, which relates to greenhouse gas (GHG) emission inventories.

Kyoto Protocol
According to the United Nations, the Kyoto Protocol was adopted in 1997 and entered into force in 2005 (with 192 Parties signed up). The protocol operationalises the UN's Framework Convention on Climate Change (UNFCCC) by committing each country to specific targets to reduce its greenhouse gas (GHG) emissions.

(continued)

Term	Definition
Last mile delivery	Refers to the very last step of the delivery process when a parcel is moved from a transportation hub to its final destination. The latter could be a customer's residence or a retail store.
Life Cycle Analysis or Life Cycle Assessment (LCA)	This is a methodology to measure and evaluate the inputs and outputs of energy and materials including the environmental impact of a product through its full life cycle. This will include extraction and processing of the raw materials, manufacturing, distribution, use, recycling and final disposal. The purpose of this is to identify improvements that could reduce the product's impacts on the environment at each stage of its life.
Marketing Mix (4Ps)	This is core to marketing theory and refers to the different aspects of marketing. Although the 4Ps has been superseded in many textbooks and organisations, it still provides a useful framework. In its most basic form, it focuses on the Product (or service), Price, Promotion (including communication) and Place (e.g. distribution).
Materiality	Relates to the assessment as to whether an issue has a major bearing on the economic, financial, legal or reputational aspects of an organisation and the provision of related information to stakeholders. If this information is considered important by a reasonable person, then it must be disclosed, and this is the core of materiality.
Microgrid	According to Project Drawdown, a *localized grouping of distributed electricity generation technologies, paired with energy storage or backup generation and tools to manage demand.*
Natural carbon storage	Many places on Earth store carbon naturally already, or could be enabled to increase their storage. This includes forests, soils, peatlands, oceans, marine agriculture etc. (See also carbon sink and technical carbon storage.)
Net Positive	Broadly means putting more back into the global system or the world than is taken out. May be viewed narrowly from a climate or wider sustainability perspective.
Net Zero	The IPCC defines Net Zero carbon dioxide (CO_2) emissions in their glossary as being achieved when *anthropogenic CO_2 emissions are balanced globally by anthropogenic CO_2 removals over a specified period. Net Zero CO_2 emissions are also referred to as carbon neutrality.* According to the United Nations this means cutting greenhouse gas emissions to as close to zero as possible, with any remaining emissions re-absorbed from the atmosphere, by oceans and forests for instance. Targets to achieve Net Zero can be set at different levels, and all types of organisations can contribute to a country's overall target.

Net Zero emissions	While we cannot achieve zero emissions, as human activities will always cause carbon equivalent emissions, we can achieve Net Zero emissions. This is where the (reduced) emissions we cause will be absorbed by natural and technical carbon storage.
Offsetting	See Carbon Offsetting.
Operational Boundary	Used in carbon accounting, these are the boundaries within an organisation which need identifying in relation to the different scopes (see Scope 1, 2 and 3 in this glossary).
Organisational Boundary	Used in carbon accounting, this should detail any branches or subsidiaries to be included in calculating an organisation's carbon footprint. It will also help determine which parts of the business organisation need to be involved in its carbon management, through the measurement of its emissions.
Paris Agreement	According to the United Nations, this is a *legally binding international treaty on climate change. It was adopted by 196 Parties at COP (conference of the parties) 21 in Paris, on 12 December 2015 and entered into force on 4 November 2016. Its goal is to limit global warming to well below 2, preferably to 1.5 degrees Celsius, compared to pre-industrial levels. To achieve this long-term temperature goal, countries aim to reach global peaking of greenhouse gas emissions as soon as possible to achieve a climate neutral world by mid-century. The Paris Agreement is a landmark in the multilateral climate change process because, for the first time, a binding agreement brings all nations into a common cause to undertake ambitious efforts to combat climate change and adapt to its effects.*
Race to Net Zero	According to the UN Framework Convention on Climate Change (UNFCCC), this is *[a] global campaign to rally leadership and support from businesses, cities, regions, investors for a healthy, resilient, zero carbon recovery that prevents future threats, creates decent jobs, and unlocks inclusive, sustainable growth.*
Ratio indicator	A performance metric relevant to the organisation and its activities (which along with the base year) provides a means for interpretation and realistic comparisons internally and externally.
REAL Talk	Mnemonic which provides structure for the #TalkingClimate handbook from Climate Outreach. Summarised, it stands for: **R**espect your conversational partner, **E**njoy the conversation, **A**sk questions, **L**isten, **T**ell your story, **A**ction makes it easier, **L**earn from conversation, **K**eep going.
Rebound effect	The idea that when something is more carbon efficient, it uses less energy and is therefore cheaper. We may therefore end up doing it more frequently, leading to the same amount or more emissions.

(continued)

Term	Definition
Renewable energy	Energy that comes from a sustainable and low-carbon source, and technologies such as solar panels, wind turbines or heat pumps that can be used with few or no carbon emissions.
Resource or activity data	Used to measure the activities that generate greenhouse gas (GHG) emissions, expressed in standard units such as kilometres driven, litres of fuel used and kilowatt hours of electricity consumed.
Reverse logistics	This is the opposite of order fulfilment and relates to how products are dealt with when they are returned to the supplier by a customer.
Science-based Target (SBT)	According to the Science Based Targets initiative (SBTi), targets are termed 'science-based' if they are in line with what the latest climate science deems necessary to meet the goals of the Paris Agreement – limiting global warming to well-below 2°C above pre-industrial levels and pursuing efforts to limit warming to 1.5°C.
Scopes of emissions	The Greenhouse Gas Protocol (GHGP) breaks down greenhouse gas (GHG) emissions into different 'scopes' according to their source.
Scope 1	**Scope 1** (direct emissions): from sources owned or controlled by the organisation.
Scope 2	**Scope 2** (indirect emissions): from the generation of purchased electricity, heat, steam or cooling.
Scope 3	**Scope 3** (all other indirect emissions): from various organisational activities from external sources, not owned or controlled by the organisation. These are referred to as 'value chain emissions' and can be both upstream and downstream of an organisation's activities.
Sectoral Decarbonization Approach (SDA)	The SDA allocates the carbon budget to different sectors, using data from the International Energy Agency's 2°C Scenario model. Organisations' own targets then contribute to the sectoral carbon budget in line with climate science.
Social marketing	The use of marketing techniques to influence social change, for example relating to health-related behaviour.
Sustainable marketing	Can be defined in various ways, but Adanma Onuoha of the Network for Business Sustainability concludes that it is *marketing activities and strategies that promote environmental wellbeing, social equity, and economic development in a manner that enhances the business.*
Task Force on Climate-related Financial Disclosures (TCFD)	According to the TCFD's own website, it was set up by the Financial Stability Board (FSB) *to develop recommendations on the types of information that companies should disclose to support investors, lenders, and insurance underwriters in appropriately assessing and pricing a specific set of risks – risks related to climate change.*

| **Technical carbon storage** | This usually refers to new technologies employed to capture emissions from power plants and other industrial sites, before they are released into the atmosphere. It can also refer to a situation where a technical solution improves a Natural Carbon Storage's ability to absorb more carbon (soil for example). (See also carbon sink and natural carbon storage.) |
| **Zero emissions** | This term is sometimes used instead of Net Zero emissions. |

INDEX

Milton Keynes UK
Ingram Content Group UK Ltd.
UKHW031135101224
452273UK00007B/25